CANADIAN PROVINCIAL POLITICS

CANADIAN PROVINCIAL POLITICS

The Party Systems of the Ten Provinces

edited by

MARTIN ROBIN

Department of Political Science, Simon Fraser University

p
PRENTICE-HALL ♦ OF CANADA, LTD.
h

Scarborough, Ontario

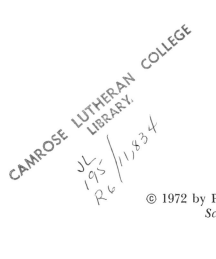
© 1972 by Prentice-Hall of Canada, Ltd.
Scarborough, Ontario

PRENTICE-HALL, INC., ENGLEWOOD CLIFFS, NEW JERSEY
PRENTICE-HALL INTERNATIONAL, INC., LONDON
PRENTICE-HALL OF AUSTRALIA, PTY., LTD., SYDNEY
PRENTICE-HALL OF INDIA, PVT., LTD., NEW DELHI
PRENTICE-HALL OF JAPAN, INC., TOKYO

Library of Congress Catalog Card No. 70-109490

ISBN

013-113217-2 (pa.)
013-113225-3 (cl.)
1 2 3 4 5 75 74 73 72

PRINTED IN CANADA

Table of Contents

Preface

This volume is intended to provide the reader with a survey of party politics in Canada at the provincial level. Federal politics and federal-provincial relations are touched upon only where they help illuminate the workings of the provincial systems. Nor do the essays attempt to outline the workings of the formal institutions of government. The emphasis throughout is on the history, structure and determinants of the party systems in each of the ten Canadian provinces.

All of the essays have been written expressly for this volume by experts in the field. As editor, I have not attempted to impose a rigid format on the authors. The reader will note a variety of different approaches, ranging from the historical and traditional, to the structural and quantitative. All, however, are informed by the common purpose of providing an original analytical survey of the provincial party scene.

M.R.

CANADIAN PROVINCIAL POLITICS

* ALBERTA *
One Party Dominance[1]

J. A. LONG AND F. Q. QUO

On August 30, 1971, one of the most important election upsets in Alberta political history occurred. The Progressive Conservative Party captured 49 of the 75 seats in the Legislative Assembly and thus ended 36 years of Social Credit rule. It is difficult to pinpoint the causes of the upset. Certainly the Socreds' lackluster campaign, marked by the absence of Ernest Manning, and the dynamic, well organized Conservative campaign were contributory factors. The Conservatives seemed able to capitalize on public dissatisfaction with existing economic conditions and the apparent desire of Albertans for political change. Moreover, the Conservatives appear to have benefited greatly from the concentration of anti-Socred votes formerly shared by the Liberal and New Democratic parties.

The Tory victory, however, does not signal any fundamental change in the basic political beliefs of Albertans for it constitutes the replacement in power of one conservatively oriented party by another. Despite the hopes of NDP supporters that Alberta would follow the trend set by Manitoba and Saskatchewan the NDP's percentage of the popular vote decreased from the preceeding election. While it is too early to predict the future direction of party politics in Alberta, it seems likely that one of two alternative patterns will develop. Following tradition, Alberta may continue to support one dominant party with the Conservatives assuming the position formerly held by the Socreds and the Socreds following in the footsteps of the U.F.A. While the Tory party may in future lose some of the votes borrowed from the

[1]This chapter is based partly on *The Government and Politics of Alberta*, which is currently under preparation by the same authors. The writers are grateful to the Canada Council and the Research Committee of the University of Lethbridge for financial assistance, and to numerous individuals who have cooperated in our research project on Alberta politics. Credit should be given also to Peter Hill, now at Queen's University, and Brian Slemko and Michael Georgeson, Research Assistants in the Department of Political Science, University of Lethbridge.

Liberals and NDP, it should eventually win the allegiance of considerably more Socred supporters. Alternatively, Alberta may see an eventual political realignment among provincial parties with an effective opposition of the left.

The size of the Conservative majority in the legislature surprised even the party's most enthusiastic supporters. The extent of the sweep, however, is not unprecedented in Alberta politics, for Albertans historically have followed a pattern in provincial elections of dramatically reversing party fortunes and giving one party a dominant majority in the legislature.

I. HISTORICAL BACKGROUND

When the first provincial legislature met in 1906, the opposition had barely enough members to move and second debate of the Speech From the Throne.[2] Leaders in the assembly of the North-West Territories had insisted that the welfare of the Territories take precedence over party politics. They particulary opposed any attempt to extend federal politics into the Territories. Although party lines were drawn between Liberals and Conservatives after Alberta came into being, the first provincial election found little disagreement between the parties. Both Liberals and Conservatives supported a successful campaign to amend the separate school system clause of the federal legislation creating the province so that it would not contravene the provisions made for minority rights in the Territorial Ordinances of 1892 and 1901. Another important issue, the question of the ownership of Crown lands, found all parties in the province agreed that the lands should belong to the province rather than the federal government, although some Liberals felt a money grant in lieu of lands would be an acceptable settlement.

This "united front" lasted for some time under the leadership of Liberal premier A.C. Rutherford. Writing about the 1909 election, the Provincial Librarian recorded: "On the important questions of the hour there was little difference in the policies of the two parties."[3] But the Alberta and Great Waterways Railway Company scandal of 1910 divided the Liberal party, providing an opportunity for the Conservatives to become a viable opposition. The scandal revolved around the sale of bonds for railway construction to the J.P. Morgan Company of New York, which resold the bonds at a considerable profit. This resulted in rumors that some members of the government received a share of the profits and eventually led to a split in the Liberal cabinet. Rutherford, unable to unite his cabinet, resigned and a new government was formed under A.L. Sifton. Aided by some loss of public confidence in the Liberals, Conservative strength rose from 5 to 32 per cent of the legislative seats in the 1913 election (see Table I).

The scandal also planted the seed of "anti-partyism" in the minds of many Alberta voters. The invasion of the Nonpartisan League movement from North Dakota during the later years of the 1910's fertilized the growth of this anti-partyism and eventually led to the capture of power by the United Farmers of Alberta in 1921.[4]

TABLE I
*Legislative Seats and Percentage of
Popular Vote by Political Party*

Election	Total Number of Seats	Social Credit			Liberal			Conservative			UFA			CCF/NDP			Others			Total Popular Vote
		No. of Seats	% Pop. Vote	% Seats	No. of Seats	% Pop. Vote	% Seats	No. of Seats	% Pop. Vote	% Seats	No. of Seats	% Pop. Vote	% Seats	No. of Seats	% Pop. Vote	% Seats	No. of Seats	% Pop. Vote	% Seats	
*1905	25				23	61	92	2	35	8									4	23,336
1909	41				36	59	88	2	32	5							3	9	7	50,004
1913	56				38	49	68	18	45	32									6	96,833
1917	58				34	36	59	19	30	33							5	34	9	151,499
1921	59				14	33	24	1	11	2	38	28	64				6	28	10	298,087
**1926	60				7	27	12	4	23	7	43	41	72				6	9	10	175,137
1930	63				11	25	17	6	14	10	39	39	62				7	23	11	188,219
1935	63	57	54	90	4	23	6	2	6	3	11								5	301,752
1940	57	36	43	63	1	.6	2							11			20	46	35	308,864
1944	57	51	52	89										2	25	4	4	23	7	282,106
1948	57	51	56	89	2	18	4							2	19	4	2	7	4	294,793
1952	61	52	56	85	4	22	7	1	2	2				2	14	3	2	5	3	298,335
1955	61	37	46	61	15	31	25	3	9	5				2	8	3	4	5	7	378,179
1959	65	61	56	94	1	14	2	1	24	2					4		2	2	3	413,515
1963	63	60	55	95	2	20	3		13						9		1	3	2	403,444
1967	65	55	45	83	3	11	5	6	26	11					16		1	3	2	498,341
***1971	75	25	41	33	1			49	46	63				1	12	1		.1		637,969

*Source: 1905-1921 Election figures: *Canadian Parliamentary Guide,* 1905-1921.
**Source: Government of Alberta, *Provincial Election Returns,* 1926-1967.
***Election data from unofficial sources.

A. The UFA Government (1921-1935)

When formed in 1909, the UFA was not intended to be a political party. Its original purpose was to provide farmers with local recreational and educational facilities. Politically, the organization purported to be no more than a pressure group for farm interests. As late as 1917, Henry Wise Wood, the leader of the UFA, still preferred working within the old party system to

2The Alberta Act came into effect on September 1, 1905. The first provincial general election was held on November 9, 1905. For a description of the first legislature see Archibald O. MacRae, *History of the Province of Alberta* (Calgary: Western Canada History Co., 1912), p. 90.

3John Blue, *Alberta: Past and Present* (Pioneer Historical Publications Co., 1924) I, 122-125.

4For the spread of the Nonpartisan League movement in western Canada, see Paul F. Sharp, *The Agrarian Revolt in Western Canada: A Survey Showing American Parallels* (Minneapolis: University of Minnesota Press, 1948).

building a new one by UFA members: "the machine is all right if it is run right, and it will be easier to run it right than it will be to build another one — another party."[5] It was not until the fall of 1919 that Wood began a vitriolic polemic against the party system and the advocacy of his theory of group government. Wood regarded the party system as an autocratic instrument of the moneyed classes and unsuitable to be a democratic movement.[6] In the place of party politics, Wood suggested "group government." In essence the theory of group government argued for a non-exploitive democracy based upon functional representation by occupational groups. Members of the legislature would be considered instructed delegates from the group that elected them.

When the UFA came to power in 1921 it was confronted with the difficulties of applying this theory in a parliamentary system. The UFA itself controlled two-thirds of the seats in the Legislative Assembly and there was no mechanism for selecting representatives from other occupational groups. Consequently, it had to fall back on its own convention organization for political decision-making. That is, the UFA leadership promised that legislation would be shaped not by a coterie of ministers but by a broadly based party convention. Because of the political realities of government, however, leadership passed quickly from the convention to the cabinet. By the early 1930's UFA convention resolutions that called for easing the farmers' debts were repeatedly rejected by the UFA cabinet. Fourteen years of UFA government only demonstrated the incompatability of direct democracy and a parliamentary system. Unable to reconcile its ideals with the practical demands of administration, the UFA was swept from power in the 1935 election by a fresher populist vision.

B. The Social Credit Movement

The idea of "Social Credit" was not new to Albertans in 1935.[7] During the 1920's the UFA had devoted considerable effort to studying credit reform and publicizing the doctrine that the state should control credit. By giving legitimacy to Social Credit's monetary proposals, the UFA helped pave its way to power. But legitimized or not, these proposals had a magic appeal in the middle of a depression that was, to many western farmers, simply incomprehensible. Social Credit seemed both to explain why the Depression had happened and to offer a solution to it: Major Douglas' so-called "A+B theorm,"[8] which possessed, in the words of C.B. MacPherson, a "false clarity which made it impossible either to understand it or refute it in simple terms" but "an almost hypnotic quality for those who were disposed to believe it and were not accustomed to close abstract reasoning."[9] The economic validity of Social Credit was not however as important as its political potency.

But the appeal of Social Credit's monetary theories only partly explains the movement's success. An important reason for that success was the leadership of William Aberhart, who brought to the movement both charisma and a genius for organization and tactics. Using his Calgary Prophetic Bible Institute as his headquarters Aberhart was able to transform his large personal religious following into a political force — and succeeded, moreover, in identifying the philosophy of Social Credit with Christian fundamentalism, offering Social Credit as a "Divine plan" for the salvation of society.[10] By 1935 Social Credit study groups had spread into nearly every part of the province. In addition to providing political instruction these groups also served as important sources of funds.

Aberhart campaigned under the slogan: "vote for results, not schemes." He rejected the UFA's notion of delegate democracy and argued instead for government by plebiscite — something quite the opposite. The electorate, he said, had the right to indicate generally, through its elected representatives, what it wished its government to do, but the choice of means and the execution of policy were properly functions of the government alone. "Don't try to tell your government everything they should do," he warned his followers. "The minute you start to talk about the policing of the country you are out of order."[11] The government would not itself formulate legislation, however; instead it would hire experts in various fields to make and execute policy in accordance with the government's interpretation of the popular will. In exchange for their right to demand "results" from his government and its hired experts, Aberhart told Albertans, it was their "duty" to support that government.

Whether or not many Albertans understood the implications of Aberhart's theory of government, or were even aware of that theory — the Social

[5]H.W. Wood, "The Price of Democracy," *Grain Growers' Guide*, June 20, 1917, quoted in Macpherson, *Democracy in Alberta*, p. 38.

[6]*Ibid.*, pp. 40ff.

[7]The background and development of the Social Credit Movement in Alberta have been studied quite extensively under a program sponsored by the Canadian Social Science Research Council. Publications resulting from the program most pertinent to the problems discussed in this paper include: C.B. Macpherson, *Democracy in Alberta: Social Credit and the Party System*, 2nd ed. (Toronto: University of Toronto Press, 1962); J.R. Mallory, *Social Credit and Federal Power in Canada* (Toronto: University of Toronto Press, 1954); W.E. Mann, *Sect, Cult and Church in Alberta* (Toronto: University of Toronto Press, 1955); L.G. Thomas, *The Liberal Party in in Alberta: A History of Politics in the Province of Alberta, 1905-1921* (Toronto: University of Toronto Press, 1959); and J.A. Irving, *The Social Credit Movement in Alberta* (Toronto: University of Toronto Press, 1959).

[8]The "A + B Theorem" argues:
1. that the cost of every unit produced consists of (A) all payments made to individuals either in the form of wages, salaries, or dividends and (B) all payments made to organizations either for raw materials, bank interests or other external costs;
2. therefore the price of goods has to be at least A + B;
3. however, only A creates purchasing power and since A is less than A + B, not all goods can be purchased; thus
4. in order to ensure that all products be purchased, purchasing power in the amount of B has to be created; and
5. this new money created can be distributed to consumers as social credit or to producers as subsidies for their lowering of prices.

[9]Macpherson, *Democracy in Alberta*, pp. 108-111.

[10]Irving, *The Social Credit Movement*, p. 338.

[11]*Alberta Social Credit Chronicle*, August 16, 1935.

Credit platform was published only a few days before the 1935 election[12] — the election returns demonstrated both the success of his campaign strategy and the desperation of a poverty-stricken province.

But aside from a half-hearted solicitation of expert advice from Major Douglas, the new government made no effort to implement Social Credit. Neither the promised $25 a month dividend nor a new economic order seemed to be forthcoming. In the spring of 1937 some "faithful" Socred backbenchers refused to support the government's proposed budget. This insurgence forced the government to establish a Social Credit Board and to appoint a commission of experts charged with the implementation of Social Credit doctrines. The Alberta Social Credit acts were, however, either invalidated by the Supreme Court as *ultra vires* or disallowed by the federal government.[13] By 1939 it was evident that Social Credit could not be implemented.

C. Transformation of the Social Credit Movement (1944-1967)

Although the Aberhart Government was able to blame the federal government rather than its own unwillingness for the failure of Social Credit, it lost some popularity. In the 1940 election the number of Social Credit seats dropped from fifty-seven (out of a total of sixty-three) to thirty-six (out of fifty-seven) and the party's share of the vote from 54.2 to 42.9 per cent. Liberals and Conservatives joined forces in many constituencies to defeat Socred candidates. Running as Independents, these fusion candidates captured twenty seats with 45.1 per cent of the popular vote. Although the advent of World War II and the return of some measure of prosperity helped the Social Credit government to survive this election, in spite of its abandonment of Social Credit economics, it clearly had to find a new justification for its existence.

In the 1944 election campaign it found a formula that has served it faithfully in every election since: evocation of the threat of socialism and the promise of clean government. The 1944 campaign was led by E.C. Manning, Aberhart's most trusted disciple, who succeeded to the party leadership upon the death of the master in 1943. The inspiration for the 1944 anti-socialist campaign was the rise of the Co-operative Commonwealth Federation (CCF), but after the war the world situation encouraged the government to identify a larger enemy: international communism. Fear of communism, or what seemed to be communism, was strong enough to rally many Albertans behind the SC government. Thus, in the spectrum of political ideologies, Social Credit can be said to have moved from a kind of right-wing populism to a more orthodox conservatism.

However, what a political party professes does not necessarily correspond to what it does. In spite of its statement that Social Credit is "a free individual enterprise movement opposed to Socialism and all other forms of Statism," the Socred government in practice created a welfare state. In 1967 it spent $446 *per capita* for public services, compared to a national average of $333 *per capita*.[14] The government continually opposed proposals for the release of the state-owned Alberta telephone system to "free individual enterprise."[15] It established a Human Resources Development Authority in order to realize the potential of Albertans who are socially and economically depressed. Premier Strom endorsed a guaranteed national income plan similar to the Social Credit monetary proposals of the 1930's.[16] On the other hand, the government was generous to large resource development industries to the point where it was often criticised as being "soft" on oil and mining companies. Its labor legislation, moreover, has been characterized as extremely illiberal.

From one election to another Social Credit of Alberta depended more and more on its administrative record as a government that served the people rather than on its appeal as a party of particular doctrine. "The major function of any government," according to the official statement of the Alberta Socreds, "is to bring to people the results which the people want in the management of their affairs."[17] Because of the revenues it harvested from the oil fields, the Socred government was able to give considerable "results" without resorting to such unpopular devices as a sales tax and extensive deficit financing. This earned it much credit for its "management." Until the 1967 election Social Credit received a majority of the popular vote in every election except those of 1940 and 1955.[18]

But the 1967 election alerted the Socreds to an erosion of their popularity. The metropolitan areas are attracting newcomers with new outlooks. The younger generation, with no memory of the Great Depression, is full of new dreams. The old image of Social Credit means little to these groups. Federally, Social Credit seems to be finished. It has never recovered from Diefenbaker's sweep of the West in 1958.[19] But before his retirement from the premiership and the Socred leadership in 1968, E.C. Manning made a last attempt to establish his ideology, if not his party, in federal politics. The social-conservatism

---

[12]Macpherson, *Democracy in Alberta,* pp. 149-160.

[13]The Dominion of Canada disallowed twelve Alberta Provincial Acts, eleven of which dealt with Social Credit monetary legislation. In 1938 the acts were declared *ultra vires* by the Supreme Court. See R. MacGregor Dawson, *The Government of Canada* (Toronto: University of Toronto Press, 1964) and Mallory, *Social Credit and Federal Power.*

[14]*Alberta: The Tax Haven* (Edmonton: Alberta Social Credit League, n.d.).

[15]The motion to transfer the government-owned Alberta telephone system to private enterprise has been repeatedly objected to by the leaders and consequently rejected in the Social Credit Conventions.

[16]*Calgary Herald,* November 1, 1969.

[17]Orvis A. Kennedy, *Principles and Policies of Social Credit* (Edmonton: Alberta Social Credit League, 1965).

[18]The 1955 election centred around the issue of the honesty and integrity of some Social Credit M.L.A.s. J.H. Prowse, the Liberal leader, led the accusations. In the constituencies where the Liberals did not run candidates they supported coalition candidates with other parties against Social Credit. Social Credit lost 10 per cent of its popular support.

[19]

	1957 Federal Election		1958 Federal Election	
	Seats	% of Vote	Seats	% of Vote
Social Credit	13	37.8	0	21.6
Progressive Conservative	3	27.6	17	59.9

advocated by Manning in his *Political Re-alignment: A Challenge to Thoughtful Canadians*[20] caused much speculation that the premier of Alberta would soon enter the federal political scene. In essence, Manning argued for a pragmatic, conservative approach to government. Moreover, he felt there were already too many federal parties and that his suggested approach should be adopted by one of the existing major parties. Since the Progressive Conservative party was at that time faced with the problem of choosing a new national leader, the interpretation that the Premier was making himself available seemed reasonable. But the Progressive Conservative response was barely audible. In his speech at the 1967 Social Credit Convention, Manning blamed this lack of interest on the undemocratic machine of the Conservative party and the unfavorable treatment of his party by the mass media. The failure of this attempt to use the existing Conservate party as a vehicle for his social-conservative ideology convinced Manning and many Socred leaders that Social Credit as a national political force was dying. The episode resulted in the desertion of the party by Socred politicians at the federal level and also led the party to decide against making any province-wide bid for seats in Parliament. In the 1968 federal election Social Credit candidates ran in only three constituencies and they received little official support from their party. All of them lost. But the myth of social-conservatism remains a ready-made justification for those who support the Conservative party federally but Social Credit provincially.

Before leaving office, Manning also gave some thought to modernizing the provincial party. There were two important aspects to his reform strategy: to attract the younger generation, and to extend Socred strength in the urban centers. But it was left to his successor, Harry Strom, to try to realize these ends. The creation of a Ministry of Youth, the appointment of young Socreds to the cabinet, and the establishment of a regional party office in Calgary were some of his efforts. These instruments of reform, however, proved to be ineffectual, for in the 1971 election the Conservatives won most of the urban seats and appear to have attracted a great number of young voters.

D. The Opposition In Recent Years:

No significant opposition to Social Credit emerged until the assumption of the Progressive Conservative leadership by Peter Lougheed, a Calgary lawyer. Though the Progressive Conservatives won only six seats in the 1967 general election, they enlarged that number to ten by winning two by-elections and absorbing two seats from other parties.[21] This increase culminated in their majority in the present legislature. It is obvious that Lougheed is a capable leader and campaigner. A 1969 publication of the Progressive Conservative Party entitled *Winning the Election* showed that the party had done a great deal of research into the techniques of organizing and campaigning.[22] The material includes suggestions for day to day campaign schedules, examples of vote probability in each poll of a sample constituency, and word-by-word formulas for making and answering telephone calls. Intensive policy seminars were conducted and brain-storming sessions for candidates and party officials were scheduled far in advance of the election. The party successfully impressed the voters that there was a need for a change in government and that it was the only rival of Social Credit with any real chance of success. Because of the weakness of the other opposition parties, the Conservatives attracted many of those who were discontented with the dominance of Social Credit. But the party itself confesses that "party labels are misleading."[23] Like Social Credit, the Progressive Conservatives of Alberta profess a belief in free enterprise and in the idea that the main function of a provincial government is to administer "welfare in relation to need without detracting from human dignity."[24] Given the party's commitment to conservatism it remains to be seen whether the Tories will start the province off in any new directions from the previous Social Credit policies.

In spite of its showing in 1968 federal elections, the Liberals are the most impotent party in Alberta provincial politics. This is evidenced by the fact that they fielded only 20 candidates during the last election. Moreover, their share of the popular vote slipped from 11% in 1967 to a negligible 1% in 1971. The image of Liberals as eastern, pro-American lawyers and professionals has alienated Albertans, who identify their province as western, agrarian, and culturally British. The party has been troubled by a lack of unity and capable leadership. In the three years since Michael Maccagno left the leadership for an unsuccessful venture in the 1968 federal election, the Alberta Liberals have had four leaders. In 1971, behind-the-door negotiations between the party leader at that time, Jack Lowery, and ex-Premier Strom led to an attempt by the former's own party executives to censure him. Bob Russell, the current leader, was unsuccessful in his bid for a legislative seat and appears to offer little hope of resurrecting the party in provincial politics. The party is split by such issues as federal patronage, campaign strategy, and, more importantly, the re-organization of the provincial party structure. At present the provincial party structure operates under the direction and control of the federal party organization. The argument that there should be a separate organization geared towards the needs of the provincial political market does not seem to interest the Liberal cadre. Many Liberal candidates in provincial elections consider the opportunity only as a trial run before their entry into federal politics.

The New Democratic Party (NDP), like the Liberals, is oriented more towards national than provincial politics. Although the old CCF supporters were unhappy with the soft line adopted by the provincial NDP's founding

[20]E.C. Manning, *Political Realignment: A Challenge to Thoughtful Canadians* (Toronto: McClelland & Stewart, Ltd., 1967).

[21]One Liberal and one Independent M.L.A. joined the Progressive Conservative caucus.

[22]*Winning the Election* (Edmonton: Alberta Progressive Conservative Association, October, 1969).

[23]*Ibid.*

[24]Peter Lougheed, "Guideposts of the Progressive Conservative Party of Alberta," ratified by the Annual Meeting of the party in November 1967.

convention,[25] the NDP is nevertheless the most doctrinaire party in the province, with the result that its policies and its leaders' statements have at times been unrelated to provincial politics. It is difficult, for example, to convince Alberta voters that they should support Grant Notley and his NDP in provincial elections because of the party's moral opposition to the United States' Vietnam policy. After two unsuccessful bids to win a seat in the Legislative Assembly, Notley was finally elected by a narrow margin. The only previous NDP member in the Legislative Assembly was defeated in the 1967 election after an attempt to destroy the Socred image of "honest government."[26] The support of the trade unions alone is not sufficient to elect NDP candidates in most constituencies since there are very few constituencies in which organized labor boasts a majority.[27] Unlike its counterparts in the other prairie provinces the Alberta NDP has been unable to attract the support of the rural voters. The fact that it suffered a decline in popular vote during the last election suggests that, while it may criticize the Conservative policies, it is very unlikely that it will become a significant opposition force.

II. PARTY ORGANIZATION: FROM POLITICAL MOVEMENT TO PARTY POLITICS

Historically, political parties in Alberta as loose multi-goaled federations of voters have been no match for single-goaled mass movements. It is also clear, however, that a political movement cannot perpetuate itself unless it is capable of developing pragmatic policies and building an effective organizational structure. In order to be successful with the Alberta electorate, a political party today must be:

1. capable of attracting the support of the young,[28]
2. willing to give emphasis to urban problems, such as housing, pollution, and traffic, and
3. capable of presenting sophisticated candidates with pragmatic approaches to provincial affairs.

These requisites for electoral success have necessitated attempts at organizational reform by the Alberta political parties.

A. The Social Credit League

Social Credit reform began at the higher levels of the party's structure, since the party is by far the most organized of the provincial parties at the grass roots level (see Figure 1). A steering committee headed by Raymond Speaker, one of the young Socred leaders and former Minister of Social Development, was in charge of the reorganization task.[29] Its main goal was "to direct the development of a complete political strategy plan for the party and for the government, leading up to the next Provincial General Election."[30] Seven "task forces" were established, each assigned to deal with special aspects of party operation.[31] The main problem was to modernize the old agrarian,

FIGURE 1

*Organization of the Alberta Social Credit League**

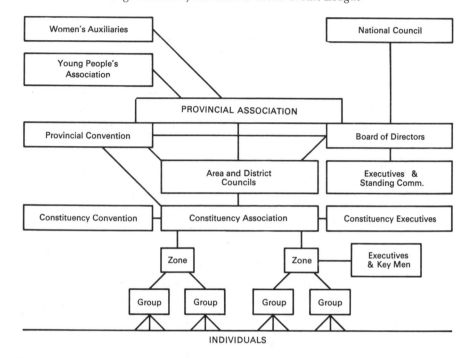

*Based on the constitution of the Alberta Social Credit League.

25At the NDP of Alberta Founding Convention there were 172 union delegates, 98 New Party Club delegates, and 85 CCF delegates. See Gad Horowitz, *Canadian Labour in Politics* (Toronto: University of Toronto Press, 1968).

26The NDP member of the Legislative Assembly, Mr. G. Turcott, attacked the Socred government for misuse of public funds and improper activities on the part of two Socred cabinet members. The incident led to the appointment of a Judicial Inquiry Commission. (See a special edition of *The Alberta Democrat*, Vol. I., No. 9 [January 1968] for details of the event.) The NDP fought the 1967 general election campaign by challenging the honesty of the Socred government.

27During the 1967 election the NDP received approximately $20,000 in campaign contributions from trade unions. See Peter Hill, "The Alberta New Democratic Party" (unpublished paper, University of Lethbridge, 1968.)

28The 1969 Alberta Legislative Assembly lowered the voting age to nineteen.

29*Re-organization of the Alberta Social Credit League,* a publication for internal circulation made available to the authors through the courtesy of Mr. Orvis Kennedy, the president of the League.

30*Ibid.,* p. 2.

31They include the Planning and Programming Task Force, Financial Task Force, Membership Task Force, Data Task Force, Policy Review Task Force, Communication Task Force, and League Task Force.

FIGURE 2

*Central Organ of the Alberta Social Credit League**

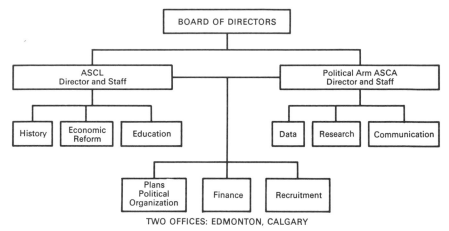

*Supplied by the Alberta Social Credit League.

religion-oriented Social Credit organization. Not long before the departure of Premier Manning the central organ was divided into two branches, the Alberta Social Credit League and the Political Arm, formerly called the Alberta Social Credit Association (see Figure 2). The League organization, which is under the control of the old guard, is now "historical" in both its influence and its operation. However, in order not to alienate the older generation, Premier Strom introduced the idea of a "second income plan" which may pacify those who retain a nostalgia for the old Social Credit "Money Plan."[32] It is evident that the party made every effort to absorb new blood as well as new techniques of organization. The Political Arm and the new task forces were designed essentially for younger talents. A key question is whether the Social Credit organization can remain viable when the party is out of power. Already a splintering between the older and the younger members appears to be taking place which could possibly signal a disintegration of the party organization. On leaving office Premier Strom commented that the Socred defeat could be attributed to the many political opportunists who saw the party as an instrument of their personal ambitions. It is rather doubtful that these young opportunists will remain with the party in its bid for a revival of power.

B. The Progressive Conservatives

The task of organizing the Alberta Progressive Conservatives has not been an easy one. Unlike the Social Credit party, which can concentrate its efforts on provincial politics, the Conservatives contest the federal as well as the provincial elections. In recent years, however, the Party has emphasized its operation at the provincial level, more or less leaving federal politics to

FIGURE 3

Organization of the Progressive Conservative Association of Alberta*

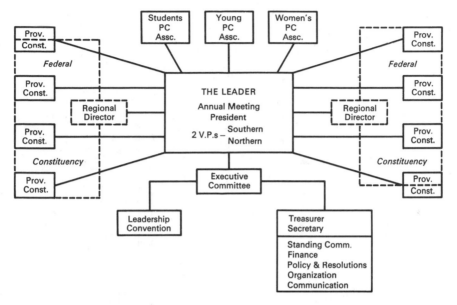

*Based on the constitution of the Progressive Conservative Association of Alberta.

its national headquarters. As Figure 3 indicates the party organization is based on both provincial and federal constituencies. However, the party constitution clearly charges the provincial leader with the responsibility in provincial politics. The leadership review has to be made "at the first Annual General Meeting of the Association following a *Provincial General Election*" by a secret ballot of the delegates.[33] The provincial and federal constituency associations operate separately, but with possible duplication in membership and officers. The separate structures not only facilitate the task-oriented operation at the constituency level but also make it possible for those who support other parties federally to join the Tory organization in provincial politics.

[32]At the 1969 Annual Convention of the Social Credit League Louis Kelso, from the United States, was a guest speaker. The "Kelso plan" is based on the argument that labor is no longer the main principal means for creating individual wealth and the individual's "right" to capital and investment is therefore in need of government protection. The plan proposes government loans to wage earners for investment, the dividends to become a second income for the individual and his family. It met with an enthusiastic response from old Social Crediters, who found a similarity between the plan and their old dream.

[33]*Constitution of the Progressive Conservative Association of Alberta,* Article 13.

FIGURE 4

Organization of the Liberal Association of Alberta*

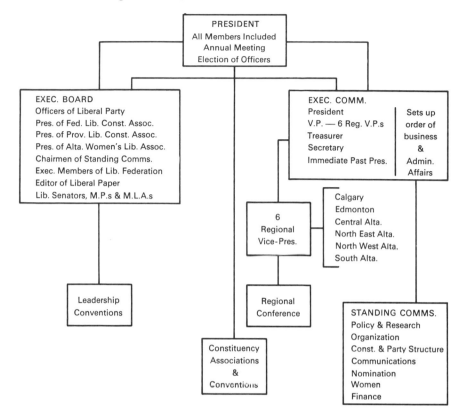

PRESIDENT
All Members Included
Annual Meeting
Election of Officers

EXEC. BOARD
Officers of Liberal Party
Pres. of Fed. Lib. Const. Assoc.
Pres. of Prov. Lib. Const. Assoc.
Pres. of Alta. Women's Lib. Assoc.
Chairmen of Standing Comms.
Exec. Members of Lib. Federation
Editor of Liberal Paper
Lib. Senators, M.P.s & M.L.A.s

EXEC. COMM.
President
V.P. — 6 Reg. V.P.s
Treasurer
Secretary
Immediate Past Pres.

Sets up order of business & Admin. Affairs

6 Regional Vice-Pres.

Calgary
Edmonton
Central Alta.
North East Alta.
North West Alta.
South Alta.

Leadership Conventions

Regional Conference

Constituency Associations & Conventions

STANDING COMMS.
Policy & Research
Organization
Const. & Party Structure
Communications
Nomination
Women
Finance

*Based on the constitution of the Liberal Party in Alberta.

C. The Liberals

As was mentioned earlier, the question of whether to organize the party on the Progressive Conservative model, *i.e.,* separate conventions and structures for the federal and the provincial constituencies, was one issue that split the Alberta Liberal Executive in 1970. At present the orientation of the Alberta Liberal organization is to federal rather than provincial politics (see Figure 4). Because of the strong regionalism of Canadian politics a provincial party operating under the direction of its federal counterpart faces many difficulties. What would the position of the Alberta Liberals be should the regional interest conflict with the national policy of the Liberal government in power at Ottawa? On what basis can Alberta Liberals solicit the support of Albertans in provincial elections while the party is in general not "pro-Alberta" in the minds of the voters?[34] In order to improve their showing in provincial elections, the Alberta Liberals would have to develop an organiza-

FIGURE 5

*The Alberta NDP Organization**

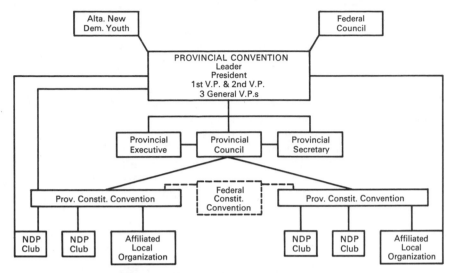

*Based on the constitution of the Alberta NDP.

tion, leaders, and policies independent of the federal party. This would, however, rule out any likelihood of the provincial party riding to power on the coat-tails of its national counterpart.

D. The NDP

Although as a provincial party the Alberta NDP is supposed to be "fully autonomous," the supremacy of the federal party is repeatedly emphasized in the constitution of the provincial NDP. Members, candidates, officers, and even the Provincial Convention, rhetorically proclaimed "the supreme governing body," are expected to act in consistency "with the constitution and principles of the Federal Party."[35] Although the party insists upon democratic practices, such as pro-rated representation of each local unit in the Provincial Convention (see Figure 5), the Provincial Council retains the authority to nullify a nomination made by a constituency convention "if the interests

[34]Robert Russell, "Alberta Needs an Independent Liberal Party," *Edmonton Journal*, January 14, 1970. See also, "Liberals Told: Only Move Left Can Save Party," *Ibid.*, November 10, 1969, referring to the so-called John Hotton paper, which advocates a move toward a "social democrat" position and a Liberal organization independent of its national counterpart; and "Alberta Liberals Consider Cutting Their Federal Ties," *Ibid.*, February 28, 1970.

[35]See the *Constitution of the Alberta New Democratic Party*, Articles 5(3), and 11(1).

of the federal or provincial party are involved."[36] The provision for disciplinary action by "warning, reprimand, or suspension for any cause" also indicates the centralist tendency of the NDP structure.

In contrast with the Liberal and the Progressive Conservative parties which are loose federations of voters, the Alberta NDP appears militant. Its constitution stipulates that "four or more members in any polling division . . . shall without fail" organize themselves "to see to it that every effort is made and every safe-guard taken to ensure the success of its candidate at the poll."[37] Emphasis on an action-group organization is reflected in the NDP clubs, which promote not only political but also "social and educational purposes." The Alberta NDP also makes provision for affiliated membership, evidently created for trade unions. This involves group membership with the provision that an individual member may opt out. As of 1971, the affiliated member organizations seem to be more effective in local political activity than the regular units of the NDP. In light of the political tradition in Alberta, the provincial NDP cannot attract significant electoral support until it achieves autonomy.

III. BASES OF ELECTORAL SUPPORT

Until recently empirical research into the voting patterns in Alberta provincial elections and of the social characteristics of provincial political party supporters has been lacking. Most studies of the Alberta electorate have dealt with the distribution of voter support among the federal political parties.[38] Because of the high incidence of alternate voting among the Alberta electorate, this research adds little to the study of provincial politics The long dominance of the Social Credit party in the province and its ineffectiveness in federal politics since 1958 is evidence of alternate voting among nearly half of Alberta voters.[39] Consequently, it is misleading to attribute the social characteristics of federal party supporters to provincial party supporters.

The result of this one-sided research is that one has had to rely upon speculative historical generalizations about the kind of people who vote for the different Alberta provincial parties. In general, there has been a tendency to assume that Social Credit draws its support mainly from the small towns and the countryside; the Liberal party from the urban, professional sector; the NDP from the workers and intellectuals; and the Progressive Conservative party from the urban middle class and some farmers.

However, data obtained in two studies of the Alberta electorate and a close study of recent provincial elections indicate that these generalizations are inadequate, obscuring what is in fact the heterogeneous nature of electoral support for each of the political parties and ignoring recent trends in provincial politics. Although these studies were made before the most recent Alberta election, they nevertheless allow us to develop a more adequate picture of the traditional bases of provincial party support among the Alberta electorate. In the following two sections we will examine the social and geographical cleavages in electoral support for each of the provincial parties.

A. Social Characteristics

The analysis in this section is based upon data taken from two surveys of the Alberta electorate, conducted in early 1968 and late 1969.[40] In both surveys, the demographic data were correlated with the respondents' recollections of their voting behavior in the 1967 provincial election. The correlations indicated a skewness in the sample in favor of the Social Credit and Liberal parties and an underrepresentation of NDP support. The Progressive Conservative party sample is very close to the actual percentage of votes the party received in the 1967 election.[41] The Social Credit and Liberal bias in the samples can be explained by the intrinsic limitations of random sampling and by the time of the surveys, which were conducted one and two years after the 1967 election. Nevertheless, the surveys are highly indicative and represent the most accurate picture yet obtained of the social characteristics of Alberta provincial party supporters.

For purposes of analysis we have classified the social characteristics of the Alberta electorate in terms of the demographic variables ordinarily used in the study of voting behavior: sex, religion, occupation, income, and education. The categories contained within the variables are dictated basically by the surveys themselves, as well as by their particular relevancy to the Alberta electorate. Data presented in Tables II through VII, except where specified, are directly from the 1969 survey.

The figures in Table II indicate that sex was not a major factor in determining allegiance to the Social Credit and Progressive Conservative parties.

[36]*Ibid.*, Article 18(9).

[37]*Ibid.*, Article 16(3).

[38]See Frederick C. Engelmann and Mildred A. Schwartz, *Political Parties and the Canadian Social Structure* (Scarborough, Ontario: Prentice-Hall of Canada, Ltd., 1967); Robert R. Alford, "The Social Bases of Political Cleavage in 1962," in *Papers on the 1962 Election,* John Meisel, ed. (Toronto: University of Toronto Press, 1964), pp. 203-234; S. Peter Regenstreif, "Some Aspects of National Party Support in Canada," *Canadian Journal of Economics and Political Science,* XXIX, No. 1, (February 1963), 59-74; and Wallace Gagne and Peter Regenstreif, "Some Aspects of New Democratic Party Urban Support in 1965," *Canadian Journal of Economics and Political Science,* XXXIII, No. 4 (November 1967), 529-550.

[39]See F.Q. Quo, "Split-Ticket Voting in Alberta," a paper delivered at the 40th Annual Meeting of the Canadian Political Science Association, Calgary, June 5, 1968.

[40]The first survey was carried out by F.Q. Quo for his study of alternate voting patterns among Alberta voters. The second was conducted by David K. Elton in conjunction with his study on electoral perception of federalism. Both studies used the proportional random probability sampling technique. The first survey, however, involved the use of mail questionnaires, whereas the second was conducted through personal interviews.

[41]The following is a comparison between actual election results and the sample returns:

	1967 Actual Results	1968 Sample	1968 Difference	1969 Sample	1969 Difference
Social Credit	44.6	52.7	+8.1	53.1	+8.5
Progressive Conservative	26.0	28.0	+2.0	24.6	−1.4
Liberal	10.8	10.3	− .5	14.7	+3.9
NDP	16.0	9.0	−7.0	7.6	−8.4

TABLE II

Party Support By Sex

Sex	Social Credit	Progressive Conservative	Liberal	New Democratic Party/CCF	No.
Male	53.6%	25.1%	11.2%	10.1%	179
Female	52.7%	24.6%	17.7%	4.9%	203

Both parties received an almost equal percentage of their electoral support from both men and women. Significant variations occurred in the support for the Liberal and New Democratic parties, where a substantially lower percentage of males voted Liberal but over twice as many males voted NDP as did females. The smaller percentage of women than men voting NDP can be related to the hypothesis that women, because of their greater traditionalism, are more likely to vote conservatively than men.[42] The total data, however, suggest that sex is of limited value as a determinant of provincial party allegiance and should be related to other demographic variables.

The breakdown of the religious vote by party in Table III emphasizes the hazards of generalizing about supporters of federal and provincial parties of the same name. Although the religious basis of both Social Credit and Progressive Conservative support is mainly Protestant, two-thirds of the province's Catholics and many members of other religious groups also voted for these parties in 1967. Catholic support is less signficant than Protestant support in terms of total party vote because there are considerably fewer Catholics than Protestants in Alberta.[43] This is true as well of those classified as "others." When we examine party support by religion for the provincial Liberal and NDP parties, Catholics gave nearly 28 per cent of their vote to the Liberal party and a neglible 3.5 per cent to the NDP.[44] On the other hand, only about 15 per cent of Protestants voted for these two parties. The NDP received the largest proportion of its support from the category "others," which includes the numerically smaller groups. This might reflect a tendency for ethnic minority groups in Alberta to support the NDP. But with the excep-

TABLE III

Party Support By Religion

	Social Credit	Progressive Conservative	Liberal	New Democratic Party/CCF	No.
Protestant*	59.6%	25.1%	9.4%	5.8%	223
Catholic**	40.7%	27.9%	27.9%	3.5%	86
Others***	47.9%	20.5%	15.1%	16.4%	73

*Includes Anglican, United Church, Baptist, Presbyterian and other Protestant sects.
**Includes Roman Catholic and Greek Orthodox.
***Includes Jehovah Witnesses, Mormons, Jewish, Christian non-affiliated, Buddhist, Hindu, etc.

TABLE IV*

Party Support By Age

Age	Social Credit	Progressive Conservative	Liberal	New Democratic Party/CCF	No.
20 to 29	48.2%	30.4%	12.5%	8.9%	56
30 to 39	44.3%	34.2%	8.9%	12.7%	79
40 to 49	52.9%	28.6%	14.3%	4.3%	70
50 to 59	56.0%	22.0%	10.0%	12.0%	50
60 and over	68.9%	20.0%	4.4%	6.7%	45

*Figures in Table IV are derived from the 1968 survey. In our opinion, the age group categories used in that survey are more meaningful for our purposes than those used in the 1969 one. The data from the 1969 sample are in general accord with the percentages listed above.

tion of this relatively high percentage of small group support for the NDP and the Catholic vote for Liberals, the Alberta electorate does not appear to be significantly divided along religious lines.

The survey data on age groups closely follow the popular impression that Social Credit derived a large part of its vote from older age groups. The percentage of electoral support given to the Social Credit party rose with the age of the voters. This generally concurs with the hypothesis that the people who supported the Social Credit party in its initial rise to power have remained constant in their party identification. The Progressive Conservative party appeared to draw nearly the same percentage of support from all age groups, with a slightly higher proportion from the younger and middle aged voters. Electoral support by age for the NDP was also scattered. The Liberal party appeared to receive a higher percentage of its vote from younger and middle age categories. This seems to be an indication that the support among younger voters for the federal Liberty party was tentatively carried over into provincial politics in 1967.

Occupation, income, and education are integrally related in determining socio-economic class and should be considered together in analyzing political behavior. As Table V suggests, the Social Credit party drew a substantial vote from every occupational group, although the percentages are highest for those occupations which require the least formal education, i.e., clerical workers, farmers, skilled workers, and housewives. Surprisingly, the proprietor-manager and professional groups gave a higher degree of support to Social Credit than to any other party. This points out that the suggestion

42Alford, "The Social Basis of Political Cleavage," p. 223.

43On this point compare Engelmann and Schwartz, *Political Parties*, p. 49. According to the Dominion Bureau of Statistics, the population of Alberta is 59.8 per cent Protestant and 28.6 per cent Catholic. Dominion Bureau of Statistics, *1961 Census of Canada, Religious Denominations*, Vol. I, pt. 2.

44This can be compared favorably with the Catholic vote for the Liberal party and the NDP in the 1962 federal election in Alberta. See Alford, "The Social Basis of Political Cleavage," p. 215.

TABLE V

Party Support By Occupation

Occupation	Social Credit	Progressive Conservative	Liberal	New Democratic Party/CCF	No.
Proprietor- Managerial	48.0%	28.0%	8.0%	16.0%	25
Professional	40.0%	35.6%	20.0%	4.4%	45
Clerical	66.7%	24.2%	6.1%	3.0%	33
Agricultural	58.1%	32.3%	6.5%	3.2%	31
Skilled Workers	63.4%	14.6%	12.2%	9.8%	41
Unskilled Workers	48.4%	22.6%	9.7%	19.4%	31
Sales Workers	46.7%	33.3%	13.3%	6.7%	15
Service Workers	54.2%	12.5%	16.7%	16.7%	24
Housewives	52.6%	24.4%	19.3%	3.7%	135

that Social Credit draws its leaders primarily from people with less education and social status than the other political parties cannot be extended to the people who vote for the party.[45] Distribution of Progressive Conservative party support among the occupational groups was uneven. It drew the greatest percentage of its strength from the non-manual occupations. The relatively low percentage of farmers supporting the Tories provincially before 1971 reflects the high degree of alternate voting in Alberta, where a large number of farmers voted for Progressive Conservative candidates at the federal level, but switched to Social Credit at the Provincial level. The small manual occupation vote for the provincial Progressive Conservatives is in striking contrast to Alford's study of the 1962 federal election, in which nearly half of the manual occupation vote went to the Tories.[46] The provincial Liberal party received its greatest support from the professional category. This perhaps reflects the dominance of lawyers and other professionals in the provincial Liberal party organization.[47] Other than clerical workers and farmers, who gave them only a small part of their vote, the Liberals received a fairly even percentage of support from the other occupations.

The occupational breakdown of support for the provincial NDP agrees with the general impression that the New Democrats are strongest among manual workers. The major exception is the relatively high percentage of support from the NDP found in the proprietor-managerial class. Again, this is in contrast with Alford's data on the 1962 federal election, where the federal NDP received a negligible percentage of the non-manual occupations vote. The fact that the NDP received some support from every occupational group indicates that in Alberta, at least, it is not a party of the poor.[48]

One would expect that the distribution of electoral support by income levels would correspond with distribution by occupation, as these two vari-

TABLE VI

Party Support By Income

Income	Social Credit	Progressive Conservative	Liberal	New Democratic Party/CCF	No.
Below $ 4,000	61.4%	22.8%	8.8%	7.0%	57
$ 4,000— $ 7,499	55.5%	22.7%	12.6%	9.2%	119
$ 7,500— $ 9,999	54.3%	29.3%	12.0%	4.3%	92
$10,000— $14,999	43.2%	28.4%	20.3%	8.1%	74
$15,000 & over	48.1%	14.8%	29.6%	7.4%	27

ables, along with education, are interrelated. The information in Table VI indicates the tendency of lower income groups to have voted for the Social Credit party. Although it is difficult to closely correlate income levels with occupational categories this tendency would seem to follow the higher incidence of voting for Social Credit among the clerical, skilled, and unskilled working groups. It must also be recognized, however, that the Social Credit party drew significant support from all income groups. Progressive Conservative strength appeared to be greatest among those individuals earning between $7,500 and $15,000, although the percentage of votes for the Tories was not appreciably less in the lower income groups. The number of responses in the $15,000 and over income category is inadequate for meaningful interpretation; a larger sample might yield a percentage figure closer to the level of electoral support the provincial Conservative party seemed to enjoy among the higher income occupations. The breakdown by income groups of support for the Liberal party seems to be related to the occupational distribution of the party's support. The large vote it receives from the higher income groups is probably additional evidence of its popularity with the professional class. The NDP appears to have received its greatest electoral support from the income groups at both ends of the scale. This corresponds with the earlier conclusion that the NDP is strongest among manual workers, service workers, and some intellectuals.

Data concerning the last variable, education, follow the pattern of electoral support by income and occupation. People with less formal education

[45]See Donald V. Smiley, "Canada's Poujadists: A New Look at Social Credit," *The Canadian Forum*, XLII, No. 500 (September 1962), 122.

[46]Alford, "The Social Basis of Political Cleavage," p. 218.

[47]Don Peacock, "Lowery Trying to Defossilize a Party of Lawyers," *Calgary Albertan*, (January 2, 1970).

[48]Regenstreif also makes this point about the federal NDP. See "Some Aspects of National Party Support in Canada," p. 62.

TABLE VII

Party Support By Education

Education	Social Credit	Progressive Conservative	Liberal	New Democratic Party/CCF	No.
Grade 9 & below	56.8%	23.4%	11.7%	8.1%	111
Some high school	56.1%	25.2%	7.5%	11.2%	107
High school	47.7%	30.8%	20.0%	1.5%	65
Technical	61.9%	19.0%	11.9%	7.1%	42
Some university	34.5%	27.6%	27.6%	10.3%	29
University graduate	44.4%	25.9%	25.9%	3.7%	27

were more inclined to vote Social Credit. The Progressive Conservative party attracted voters at all educational levels. Not unexpectedly, the Liberal party received more votes from the upper educational groups than from the lower ones. NDP strength appears to be polarized in the low and high educational group categories.

The preceding analysis reveals that popular assumptions concerning the social bases of provincial party support in Alberta tend to over-compartmentalize the Alberta electorate. When considered in terms of demographic variables, Alberta voters appear to exhibit a high degree of catholicity. Although different provincial parties can expect to receive a higher percentage of votes from certain socio-economic groups, these margins are not significant enough to divide the electorate on a class basis. The fact that the parties received a fairly even proportion of electoral support from all socioeconomic groups indicates not only a lack of class voting, but also a high level of satisfaction with the Social Credit administration during the sixties. The Social Credit party, despite its evolution from a political movement to a pragmatic, administrative kind of party, retained its appeal to all voter groups and was able to rely upon a "politics of consensus" within the Alberta electorate. It had, however, rebuilt this consensus in a society which is no longer dominated by the small independent farmer but has become socially and economically heterogeneous.

B. Geographical Bases of Party Support

Like most other Canadian provinces Alberta has experienced increasing urbanization. At present nearly 50 per cent of its population resides in the two major urban centres, Calgary and Edmonton.[49] Alberta has always had a comparatively large urban population, but the ratio of urban to rural population has shifted considerably in the last two decades, a shift accentuated by our absolute decline in population in many rural areas. The effect

TABLE VIII

Province-Wide Vote by Party*

Election Year	Social Credit			Liberal			Conservative			CCF/NDP		
	Major Urban**	Small Urban***	Other Districts	Major Urban	Small Urban	Other Districts	Major Urban	Small Urban	Other Districts	Major Urban	Small Urban	Other Districts
	%	%	%	%	%	%	%	%	%	%	%	%
1944	23	5	72	—	—	—	—	—	—	25	5	70
1948	25	8	67	32	5	63	—	—	—	24	6	70
1952	28	9	63	27	5	68	100	—	—	32	4	64
1955	31	8	61	41	4	55	68	15	17	31	6	63
1959	34	8	58	39	4	47	43	9	48	48	3	49
1963	38	8	54	47	8	45	54	9	37	48	6	46
1967	41	8	51	53	9	38	62	9	29	44	6	50
1971****	47	7	46	61	16	23	54	6	40	57	7	36

*Source: Government of Alberta, *Provincial Election Returns*.
**Includes voters in the Calgary, Edmonton, and Strathcona (Edmonton) constituencies.
***Includes voters in the Lethbridge, Red Deer, and Medicine Hat constituencies.
****Election data from unofficial sources.

of this population shift is that new patterns of urban-rural distribution of electoral support for the provincial parties have emerged.

Over the span of the last twenty years an increasing proportion of each party's total vote has come from Calgary and Edmonton. As Table VIII indicates, between the elections of 1952 and 1971 the proportion of total Social Credit vote from these areas increased by 19 per cent, Liberal support by 34 per cent, and NDP vote by 25 per cent. The relative growth of Progressive Conservative strength should be traced from 1959, because in the 1952 election the party ran no candidates in rural constituencies and in 1955 it contested only fifteen constituencies in addition to those in Calgary and Edmonton. Since 1959 the urban proportion of its total vote has increased by 11 per cent.

The breakdown of electoral support by area given in Table IX, however, shows that the growth of the Conservative vote in Alberta's major urban centers has been far more rapid than for the other parties, to the point where the Conservatives are now the dominant urban party, having won all 16 seats in Edmonton and nine out of thirteen in Calgary in the last election. Table IX also indicates that the Tories' province-wide strength increased and that the party captured the most votes or an equal share in every area except the small urban districts in Southern Alberta. A highly significant aspect of the

[49]Dominion Bureau of Statistics, *1966 Census of Canada*, I (1-8), March 1968.

TABLE IX

Percentage of Vote by Party in
*Major Urban, Small Urban, and Rural Areas**

| | Major Urban Districts** | | | | | Small Urban Districts*** | | | | | All Other Districts | | | | |
Year	Social Credit	Liberal	Conservative	CCF/NDP	Other	Social Credit	Liberal	Conservative	CCF/NDP	Other	Social Credit	Liberal	Conservative	CCF/NDP	Other
1944	43			22	35	47			20	33	56			27	17
1948	49	20		15	16	66	15		19		58	17		21	4
1952	50	19	12	14	5	74	18		8		58	24		14	4
1955	40	35	17	7	2	53	20	20	7		50	30	3	9	8
1959	51	15	28	6	.3	64	7	27	2		57	14	21	4	4
1963	49	22	16	11	2	57	21	15	7		59	17	9	9	6
1967	38	12	34	15	.2	44	13	30	13		51	9	17	18	5
1971****	38	1.5	49	12	.01	47	3	39	11		45	.6	45	9	.08

*Source: Government of Alberta, *Provincial Election Returns*.
**Includes voters in the Calgary, Edmonton, and Strathcona (Edmonton) constituencies.
***Includes voters in the Lethbridge, Red Deer, and Medicine Hat constituencies.
****Election data from unofficial sources.

Conservative victory is the successful invasion of the traditional stronghold of Social Credit, the rural ridings. For the first time in Alberta political history the Conservatives have been able to gain a province-wide base of electoral support. The Liberal party suffered severe losses in all parts of the province. The NDP vote declined most heavily in the rural areas, but the party also lost support in the rest of the province. The proportionate distribution of a party's strength will become increasingly important in assessing its fortunes in future Alberta provincial politics.

IV. CONCLUSION

Our analysis of contemporary Alberta provincial politics suggests that it is no longer possible to view the Alberta party system solely in the context of Macpherson's theory of a "quasi-party" system.[50] Although his *Democracy in Alberta* still represents the best historical explanation of the rise of political movements in Alberta, his quasi-party thesis, which argues the existence of one dominant party within a homogeneous electorate, had greater validity two decades ago than it does today. It is doubtful whether the two conditions necessary for the existence of a quasi-party system — quasi-colonial status and a predominately *petit-bourgeois* society — still exist in Alberta. Alberta no longer has to battle the federal government for natural resources; she now controls and has developed her own natural resources, becoming one of the richest provinces in Canada. Moreover, Alberta voters seem satisfied with having their representation in Ottawa channeled through the traditional national parties. Although Alberta still confronts the national government in the areas of grain marketing, allocation of tax revenue, language rights, and other issues, these conflicts add very little to a party's strength in provincial politics. Conflicts between Ottawa and the provincial governments have been a rather common phenomenon of Canadian federalism in recent years and cannot be considered peculiar to Alberta. Regarding the second condition, the majority of the present Alberta electorate cannot be characterized as having an "independent producer outlook." The last two decades have witnessed an extensive diversification of the Alberta economy.[51] The number of Albertans engaged in farming is continually declining, while the resource extraction, service, and light manufacturing industries are expanding. Accompanying this economic diversification is the growing trend toward urbanization and the development of political attitudes more characteristic of urban voters. The Alberta of today is a socially and economically heterogeneous society. Consequently, Macpherson's homogeneous class theory as the basis for a quasi-party system needs substantial modification. Very little class voting exists. All provincial parties attract some votes from every socio-economic group in the Alberta electorate. The fact that the Social Credit party drew, prior to the last election, a larger proportion of support from each of these groups than any of the other provincial parties indicates that its electoral success was not due primarily to an image as a party of the *petit-bourgeois,* but rather that it governed sufficiently well to satisfy most of the social and economic groups in the Alberta electorate.

It can be argued that the political structure of Macpherson's quasi-party system only partly exists in the present Alberta political system. Lipset is basically correct in his contention that the large legislative majorities in Alberta political history have been partly the result of the opposition vote being divided among a number of parties.[52] As we have pointed out above, moreover, the size of a legislative majority can also be related to the degree of maldistribution in the electoral system. Rural areas have until the last election always been overrepresented in the Alberta legislature and Social Credit has been the major beneficiary of this maldistribution.[53]

[50]Macpherson, *Democracy in Alberta,* pp. 237ff.

[51]The following socio-economic indices clearly indicate the changes which have taken place in Alberta in recent decades:

	1931	1961
Population engaged in agriculture	56.41%	25.16%
Net value of production: agriculture	52.85%	18.7%
Population living in urban areas	31.1%	63.9%

As of 1966 the oil industry provided 27 per cent of the productive value of industries in Alberta. Alberta Bureau of Statistics, *Alberta Industry and Resources,* 1968.

[52]Seymour Martin Lipset, "Democracy in Alberta: Part I," *Canadian Forum,* November 1954, 175-177.

[53]See John Anthony Long, "Maldistribution in Western Provincial Legislature: The Case of Alberta," *Canadian Journal of Political Science,* II, No. 3 (September 1969), 345-355.

For a dynamic interpretation of the recent history of party politics in Alberta we suggest the use of the "developmental approach," designed originally for the study of developing political systems.[54] The main advantage of applying the developmental approach to Alberta is that changes in provincial politics can be explained in light of the necessity of the party system to adapt itself to a modernizing society. The demise of Social Credit as an ideological movement and its transformation into a success-oriented administrative party with a differentiated structure is a reflection of this adaptation process. This process is of course conditioned and directed by the strong tradition of democracy in Alberta. That is, democracy is a framework within which the development of the Alberta party system must take place. Albertans may respond favorably to a charismatic leader in times of unusual social stress, as they did to William Aberhart, but they do not hesitate to demand that charisma be accompanied by pragmatic governing ability. Furthermore, a strong identification with the rest of Canada also limits the directions party politics will take. Albertans did not seriously threaten to separate from confederation during the 1930's, nor does it seem likely that they will do so in the future.[55] Within these limitations one can draw a meaningful analogy between the course of political development in Alberta and a developing nation.

Another advantage of such an approach is that it complements Macpherson's quasi-party thesis by adding to it an explanation of recent developments in Alberta provincial politics. That is, the quasi-party system should be considered as a stage in the development of the Alberta party system, a stage the party system has now passed beyond. Finally, the developmental approach may facilitate comparative study of provincial politics in Alberta and in other provinces. Instead of over-emphasizing the idiosyncrasy of Alberta provincial politics, the developmental approach may provide common measures for cross-provincial comparison.

[54]G.A. Almond and G. Bingham Powell, *Comparative Politics: A Developmental Approach* (Boston: Little, Brown and Company, 1966).

[55]See David K. Elton, "Electoral Perception of Federalism: A Descriptive Analysis of the Alberta Electorate," a paper presented at the One Prairie Province Conference, May 10-13, 1970, Lethbridge.

* BRITISH COLUMBIA *

The Politics
of Class Conflict

MARTIN ROBIN

I. SOCIAL STRUCTURE

The British Columbia party system has evolved from and reflects a unique social environment. Frequently designated a fragment of western Canadian society, British Columbia is as distinct in social structure and party politics as it is in ideology and culture. British Columbians are westerners, but they share little in common with the Prairie provinces. They are Canadians, but only half-heartedly attached to their loose and variegated federation. British Columbians cultivate and feed on a sense of uniqueness and they are aided immeasurably in their narcissistic idolatry by the great Rocky Mountain divide which separates this remarkable land of mountains, forest, and sea from the flattened land mass to the east.

Western Prairie politics in Canada have been indelibly stamped with the ideology of agrarianism. Industrialism, with its concomitant changes in class structure, is a latecomer to the Canadian prairies, and the western provinces, outside of British Columbia, have been until the Great Depression predominently rural expanses populated by independent commodity producers. In all three provinces, Manitoba, Saskatchewan, and Alberta, indigent farmers have banded together in social and economic organizations to oppose the railways, the urban middlemen, and the eastern financial interests that controlled the institutions and made the decisions that affected their lives as consumers and producers. They organized politically as well to oppose the major national parties traditionally responsive to the eastern financial and industrial interests. The centre of gravity of the Progressive movement was in the Prairies and the contemporary culture and politics of these provinces, although markedly changed from an earlier day, still bear the certain stamp of agrarianism.

The British Columbia frontier differs from the Prairie frontier. The latter was settled by independent commodity producers who owned the means of production they worked with, produced agricultural commodities for sale to a largely external market, and refrained from employing wage labour except on a small scale. British Columbia society developed as a corporate frontier and the agrarian sector has always played a smaller part in the economy, and in the society and politics of the province, than has its equivalent in the Prairies.

The British Columbia economy is peculiarly dependent, directly and indirectly, on the extraction of natural resources, particularly forest, mineral, and water resources. The primary extractive industries, producing goods and services for sale outside the province and the country, form the hub of the economy. Auxiliary industries which supply goods to the other industries of the province, and the consumer-oriented industries, are both dependent on the primary industries. The auxiliary industries exist only to service the basic industries, and without the income and employment provided by these two classes, the local consumer-oriented industries would have no market.

The basic outline of the British Columbia economy has not changed since the turn of the century. The fortunes of different industries have risen and fallen with economic expansion. The relative importance of some industries such as agriculture and fishing have declined while other industries, such as petroleum and natural gas, have flourished. But the structure of the economy, tied to the foundations of the primary-resource-extractive industries, has remained unaltered. Enjoying the economies of large-scale production, British Columbia has long been a "company" province and the large enterprise, rather than the small family homestead, is the dominant shape on the social landscape. Scattered throughout are company towns, single-enterprise communities subsisting on the activities of resource extraction which provide the goods for an economy serviced and administered by the heavily populated area of metropolitan Vancouver.

Along with the rise of an industrial economy based on resource extractive industry there has grown a labour movement stronger and more articulate than any in Western Canada. Agrarianism has coloured the economy and culture of the Prairie provinces. The labour movements in all three provinces, with the possible exception of Manitoba,[1] have been relatively weak and wielded little effective political power. Socialism emerged as a strong political force only in Saskatchewan, where the farmers' movement provided the principal, although not the only, social base of the Co-operative Commonwealth Federation. In British Columbia there grew steadily, from the onset of industrialism, a virile labour movement intent on checking the powers of the employing class in a company-dominated province. Carried by radical British and American workers, socialism emerged as a viable ideology and movement around the turn of the century, at a time when the movement was weak and ineffective in most other Canadian provinces.

Large-scale production and the structure of employment in the coal- and metal-mining industries assured that industrial unionism, with its radical ideology, was well represented within the provincial labour movement. The British workingmen who first led the unions and worked the coal mines of Vancouver Island were not the highly skilled and exclusive artisans who dominated the trade assemblies of Ontario during the 1880's. They were men from the North of England who brought to Canada organizational skill and a marked propensity toward independent politics characteristic of the English and Scottish northern mining communities. Equally militant were the many American workers who provided the early constituency of radical unions like the Western Federation of Miners. The frontier labour conditions prevailing in the metaliferous mining areas of the Pacific Northwest shaped the outlook and temperament of many of the miners who settled in the B.C. interior. The employing class's views of property rights were narrowly and rigidly defined. The proliferation of company towns, the struggles of the hardrock miners, the millmen and smeltermen within the bowels of the earth, the rapid proliferation of militant employers' associations and the frontier tradition of violence as a solution to social conflicts, contributed to the creation of a "heritage of conflict" between capitalists and workers.[2]

The legacy of class opposition, forged over decades of bitter struggle, persists in virile form today and colours the ideology of contemporary workers. The coastal labour movement is highly politicized. Labour has unabashedly engaged in partisan politics, not simply the Gompersian variety of rewarding friends and punishing enemies, but ideological politics. Since the turn of the century, important sections of the organized labour movement have formed the primary electoral base of socialist parties, militant by Canadian standards, which have been within reach of power for decades. The question of labour's political action, together with a host of issues arising from working-class participation, form enduring themes of the British Columbia political culture.

British Columbia labour leaders have acted politically, in both pragmatic and ideological ways, because they correctly perceived that the problems the workers faced were insoluble except by state intervention through partisan alignment. Workers organized politically to overcome problems and lessen insecurities which could not be remedied by industrial organization alone. The problems and insecurities facing coast workers were legion and their political response was correspondingly strong. "The labour movement in British Columbia," one close observer has written, "has always faced a high degree of insecurity, greater than in most areas of the country."[3] The perceived insecurities of coast workers stemmed from a variety of causes and circumstances. The province has been subject to waves of immigration — Oriental, central and eastern European, and American — which have created an unstable labour market. For decades, trade unions sought to restrict the

---

[1] Winnipeg has a history of trade union militancy.

[2] See Vernon J. Jensen, *Heritage of Conflict* (Ithaca, New York: Cornell University Press, 1950), p. 11.

[3] Paul Phillips, *No Greater Power: A Century of Labour in British Columbia* (Vancouver: British Columbia Federation of Labour, Boague Foundation, Broadway Printers, 1967). The central European and Oriental employee, as opposed to the more militant British worker, was preferred by mine owners like Edmund Kirby, manager of the large War Eagle Mine in the Kootenays, who wrote "In all the lower grades of labour and especially in smelter labour it is necessary to have a mixture of races which includes a number of illiterates who are first-class workmen. They are the strength of an employer, and the weakness of the union." Kirby's views applied to coal mining as well where Oriental labourers occupied the lower rungs of the social ladder.

influx of oriental immigrants, who were used by the employing class to break strikes and lower wage rates in mining and other employments.[4]

The insecurity that many workers felt in the face of foreign labour was reinforced by the employment and wage fluctuations of a specialized resource-based economy directly responsive to and dependent upon the vagaries of external markets. A much larger percentage of the wage income of British Columbians, as compared to Canada as a whole, derives directly from the export of goods and services and is subject to the rise and fall of world prices.[5] Construction, mining, and lumber workers have been particularly vulnerable to seasonal and cyclical unemployment and to high job turnover. Workers quickly understood that the problems of cyclical unemployment could not be solved by union action alone. During depressed periods large groups of unemployed became radical and when conditions improved they brought their militant ideology into the organized labour movement.[6] Workers became equally restive during inflationary periods, when real income fell; socialist and labour parties enjoyed their greatest support during periods of rising prices rather than during periods of recession.[7]

Large sections of British Columbia industry have been prone to conflict and the frontier conditions which obtained in the American Pacific Northwest and Mountain states were equally in evidence across the international boundary. The maritime, mining, longshoring, and lumber industries were plagued by harsh conditions: a high accident rate, geographical and social isolation, a high turnover rate, and unstable family circumstances. The closed nature of many homogeneous single-industry mining communities with no middle-class to mediate industrial conflict, in which class lines were clearly drawn, contributed to the development of an intense working-class consciousness freed from the restraints of traditional conservative institutions like the church, family, and an "enlightened middle class." A significant portion of the west coast labour force has been located in non-urban areas where little contact is maintained with the urban middle classes. Workers in these outlying communities developed an intense group consciousness, a cohesive isolation experienced by miners, loggers, and fishermen who lived and worked on "the periphery of modern society."[8] The employers in these industries tended to be robust newly-risen capitalists intent on extracting as much surplus profit as circumstances would allow. Men like James Dunsmuir, proprietor of a vast industrial empire on the Island at the turn of the century, were captains of industry untroubled by a conservative ethic of social obligation.[9]

Institutions for regulating industrial conflict grew slowly in British Columbia and collective bargaining procedures remained poorly developed for decades. Since World War II, the adoption of compulsory recognition of unions and the provision of machinery for channeling conflict has dampened the overt struggle, but the increasingly widespread use of the injunction and of other legal restrictions on collective bargaining "has tended to destroy the ability of the bargaining process to control conflict within institutional channels."[10]

The industrial class struggle in British Columbia has necessarily involved a struggle for political power. The early union of industrial captains and political parties was fruitful and the state was used to create and consolidate company empires which flourished in the ruggedly individualistic environment of the mountain province. Many labour leaders quickly realized that what the state granted the state could take away, and they worked to curb businesses' hold on government by exerting influence within the non-socialist parties through support of "independent" candidates sympathetic to labour's claims. They did this in industrial constituencies with a high concentration of politically active unionists. A significant section of the labour movement has, for many decades, by-passed the non-socialist parties and candidates altogether, and channeled the resources of organized labour into support of socialist parties that aim to restructure British Columbia society in a fundamental way.

In contrast to the labour movement in the coastal province, and to the farmers' movements in the other western provinces, British Columbia agrarians have never paraded a myth of social regeneration and have rarely strayed from the quiet confines of the major non-socialist parties in their search for economic redress. The major struggle in the fractured coastal community, aside from regional disputes of varying intensity, has been the class struggle between worker and capitalist. The British Columbia agrarians have not viewed themselves as an oppressed class and have refrained from importing or creating on their own a social philosophy, or myth of agrarianism, which would articulate their desire for a new golden age of blissful cultivation. Thomas Jefferson, William Jennings Bryan, and Henry Wise Wood have received a cold reception in the sunny orchards of the Okanagan and pretty greenery of Saanich.

In a society as industrialized as British Columbia, the farming class has rightly never seen itself as a majority, or as being synonymous with "the people." Farmers have been reluctant to parade under the banner of "agrarian power" or any other physiocratic slogans. In Alberta and Saskatchewan, the farmers' movements spoke for a large majority of the population and both

4Letter of Edmund S. Kirby to T.C. Blackstock, *Laurier Papers* (Public Archives of Canada, January 31, 1901).

5R.A. Shearer, "The Development of the British Columbia Economy: The Record and the Issues" (unpublished manuscript, 1967), p. 16.

6Phillips, *No Greater Power,* p. 162.

7*Ibid.*

8Stewart Jamieson and P. Gladstone, "Unionism in the Fishing Industry in British Columbia," *Canadian Journal of Economics and Political Science,* XVI, (February 1950), 2.

9Much of British Columbia wealth, today as well as in early days, was newly acquired and "no man is so cruel to the poor as a poor man grown rich . . . ." G.S. Williams, "The Labour Unions in Relation to Mining," *Westward Ho,* July 1907, p. 36.

10Phillips, *No Greater Power,* p. 164. The B.C. labour movement is today the most highly organized and strike prone in the Dominion. About 43 per cent of the paid labour force are in trade unions compared to about 33 per cent for Canada as a whole. From 1949 to 1959 the non-agricultural labour force in British Columbia, comprising 10 per cent of the total force of the country, contributed 15 per cent of all strikes and lock-outs. Industrial disputes in British Columbia have been longer and more difficult to settle than in other parts of the country.

provinces were governed for years by farmers' parties. The outstanding feature of the class composition of these provinces has been the high number of independent commodity producers which, in Alberta, formed about 48 per cent of the gainfully employed occupations between 1921 and 1941, while in British Columbia the same number in 1941 stood at no more than 13.1 per cent, a figure which declined to 4 per cent in 1961.[11] Independent commodity producers in Alberta continued to outnumber industrial employees and, in 1941, farmers constituted about 45 per cent of the gainfully employed and industrial employees 41 per cent. Since the beginning of the century, industrial workers in British Columbia have greatly exceeded the farmers in number.

An indebted rural peasantry or tenantry, or an impoverished rural proletariat have been traditional seed-beds of discord. British Columbia farmers stress ownership: only 4.1 per cent of the farms were rented in 1961.[12] Approximately 85 per cent of the farm operators in 1961 held the title to their land with 75 per cent of the total number of farms free from mortgages or agreements for sale. British Columbia agriculture resembles in some respects the farm regions of the Maritimes, another area of rural political quiescence, with a large number of farms being on a small scale (30 per cent) or part-time (50.9 per cent) and only 54.8 per cent commercial farms.[13] Since farming in British Columbia is still basically a family affair, the wage bill related to gross output is not high and the rural proletariat remains a small inarticulate group.

Farming in British Columbia has been a relatively successful operation and the ample monetary returns cooled whatever ardour agrarians may have had for social reform. Favourable climatic conditions and cost structures have allowed common B.C. farm commodities like fruit, milk, and vegetables to compete successfully in foreign markets, and the internal market for these commodities has been stable. Tree farming and ranching attracted capitalistically oriented farmers, some of whom began operations with substantial investments. Their native conservative sentiments were reinforced by the discipline of occupations that placed a premium on patience and long-term planning.

British Columbia agriculture is highly varied and the great regional and occupational diversity has retarded the development of common rural culture and group consciousness. Unlike Saskatchewan, where farmers were common residents of a great wheat culture, the perceived particular interest of regional rural groups, wedded to a common employment, superseded any generalized conception of the farmers as a class, with a separate class interest. "Strictly speaking," wrote Louis Aubrey Wood in his pioneering study of Canadian farm movements, "the physical characteristics of British Columbia and the diversity of its occupations have been, and still are, the main hinderances to an evolution of class-consciousness among its rural dwellers."[14]

There is considerable diversification both within and between the major agricultural areas of the province concentrated in the Peace River, Okanagan, Vancouver Island, and Lower Fraser Valley regions. The Peace River region is the grain basin of the province with over 68 per cent of all acreage devoted to the growing of wheat, oats, and barley. The Okanagan region is intensively farmed and highly diversified. In the north, the emphasis is on livestock, cultivated grains, grass, and commercial vegetable and potato growing. From the northern limit to Kelowna the emphasis is on apple production. Specialized crops such as fruit trees and vegetables are grown on the irrigated lands throughout lower Similkameen and the Okanagan valleys. The Okanagan provides for 90 per cent of all fruit production in the province and is a major supplier of hot-weather crops such as tomatoes, peppers, etc. The Lower Fraser Valley is the major vegetable producing area and also the principal centre of small fruit production. A wide variety of cereal, fruit, and vegetables are grown on Vancouver Island. Dairy production is scattered in the Okanagan, Lower Fraser Valley, and Vancouver Island regions while beef cattle are raised in the Cariboo region.

The types of farmers that settled and cultivated these agricultural regions varied considerably but they generally shared an ideological and cultural conservatism which effectively prevented any fusion or co-operation between the farm and labour movements. The fruit farmers were described by Lord Grey as "par excellence Nature's Gentlemen," and when radical American unions began to expand in the interior at the beginning of the century, Grey confessed to Laurier that he felt "like an Elizabethan in the face of Papal Domination — and I look to the fruit growers to save the situation."[15] Bruce Hutchison, in his *Unknown Country,* described many of the Okanagan farmers as gentlemen Tories living in "cheerful well-groomed towns" and possessed of rich fields and fat cattle. "Here is a refuge . . . here is the true sanctuary of British Columbia. Here is a distinct race of men, basically English, running the largest fruit industry in British Columbia."[16] There settled in the Okanagan as well as in certain areas of Vancouver Island like Duncan, Victoria, and Saanich, many remittance men and other delinquent colonial offshoots of the British upper class. A.C. Bradley wrote of attractive districts in the Cowichan valley where retired military and naval men, "or what is generally known as the young son" lived comfortably on small incomes or pensions and casually farmed.[17] *The Week* reported in 1905 a large influx of remittance men whose "real home is in British Columbia

[11]See C.B. McPherson, *Democracy in Alberta* (Toronto: University of Toronto Press, 1935), p. 15, for the figures on Alberta; and Joseph J. Richter, *The Developing Pattern of British Columbia Agriculture,* Inventory of the Natural Resources of British Columbia, British Columbia Natural Resources Conference, 1964, p. 153.

[12]Richter, *Developing Pattern,* p. 153.

[13]*Ibid.* The number with more than 240 acres as well as those under 3 acres show an increase and the traditional smaller commercial farms of less than 7 acres are rapidly decreasing in number.

[14]Louis Aubrey Wood, *A History of Farmers Movements in Canada* (Toronto: Ryerson Press, 1924), p. 307.

[15]Grey to Laurier, September 13th, 1907, Grey Papers.

[16]Bruce Hutchison, *The Unknown Country* (Toronto: McClelland & Stewart, Ltd., 1948), p. 269.

[17]A.C. Bradley, *Canada and the Twentieth Century* (Westminster: n.p., 1903), p. 382.

which seems to afford them their real resting place."[18] The British influx into British Columbia's agricultural regions had the opposite effect of the migration from the "old country" into urban and industrial areas. The British worker formed the vanguard of coastal trade unionism and provided a ready radical constituency for union organizations in industries like coal mining. Rural areas in the Okanagan and on the Island, on the other hand, provided the gathering place for strange and exotic remnants of the British upper classes.

While the Peace River and Lower Fraser Valley regions contained fewer refined escapees from imperial England, and could even boast of a share of Alberta and Prairie radicals, most residents of these areas remained as conservative as their Okanagan and Island counterparts. "From Chilliwack to the Sea," Bruce Hutchison wrote, "the Fraser's earth has bred the kind of folk who live in the St. Lawrence Valley and are different in their life and in their ownership of land from the cereal farmers who work the open stretches of the prairies . . . these are peasants in the old fashioned and best sense of the term — people who live and cling to the soil, and maintain its virtues, asking no more than the fruits of their labour, but people who enjoy a standard of living high among the farmers of America . . ."[19]

The high standard of living of British Columbia farmers derived not merely from careful cultivation and favourable market conditions. Since the 1920's, the farmers have been recognised by the major parties and agrarian lobbyists have gained a host of important legislative enactments. Coast farmers have not formed broad class organizations campaigning under broad slogans of social reform, but they have organized interest groups like the British Columbia Fruit Growers' Association and the Fraser Valley Milk Producers' Association which effectively regulated standards of production and shaped the course of government legislation. A number of premiers — Oliver and Tolmie, for instance — were drawn from the rural classes. This over-representation of the rural interest in the electoral system, a conservative device up to the present day, has assured the presence of many vocal spokesmen for the rural interests in the legislature. Traditionally a major voice in the early Liberal and Conservative parties — and today effectively represented by the governing Social Credit party — the farmers have steadfastly refrained from engaging in any futile third party ventures. The province of British Columbia, according to Louis Aubrey Wood, remained until 1917, "entirely outside the sphere of influence of agrarian movements in Canada. . . ." Both the populist and progressive movements found little favour in rural British Columbia and the few radicals who propagated the faith of Henry Wise Wood and his predecessors could never find a wide and meaningful audience. A few locals of the Farmers' Alliance and Grange sparked and sputtered briefly in the years preceding World War I. A more important venture occurred after the war when the United Farmers of British Columbia briefly flirted with a motley and dissident bag of crank Conservatives in the ill-fated Provincial Party, which quickly passed from the provincial scene following its defeat in the 1923 provincial election. The Provincial Party fiasco proved the last real entry of rural British Columbia into third party politics until the peculiar Social Credit explosion in 1952.[20]

The quixotic and halfhearted Provincial Party venture attested to the essential bankruptcy of British Columbia rural progressivism. Unlike the Prairie Progressives, British Columbia farmers "seemed to see nothing in the nature of party as had developed in the province to account for the conditions against which they were protesting."[21] What the farmer seemed to be campaigning for was a party of "moderately honest people,"[22] and the slogan of the Provincial Party, "turn Oliver out and don't let Bowser in," amply testified to the ideological vacuousness of the movement. Third party adventurism failed basically in rural areas because the farmers had been able to wrest substantial gains from the major parties. "Largely because the various agricultural interests," Edith Dobie wrote in her pioneer survey of B.C. parties "have been organized and reasonably successful in gaining their demands upon the government, third parties have not played so large a part in British Columbia as in the prairie provinces."[23] Premier John Oliver played Mackenzie King to the rural Progressives in the late 1920's. The Oliver government recognized the power of the farmers and devised many policies to aid them. The *Province* reported on August 31, 1929, that ". . . the legislature has swelled the statute books with enactments for the relief of the farmers."

Today the farm communities receive priority treatment from the Social Credit government. The farmers enjoy, in addition to special land purchasing rights, a variety of fiscal concessions (especially under Property and Income Tax laws), special credit facilities, technical and marketing assistance, certain direct subsidies to agricultural products, and a large number of privileges and priorities not available to other industries.[24] Provincial legislation relating to forest, water, game, trespass, motor vehicles, and so on, all provide special privileges to farmers.

II. POLITICAL CULTURE

British Columbia has long been a fractured community. The major divisions in coast society are class and regional. A religious or racial cleavage, such as existed in Canada as a whole between the English and French, or in

---

[18]*The Week,* October 28, 1905.

[19]Bruce Hutchison, *The Fraser* (Toronto: Clarke, Irwin & Co., 1950), p. 210. By permission of Holt, Rinehart and Winston, Inc., New York.

[20]In 1936 the United Farmers of Canada (British Columbia section) announced its intention to coordinate efforts with the People's Party and Technocrats in Vancouver under the banner of the British Columbia Social Credit League, but little came of the venture.

[21]Edith Dobie, "Party History in British Columbia, 1903-33," *Pacific Northwest Quarterly* (1934), p. 158.

[22]*Vancouver Daily Province,* January 15, 1923.

[23]Dobie, "Party History," p. 158.

[24]P.H. Pearse, "Natural Resource Policies in British Columbia: An Economist's Critique" (unpublished manuscript), p. 10.

the province of Quebec between the two groups, has never taken root in the ethnically polyglot coast community.[25] This is not to suggest that ethnic and religious differences do not exist or fail to motivate people politically. Party support varies significantly among the different ethnic groups and religious and ethnic questions occasionally bubble to the surface as did the Catholic school question during the historic 1952 election. But, as studies have shown, class rather than religious or ethnic identification is a greater determinant of political preference, and ethnic and religious issues have not been major political questions dividing the political parties. British Columbia's separation from Canada is not a religious or ethnic difference, and group splits within the province revolve more around regional and economic issues than around ethnic or religious questions. Only one of the two ethnic elements which have divided federal and provincial politics in Canada — the English — is present in any number in British Columbia. The French-Canadians remain a tiny group little different in number and consciousness from the many other specimens of ethnic exotica which honeycomb the province.

It is difficult to say which cleavage, class or regional, is more critical in determining the structure and course of British Columbia politics. Divided as it is into distinct and separate cultural and geographic entities, enjoying different rates of growth and histories, and only slowly brought into greater union through the expansion of the provincial communication system, British Columbia is a society rife with xenophobia, with anxieties and antagonisms between regions which often rely only on the honeyed words of the party politician or the insular prose of the local press to gain mutual knowledge. The manipulation of regional antagonisms is a prime requisite of any successful coast politician and the Social Credit party have proved themselves experts in this ancient political game. The earliest significant split was between the Island and Mainland and rivalry between the two regions provided ample fuel for politicians in the decades following confederation. Subsequent population explosions increased the claims of new regions for representation and legislation. British Columbia today displays a high degree of concentration with about two-thirds of the population crowded into the Lower Mainland region. Although it has made significant inroads into the Lower Mainland region since 1952, an advance which assures its retention of power, the Social Credit party has enjoyed great and consistent support in the rural interior, in the north, and in the metropolitan area of Victoria. The Vancouver area has never been a happy hunting ground for the governing party.

British Columbia exhibits a high degree of nodality and the conflict between the centre and the periphery is sometimes severe and bitter. Metro Vancouver, the central place of the economy, exists in a state of symbolic tension with the hinterland. The city of Vancouver is the administrative centre of the provincial economy, the locale of the regional head offices, business firms, and financial institutions. Here too are concentrated the major auxiliary service industries and distribution facilities. The port and major overland transportation routes all radiate from the metro area. Whatever its role as a provider of services for the real producers of the interior, Vancouver is often seen by the plain folks in non-urban areas as a threatening parasite rather than a symbiotic partner and politicians like Phil Gaglardi have been careful to preserve this view.[26] The brashness and vulgarity of the Vancouver elite have done little to improve their public relations.

Regional and class divisions have both contributed to the persistence of a negative community in British Columbia. The British Columbia community exists only in the negative conviction shared by many that coast society is somehow different from the larger Canadian society. Otherwise there are few effective bonds tying estranged and conflicting groups into greater communion. An important factor guaranteeing the persistence of the negative community is the high immigration rate. In 1961 more than half of the local residents were born outside the province. Existing at the periphery of the western frontier, British Columbia has served as a magnet for persons discontented with their lot, personally, economically, and politically. It is peopled by a mass of individuals who have escaped from communities from which, for one reason or another, they had become estranged. Being a high income region, the coast province is an open arena both for fortune seekers and for ordinary people seeking a modest improvement of their standard of living. The per capita income of the province is significantly higher than the national average; in 1965 the provincial per capita income was $2,263, as compared to a national average of $1,983, a differential of 14 per cent over the national average and perhaps 60 per cent over the per capita income of the Atlantic region.[27]

British Columbia is the true home in Canada of the acquisitive spirit. From the days of Captain Vancouver when the white men came and traded beads for otter with the Indians, to the 1850's when the province was flooded with "off-scour-rings of the world" in search of gold, up to the present day, when rustic buccaneers like Ben Ginter build strange empires in the northern wilderness, the province has provided a happy haven and intoxicating climate for fortune seekers, boodle hunters, and promoters with questionable pasts and devious ways. Poets and plunderers have sung hymns of praise to the vast beauty and fleshly delights of the northern land and celebrated the great opportunity for every man there to become a king. While many perished in the uncertain hunt for the golden calf, and still more languished in a state of proletarian torpor from which they had tried desperately to escape, not a few became rustic emirs who wielded their new power with all the brash abandon of the parvenue. "Hobos in evening clothes," Joseph Martin described a motley gang of nabobs in Rossland, the early Johannesburg of British Columbia.

[25]This, of course, ignores the long history of strained relations between the white man and Indian, and between the whites and Orientals. In both instances, the minority group was vastly fewer in number and possessed little political power.

[26]Margaret Ormsby writes that the mass media emanating from Vancouver could never completely dominate the thinking of the people of the province, "for the residents of the hinterland are strong individuals who had arrived at their own set of values." Margaret Ormsby, *British Columbia: A History* (Toronto: Macmillan Company of Canada, Ltd., 1958), p. 439.

[27]Shearer, "British Columbia Economy," p. 19.

It is a common view that buccaneer capitalists, striving in a competetive state of nature, prefer that state which governs least. Capitalists have traditionally warned of the danger of state intervention, but the state action they have in mind is the kind that redistributes opportunities and incomes in favour of the lower classes. Government action that guarantees further opportunities and greater incomes for the upper classes has never met with much opposition but, on the contrary, has enjoyed considerable favour in Canada as a whole and in British Columbia in particular. Neither God, nor the exceptional financial or industrial talents of particular individuals who claim to be favoured by God, created the great bulk of corporate wealth in British Columbia. It arose instead from the monopolistic advantages conferred by governments on favoured persons through mineral grants, forest management licences, public utility franchises, land grants, public contracts and so on.[28]

With minor exceptions the Canadian constitution vests responsibility for natural resources in the governments of the provinces. The British Columbia government, therefore, is and has been in the position of being the grantor and regulator of the greatest material prizes this economy has to offer. No more evidence of the hypertrophy of the acquisitive spirit in British Columbia is needed than the fact that industrial magnates have striven, in large measure successfully, to acquire governments as well as economic resources. From the earliest days of the province, they realized that ownership of the first was a prerequisite to possession of the second and they quickly went about the task of buying governments with the same dedication and ingenuity displayed in purchasing lands or floating mine companies. Without a friendly government oriental labour could not be imported at lower wage rates, unions could not be easily combatted, and new timber licences and railway charters gained in ample number. "The people will always accept a railroad," commented one knowing local observer at the turn of the century, "if it is vigorously thrust down their throats." Investment in politics in British Columbia has always been good business.

The reckless political intervention of the economic buccaneers, with the resultant buying and selling of politicians, has debased the level of political morality in coast politics. In British Columbia there is a curious tension between the inherited British ideal of constitutional and democratic government operating through a parliamentary system, and a furious commerce intent on creating its own rules and rendering the political system subservient to its goals. In some respects the low level of political morality, the disregard for rules and established procedures, the rampant patronage and punitive political expeditions — civil liberties have never been greatly respected in B.C. — and the accompanying mass resentment and apathy, resemble pre-revolutionary Quebec, to which the coast province has sometimes been compared. There too, British political institutions were introduced but were hardly revered or made workable due to economic and cultural clashes between the English-Canadian elite, working with their French-Canadian counterparts, and the French-Canadian masses. In British Columbia, the mockery of the British ideal of fair and constitutional government has derived from a rampant and heady commerce industrializing a society with immature and poorly formed political institutions. This was clearly understood by Frances MacNab, who wrote a *Handbook for Settlers* in the coast province at the turn of the century. Being a good Englishman, MacNab attributed the coast's wild acquisitive spirit to the presence of American speculators and noted that while British Columbia was part of the empire of Great Britain, the province was similar to parts of the southern United States or California, ". . . inasmuch as there is a sudden enormous increase of wealth in a country whose constitution is scarcely hatched — whose system of administration is half-fledged, and whose laws have to be framed without the light of previous experience."[29] MacNab felt that the experience of older states like Britain cannot "offer much assistance in solving the political and economic problems relating to a highly advanced commerce which invariably shows a determination of establishing and creating a code for itself."[30]

The code dictated by a highly advanced commerce, which shaped political institutions in its own image, was not a pretty one, and British Columbia is possessed of a politics more corrupt than most in the country. Many observers have pointed to the materialism of coast politics. If, as Harold Lasswell has written, the science of politics is the study of who gets what when and how, then the "what" at stake in British Columbia is material goods, pure and simple. "British Columbia," commented the *Kaslo Kootenaian* in 1903, "has been in her political life cursed with a horde of hobos, who are utterly inconstant and apparently without the remotest sense of responsibility."[31] Since the inception of self-government scarcely an administration has survived without a serious financial scandal and British Columbians have become so accustomed to scandal during good times that the fate of governments seems unaffected by the financial misdemeanors of its ministers. The present government has survived a number of serious scandals, and when it is turned out of office, it will probably be defeated on issues other than political morality. In October 1958, Robert E. Sommers, former Minister of Lands, was convicted and sent to prison for being part of a conspiracy to accept bribes while serving as a minister of the Crown. The Sommers scandal had received full publicity for over two years, yet a by-election held in Sommers' Trail constituency soon after his conviction was easily won by Socred Donald Brothers, a lawyer who had managed Sommers' campaigns.

[28]*Who Owns B.C.?*, (Vancouver: Trade Union Research Bureau, 1965), p. 22.
[29]Frances MacNab, *British Columbia for Settlers* (London: Chapman and Hill Limited, 1898), p. 9.
[30]MacNab attributed the undermining of British institutions to American speculators — "right along the southern border of British Columbia is the northern boundary of the United States of America. This means the juxtaposition of a people composed of the restless dissatisfied fractions of many nations. They are a people prepared for anything, because they had nothing, and greedy to be rich; loving both wealth and the pursuit of wealth, till the value of everything is gauged by cents and dollars alone. British Columbia could find and had attracted the brave, hardy speculators, men who faced the difficulties of mountaineering in a country scantily supplied with food and possessed of a severe climate. The Americans came in as promoters and mining brokers, and companies were formed chiefly by capital which was drawn from the States . . . ." *Ibid.*, p. 5.
[31]*Kaslo Kootenaian*, June 4, 1903.

British Columbians are tolerant of corruption in prosperous times. During depressed periods, the ire of the masses is aroused. Liberal party organizer Harry Perry wrote to T.D. Pattullo in 1932 that "the patronage is the coarsest that ever existed in any state and is fast developing in the minds of the people a disgust that is leading to socialism or any other ism that is newer and affords a change."[32] The moral apprehensions of the working and middle classes were aroused early in the province's political history and socialism as a political philosophy and movement became a strong indigenous force at the very onset of industrialism. To the poets and plunderers, British Columbia is a province of promise, but to many who tasted the bitter fruits of exploitation and unemployment, it became a province of disappointment. Two philosophies and value systems exist in polar opposition within the coast society and are reflected in the party system. The extremity of each and the extent to which they have become engrained in the social fabric makes the concept of consensus, a favourite word of liberal political scientists, very tenuous in its application to the local scene. An extreme acquisitive individualism, which advertises a dynamic approach to the development of natural resources through private enterprise, with the government's role reduced to that of handmaiden, is opposed by a strong collectivism, engrained in the strong trade union and socialist movements and supported by other groups like the conservationists, who maintain that private enterprise tends to exploit resources, human and material, wastefully and immorally, and who advocate restraint and preservation of resources in the interests of society. The two value strains are represented by the major political parties: the Social Credit Party bent on the preservation of private enterprise, and the New Democratic Party imbued with the values of collectivism. The parties have, of course, moved closer over the last decade, with each absorbing a little of the other's policies. But their world-views remain significantly different because they reflect real divisions within the body politic.

The persistence of the negative community, aggravated by the spirit of acquisitive individualism and by the strong regional and class sentiments, has shaped the structure of the party system. Group loyalties to class and region are strong in the coast society, but partisan loyalties are, with some notable exceptions, relatively weak. Within the free enterprise sector of the electorate, party is seen less as an end in itself than as a means to an end: material gain — patronage or payola — or preventing the socialists from gaining power. When Goldwin Smith, at the turn of the century, enquired of a local citizen what his politics were, the reply given was not Grit or Tory, but "government appropriations." The failure of the Social Credit party to win the hearts and loyalties, as opposed to the votes, of the electorate is common knowledge, yet the government has remained in power since 1952 despite this reticent endorsement.

The British Columbia electorate, traditionally volatile and changeful, differs markedly from that of the Maritime provinces, which are characterized by stable populations and established party traditions. Old party loyalties were late established in British Columbia and were constantly eroded by a high rate of demographic growth. The scattered nature of the population over many diverse areas together with the peculiar nature of the principal industries, which keep a large number of persons continually moving from point to point, have further reduced the hold of party over people. The presence of a tradition of nonpartyism is evidenced by a number of factors: the long persistence of group as opposed to party government, the lengthy support for a coalition government and the currency of coalition ideas for decades, the reluctance of many government voters to describe themselves as party supporters, the difficulties with which most coast parties have maintained control over dissident factions. Party lines developed in British Columbia decades after the entry into confederation and early governments consisted of a shifting galaxy of uncertain factions. The high immigration rate, the great size and diversity of the province, and the perpetuation of strong social divisions not amenable to political conciliation have weakened party organization and contributed to the existence of both a non-partisan and multi-party tradition.

The task faced by governing parties of building a majority in a fractured community has been onerous and the governing party has attempted, like all ruling groups of the past, to propagate policies and ideologies consistent with the values of the masses of the people. Because the society has been divided into classes with differing values, this has been difficult but it has been accomplished to the degree that different groups share the same values common to British Columbia and to the degree that policies are flexible to suit needs of different groups. The Social Credit government has successfully advertised the ideal of *stable government* and pleas for political stability strike a chord of sympathy among numerous electors. Stable government in the British Columbia context means a number of things. Firstly, it means majority government. In a society torn by social antagonisms in which secure party lines were only lately and tenuously established, where a multitude of parties have flourished in a changeable climate, the desire of many for the security of a majority government is strong and the Social Credit government has satisfied this felt need. Secondly, stable government means strong government. Here too, the fragmentation of political support, together with the acquisitive frontier individualist's desire to get things done without due regard to how they are done, has convinced many of the need for strong executive leadership.

The desire for strong executive leadership in British Columbia may be thought to be a political legacy from Britain, where the authoritarian and deferential norms found in the social system buttress the support of strong leadership in the political system reflected in cabinet government. But it is, in British Columbia, more likely due to the effects of the acquisitive frontier culture. Action, not deliberation, results and not methods, are important in a society where the British respect for legality and due process has been undermined by the American frontier's thrust to possess and hold no matter what. Not the freedom to deliberate and communicate, but the freedom of the political and economic elite to act and get results is respected by people

[32]As quoted in Ormsby, *British Columbia,* p. 446.

concerned with achievement to the exclusion of rights. The opposition and the press cause little stir among the electors when they rant about government by Order-in-Council, a weak legislative committee system, the absence of a Hansard, and truncated legislative sessions. Like the captains of industry, the political lieutenants get things done and do not feel they should be obstructed by the wasteful activities of a deliberative assembly.

Finally, a stable government in British Columbia, where socialism is a bogey as well as a movement, means government that provides a favourable investment climate. Political stability, a majority government by a free enterprise party, is a guarantee of high employment and economic growth financed and engineered by private enterprise. Among large sectors of the electorate, concentrated in the middle- and upper-classes, and in prosperous rural areas, there exists a latent hysteria which is freely manipulated and exploited by the free enterprise parties during times of stress. Socialism is viewed not merely as a pernicious expropriative philosophy, but as a device for stunting economic growth and undermining full employment. A socialist society is defined as an economic wasteland, in which a boisterous and heady commerce, which provides goodies for all, has been rudely emasculated. The current premier, like many of his predecessors, is viewed as a successful promoter, a type much beloved in a society replete with ardent salesmen and devious manipulators. Social Credit has been viewed as a break with the traditions of British Columbia, but there are vast similarities between Sir Richard McBride, the collosus of the roads and father of great railway enterprises, and W.A.C. Bennett, the master builder of highways and great power projects. Both were cut from the same cloth; both conjured a vision of a great northern empire based upon construction of vast economic and transportation enterprises. British Columbia has been likened to California, but in some respects it more closely resembles Texas, where the wheeler-dealer, the devious promoter of grand scale enterprises, both political and economic, is a type much admired. Duelling with whirlwind salesmen in elections, opposition party leaders have appeared as the dismal prophets of economic doom. British Columbians much prefer the breezy optimism of a happy promoter.

Political promoters are frequently obstructed by alien persons and groups who lay claim to the stuff out of which empires are built. Socialist and labour leaders have been particularly troublesome. An equally obstructive force has been the federal government, which has served as a favourite whipping-boy of provincial politicians. By doing battle with the federal authorities, the premier preys on and activates regional sentiments and deflects internally divisive sentiments on to an external enemy. The community created is an artificial community, a negative unity that exists only in tenuous opposition to the federal government. The community is tenuous because regional sentiments in British Columbia are not, as in Quebec, passionately held. British Columbia has a distinct society, history, and political tradition, and it has a unique ethos. But British Columbians are not ardent anti-federalists and anti-nationalists. Their separatist sentiments are not reinforced by ethnic, religious, or national differences. Quebeckers see themselves as a nation, a conquered nation, and French Canadians are rightly concerned with the preservation of their language and culture. British Columbia is an ethnic hodge-podge with a majority of the contemporary population born outside of the province. When claims are pressed on the federal authorities, they are couched in material rather than cultural or nationalist terms. British Columbia wants "better terms" and a fair deal, rather than an opportunity to develop its cultural personality. Being more regional than cultural, coast separatist sentiments are only mildly held, but they have been prone to effective manipulation by resourceful premiers who, by arduously tilting at federal windmills, pre-empt feelings of regional patriotism and isolate opposition groups as alien apologists of a hostile external authority. Being residents of a resource-rich province, many British Columbians are disappointed that the promise of the happy frontier has not been fulfilled for them. Bennett is the last of the long line of premiers to blame all miseries on the federal government. He often speaks of the people of British Columbia as exploited rich men, residents of a "have" province unfairly treated by a central government caring for the poor of less industrious provinces. Just as reactionary sections of the middle classes flock to the standards of politicians who condemn the transfer of resources through taxation from the industrious to the idle needy, so the premier has received the support of people convinced that the earned wealth of British Columbia is being commandeered by a federal government solicitous of the unjust claims of the poor of the Maritimes and other provinces. In his more plaintive moments the premier speaks of British Columbians as a heap of forgotten men.

III. HISTORICAL DEVELOPMENT

Firm party lines with federal labels were not established in British Columbia until thirty-two years after the achievement of responsible government in 1871. From 1856 until the entry of British Columbia into Confederation, British Columbia was ruled by a governor and legislative council not responsible to an elected legislative assembly. But the 14th article of the Terms of Union pledged the Dominion to the establishment of a system of responsible government and the Constitutional Act of 1871 provided for the creation of a legislative assembly of twenty-five to be elected by a system of oral nominations and open-voting.[33]

The legislatures that met over the next three decades were organized along personal and sectional rather than party lines. Governments were coalitions of "interested" M.L.A.s who were nominated and elected by small constituency associations and who sat as representatives of sectional groups, geographical and economic, to some extent free from the fetters of party discipline. The legislature was a school of loose fish who dashed from group to group depending on the directions in which the political and economic currents flowed. "Perhaps the most confusing element in our political history," Howay and Schofield report, "is the constant change of the members

[33]F.W. Howay and E.O.S. Scholefield, *British Columbia* (Vancouver: S.J. Clark Company, 1914), II, 327.

of the Legislature from the support of one side to the support of its opponent . . . in none of these cases did the members receive any mandate from their constituencies to change their support."[34] The fate of the government hung upon the speaker and upon the presence of every government supporter when the division bells rang and rudimentary instruments of party discipline like the whip were absent.

Group government persisted in the coast province until 1903 when party lines, roughly drawn on the federal model, were introduced. For decades the British Columbia electorate viewed the rise and fall of personal dynasties built on the short-run collusion of promotional interests. The ruling regimes were business dynasties intent on using the state to further the interest of a particular economic group of enterprise — through the grant of land, mineral and timber rights, and railway charters. The legislature was composed largely of acquisitive merchants, lawyers, industrialists, and landed proprietors whose wealth derived chiefly from investment in land, transportation, mines, lumbering, salmon canneries, and flour mills.[35] The transportation interests were particularly powerful and well represented. There used to be a saying in Vancouver that the C.P.R. was the "government on wheels" and the same was said about the B.C. Express Company in the district from Ashcroft to Barkerville. John A. Mara, promoter of a number of transportation enterprises, held court in Kamloops and Revelstoke, while Robert Dunsmuir constructed a mighty empire on Vancouver Island. The Dunsmuir family, which owned the Esquimault and Nanaimo Railroad and Island Coal Mines, retained great power during and after the Smithe Dynasty. Robert Dunsmuir, founder of the family fortune, was a leading M.L.A. and cabinet minister until his death in 1889, while his son, who graced the office of prime minister at the high tide of his political fortunes, was politically prominent in the decade following. Many Island representatives, including prominent politicians like R.H. Pooley and Dr. Walkem, swore allegiance to the Dunsmuir interests. Representatives R.P. Bethel and H.D. Helmcken protected the interest of the British Pacific Company and Colonel Baker helped the British Columbia Southern Railroad Company at a time when both of these companies were cashing in on the railway boom.[36]

Group government survived in British Columbia in reasonably healthy condition until 1898, when began a period of extreme instability that resulted in the coalescence and hardening of party lines. The crisis started in the provincial election of 1898 in which the Turner government — "the government of industrialists, coal-barons, wholesalers and importers, and lumber and salmon canning capitalists" — failed to gain the support which for so long had been given to the Smithe Dynasty.[37] The Turnerites were returned with seventeen out of thirty-eight seats in the House and proved unable to form a stable government. Until the accession of McBride to the premiership in 1903 there followed in quick succession a series of governments unable to command a stable majority in an assembly composed of "as many leaders, or would be leaders, as followers."[38] When Lieutenant Governor T.R. McInnes found that the Turnerites were unable to command a majority he called upon Robert Beaven to form a government. Beaven, however, failed and was quickly succeeded by Charles Semlin, whose short-lived regime instituted a number of reforms hotly demanded by the growing and articulate labouring community. In February 1900, McInnes dismissed Semlin who had been defeated on a re-distribution bill, and appointed the hot-headed and reform-minded Joseph Martin as premier. Martin constructed a make-shift cabinet and held office for three months without meeting the legislature, then composed of at least five groups, the straight Conservatives, the Turner party, the Cotton party, Independent Liberals, Independent Conservatives, and Labour.[39] Martin's tenuous and unpopular government did not last through the next election, which resulted in the choice of James Dunsmuir as premier by the new Lieutenant Governor Sir Henry Joly de Lotbinière, who had replaced the frustrated T.R. McInnes as the Crown's chief officer in the province. The new Dunsmuir cabinet was a temporary stop-gap supported briefly by a group of twenty-five in the legislature until a more stable cabinet could be constructed. Hopes were high when Edward Gowler Prior assumed the premiership, but the old black ghost of scandal chased the new premier from office after a select committee of the House discovered that he had profited personally from a deal between the government and a firm that he owned.

With the demise of the Prior government, there grew a demand from an influential section of the electorate for an end to the old uncertain system of personal alignments and for the achievement of stable government through the adoption of disciplined parties. Both of the federal parties were represented in the coast province in the decades preceding the turn of the century. Liberal-Conservative associations were strong during the Macdonald era and the importance of the C.P.R. to the British Columbia economy was enough to ensure solid support for the Liberal-Conservative party for many years.[40] The Liberals, who opposed the railway, were in great disfavour with coast residents and it was not until 1889 that a Liberal Association was formed in the province. In the early 1890's, Laurier encouraged the growth of Liberal party feeling in British Columbia and a loose provincial association was formed in 1894.

The pressures to develop provincial counterparts of the federal parties increased at the turn of the century as the provincial government drifted in a sea of political instability. The Conservatives convened in Revelstoke in September 1902 and passed resolutions favouring participation in provincial politics. A provincial party constitution was drafted and M.L.A.s

[34]*Ibid.*, p. 401.

[35]Ormsby, *British Columbia*.

[36]Eleanor B. Mercer, "Political Groups in British Columbia, 1883–1898" (M.A. thesis, University of British Columbia, 1937), p. 204.

[37]Ormsby, *British Columbia*, p. 318.

[38]Letter of L.G. McGinnis to Sir Wilfred Laurier, June 14, 1903, quoted in *Ibid.*, p. 323.

[39]*Ibid.*, p. 322.

[40]Edwin Robert Black, "The Progressive Conservative Party in British Columbia: Some Aspects of Organization" (M.A. thesis, University of British Columbia, 1960), p. 8.

who supported the Tories in federal politics were asked to work as a disciplined group in the provincial legislature. When Sir Richard McBride, who had served as Minister of Mines in the Prior government, was summoned by the Lieutenant Governor to build a cabinet and assume the reins of power after Prior's resignation, a frankly conservative government was formed. Candidates contested the 1903 election as Liberals and Conservatives, and when the election results were in, the McBride Conservatives commanded enough votes in the House to form a government more stable than any in the past, although the support of two Socialist M.L.A.s was needed on occasion to maintain a majority. In the election of 1903, the Tories won twenty-two seats and 40 per cent of the total vote, the Liberals were second with seventeen seats and 38 per cent of the vote, and the Socialists and Labourites, with three seats in the legislature, gained 15 per cent of the votes.[41]

The five years of instability (1898–1903) formed a critical period in British Columbia history for two reasons. Firstly, legislative representatives and party officers became disillusioned with the old system of government through personal alignment and steps were taken to develop disciplined parties operating under federal party labels. Secondly, a strong Socialist and Labour movement emerged to threaten the traditional political beliefs at a time when socialism was only a minor and insignificant force in most of the other provinces of the Dominion. The two developments were not unrelated. The Socialist explosion at the turn of the century, preceded by over two decades of working-class political action in the coast province, impressed upon the economic and political elites the need for strong party government as a guarantee of a stable investment climate that would ensure the orderly economic development of the province through private enterprise.[42] Pro-Labour M.L.A.s elected in the 1898 provincial election and later were able to wield considerable influence as a power group in the unbalanced system of group alignments, and bits of legislation inimical to the powerful mining interests were put through during the Semlin and Martin regimes. Equally convincing of the need for stable strong government was the long series of strikes which swept the province at the turn of the century. Businessmen were dejected at the new prospects of Labour and Socialist power, investors began transferring their funds elsewhere, and the Canadian Manufacturers Association warned of the curtailment of investment capital if matters were not righted. The *Canadian Annual Review* correctly noted that labour unions had become so influential by 1903 that fear lest the voters align themselves as labour and anti-labour was one of the factors in the move to introduce party lines.[43]

The McBride victory began a period of Tory ascendancy that lasted until the 1916 provincial election. Under the premier's strong leadership, the Tories became the party that guaranteed stability and positive growth through the encouragement of railway development, Asiatic exclusion, and better terms for British Columbia through the application of a methodical "Fight Ottawa" policy. The majority was steadily increased in all provincial elections preceding World War I. Dependent upon the support of the two Socialist M.L.A.s, Parker Williams and J.H. Hawthornthwaite, following the 1903 election, the Tories were able to gain an absolute majority in the 1907 election in which twenty-seven Conservative members were returned. In the 1909 election McBride swept back into power with a majority of thirty-four seats in a campaign that witnessed the defeat of all opposition members save two Liberals and two Socialists. Liberal representation was reduced to nil in the 1912 provincial election and a simple evaluation of legislative representation in the years following yields the view that British Columbia was blessed with either a modified one party system — Conservative — or a two party system — Conservative and Socialist. But the Tory ascendancy was rudely halted in the provincial election of 1916. The death of McBride in 1915 and his succession by the heavy-handed W.J. Bowser as premier, the recession of 1912–1915, which resulted in a high rate of unemployment and acute industrial failures, and the new winds of progressive reform focusing on the issues of women's suffrage, temperance, and honest government, conspired to bring down the Conservatives.

The 1916 election was important not merely because it ended Conservative rule, but because the Liberals, who organized and channeled the new urban progressive forces, gained a majority and formed a government in a legislature in which they had had no representation since the preceding election. The Socialist Party of Canada, whose two representatives formed His Majesty's Loyal Opposition following the 1912 election, had missed a golden opportunity to firmly establish itself as a replacement for either of the major parties. Observers like Ramsay Macdonald, who visited the coast province in the years before the outbreak of the War, were convinced that conditions were then ripe for the Socialists to gain power. But internal divisions within the Socialist party, aggravated by the party's sectarianism, the increasing alienation of the Socialist elite from organized labour, together with the virulent anti-Labour and Socialist scare campaigns launched by the press on behalf of the political and economic elites, ensured that the Liberals, who effectively reorganized after the 1912 debacle, channeled the rising tide of protest against the Conservative party along moderate and gradualist lines. The 1916 election witnessed the rejuvenation of the British Columbia Liberal party, which elected thirty-seven members to the provincial legislature as compared to only nine by the prostrate Conservatives.

The resurgence of the Liberal party was not, however, complete enough to destroy the protest vote, which was strong in the years preceding the war and revived with the return to normalcy following the end of hostilities. The Liberals won twenty-six of the forty-seven seats in the election of 1920 but the Tories raised their total to fourteen and Labour elected four candidates.

[41]T.A. Sanford, "The Politics of Protest" (Ph.D. thesis, University of California at Berkeley, 1961), p. 76.

[42]See T.R. Loosemore, "The British Columbia Labour Movement and Political Action, 1879–1906" (M.A. thesis, University of British Columbia, 1954), and the author's *Radical Politics and Canadian Labour* (Kingston, Ontario: Queen's University, Industrial Relations Centre, 1968), chs. 3 and 4, for an analysis of early working class politics in British Columbia.

[43]*Canadian Annual Review* (1901), J. Castwell Hopkins, ed. (Toronto: Annual Review Publishing Company Limited, 1902), p. 434.

The protest vote in the 1923 election, which exceeded 35 per cent of the total ballots cast, was split between Labour and Socialists on the one hand, and the curious Progressive-Conservative alliance known as the Provincial Party on the other. The Provincial Party resulted from a temporary alliance of young Conservatives who resented the re-election of W.J. Bowser as leader at the 1922 Provincial Convention, rural progressives who felt that the farmers' interests were being neglected by both major parties, and dissatisfied businessmen and millionaires like General A.D. McRae who bellowed about corruption and "injected a shot of gold cure" into the infant party to ensure its survival for at least one election.[44] Provincial Party supporters believed that "there was an underground sewer connecting the two old parties."[45] and campaigned earnestly for "honest and economical government" by a party free of any unsavoury ties with the corrupt federal parties. Although only three candidates were elected, the Provincial Party gained 24 per cent of the popular vote and achieved the short-run objective of keeping Oliver out and not letting Bowser in. The defeat of both major party leaders and the high protest vote testified to the extreme tenuousness of party ties in the coast province. The CCF explosion in the following decade, and the Social Credit rise twenty years later, both stemmed from a similar disillusionment with the prevailing structure of partisan politics by alienated social groups of both the left and right.

The ascendancy of the Conservative liberalism of John Oliver ended in the 1928 provincial election. By then, the Provincial Party had quietly and unobtrusively expired and the Conservatives had temporarily laid aside their daggers to elect Simon Fraser Tolmie as party leader. Tolmie led the Tories to victory against the Liberals headed by John Duncan Maclean, who, as a successor to Oliver after the 1927 convention, failed to kindle any enthusiasm among electors for policies basically similar to those of the former premier.

The Liberal defeat in the election preceding the Depression was a Godsend because the Tories were left holding the reins of government at a time of serious social dislocation. The Tolmie government proved unable to meet the challenge of unemployment and falling prices and when election day approached in 1932 the Conservatives were in the worst condition they had ever been in. Faced with a great clamor for reform, but possessed of few ideological tools or policies to mend the social fabric, the Conservative party faced the election as an amorphous and dissident mass rather than as a cohesive and purposeful organization. The Tory trouble began with a deputation in April 1931 of representatives from a cross-section of the provincial elite representing such organizations as the Vancouver Board of Trade, Victoria Chamber of Commerce, and the Retail Merchants' Association. A cabinet advisory committee was formed to inquire into government expenditures. The document that emerged, known as the Kidd Report, constituted a scathing indictment of the party system from a business viewpoint and lent support to Premier Tolmie's appeal to the Liberal opposition to form a nonpartisan union government. The Liberals sensibly refused and the provincial executive of the Conservative association decided, in conjunction with the legislative caucus, to take no official part in the impending election campaign, allowing the local associations to fight the election under whatever label they deemed fit: Union Conservatives who supported Tolmie; non-partisan Conservatives, composed of ex-Tolmieites and Bowserites; and Independents, who preferred to present themselves as non-partisan eunuchs.

The desolate state of the smitten Tories made things easy for the rejuvenated Liberals, now led by the able and urbane T.D. Pattullo, who had also served as mayor of Prince Rupert. Pattullo campaigned on a reform new deal program of "work and wages" which promised a new social order through progressive labour legislation, social welfare supports, increased aid to municipalities, state health insurance, a public utilities commission, and an economic council which would mobilize expertise to the cause of social reform. The Premier described his program as "practical idealism" as opposed to the visionary socialism of the resurrected Socialist Party.

The 1933 election was a watershed because it resulted in the elevation of a socialist party to major opposition status, a new position briefly relinquished in the subsequent election, but thereafter steadfastly maintained up to the present day. The major fight in the campaign was not between the Grits and the floundering Conservatives, who were politically bankrupt, but between the Liberals and the CCF, which broadened and deepened its base in the early depression years.

Because an institutionalized left had existed in the decades preceding the Depression, the new task of reconstruction was easily accomplished. The Socialist Party of Canada, which was a fusion of the Federated Labor Party and the old Socialist Party, represented British Columbia at the Western Conference of Labor Parties in Calgary, and when the Regina convention gave birth to the Co-operative Commonwealth Federation, the Socialist Party of Canada acted as a provisional provincial executive committee of the new party. At the outset, the Socialist Party of Canada was the sole party affiliate of the CCF, but the Reconstruction Party, which grew out of the League for Social Reconstruction, a middle-class radical group, soon became a second party affiliate. The Reconstruction Party combined in August 1933 with the various unaffiliated CCF clubs organized by an energetic doctor named Lyle Telford to form the Association of CCF Clubs. These, in turn, merged with the Socialist Party of Canada two years later to form the CCF. The 1933 election was conducted under various labels by the socialist candidates, who won seven seats and 31.5 per cent of the popular vote.

Pattullo liberalism survived, with varying success, until after the provincial election of 1941. The reform ardour of the new regime cooled with experience in office and as opposition to the progressive reforms of people like George Pearson, Gordon Sloane, and George Weir increased both within the legislative caucus and across the province. The Liberals were returned with thirty-eight seats in the 1937 election and the Tories, who once again sheathed their knives at their 1936 convention long enough to elect Dr. F.B. Patterson as party leader, replaced the CCF as the second largest party in the legislature by winning eight seats to the Socialists' seven. The drop in CCF

[44]James Morton, *Honest John Oliver* (London: J.M. Dent & Sons, 1933), p. 179.
[45]*Ibid.*, p. 181.

support was facilitated by a serious schism within the party at the 1936 provincial convention, which adopted a radical program in opposition to party leader Robert Connell, an Anglican minister and Victorian gentleman who inadvertently stumbled into a party dominated by proletarian Marxists. Connell, together with three other M.L.A.'s, left the CCF and created their own party, the Social Reconstructives, which was supposed to be true to the principles of the Regina Manifesto, betrayed, the Reconstructives claimed, by sinister Communists within the CCF.

The brief Tory advantage over the CCF ended in the election of 1941, a fateful contest which resulted in the union of the old parties in opposition to the growing socialist threat. Pattullo liberalism began to falter badly after the 1937 election and the reform vigour needed to command a society in ferment slowly dissipated. The abandonment of relief payments to unemployed single men, the failure to implement the comprehensive medical insurance scheme long advocated by progressive Liberals, and the ineffective fight with oil companies over rising gasoline prices, were evidence that the "practical idealism" dramatized by the slogan "work and wages" had somewhere faded in the long trek through the hard Depression. Liberal representation was reduced from thirty-one to twenty-one in the 1941 election, the Tories increased their support to twelve, and the CCF, with restored party unity, elected fourteen representatives and gained 33 per cent of the popular vote. Faced once again with the socialist threat, businessmen and politicians within both old parties began to pressure for a coalition to ensure stability, i.e. stable majority government, and, by keeping the CCF from power, a favourable investment climate. The coalition idea was heatedly opposed by Pattullo, a curious constitutional Grit whose hatred of the Conservatives seemed to far exceed any fear of the CCF. Pattullo felt that the CCF was a party of well-meaning idealists that could be effectively checked by a progressive centre party. Exhausted by a furious battle with the oil companies over price-fixing, and with the federal government over the Rowell-Sirois Report, Pattullo resigned after the Liberal convention of December 1941, which supported the principle of coalition with the Tories. Foremost in the minds of the coalitionists was the task of avoiding a quick election, contested by three parties, which the CCF could win. The Liberals needed Tory support to stay in power but the price of support was cabinet representation. When John Hart assumed the premiership in December 1941, one of his first tasks was to find a place for his Conservative colleagues.

The coalition arrangement worked admirably in the next two elections and the CCF found itself engaging in two-party contests in constituencies with strong socialist support. The CCF won only ten seats in the 1945 election: nine of the seats taken in 1941 were lost in 1945, and in seven of these nine electoral districts the CCF percentage of the popular vote was increased.[46] The CCF would probably have attained power in 1945 had it not been for the coalition arrangement. In twenty-one of the forty-eight electoral districts, CCF candidates received between 40 and 50 per cent of the vote; a percentage high enough to win in most three-way election contests.

The coalition device was equally effective in the 1949 election, which witnessed a diminution in CCF representation and popular support. The election contributed to the development of a defeatist mentality that often characterizes parties who have been political bridesmaids too long. Once again, a common coalition platform was constructed, a collective war chest gathered, joint nominations effected in dual ridings, and saw-offs arranged in single-member ridings, with one or the other party organization performing the nomination function.

But the very success of the coalition arrangement contributed to its abandonment before the fateful 1952 election. The CCF dragon began to appear less awesome than in older days and the temptation to go it alone correspondingly increased among politicians who still thought jealously in partisan terms. After all, the coalition had been an arrangement, not a marriage, and like most lengthy engagements, severe tensions built up which led to rupture. The coalition was constructed and made workable by John Hart and R.J. Maitland, but when Maitland died in 1946 and Hart resigned a year later, two new leaders were chosen — Herbert Anscomb by the Conservatives and Byron Johnson by the Liberals — who were considerably less enamoured of the coalition. The Tories complained of too few cabinet posts and were especially incensed at the retention of the coveted Attorney-General portfolio by the hated Gordon Wismer. They were equally upset by the pressure to move left by the Liberals who sought to take the wind out of the socialists' sails by instituting a hospital insurance scheme without taking into account the profound opposition of the laissez-faire Tory Minister of Finance, Herbert Anscomb. The hospital scheme was hopelessly mal-administered and the principle of comprehensive free coverage was quickly abandoned. Federal Liberals and Conservatives were never very happy with the coalition and their persistent opposition began to meet with results after the 1949 election. They understandably had difficulty establishing separate and credible party images among the electors bombarded with propaganda in provincial elections which emphasized similarities, not differences, between the two old parties. Matters were aggravated in 1945 and 1949 when federal and provincial elections were held in the same year and, in the case of 1949, practically at the same time. Federal candidates were upset when they discovered their local association had lapsed in ridings controlled in provincial elections by the other party.

Few in British Columbia were surprised, therefore, when Byron Johnson dissolved the coalition by firing Tory leader Herbert Anscomb as Minister of Finance in January 1951. Facing the prospects of an election replete, once again, with three-party contests, Liberal and Conservative politicians were fearful of a CCF victory through a split in the free enterprise vote; an apprehension that was a major determinant of the formation of the coalition in the first place. The coalition politicians wanted both a dissolution of their partnership and a CCF defeat in the impending election. They were convinced that this prodigious feat could be achieved by the institution of a system of alternative voting. During the 1951 legislative session amendments were made to the Provincial Elections Act providing for the replacement of the

[46]Sanford, "Politics of Protest," p. 152.

old simple majority type by a system of preferential voting known as the alternative vote. Their calculations were simple. The CCF would be able to gain an absolute majority on the first ballot in only a few constituencies. The electorate, enamoured of free enterprise, would deny the socialists second preferences. Grits would specify Tories as a second choice and Tories would specify Grits as their second preference. The CCF would be robbed of victory by the miraculous workings of the new voting system. "Without the alternative vote," declared Attorney-General Wismer, "it would have been possible for one party which wanted to upset our whole system to have become the government on a minority vote."[47]

The coalitionists were somewhat correct. The CCF was unable to overcome the system and remained the major opposition party with eighteen seats and 34.3 per cent of the popular vote. But both the Liberals and Conservatives suffered crushing defeats: the Liberals gained six seats and 25 per cent of the vote and Conservatives won four seats and 9 per cent of the vote, a meager total which they barely exceeded in subsequent elections. The victor was the strange new Social Credit party, which elected nineteen seats and proceeded to form the government.

The rise of the Social Credit party to power is a simple tale of perseverance and luck. Before 1950 the Social Credit group in the province remained an inconsequential political sect with a tiny following. Although all provincial elections since 1937 were contested by Social Credit nominees, few candidates gained sufficient votes to save their deposits. A Social Credit Study Group was first formed in 1934 and two years later a monetary reform organization known as the Social Credit League of British Columbia came into existence. The new sect was a composite of various cranks, monetary reformers, religious fanatics, and professional anti-Semites. Like all such groups, the new movement underwent numerous schisms until taken in hand by Lyle Wicks, an ex-railway conductor who perceived that the political vacuum foreseen by T.D. Pattullo was imminent. Wicks and others streamlined the party in 1949, excommunicated many of the cranks and troublemakers, and rid the platform of the extremist planks abandoned by the Alberta Social Credit party decades earlier. With the coalition floundering and the electorate still fearful of the Socialist bogey, a golden opportunity presented itself to the new band of reformers. Funds and personnel were sent into the province from Alberta and a great and successful expansion drive was launched in 1951 in rural areas that counted a high percentage of Alberta emigrees. Devoid of practical political experience, the new movement welcomed, though reluctantly, two dissident M.L.A.'s, Tilly Rolston and W.A.C. Bennett, who were only recently converted to the new cause. Bennett, who quarrelled with his Tory party rulers over many issues, had crossed the floor and sat as an Independent in 1951 after unsuccessfully contesting the Conservative party leadership twice. He quickly perceived the opportunity presented by the new movement.

Social Credit's accession to power was derived less from economic discontent than from political disillusionment due to the constant bickering and dissidence within the coalition, the unsavoury ties with liquor and other interests openly maintained by Anscomb, Wismer, and others, the bungled hospital insurance scheme, the failure of the government to aid separate Catholic schools, the stalled Pacific Great Eastern railroad enterprise, the ineffective Labour Relations Act, and the credibility of politicians who hurled knives at one another after reclining in an amourous embrace for over a decade. A mighty stench, as thick as a Port Moody fog, lay heavy over the coastal political scene in the declining coalition years, and the new party of Christian purity found ready support among the many disillusioned with the old parties but frightened of the CCF.

The mechanics of the alternative voting system favoured the Socred parvenus. Liberal and Conservative mutual hostilities were so great that in some constituencies, the second choice of voters went to the latest free enterprise alternative — the Social Credit party — instead of to the other old party. In thirteen constituencies there was a transfer of first choice CCF votes to other parties and in many of these ridings those votes went to the Social Credit candidate instead of to the old parties. Hatred of the old free enterprise villains among CCF supporters far exceeded any mistrust of the unfamiliar new group which, after all, opposed the old system. The net effect, therefore, of the ballot system was to channel resentments against the old parties into support for the newcomers. The surprise and disillusionment of the Liberals and Tories, whose best laid plans had gone awry, was matched only by the wild elation of the motley bag of merchants, ministers, salesmen, and real estate agents who made their way into the legislature. The Social Credit party had fought the campaign without an official leader: Ernest Hansell, an Alberta M.L.A. and president of the national Social Credit League acted as the temporary campaign leader. And they had gone to the public on a platform thrust upon them, and accepted without debate, by the Alberta movement, which managed, like a marionette show, the entire party convention of April 1952.[48] But the new M.L.A.s, practised in the petty arts of small business, were now faced with the serious task of running a large enterprise. They turned to the successful hardware merchant and experienced Tory politico W.A.C. Bennett for guidance. Bennett accepted the invitation and earnestly applied himself to the hard business of retaining power.

IV. THE CONTEMPORARY SYSTEM

The realignment of the provincial party system, begun in the 1952 election, was completed the following year. The Bennett minority government pursued a strategy of early dissolution, courting defeat in order to capitalize on the prevailing public yearning for political stability. Social Credit strategists hoped to appeal early for a majority government in order to "get things done." "Social Credit has one clear advantage," Maclean's magazine wrote on June 1, 1953, "the average voter's desire for a stable government. No one, not even the Liberals and Conservatives themselves, will go so far as to predict a Liberal or Conservative victory. Therefore, the only non-Socialist

[47]*Vancouver Sun,* June 13, 1952.
[48]*Ibid.,* April 28, 1952.

government with any hope of a majority is the present Social Credit government."[49] The budget was not yet through and some eighty bills hung in suspension when the government was defeated on a bill containing the so-called "Rolston formula" providing for a new system of financing education. Bennett's calculations proved correct and both Liberals and Conservatives were decimated by the new free enterprisers in the election that followed. The Social Credit majority was increased to twenty-eight, Liberal representation plummeted to four, while the Tories obtained one seat. The CCF representation stood at fourteen. The alternative ballot system once again worked in favour of the Social Credit party. CCF electors, shocked by the twisted results of the previous contest, learned from their errors, recognized the Socred bogey and either plumped on their second choice or cast most of their votes for the Liberals. But the movement of supporters away from the traditional parties, only begun in the 1952 contest, became a landslide and both Grit and Tory voters rushed to vote for the Social Credit candidates. The second preferences of old party supporters finally overwhelmed the former coalition partners.[50] The preferential voting system had worked to keep the CCF out, but not to keep the Liberals and Conservatives in. Now that they had achieved a majority, the system was wisely abandoned by the Social Credit party in favour of the simple majority system in the 1956 election.

What emerged in the early 1950's was a party system different in structure and composition from any in the country. British Columbia was the only province in which the two federal minor parties became major parties in the legislature. Some preferred to label the new system, and persist with their definition to the present day, a protest party system. But this designation is far from accurate. The strange band of protesters campaigning under a vague platform imported and swallowed whole in 1952 quickly became a conservative party although, admittedly, an unorthodox one, and the tradi tional balance of the party system between left and right was preserved. According to W.A.C. Bennett, what occurred in British Columbia in the mid-fifties was a "return to the two party system . . . a Socialist party on the one hand and our Social Credit free enterprise party on the other."[51]

The Social Credit explosion in British Columbia bore some similarities to the earlier one in Alberta. Both movements grew rapidly in the period immediately preceding their advent to power, both exploited mass sentiments of disillusionment with politics, both contained significant elements, though in different proportions, of religious zealots who sought to purify the dirty political world. But the differences between the two movements exceeded their similarities. Social Credit in Alberta was born in the Depression and purported, in its protest phase, to provide a populist Utopian answer to the extreme deprivations people were experiencing. Although power had a sobering effect on Social Credit governors, the Alberta party, from the top down, contained many monetary fetishists who believed that all social and economic ills could be solved through adjustments in the monetary system, just as some chiropractors are convinced that all human bodily ills can best be cured through manipulation of the spinal column. The Alberta party became a prosperity party only after the Depression and the happy discovery of oil which transformed Alberta into an affluent province. The chiliastic strain in the Alberta movement, expressed through the charismatic person of Aberhart, was powerful and the party in its early phases was a political emanation of a personal religious movement built up by Aberhart through his church and radio broadcasts.

The British Columbia movement, despite its mushroom growth, was more politically orthodox than its Alberta counterpart. The party came to power during a period of relative prosperity and received support from groups in both rural and urban areas free from severe economic stress. Bennett was not a charismatic messiah born to free the masses from economic slavery. Economic renovation, though of a different variety, was the exclusive province of the CCF, which had advocated socialist Utopian ideas for decades. Coming to power almost two decades after the Alberta group, British Columbia's Social Creditors and their supporters were well aware of the conservative effects of power and responsibility on the Alberta government. The 1952 platform, handed down from Alberta, talked about voluntary hospital insurance, old-age pensions, better tax rental arrangements and a "pay as you go" policy in provincial expenditures, but there was nothing said about revamping the financial system or instituting a technocratic system of government by experts.[52] Alberta was cited in the 1952 campaign and beyond, not as a reform Utopia but as an affluent, well-run, and debt-free province; the model of a well-run enterprise but hardly the petty bourgeois paradise conjured up by Major Douglas. British Columbia Social Credit triumphed despite the absence of a charismatic leader like Aberhart who exploited the feelings of despair in a society of acute scarcity and high unemployment. Ernest Hansell, an Alberta export, who served as temporary campaign leader, lent a certain religious flair to the 1952 campaign,[53] but he left the provincial party and government after the election to W.A.C. Bennett, a recent party supporter ignorant of Major Douglas's theories, who had administered hardware rather than grace most of his life. "I make you only one promise," Bennett informed the electors before the 1953 election, "if you vote 'Social Credit', we will give you good government."[54] Finally, British Columbia Social Credit was not a religious movement and the fundamentalist strain in the party, still present today, is much less accented than in the Alberta party. ". . . Social Credit was regarded by Mr. Aberhart as a way of life," Ernest Hansell told the farmers in Vernon in May 1952, "it is a subject involving the destiny of the human race."[55] But to the many thou-

---

49*Ibid.*, June 2, 1953.

50According to the *Vancouver Sun*, Liberal party leaders quietly suggested to their voters that they give their second choices to the CCF, so anxious were they to see Bennett and his cohorts defeated. But the Liberal voters decided to stay free enterprise. *Ibid.*, July 2, 1953.

51*Ibid.*, September 20, 1956.

52*Vancouver Province*, July 12, 1952.

53Witness Hansell's speech in Oliver which opened the 1952 Socred campaign: "Politics doesn't have to be dirty — it's only as dirty as the politicians make it, and it would help a lot if governments would take Almighty God into their plans . . ." *Vancouver Province*, May 30, 1952.

54*Vancouver Sun*, June 2, 1953.

55*Vancouver Province*, May 31, 1952.

sands of Liberals and Conservatives who cast their votes for the new party, and to W.A.C. Bennett, who lived most of his life as a Conservative, Social Credit was not a way of life but a vehicle for attaining power and for keeping the CCF out in the cold.

It is undeniable, however, that the fundamentalist strain was present at the time of the party's accession to power, and it still provides an interesting gloss today. Party conventions are opened with hymns and candidates are careful to present Social Credit as a Christian party, especially in constituencies like Chilliwack and other towns of the interior where religious feelings are salient. "I don't know as much about your party as I should," Tilly Rolston told a nominating convention in 1952, "but I believe in a return to honest Christian principles in government."[56] The Christian orientation of the Social Credit party is sharply contrasted by confirmed Social Creditors with the alleged atheism of the NDP. Despite the subsidence of the wave of religiosity which spilled into the interior in 1952 at the behest of Alberta sorcerers like Hansell, and which helped elect Social Credit candidates on the first ballot in Chilliwack, Langley, and the Okanagans, Social Credit continued to receive strong support in areas with a high representation of sectarian religionists and still recruits a small and dwindling section of its elite from the fundamentalist clergy.[57] Included among the group of '52 swept into the legislative assembly were three fundamentalist preachers: Reverend Charles W. Parker (Church of Nazarene), and Reverends H.D. Frances and P. Gaglardi (Pentacostal Assemblies). One-third of the caucus of eighteen elected members was affiliated with fundamentalist sects: four were Baptist M.L.A.s and two were affiliates of the Holiness Movements. By 1945, fundamentalists' representation in the caucus was restricted to two members of the Pentacostal Assemblies and one Full Gospel member. There were no Baptist M.L.A.s. A study made of clergymen in the Vancouver area in 1959 revealed that ministers affiliated with the smaller denominations preferred Social Credit to the other major parties.[58] Electoral support remains high for Social Credit in areas like Chilliwack, Langley, and the Cariboo, with their relatively high proportion of religious sectarians. But the religious element is not as predominant in the caucus as it is in Alberta, where the high priest Aberhart was succeeded as party leader by his equally religious apprentice Manning, the first graduate of Aberhart's Prophetic Bible Institute. Much of the leadership cadre was recruited from fundamentalist ministers and lay preachers. As late as 1965, seven Alberta M.L.A.s could be counted as members of the radical sects (Evangelican Free Church, Christian Science, Latter Day Saints), while another seven were of Baptist persuasion. The predominant part of the British Columbia Social Credit caucus is affiliated with the Anglican and United Churches and the movement represents, both in terms of elite recruitment and electoral support, a coalition of the former Conservative Anglican elements, United Church supporters, and the rising fundamentalist sects.

But religion is not a major factor in British Columbia politics; religious affiliations are not as determining a political preference as in other parts of the country and religious issues have rarely provided the stuff and substance of political debate.[59] A more important element is economic position which,

Robert Alford points out in his study on voting, is a key determinant of voting in British Columbia and in Ontario, the two regions where class voting is higher than the national average.

There are current in British Columbia three theories about Social Credit's relation to the class system: one advertised by the premier and his colleagues, the second finding favour among liberal intellectual critics of the governing party, and the third held by the traditional socialist opposition. According to Premier Bennett, who revels in the glib cliché as much as some politicians prefer good cigars or fine scotch, Social Credit is not a class party but a people's party. Like the United Nations, the party draws support from many and diverse groups and walks of life and, like the good King Solomon, the government dispenses justice and favours in fair proportion to all sections of the realm. In the eyes of the Premier, the opposition parties are exclusive class parties; only Social Credit is an inclusive party that represents and cares for the masses as opposed to the classes. "The aim of the Social Credit government," Bennett stated in the 1953 campaign, "is to enlist the united support of British Columbians who believe in a free way of life, and we will oppose equally as strongly the forces of monopoly and the forces of socialism."[60] Liberal critics of the governing party, frightened and dazzled by Social Credit's idiosyncratic style, prefer to define Social Credit not as a political and legislative conglomerate which *represents* the different groups and balances one interest against the other, but as a blind and unpredictable band of Poujadists and political nihilists who have no purpose in mind except to retain power (as if this is not the concern of all political parties!) and do so by cynically waging war on all established elites whether of the left or right. The Socialist critique abjures both views and defines Social Credit in a more traditional way as a spokesman and representative of the established economic elites, both within and without the province.

Bennett's definition of Social Credit contains a little truth but does not hold up to examination. Without a reasonable spread of regional and class support, Social Credit would not, of course, have retained power as long as it has. A primary base of party support, from the very onset of the growing movement in 1950 until the present day, has been the rural constituencies. The conservative farmers have never deserted the Socred party and the party counts its greatest strongholds in rural areas, retaining strong support in the towns as well as in the farming areas of the regions. Chilliwack, Cariboo, Langley, North and South Okanagan, and North and South Peace River, form the bastions of Social Credit support. These areas, since the Social Credit explosion, have never been centres of rural unrest and Socred candidates were not returned at the outset to remedy economic or social distress.

56*Ibid.,* May 3, 1952.
57A liquor plebicite was held in conjunction with the 1952 election and, significantly enough, those areas which favoured the restriction of sale of liquor by the glass were strongholds of Social Credit support.
58Walter Ellis, "Some Aspects of Religion in British Columbia Politics" (M.A. thesis, University of British Columbia, 1959), p. 85.
59R. Alford, *Party and Society* (Chicago: Rand-McNally & Co., 1963), pp. 265-270.
60*Vancouver Sun,* June 2, 1953.

High Social Credit representation in key rural and northern strongholds has been preserved by the persistent discrepancy in constituency sizes. Rural and sparsely populated northern areas have been traditionally over-represented in the legislature; the Lower Mainland area, with over 65 per cent of the population, has been grossly under-represented. Until the 1966 redistribution, it was possible for one party to sweep the rural areas and leave the ridings in Greater Vancouver, New Westminster, and Victoria with no representation on the government side of the House. There were as many voters registered in the three largest provincial ridings — Point Grey, Vancouver East, and Delta — as there were in twenty-six non-urban ridings. The three urban districts elected only seven M.L.A.s, the twenty-six non-urban seats elected twenty-six M.L.A.s. One vote in Atlin counted as thirty in Vancouver East. Thirty per cent of the voters in Vancouver received only nine members or 17.3 per cent of the legislative representation.[61]

The 1966 redistribution, accomplished after years of public pressure, has rectified rural-urban disparity somewhat but not nearly to the extent wished for by the opposition parties. In British Columbia there was no legal requirements for any sort of regular adjustment of constituency boundaries and the Social Credit government stalled for years before setting up a Royal Commission to recommend changes in the electoral map.[62]

The Angus Commission, which began deliberations in August 1966, recommended important revisions of the electoral boundaries; eight more members were to be added to the Lower Mainland area and the representation of outlying areas in the interior and north coast reduced from twenty-eight to twenty-one.[63] The Commission cut northern representation from seven to five. The Commission's recommendations were modified by the Social Credit government for partisan purposes. Under the new Bennett plan instituted in time for the 1966 election, the legislature was increased from fifty-two to fifty-five seats, and Vancouver's representation grew to twelve members sitting for six dual ridings.[64] Representation of the sparsely populated north was maintained and a new constituency was carved out of the Social-Credit-held Columbia River riding. Bennett was careful to keep intact the northern constituencies that complemented rural constituencies like the Okanagans as party strongholds, but he took care to wipe out NDP and Liberal citadels in the Kootenays, whose representation was reduced from seven to four.

Rural and northern non-urban areas, populated by farmers and by small businessmen flourishing in the growing towns, have been a primary base of Social Credit support. Social Credit receives some support today in the urban areas of Victoria and Vancouver, but urban support is not nearly as certain as non-urban. A breakdown of constituencies in terms of party strongholds — a party stronghold being an electoral riding that elected the same party in every election since 1952 — reveals that not one Socred stronghold is in a metropolitan area. In the 1966 election, five out of six Liberal members came from metro Vancouver and the sixth came from metro Victoria. The NDP gained ten of its sixteen seats in metro Vancouver. The Social Credit party had only seven of its thirty-four victories in metro Vancouver and another four in metro Victoria. Areas of Social Credit support in urban constituencies have a relatively high proportion of clerical, sales, and lower management personnel as well as small business owners.

Social Credit policy has actively fostered and defended the interests of these groups. "It is the small matters of individual and local interest," declared Mr. Maclean, Oliver's Provincial Secretary, "that determine the fates of governments."[65] The Bennett government has very enthusiastically pursued a policy of *bouts de chemin* in a province where inter-regional communication is minimized by hostile geographical barriers. The Premier and his maverick highways minister have earned the reputations of being master road builders. Numerous highway extensions have been constructed and re-built on both the mainland and Vancouver Island. The Trans-Canada Highway has been finally completed, with substantial federal aid, linking Vancouver with the western rim of the Rockies. Numerous bridges and tunnels — the Lions Gate Bridge, Kamloops Floating Bridge, Deas Tunnel — have been built to provide key links in the road system. The ferry systems have been taken over by the government, up-graded with new equipment, and expanded to serve outlying coastal communities. The Pacific Great Eastern Railway, that running political sore, was completed after decades of intrigue, scandal, and commissions of inquiry, and the productive mineral basins of the north and interior were linked with Vancouver.

Transportation construction has made good politics. The tourist industry is indebted to the government for good roads. Contractors have filled the party coffers with contributions and working men, provided with jobs in a period of high prosperity, have ignored NDP propaganda and voted for the government. Trucking competition with the railroads has been facilitated and transportation costs reduced. The improved transportation system contributed to the development of a series of small cities as regional service centres close to centres of resource extraction. The service industries are the mecca of the small businessman and the rapid expansion of cities like Prince George, Kamloops, and Chilliwack during the past decade coincides with their emergence as strongholds of Social Credit support.[66] Outlying and isolated communities in the north and coastal areas have been indebted to the government for transportation links, whether by ferry or by road, with the outside world, and have expressed their gratitude through the ballot box.

61*Ibid.*, May 4, 1961.

62Nothing is said in the Constitution Act about redistribution. The electoral map was redrawn five times in the first thirty-two years after B.C.'s entry into Confederation, but in the thirty years preceding the present redistribution there had been only two electoral re-apportionments despite the population growth during the same period from 700,000 to 1.7 million. The Social Credit party made only one change before the present redistribution: in 1955, when four seats were added, one in Peace River and three in the Lower Mainland.

63See *Vancouver Sun*, January 28, 1966.

64It was the government's intention to run cabinet ministers, four of whom already sat in Vancouver in the urban ridings who would, presumably, drag lesser men into office on their lustrous coattails.

65Ormsby, *British Columbia*, p. 412.

66Edwin Black, "British Columbia: The Politics of Exploitation" (unpublished manuscript), p. 21.

The political acceptability of intensive road construction has been facilitated by the peculiar bookkeeping of a government whose premier delights in accounting double-talk. Highway and bridge construction are costly and involve a high level of government borrowing. But government indebtedness is minimized to the public by classifying the borrowing of government agencies such as the Highways and Bridges Toll Authority, the B.C. Hydro & Power Authority, and the B.C. Ferries Authority as "contingent liabilities." Government protestations about being debt-free are belied by the huge indirect debt incurred through these borrowing agencies whose accounts are often misrepresented. But the idea of a balanced budget and a debt-free province, widely advertised by the Premier, caters to an old faith in financial status long outdated among economists, but still heartily endorsed by the bingo set inhabiting the Canadian Legion halls of Kamloops and Vernon.

Equally pleasing to the middle classes have been the Homeowner's and Home Purchase Grants, British Columbia's version of the Social Credit dividend, made available by a government that prefers to distribute benefits — and collect appropriate credits — to people directly rather than through intermediate authorities such as municipal governments. The Home Owner Grant program gave to every homeowner in the province a flat grant that is deducted from his tax bill. It was applied first to school taxes, for the sharply rising educational costs have been cited by Bennett as a primary reason why the homeowner has to be relieved of some of his tax obligations. To make certain the recipients remember from whom the sweets come, they have to apply for their money to the provincial government. The government whets the possessive appetites by raising the grant every year. The grant has benefitted mostly the lower middle class. By owning more of their own homes on a per capita basis than the working class, the local bourgeoisie benefited more from the government's munificence; by having smaller incomes than the upper classes, the middle classes were more appreciative of the government's generosity. The Homeowner Grant meant little to those who paid rent or to those who languished in high-priced homes in Oak Bay or West Vancouver. As a sop to the young marrieds who wished to stop renting and start buying, an increasingly difficult task in metro Vancouver's inflated market but more feasible in smaller centres in the interior, the Home Purchase Grant has been made available as a modest subsidy.

Social Credit's marriage with the middle class — urban and non-urban — has been a joyful and tranquil affair which belies the excited accusation of some Liberal critics that the governing party has blindly waged war at different times on all sections of the population and against all established elites. The British Columbia Federation of Agriculture, the various agricultural co-operative associations, the Junior Chambers of Commerce, the dull assemblies of merchants, businessmen, real estate and insurance salesmen, and the learned societies of notary publics and chiropractors have never tasted the Socred whip but, on the contrary, have provided the active supporters from whom the party recruits electoral supporters, party activists, and its political elite.[67]

Social Credit's relations with sections of the economic elite have been strained and difficult on occasion but the party has basically performed the functions expected of all free enterprise parties in British Columbia; it has provided stable government and a favourable investment climate for the private capital of economic buccaneers fearful of the demon of Socialist expropriation. The Social Credit movement was not, at the outset, a creation of the business tycoons who had found a safe abode in the Liberal-Conservative coalition, a marriage that big business had avidly encouraged in the early 1940's as an answer to the Socialist threat. Until 1950–1951, the Social Credit party was an assemblage of monetary faddists who feared the domination of the financial interests as much as they quaked at the thought of a Socialist state. Party leaders like Hansell and Bennett at times used the theory of Invisible Government, with its moral overtones of deceit, corruption, and graft, to exploit the realistic observations and suspicions of ordinary people that political parties were facades that hid the real rulers from public view. "There is a government," Ernest Hansell told the citizens of Vernon in 1952, "more powerful than governments, this great monetary power that knows no international boundaries. That is what we are attacking, and everyone who opposes Social Credit is either ignorant of that power or a party to it."[68] Bennett knew as well as Hansell the fears of ordinary middle-class people when he promised during the 1953 campaign that Social Credit would "oppose equally as strongly the forces of monopoly and the forces of socialism."[69] Catapulted into power by a swift and peculiar conjunction of circumstances, and devoid of initial support from any established interests, the Social Credit regime found itself free of any incurred political obligations. The new political lords ruled a domain rich in resources and conferred privileges on favoured barons in return for an oath of allegiance and economic support. The coffers of the Liberal and Conservative parties were rich in funds in the 1949 and 1952 elections, but by 1953, the dolorous moans of Grit and Tory money collectors were heard everywhere. "Many large and small industries are awaiting the outcome of this election," Bennett informed the electors in 1953. "If the Social Credit government has a good working majority new industries will be commenced with increased payrolls and benefit to all . . . the issue is clear: it is Social Credit or chaos." Businessmen, who equated socialism with chaos, got the word and fell into line to the point where party collector Al Williamson could admit to the court at his trial a few years later that he had not been refused once in his many requests for funds from assorted businesses. Campaign contributions went into a fund administered by Einar Gunderson and W.A.C. Bennett known as the British Columbia Free Enterprise Educational Fund. This fund is in no way

[67]Professor Donald Smiley, in a clever and illuminating article on Social Credit as a Canadian expression of Poujadism, traces the Social Credit elite's idiosyncracies, disregard for traditional liberal decorum and procedures, and sensitivity to the feelings of the electoral masses, to a lack of group experience. But biographical material gathered on the background of Social Credit M.L.A.s in the 1963 legislature revealed that over 65 per cent of the legislative group held office in various political and social organizations before entering the legislature.
[68]*Vancouver Province,* May 30, 1952.
[69]*Vancouver Sun,* June 2, 1953.

accountable for receipts and expenditures to Social Credit conventions or party organization. This arrangement, of course, immeasurably strengthens the hand of the premier over the party. The Liberal and Conservative parties have been starved for funds since the 1953 election. The new direction of the flow of business funds was described by a Tory member of the House of Commons who complained that:

. . . [the] thick-headed tycoons out in British Columbia . . . pushed us into a coalition that we didn't want, and ruined us as a party in B.C., because they said that was the only way to stop the CCF. Then they finance this Social Credit movement because it, now, is "the only way to stop the CCF."

Big business has hitched its star to the Social Credit government not because of customary partisan predispositions, or through love of the Premier's grey flannel wardrobe, but because Social Credit is the only effective and available free enterprise alternative. A shift of support back to one of the floundering old parties is liable to have a short run effect of bringing in a New Democratic government through a split in the free enterprise vote. But big business supports Social Credit not merely because it has nowhere else to go; the Social Credit Party has done much over the years to preserve and encourage the corporate pursuit of profit in the province. The governing party has provided what businessmen like to call a favourable investment climate by maintaining restrictive labour legislation, reducing the mining tax, and managing British Columbia forest industries with considerable solicitude for the interest of large companies.

But Social Credit is not an emanation of the fashionable areas of Oak Bay, West Vancouver, and Point Grey. The residents of these places prefer the Liberals to the rude new men of power. Social Credit's accession to power ruptured the easy traditional relationship between the economic and the political elites and while a working arrangement has been partially restored, there has never developed the same easy familiarity that characterized the old system, a closeness born of interaction at fashionable debutante parties and quiet evenings at the Union or Royal Victoria Yacht Clubs. Because Social Credit politicians inherited few obligations of office, having raised themselves to power by their own electoral bootstraps from undistinguished middle-class circumstances, they have freely mixed their favours towards the old giants with largesse towards rising new entrepreneurs. The Capozzis, Gaglardis, McMahons, Gundersons, and Ginters constructed little economic empires under the friendly tutelage of the Bennett government and their children will soon enter the private school system, where they will rub shoulders with scions of the old rich and absorb, secondhand and in watered Canadian form, some of the rudiments of British haute culture propagated by maiden schoolteachers and prissy masters.

Not everything the Premier has done has met with the firm approval of the business tycoons. Liberal critics of the government have eagerly pointed to the takeover of B.C. Electric as evidence of Social Credit's ambivalent attitude to big business and lack of principled support for free enterprise. But by nationalizing B.C. Electric, one of the last of the giant, privately-owned power companies in the country, and a great provider of Social Credit campaign funds, the provincial government was only doing what had been done much earlier in most of the other provinces of the country. The corporation was nationalized for pragmatic reasons, political as well as economic. Through expropriation, the provincial government could retain the share of profits being paid to Ottawa for private corporate income tax and strengthen its hand in the fight with Ottawa over the development of hydro-electric power in British Columbia. This resulted in the successful execution of Bennett's two-river policy, and took the wind out of the sails of the NDP and Liberals who had supported the expropriation of a private company which laboured under an unfavourable public image, charging higher rates than the publicly-owned systems of Ontario, Quebec, and the American Pacific Northwest.[71] Bennett did not betray the principles of free enterprise with the power take-over; he merely proved that the government was as flexible as other twentieth century Canadian provincial governments. The Portland *Oregonian* compared Bennett with Castro as a confiscator of private property. The analogy becomes doubly absurd when it is considered that the premier did his utmost to keep the case out of the courts in the final phases of the battle because it might reveal that the stockholders, who were rewarded at the current market value of B.C. Electric shares rather than at the lower value assessed by the Public Utilities Commission, were grossly overpaid.[72]

It was not merely the fact of the power takeover itself that excited Liberal critics but the manner in which it was done. To opponents, the power take-over was but another example of the government's contempt for accepted procedure and public opinion, and confirmation of the development of the Social Credit government as the personal dictatorship of W.A.C. Bennett. The Premier's sudden decision, taken apparently without informing many of his cabinet ministers, who were singing the praises of free enterprise and damning nationalization as a Communist device unworthy of free men, to-gether with the tactics used to keep the matter out of the courts, seemed to support claims of "arbitrary government and personal dictatorship." That these charges have been greatly exaggerated and therefore have aided the government by adding a certain dash of recklessness to its image does not vitiate the observation that the Social Credit government has on occasion gone about its business in an odd way and with the help of some very strange people. It was revealed, for instance, during the 1953 election that Socred League President, John Perdue, had been convicted three times and had spent a year in jail between 1928 and 1933.[73] The 1956 election featured the Sommers case which resulted in the incarceration of a cabinet minister for graft and corruption. In 1960, another party candidate admitted serving

[70]*Maclean's*, January 15, 1953, p. 59.

[71]Stewart Jamieson, "Expropriation of the B.C. Electric," *Canadian Forum*, March 1962, p. 272.

[72]"Fidel Castro is no more dictatorial than Premier Bennett in the expropriation field. Both call it expropriation as a courtesy, but confiscation is a better word." As quoted in Paddy Sherman, *Bennett* (Toronto: McClelland & Stewart, Ltd., 1966), p. 253.

[73]*Ibid.*, p. 137.

a jail sentence. Two years earlier, a Social Credit federal candidate confessed holding up two banks and being caught as he tried to rob a third. He performed these misdemeanours, he confessed, in order to pay off a $14,000 gambling debt.

The antics of the former highways minister, P. Gaglardi, have contributed to the government's maverick image. Gaglardi has courted popular favour and exploited both repressed and overt hostility towards legal institutions and procedures by engaging in a running battle with courts and police. He received a number of speeding convictions and a great deal of publicity for his cavalier treatment of arresting officers, whom he described as "a couple of punks." The highways minister was fined $1,000 in contempt of court for ignoring a court order stopping payment of department funds to a bankrupt highway contractor, and rarely has a legislative session been completed without suggestions of graft and corruption being made by the opposition. A number of legislative committees of inquiry, loaded with government supporters, have been convened to look into some of the more severe allegations of sordid dealings in the highways department. The recent storm, which involved the amassing of huge profits by the minister's sons in shady land deals involving oil companies and the highways department — activities which Gaglardi dismissed as "trying to make a living like everyone else" — was severe enough to occasion his removal from the highways portfolio.

Opposition critics have focused as well on the Premier's alleged contempt for the legislature and the opposition as evidence of Social Credit's "arbitrary government." The legislative committee system is weak and ineffective. There is no official record of debate in the assembly and cabinet ministers can plead they have been misquoted when confronted with unpleasant quotations in the newspapers. Legislative sessions run in mid-winter for only eight to ten weeks, during which time bills are rammed through without proper consideration in late night sessions that follow one another in quick succession. Former Liberal leader Arther Laing designated the government penchant for presenting the departmental estimates at one a.m. for intelligent discussion as "legislation by exhaustion," and the Premier's statement, which often accompanies the late night sitting, that British Columbia is a democracy and the opposition can take as long as it wants — all night — to discuss matters, has supported claims of contempt of parliament. Important policy pronouncements are usually saved until after the truncated legislative session has ended and the opposition M.L.A.s have scattered to the far ends of the province. The government then embarks on an orgy of Orders-In-Council.

All of this, together with the Premier's domination of the Social Credit party organization, both parliamentary and extra-parliamentary, have lent some substance to opposition claims of personal and arbitrary government. But the accusation should be viewed in proper perspective: within the British Columbia context and within the context of western liberal democracy. The decline of parliament and the consolidation of cabinet rule are general developments found elsewhere and are not demonic concoctions of the present regime. The coalition government that preceded Social Credit government was equally contemptuous of the opposition and of the rights of parliament. And British Columbians, who prefer results to methods and action to deliberation, have always been more respectful of the claims of strong leaders than of the liberties of their opponents.

The one social group which the government has fought, consistently and zestfully, has been the organized labour movement. The Social Credit platform in the 1952 election contained few references to labour problems and the candidates returned were not elected on a wave of anti-labour sentiment. Having gained power, however, the government of merchants, shopkeepers, salesmen, and ministers soon ran full steam into a trade-union movement, strong, militant, and socialist by national standards. Labour leaders are incensed with heavy-handed government labour legislation that has sought to restrict the organizational power of unions. The first major Social Credit labour legislation, the Labour Relations Act, known as Bill 28, was passed in 1954. It provided fines and penalties for a union and its officers for contravening the new restrictive provisions regarding the legality of strikes and it decreased the power of the Labour Relations Board established under the province's Industrial Conciliation and Arbitration Act of 1947, in favour of the Minister of Labour and the courts.[74] The effect of the new act was to bring industrial relations more into the political sphere and thereby heighten the exploitation for electoral purposes of widespread middle-class fears and resentments of organized labour. The government built on the foundation provided by the Labour Relations Act. Bill 43 was passed in 1958, forbidding the secondary boycott, limiting picketing to a union or plant directly involved in a strike, and making the unions liable entities in offences committed by individual members in strike situations. The secretary of the militant I.W.A. described the act as "another Pearl Harbor attack by the Social Credit government" and one which brought the province a step closer to fascism. Labour leaders, who believed the only way to change the law was to change the premier, consolidated politically and moved closer to the NDP in order to better oppose the new legislation. The government responded by bringing in Bill 42, which forbade the use for political purposes of any money collected in unions by payroll deduction. Organized labour also collided with the government over Bill 33, passed in 1967, which established the principle of compulsory arbitration in major industries. The B.C. Federation of Labour described the new bill as a "club over the head of every employee and every worker's family in B.C."

In defence of their restrictive union legislation, Premier Bennett and his colleagues have advanced a peculiar Okanagan variant of Marxism. They agree with Marxists that workers are exploited, but violently disagree as to who are the exploiters. To Social Credit ideologists, the exploiters of labour are union leaders rather than capitalists. The function of the state is not to save the worker from the capitalist but to rescue him from his leader. Left to their own devices in a prosperous state in which private enterprise freely pursues its ends in an economic climate guaranteed free and healthy by a Social Credit government, workers could live and work in a state of blissful contentment. As it is, they are constantly misled by their leaders

[74]Phillips, *No Greater Power*, p. 146.

who impose their own political aims on the unsuspecting masses. Social Credit politicians by-pass labour leaders and appeal directly to the masses. The government has bitterly fought and restricted the organizational demands of labour, which enhance the power of labour leaders, and at the same time wooed the masses with political sweets like the Homeowner's and Home Purchase Grants, medicare, and annual vacations with pay. Social Credit has not been entirely unsuccessful in its bid for the labour vote. Workers who enjoy high wages and prosperous times, who see little benefit from belonging to a union, who are forced to join unions through closed or union shop regulations, who resent the proliferation of union bureaucracies, who dislike having part of their dues channeled to support an opposition party that has never tasted power, quietly cast their vote for Social Credit leaders whose anti-establishment style often strikes a sympathetic chord with their own feelings of alienation.

Possessed of a restricted but faithful social and electoral base, the Social Credit government has been able to survive longer than all previous governments in British Columbia. It appears unlikely that either of the old parties, Conservative and Liberal, will rise to defeat the government. The Tories are moribund and received over 10 per cent of the vote in only one election since 1952. This was in 1963, when Davie Fulton, the brahmin from Kamloops, quit federal politics and returned to lead the party. The party ran a few token candidates in the 1966 election, which it contested without an official leader, but it has no representation in the House.

The Liberals, much stronger, gained around 20 per cent of the votes in the last few elections, but will have to expand their base considerably to attain office. At the moment, the Liberals remain a high-priced oceanfront party drawing strong support in constituencies in and around Vancouver's Point Grey, West and North Vancouver, and Victoria's Oak Bay, which all boast of traditional wealth, a high per capita income, and a high incidence of Anglicans. Ideologically, the Liberals are confused, striking a middle way between the free enterprise Social Credit approach and the moderate socialism of the NDP. Party devotees like the *Vancouver Sun* define the Liberals as the only reliable grey-flannel alternatives in the Social Credit party, which they consider to be recklessly irresponsible and opportunistic, and to the NDP, which they regard as the Trojan horse of power-hungry labour leaders.

The New Democratic Party is the problem-child of British Columbia's party system. The party has been at the brink of power for decades, waiting for the great opportunity that has never come. Despite numerous defeats the NDP has maintained a high level of support and retained its position as the major opposition party. CCF-NDP has rarely dropped below 30 per cent of the popular vote since 1933 and the party gained 34 per cent of the popular vote in the 1966 provincial election.

The NDP's social and electoral base, although secure, is not quite wide enough to yield the extra 4 or 5 per cent of the vote in marginal constituencies necessary to bring in a minority socialist government. The party's electoral base is still strongly riveted to the wage-earning class and the major party strongholds — Cowichan-Malahat, Burnaby-North, Burnaby-Willingdon, Burnaby-Edmonds, New Westminster, and Vancouver East — contain a high incidence of working men and trade unionists. It may be safely said that the party derives its major support from the Vancouver area and from non-urban industrial constituencies that contain a high percentage of trade unionists. Although NDP support has risen across the country, Vancouver remains, like Toronto, one of the strongest areas of party support in the country.[75]

The highest proportion of working-class votes has come from the organized sections of the labour movement: the trade unions. When the voting habits of workers from union and non-union households were compared in a national sample that included Vancouver, there was a much stronger tendency for those of union households to support the NDP.[76] The same study indicated that the tenuousness and fluidity of partisan loyalties, which seem to uniquely characterize the British Columbia electorate, are less characteristic of NDP supporters, who strongly identify with the party as a "working-class party" and are less likely to bolt their group than other party adherents. A study of New Democrats in the federal constituency of Vancouver-Burrard showed a strong continuity in NDP support — "about three-fifths of the group support the party for which their parents voted, either provincially, federally, or both."[77]

Union support for the NDP is not restricted to the votes of union members. The financial contributions of unions such as the I.W.A. and packing-house and steel workers are substantial, although restricted by the provisions of Bill 42, and are manifest in many ways: directly through voluntary contributions and indirectly through political education within the union and the loan of resources, human and material, both during and between election campaigns.

The strong union orientation of the NDP, reflected in the big labour vote, the prominence of union officials on the provincial executive committee and in the caucus, and in the party's policy orientation, which is broadly pro-labour, have both aided and hurt the party. Without the strong backbone of labour support, the NDP probably could not have survived the many vicious electoral wars fought against the free enterprise parties. But the close and visible ties with labour in a province in which industrial relations have always been in the political limelight, and where the possessive instincts of the middle classes have been both threatened and aroused by truculent labour leaders, have contributed to the failure of the NDP to make significant inroads into the middle-class electorate — urban and rural.

The actions and legacy of a militant labour movement and traditionally radical socialist party have fed the anxieties of the middle and upper classes, replete with nouveau riche, who feared losing what they had gained and held in the Hobbesian scramble. The coastal electorate have been treated to high-tension scare campaigns since the CCF became the major opposition.

[75]See Wallace Gagne and Peter Regenstreif, "Some Aspects of New Democratic Party Urban Support in 1965," *Canadian Journal of Economics and Political Science,* XXXIII, No. 4 (November 1967), 539.

[76]*Ibid.,* p. 538.

[77]Thelma Oliver, "Political Socialization and Political Culture: A Case Study" (M.A. thesis, University of British Columbia, 1967), p. 22.

The pleas of Gerry McGeer, who quoted Marx to prove that "free love and atheism" were basic CCF doctrines, and the dire warnings of R.L. Maitland that a system of companionate marriage would quickly follow CCF rule, have been echoed by contemporary politicians like Gaglardi and Bennett who assure the people that the NDP would take away everything they had soon after gaining office.

The latent hysteria about the NDP and socialism was not manifest in the 1963 and 1966 provincial elections. The NDP strained terribly in the 1963 contest to present itself as a nice middle-class party and leader Strachan appeared everywhere mouthing pleasantries and attired in the garb of a Royal Trust Company bond salesman. The 1966 campaign was fought on a low key with the government waging a restrained non-campaign in the new mode of focusing on local issues while ignoring the opposition. But this strategy was abandoned by the government in favour of the total war concept during the 1969 election. Once again, the NDP donned a sheepskin guise as candidates nodded assent to leader Tom Berger's assertion that free enterprise — "responsible free enterprise" — would find a safe and comfortable home in the liberal socialist commonwealth. All of this, however, did not deter the premier from launching a loud and boisterous campaign against the spectre of "Marxian Socialism," a foray which resulted in a renewed government mandate, a sharply reduced opposition representation, the premature retirement of Berger from provincial politics, and his replacement as party leader by Dave Barret.

* MANITOBA *

Ethnic and Class Politics in Manitoba

T. PETERSON

It might be argued that the low level of class voting in Canada implies that it is in the forefront of a trend in all of the Anglo-American countries away from class politics. . . . I suggest, on the contrary, that class voting in Canada is less than should be expected in a country with its type of stratification, and that therefore class voting may be expected to increase if social changes follow certain paths.[1]

The development of party politics in Manitoba has been influenced by the interaction of two social and economic classes. One of these has generally been more prosperous and culturally more secure. Most of its members were of British origin and many of them originally came to the province from Ontario. For almost a hundred years, this class controlled political and economic power. The second or lower class was more heterogeneous, comprised of several cultural groups including working-class immigrants from Britain, various other immigrants of non-British origin and the province's native Indians and Métis. The members of this class were generally poorer, less secure and more submissive; although at times, when spokesmen expressed their discontent, there occurred conflict and violence. By the 1960's, the ethnic and other divisions within this lower class were declining. There were indications of assimilation in some cases, and more militant political attitudes in others. This contributed to a polarization of party politics partly along class lines. Also, as the traditional ruling group showed signs of age and diminishing vitality, its capacity for maintaining control wavered. As a result, there emerged a new political environment in which the two rival groups were more evenly matched.

One of the initial bases of the province's class division was the uneven distribution of good land. When the glaciers of the Ice Age passed over northeastern Manitoba, they left it scarred and barren. Along the Shield's southern edge, extending diagonally from Lake of the Woods in the southeast to the Swan River Valley in the northwest, are numerous marshes, bogs, and gravel ridges. Coarse stones litter the fields, and the soil is shallow and poor. The

[1] R. Alford, *Party and Society* (London: John Murray, 1964), p. 25.

area to the south and west, comprising about one-seventh of the province, is more attractive. Rolling plains extend from the Red River valley to the western prairie uplands. The soil is fine textured and fertile, average temperatures are higher, and spring rains more reliable.[2] When they first saw this region, La Vérendrye and his sons were struck by its beauty:

It is all very level, without mountains, all fine hard wood with here and there groves of oak . . . everywhere there are quantities of fruit trees, and all sorts of wild animals . . . the savage tribes are there very numerous. There are some magnificent plains. . . . Trees grow only on the banks of the rivers and the prevailing kinds are white oak, elm, ash . . . bass and birch. All the rest is prairie, with here and there clumps of oak and wild plum.[3]

When Manitoba became a province in 1870, the population numbered about 13,000 and consisted mainly of Indians and Métis. After Louis Riel's failure to secure their rights, they were forced to move further west or north into the Shield. Their claims to the southern region were extinguished by treaties in 1871 and their eviction completed by 1890.[4]

The British settlers who displaced them came mainly from Ontario:

Nearly all were practical farmers with means, a few were graduates of the Ontario Agricultural College at Guelph, and they brought to the parklands . . . a high degree of agricultural experience and skill.[5]

Others came directly from Great Britain:

Including among their numbers graduates of British universities, and, as well, people of sufficient means to permit of their living the life of the English country gentlemen, so far as it might be lived on the prairies, these settlers, by their love of good books, art, music, flowers . . . made a contribution to the life of Manitoba.[6]

A local history of Carman, a British settlement begun in 1878, later commented on the removal of the original inhabitants:

The time . . . was not favourable for the Métis, who were such a contented people. . . . Today there is not one Métis left from the many that used to be here. They dispersed in all directions.[7]

During the winter of 1891, an editor reported that "an untutored child of the Plains came into the *Free Press* on Saturday and left the following letter":

We are very poor. Simpson [an Indian commissioner] told us at the Lower Fort that the treaty would not be broken so we hope the authorities will keep their word. We are kept from killing moose and those who have no crop will starve. We have no school house nor anything which the Queen promised us.[8]

Mr. E. McColl, the Indian agent in Winnipeg, responded that the Indians were "most indolent and improvident" and that their annuities had already been increased from three to five dollars.[9]

During the 1870's and early 1880's, a few non-British immigrant groups also arrived in the province. About fifteen hundred Icelanders, obliged by an active volcano to emigrate, moved into a bleak district north of the provincial boundary alongside Lake Winnipeg and named their new community Gimli, meaning Paradise. Escaping Czarist conscription, an estimated seven thousand German-speaking Mennonites settled south of Winnipeg along the American border. An English visitor to their community reported:

The Mennonites do not give a great impression of cleanliness . . . the same roof covers the horses and the chickens and the rest of the family. As a race they are thrifty and industrious but their neighbours say that the women do most of their work. The great drawback of the Mennonites seems to be their poverty.[10]

To the northwest, a party of Hungarians settled at Stoney Creek, which came to be called Huns' Valley. From Quebec, a few French-Canadians came to St. Boniface and villages in the southeast. Also about 350 Jewish refugees from Russia spent a winter in makeshift sheds in Winnipeg and then moved north to a barren Interlake settlement at Narcisse. After watching Jewish women "picking up odds and ends of food and clothing" in Winnipeg streets before their migration north, a writer concluded:

A more helpless and useless lot never crossed the Atlantic. . . . It will cost our people more to keep them than to send them back to Europe.[11]

By the mid-1880's, the province's ethnic and class structure was thus being established by the pattern of immigration and settlement. A relatively prosperous British majority occupied much of the best land in the southwest while through generally less promising areas were scattered various poorer non-British minorities.

In the first years after Confederation, political parties were little more than primitive factions.[12] With federal help, a stable Conservative ministry was formed in 1878. Its leader was John Norquay, a 300-pound Métis who could astonish English visitors with a high-kicking Red River jig. To the British immigrant settlers from Ontario, confidently rooted in a rural Grit tradition, Norquay seemed little better than a federal puppet: as their settlements grew, his government weakened. He narrowly won re-election in 1886 but lost the new British ridings. The next year, their dissatisfaction with federal railway policy drove him to desperate efforts to borrow money for the construction of a provincial railway.[13] His failure forced his resignation

[2]*Economic Atlas of Manitoba*, T. R. Weir, ed. (Winnipeg: Queen's Printer, 1960), pp. 12-13.

[3]Quoted in *The Western Interior of Canada*, J. Warkentin, ed. (Toronto: McClelland and Stewart Ltd., 1964), pp. 44-48.

[4]J.H. Lagasse, *et al.*, *The People of Indian Ancestry in Manitoba, A Social and Economic Study* (Winnipeg: Queen's Printer, 1959), I, 32-35 and 58-67.

[5]W.L. Morton, *Manitoba, A History*, 2nd ed. (Toronto: University of Toronto Press, 1967), p. 179.

[6]M. McWilliams, *Manitoba Milestones* (Toronto: J. M. Dent and Sons, 1928), p. 165.

[7]Carman Centennial Committee, *Up To Now, A Story of Dufferin and Carman* (Altona, Manitoba: D. W. Friesen and Sons, 1967), pp. 7-9.

[8]*Manitoba Free Press* (Winnipeg), February 2, 1891.

[9]*Ibid.*, February 3, 1891.

[10]*Ibid.*, September 2, 1881.

[11]*Winnipeg Daily Times*, August 9, 1882.

[12]R.O. MacFarlane, "Manitoba Politics and Parties after Confederation," *Canadian Historical Association Annual Report, 1940*.

[13]J.A. Jackson, "The Disallowance of Manitoba Railway Legislation in the 1880's" (M.A. Thesis, University of Manitoba, 1945), pp. 90-102.

and, broken and exhausted, he died eighteen months later. Ontario democracy triumphed.[14] The new Liberal premier was Thomas Greenway, a prosperous farmer originally from Centralia, Ontario. After winning the election of 1888, his government took decisive action against the French minority. The printing of government documents in French was ended and public financial support withdrawn from Catholic schools. The French sought help from the courts and the federal Conservative cabinet but without success. The Greenway government remained secure, partly by appointing clerks to control the voters' lists and by a gerrymander in 1892.[15]

Only after the federal Liberal victory of Wilfrid Laurier in 1896 did Greenway become suspect to his British supporters. Under federal pressure, he agreed to permit limited Catholic religious instruction and the use of languages other than English in Manitoba public schools. A new Conservative newspaper now accused him of "treachery and hypocrisy" and condemned "the special privileges now enjoyed by the French."[16] More vigorous Conservative leadership was provided by Hugh John Macdonald, son of former Prime Minister John A. Macdonald, from Kingston, Ontario. He blamed Greenway for the federal Liberal immigration policy directed by Clifford Sifton, one of Greenway's former ministers, and warned that "the wholesale importation of undesirable immigrants," particularly from Eastern Europe, threatened the province's newly asserted British character.[17] His speeches on this issue secured a good response:

Discussing Mr. Greenway's approval of Galician and Doukhobor immigration, Mr. Macdonald made a vigorous protest against importing this class of immigrants in preference to immigrants of Anglo-Saxon racial stock.

His remarks on this point were received with prolonged applause.

The people of the West, at any rate, are not going to place the government of this intelligent and British community at the mercy of a horde of Slavs.[18]

The *Manitoba Free Press,* in which Sifton purchased a controlling interest,[19] defended the Liberals by claiming that the Conservatives were really to blame for the "foreign colonies" in Manitoba since Slavic immigration had begun in 1892.[20] But Macdonald won the election by capturing most of the British ridings in the southwest. To the extent that they were politically active, the other ethnic groups tended to vote in separate blocs. Many of the Mennonites regarded any government as a threat and their religion opposed holding public office. Few welcomed the right to vote and a small turnout in their district of Rosenfeldt elected Wilhelm Hespeler, the German consul in Winnipeg, as an Independent. The contest in Gimli was narrowly won by a former Conservative immigration agent, Baldwin Baldwinson, who answered charges that he bribed his way to victory by claiming "it was the Liberals who sold themselves."[21] For the French, survival required solidarity:

D'un commun accord les electeurs, conservateurs comme libéraux, ont cru qu'il ne fallait pas introduire ces divisions dans nos luttes provinciales. . . . Notre peuple est trop faible pour se payer le luxe de luttes fratricides.[22]

They voted Liberal in 1899 partly because of Laurier's appeal and partly because they expected Greenway to win and thought they would be safer on the winning side.[23] Nine months after the election, Macdonald resigned and was succeeded by Rodmond P. Roblin, a grain merchant in Carman originally from Picton, Ontario. To the Catholic clergy, Roblin's accession was reassuring and he shortly secured French allegiance. Like Macdonald, however, he considered foreign immigration objectionable:

He regarded it as of vital importance that Canada should exercise the greatest care in the selection of those admitted to her shores. The folly of paying agents and corporations a bonus for using the dragnet through Europe to gather up those who could be induced to settle in Canada, regardless of all considerations of suitability, appealed to him as not only dangerous to the future state but absolutely un-British.[24]

Paradoxically, his government came to be based upon the support of non-British immigrants.

Between 1901 and 1911, the province's population nearly doubled, becoming almost half a million.[25] Thousands from Central and Eastern Europe were settled by immigration officials along the fringe of existing northern settlement on "marginal lands which demanded much more work and gave fewer returns than any of the lands hitherto settled."[26] Clifford Sifton later commented:

For thirty years Canadian and British settlers had been coming to Manitoba, but none would go on those lands where I as a boy with my father, who was a railway contractor, had sunk into the swampy muck. Perhaps it was hardly fair to place those people there but it was . . . like their old home and they went there willingly.[27]

Albert Smith, a Methodist minister in the northwestern town of Dauphin, witnessed the arrival there in 1898 of the first Ukrainians who "were conducted by government agents" to homesteads further north in "an area of low, cheap land covered with willow scrub."[28] The remoteness and hardship

[14]Morton, *op. cit.*, Chapter 9.

[15]J. Holmes, "Factors Affecting Politics in Manitoba: A Study of the Provincial Elections, 1870-1899" (M.A. Thesis, University of Manitoba, 1936), pp. 94-96.

[16]*Winnipeg Telegram*, January 26, 1899.

[17]*Ibid.*, July 11, 1899.

[18]*Ibid.*, August 11 and September 5, 1899.

[19]M.S. Donnelly, *Dafoe of the Free Press* (Toronto: The Macmillan Company of Canada, 1968), p. 35.

[20]*Manitoba Free Press* (Winnipeg), September 2, 9, and 12, 1899.

[21]Quoted by W. Kristjanson, *The Icelandic People in Manitoba* (Winnipeg: Wallingford Press, 1965), p. 295.

[22]*Le Manitoba* (St. Boniface), January 22, 1896, quoted by R. Turenne, "The Minority and the Ballot Box, A Study of the Voting Behaviour of the French-Canadians of Manitoba, 1888-1967" (M.A. Thesis, University of Manitoba, 1969), p. 35.

[23]*Ibid.*, pp. 42-57.

[24]Hugh Ross, *Thirty-Five Years in the Limelight, Sir Rodmond P. Roblin and His Times* (Winnipeg: Farmer's Advocate Press, 1936), p. 85.

[25]Canada, Dominion Bureau of Statistics, *Census of the Prairie Provinces, Population and Agriculture, 1916* (Ottawa: King's Printer, 1918), p. 22.

[26]*Economic Atlas of Manitoba*, p. 28.

[27]Quoted by V. Lysenko, *Men in Sheepskin Coats* (Toronto: The Ryerson Press, 1947), pp. 123-124.

[28]A.E. Smith, *All My Life* (Toronto: Progress Publishing Company, 1949), p. 27.

of these new communities confirmed their natural disposition: they became isolated by poverty as well as language.[29] As the province thus became more clearly divided along ethnic and class lines, so did Winnipeg become two distinct cities. The more prosperous British families moved southward and westward along the Assiniboine River and built impressive homes amid boulevards and parks in the new districts of Crescentwood and River Heights. Much of the city's north end, in contrast, became a noisy, crowded ghetto. In 1906, a delegation of ladies from the Winnipeg Ministerial Association, accompanied by a private detective, visited a Jewish district, identified as "Jerusalem number one," and reported back to a meeting:

Forty-five families inhabited a very small space, living in a manner that was to say the least disgraceful. Diseases of all kinds were common. . . . It was just the spot for a plague to begin and sweep over the city, and it was a providence that such had not occurred.[30]

After discussing the possibilities of confining the immigrants to an industrial farm or at least curbing their beer consumption, the meeting went on to hear a lecture on "The Christology of Paul." James Woodsworth, a Methodist minister from Ontario who organized missionary work in Winnipeg's north end, also characterized some of the new immigrant groups:

Even those who detest 'foreigners' make an exception of Germans, whom they classify as 'white people like ourselves'.

Most of the Poles who reached this country are peasants or workingmen . . . far from the best class. They are poor, illiterate, and with a code of morals none too high. . . .

The Galician figures, disproportionately to his numbers, in the police court and penitentiary. Centuries of poverty and oppression have, to some extent, animalized him.

The large majority of Jews . . . come here wretchedly poor . . . and yet in some way they exist and make money. . . .[31]

Having come from villages where vestiges of feudalism persisted, most of these immigrants tended to be deferential to authority, fearful of giving offence, and more than willing to cooperate with their new government.

On this foundation, Premier Roblin and his minister of public works, Robert Rogers, built a powerful party machine. Undecipherable Slavic names made voters' lists elastic and impersonation unchallengeable. In 1914, the *Free Press* investigated voter registration at Komarno, a village in the Interlake district:

Wasyl Krucekowski appears again on the same list as Wasyl Kluczkowski. . . . Alex Cymbaluk blossomed forth twice as Alex Cybulak. John Blowatczuk admitted that he was on the list again as John Glavacz. Leon Ukramik was first on the list as Leon Szpakowski. . . . There were dozens of others like him. A large measure of the credit for this is freely given to F.S. Szablewski, the debonair land inspector, whose success in "organizing" is giving him a "stand-in" with the bosses of the Conservative machine.[32]

Platoons of such inspectors exchanged kegs of beer for votes. Contributions squeezed from government contractors paid the bills, newspapers multiplied and fattened on government printing orders, and when necessary, most of the annual road appropriation for the province could be spent in one district to win a difficult by-election, as was done in Gimli in 1913.[33] Above it all, Premier Roblin invoked Biblical phrase and patriotic sentiment to roast his opponents. Proclaiming that "in Western Canada all roads lead to Winnipeg,"[34] his government initially showed great energy. An agreement with the Canadian Northern secured another grain outlet to the lakehead in 1902, and resulting competition cut freight charges. Before 1905, Roblin almost acquired the North-West Territory as a Manitoba empire, and despite the local popularity of reciprocity in the 1911 federal election, he delivered eight out of ten Manitoba seats to the Conservatives and won a massive northward extension of the provincial boundary in 1912. Pioneering in public ownership, he bought out Bell Telephone in 1907 and three years later launched a public grain elevator scheme that became a fiscal nightmare. Economic growth and prosperity, based in part on the abundance of cheap immigrant labour, were unprecedented. But even so, provincial expenditures threatened to become unmanageable. Roblin himself was wearing out: his platform performances became unpredictable, his rhetoric more florid. After Rogers entered federal politics, the party organization also faltered. Its final glory was the 1914 election victory. With only a minority of the popular vote, it won a majority of seats by sweeping the non-British ridings.

In their frustration, the Liberals urged higher public morality and attacked the foreign immigrants for being constitutionally inferior, if not depraved. A temperance movement, undeterred by Roblin's defence of saloons as centres of good-will, blamed electoral corruption on immigrant vice. After observing the 1914 campaign, a Presbyterian minister reported: *They come to Canada and huddle themselves off in colonies and are subject to evil influences. From the conditions in which they live, they are brought up to expect remuneration for their votes. Unfortunately it is difficult, I have found, to separate drink from the foreigners. During this election, it was not an uncommon sight to see these new arrivals lying around soaked in whiskey that was carried in suitcases by ardent politicians. Thousands of foreigners have been given the ballot who have certainly no right to it, and thousands of intelligent women have been denied the right.*[35] Illustrating a common tendency to unite the emerging question of female suffrage with the need to curb immigrant influence, there was hearty agreement with the Britisher who declared: "Surely my wife is more capable of

29C. Dawson and E. Younge, *Pioneering in the Prairie Provinces: The Social Side of the Settlement Process* (Toronto: The Macmillan Company of Canada, 1940), p. 36.

30*Manitoba Free Press* (Winnipeg), October 9, 1906.

31J.S. Woodsworth, *Strangers Within Our Gates* (Toronto: Missionary Society of the Methodist Church, Canada, 1909), pp. 100, 136, 141 and 156.

32*Manitoba Free Press* (Winnipeg), May 21, 1914.

33L. Orlikow, "A Survey of the Reform Movement in Manitoba, 1910-1920" (M.A. Thesis, University of Manitoba, 1955), pp. 136-140.

34R.P. Roblin, *et al.*, *A Handbook to Winnipeg and the Province of Manitoba* (Winnipeg: Sanford Evans, Ltd., 1901), p. 45.

35*Manitoba Free Press* (Winnipeg), May 18, 1914.

voting than the ignorant Galician."[36] Another non-British group was treated with humour:

The wildest excitement prevails among the Indians . . . over the election campaign. On Thursday, the whole thing was made plain by the arrival from Winnipeg of a party of expert naturalization and registration operators, who explained that the scheme is to put through bogus naturalization papers making the Indians citizens.

One group will have their faces darkened and will be naturalized and registered as Hudson Bay Railway sleeping car conductors; other groups will be naturalized as newcomers to this country from continental Europe.[37]

When the government tried to assist urban Catholic schools and in 1913 admitted a French-Canadian to the cabinet, it incurred the wrath of the Orange Lodge, which joined the Liberals in attacking Roblin. The onset of World War I increased these racial and religious tensions. North and east of Winnipeg, there had developed a substantial settlement of German Catholics just prior to the war.[38] After their newspaper advised them to return to Germany, the *Free Press* reacted by charging it with "active and flagrant treason" and also warned that "agitators have imported into this country the lingo and catch cries of the nationalist crusade in Galicia."[39] The war placed both East European and German immigrants on the defensive, while Mennonites henceforth identified themselves as being of Dutch origin.

In 1915, a scandal involving the construction of the provincial legislative building finally finished Premier Roblin's political career. He was forced to resign and in the resulting election the Liberals won almost every seat. Their leader was Toby Norris, a farmer and auctioneer who had come to Manitoba from Brampton, Ontario, and settled near Brandon in the southwest. Women were given the right to vote in 1916 and became an important source of Liberal support. Regarding non-British women, Nellie McClung, a leading suffragette, advised that there was nothing to fear:

Mrs. McClung declared she was not afraid of the way in which the foreign women of Manitoba would cast their vote. She knew many of the Mary's and Annie's among the foreign-born women and she loved their honest faces. The women who had fought for suffrage would take upon themselves the task of instructing their foreign-born sisters in the duties and privileges of citizenship.[40]

The persistence of sharp racial divisions was shown by the conflict in 1917 over Quebec's opposition to conscription. At a mass rally in Winnipeg's Walker Theatre, Mrs. Edward Brown, wife of the provincial treasurer, declared:

It is a proud boast for anyone who can say today: I am of the British race, I am of Canada! I have absolute confidence in the people of Canada, outside of the unspeakable French-Canadians.[41]

In this spirit, the Norris government moved to accelerate assimilation of the non-British groups. Primary school attendance became compulsory and the use of languages other than English in the public schools was prohibited. To escape the school law, about 6,000 Mennonites, a third of their community, emigrated to Mexico and Paraguay after 1918.[42] The Ukrainians made little protest since they were internally preoccupied with a deepening struggle between Greek Catholic and Greek Orthodox congregations.[43] But for the French, protection of their language became an overriding goal that absorbed their attention to the virtual exclusion of all else, and a new educational association, allied with clerical leaders, replaced their political representatives as guardian of the group's survival.[44]

Other reforms also cut against the non-British minorities. With the establishment of a Civil Service Commission empowered to hire on the basis of competitive examinations, their access to jobs by the back door of patronage was blocked. A new electoral system of transferable ballots which was designed to assure that winning candidates had majority support proved advantageous to the more experienced British voters. A temperance referendum, that split the electorate along ethnic lines, was won by the British; and after moderate control reportedly failed to curb drunkenness in the non-British districts, it was followed by total prohibition in 1920. The problem of absorbing or containing the foreign element invariably became entangled in such questions. To provincial Liberal leaders, reform and assimilation seemed nearly synonymous: the non-British evidently needed civilizing and in practical terms this meant that they needed to be Anglicized. Few of the non-British were in a position to oppose this view and many indeed welcomed and pursued Anglicization as a step toward economic survival. Beyond this ethnic issue, the Norris government also introduced other reforms including allowances for deserted or widowed mothers, improved workmen's compensation for industrial injuries, more effective factory inspection and a fair wage board to consider requests for higher pay. It proved unwilling to recognize collective bargaining rights, however, and on this issue rising working-class discontent shortly erupted.

Protest came from British workingmen in Winnipeg. After forming a labour party in 1895, they entered the 1899 provincial election with resolutions advocating free compulsory education, a minimum wage and a maximum 48-hour work week, abolition of child labour, orderly negotiation of wage disputes, public ownership of utilities and abolition of the federal Senate.[45] Arthur Puttee, a printer from Folkestone, England, won a labour

36*Winnipeg Tribune*, February 2, 1912.

37*Manitoba Free Press* (Winnipeg), June 27, 1914.

38C. Dawson, *Group Settlement, Ethnic Communities in Western Canada* (Toronto: The Macmillan Company of Canada, 1936), p. 277.

39*Der Nordwesten* (Winnipeg), August 5, 1914; *Manitoba Free Press* (Winnipeg), August 10, 1914.

40*Manitoba Free Press* (Winnipeg), August 14, 1915.

41*Winnipeg Telegram*, December 14, 1917.

42E.K. Francis, *In Search of Utopia* (Altona, Manitoba: D.W. Friesen and Sons, 1955), p. 187.

43O.S. Trosky, *The Ukrainian Greek Orthodox Church in Canada* (Winnipeg: Bulman Bros., 1968), pp. 8-16.

44Turenne, *op. cit.*, pp. 101-105.

45*Winnipeg Telegram*, July 16, 1899.

seat in a federal by-election in 1900 and held it until 1904.[46] The first labour victory in provincial politics was in 1914, when Fred Dixon, an engraver who arrived from England in 1904, won in Winnipeg Centre. Like Puttee and Dixon, other labour leaders were also recent immigrants from Britain: William Ivens came in 1896, John Queen in 1906, Bob Russell in 1911 and R.J. Johns in 1912. Dixon was joined in the legislature in 1915 by Richard Rigg, a Methodist preacher and bookbinder, who immigrated from Lancashire in 1903.[47] But despite this common background, disputes occurred within the movement and splinter groups appeared, such as a socialist party in 1902. Another limiting factor was the non-British working-class group, considered more an economic threat than a possible political ally. The Winnipeg Trades and Labour Council made this clear in 1899:

A protest was sent to the Dominion government against the expenditure of public funds for the wholesale importation of Galicians and Doukhobors to this country and thus bringing unjust competition against the industrial classes . . . [with immigrants] accustomed to starvation wages.[48]

As heavy immigration continued over the next decade and a half, so did similar complaints.

Far from going to a labour party, most non-British voting support was captured early by the Liberals and Conservatives. Both parties organized Jewish political clubs in Winnipeg in 1896. The first Jewish political representatives were Conservative businessmen: Moses Finkelstein and Altar Skaletar, elected as city aldermen in 1904 and 1912. The Liberals countered by launching the *Canadian Israelite* and their efforts secured the 1910 election to the provincial legislature of Solomon Hart Green, a prominent lawyer originally from New Brunswick.[49] Both parties sent speakers to address Jewish meetings on such topics as "Courage," "Our Patriotism," and "Equal Suffrage for All."[50] Labour candidates made no such appeal and their early successes in the north end came from British working-class support, in spite of non-British opposition. Thus Richard Rigg's victory in 1915 was possible partly because the Jewish vote split between Green and Elias Levinson, a prominent Conservative lawyer from Australia appointed Crown prosecutor in 1912. When Rigg resigned to contest a federal seat in 1917, the Jewish vote again elected a Liberal, Robert Jacob, although there was uncertainty about his background:

At some meetings, Mr. Jacob has been referred to as a Hebrew, the speakers evidently thinking that he is of Hebrew extraction. To this Mr. Jacob has had to explain that he is an Englishman by birth.[51]

In 1917 a radical Jewish upholsterer, A.A. Heaps, won election as an alderman, but at the provincial level there was no Jewish representation from 1915 to 1927, when Captain William Tobias, a prominent city "lawyer and sportsman" was elected as a Conservative.[52]

A similar pattern of allegiance developed in the Slavic community. From the outset, its newspapers were directed by Conservative and Liberal publicists. When the Liberals organized the *Canadian Farmer* in 1903, John Dafoe, editor of the *Free Press,* wrote to Clifford Sifton:

Our Galician paper has at last made its appearance. J. Obed and John Appleton with the assistance of a Galician interpreter are keeping an eye on the matter that goes into it. It has been thought desirable to keep contentious matters out of the first few issues: later on we shall give a few knocks to the Tories.[53]

In 1910, another paper, the *Ukrainian Voice,* was organized by a school teacher, Taras Ferley, who won as a Liberal in Gimli in 1915. By this time, Ukrainians were under attack from two sides. As aliens, many were disfranchised, interned and suspended from applying for naturalization.[54] For their service as pawns of the Roblin machine, they were also blamed for its corruption. To escape this stigma, a new Ukrainian political club emphasized in awkward English its dedication to a higher level of politics:

The lack of such organization has been painfully felt in the past by Ruthenian-Ukrainians themselves as on account of such a state of affairs existing, there has not been clear political ideas and from this, quasi politicians drew advantages of all kinds through their persistency in the bartering of people, entailing disgrace for the whole nation.[55]

Similarly, the *Canadian Ruthenian,* a Conservative and Catholic paper formed in 1911, now disavowed its previous political association which it blamed on the "French Mafia":

Every true Ruthenian-Ukrainian considers it from now on his sacred duty . . . to protest against the running of a Ukrainian paper by the French with the following words: Down with the French Conservative hirelings![56]

Thus, when under political attack, one non-British group would seek respectability by attacking another non-British group.

For their part, the French sought respite by retreating from partisan politics altogether. The only other numerically significant non-British group, the Icelanders, became increasingly Liberal, particularly after the appointment of Thomas Johnson, a prominent attorney, to the Norris cabinet in 1915 and the placing of a statue of one of their national heroes, Jon Sigurdson, on the legislative grounds. By the end of the war, the roster was virtually complete: the major parties, especially the Liberals, enjoyed the allegiance of most non-British voters, both rural and urban. In Winnipeg, the lower class was thus divided into British workers prepared to protest economic conditions and non-British workers, amounting to almost a third of the city

---

[46]*Manitoba Commonwealth* (Winnipeg), April 28, 1945; Cp. A.R. McCormack, "Arthur Puttee and the Liberal Party: 1899-1904," *Canadian Historical Review,* June, 1970, pp. 141-163.

[47]*Winnipeg Tribune,* January 28, 1916.

[48]*Winnipeg Telegram,* August 4, 1899.

[49]A. Chiel, *The Jews in Manitoba* (Toronto: University of Toronto Press, 1961), pp. 124-128 and 176-177.

[50]*Ibid.,* p. 155; *Manitoba Free Press* (Winnipeg), July 23, 1915.

[51]*Winnipeg Telegram,* January 12, 1918.

[52]Chiel, *op. cit.,* p. 177.

[53]Dafoe-Sifton Correspondence, November 3, 1903 (Provincial Archives of Manitoba).

[54]P. Yuzyk, *The Ukrainians in Manitoba* (Toronto: University of Toronto Press, 1953), pp. 177-178.

[55]*Manitoba Free Press* (Winnipeg), July 24, 1915.

[56]*Ibid.,* August 5, 1915.

population, who were either intimidated and politically inert, or securely harnessed to the support of the existing system. This ethnic division shaped the outcome of the city's crisis in 1919.

By early 1918, trouble was imminent. The cost of living index had doubled during the war from 137.5 to 290.9, while wages increased only about 20 per cent.[57] The government fair wage board's hesitant recommendations nonetheless encountered business opposition. When it raised the minimum wage for female restaurant employees by 50 cents to $12.50 a week, owners protested:

It means that we will have to raise prices . . . and higher prices will deprive the girls of the generous tips the girls now receive.[58]

Wage increases sought in most trades were about fifteen or twenty cents an hour, amounting to raises of 20 to 30 per cent. When these were rejected, a series of strikes began in the spring of 1918 and unrest mounted to desperation the following winter. A typical delegation to the premier complained just before Christmas that "married men with families were finding it impossible to live on $75 a month."[59] As mass protest meetings developed, the federal government sent two hundred cavalry to reinforce the police.[60] The first riots began in January. They attacked the non-British who were blamed for the low wages and lack of jobs:

The outbreak developed into a general display of feeling against foreigners, who were supposed to be of alien enemy sympathies, and about a score of buildings, principally stores in the central and northern parts of the city, suffered at the hands of mobs, which were composed of returned men and youths. In the attack . . . a number of people of foreign nationality were somewhat severely mauled.[61]

In February a provincial alien board began deportation proceedings against foreigners and the department of education gave assurance that it was "stamping out" foreign languages in the schools.[62] Unemployed veterans forced "bohunks" on downtown streets to kneel and kiss the Union Jack and obliged Premier Norris to send a telegram to Ottawa:

Deputations of returned soldiers . . . urging immediate internment and deportation of alien enemies. Also want all property belonging to aliens confiscated.[63]

In this atmosphere, when a new wave of strikes began in May, the non-British became the scapegoat. To no avail did one group insist that "we have always been loyal and law-abiding citizens of this country and shall always stand for the preservation of peace and order."[64]

By early June, the *Free Press* asserted that the strikes were a lesson to workers to avoid "subjugation to the mass of rough labour, mostly foreign born," and, focusing on the interrupted delivery of milk, charged that the strike leaders "have deprived the babies of this town of milk; that is they have condemned a very large percentage of them to death — did the Returned Soldiers, in all their overseas experience, ever hear of a more Hunnish trick than that?"[65] The *Winnipeg Citizen,* issued by a businessmen's committee, went further:

Are Austrians, enemies of Canada, to be allowed to attempt to murder loyal soldiers, heroes, true Britishers upon the streets of Winnipeg?

There is no middle ground. Let all this twaddle about "collective bar-gaining" drop in the face of bloodshed!

There is anarchy and revolution abroad in Winnipeg . . . and organized labor has been betrayed into a position which gives the alien enemies, the Austrians and the Germans, cowards that they are, the chance to do their bloody work.

Sam Blumenberg, one of the few non-English spokesmen active in the strike, was singled out for criticism:

Agitator Blumberg [sic], the man who is keenly interested in turning "wage slaves" into automobile owners . . . is not noted as a worker himself. In fact he never slaves at anything unless it is on a platform with an alien audience where he slaves for an hour in broken English to tell them that they are the salt of the earth and that the earth belongs to them.[66]

James Woodsworth, who returned to the city on a lecture tour and helped raise money for strikers' families, later commented:

Without hesitation I say that there was not a single foreigner in a position of leadership, though foreigners were falsely arrested to give color to this charge. . . . In short it was the biggest hoax that was ever 'put over' any people![67]

While the strikes came to be called a general strike, whatever coordination they had was improvised and haphazard. The *ad hoc* leaders fumbled through the crisis and "never made the slightest effort" toward militant action.[68] Their paper, the *Western Labour News,* repeatedly tried to escape the alien taint and the charge of plotting revolution:

Keep your heads. Keep away from trouble makers. Leave no loophole for the other side to foment trouble.

Don't play their game. Keep out of their trap. Keep quiet.

The workers are dissatisfied, but they are not revolutionists. And their [sic] will be no revolution.

Beware of the stump orator who jumps on a box and talks Bolshevism. Beware of the fellow who tries to raise a row . . . because he is a stool pigeon.

The bosses love the alien when they can use him to break strikes. In fact in many cases he was brought here for that purpose.

Who brought the alien to Canada? It was not the workers. They opposed

57*Ibid.*, December 16, 1918.

58*Winnipeg Telegram*, April 9, 1919.

59*Manitoba Free Press* (Winnipeg), December 20, 1918.

60*Ibid.*, December 17, 1918.

61*Winnipeg Telegram*, January 27, 1919.

62*Manitoba Free Press* (Winnipeg), February 22, 1919.

63*Winnipeg Telegram*, May 2, 1919.

64*Manitoba Free Press* (Winnipeg), May 3, 1919.

65*Ibid.*, June 6, 1919.

66*Winnipeg Citizen*, June 11, 12, and 16, 1919.

67Quoted by K. McNaught, *A Prophet in Politics* (Toronto: University of Toronto Press, 1959), p. 116.

68D.C. Masters, *The Winnipeg General Strike* (Toronto: University of Toronto Press, 1950), p. 131.

it by might and main. We will support all efforts on the part of the authorities to deport all the undesirable aliens.[69]

Yet the opposition persisted in its charges of "murderous assaults by riotous aliens,"[70] and ultimately the tactic proved successful. On June 21, cavalry armed with baseball bats and revolvers charged a gathering of strikers, some carrying placards that declared "Britons Never Will Be Slaves." A spectator was killed outright and about twenty-five others were injured. Five days later, the strike collapsed, its leaders in prison and its press banned.

The use of racism in breaking the strike further isolated the non-British. Foreign agitators were blamed for the trouble, although, as an objective inquiry later concluded, its basic causes were low wages, high living costs, unemployment and the evident class division in the city.

Winnipeg unfortunately presents a prominent example of these extremes. There has been, and there is now, an increasing display of carefree, idle luxury and extravagance on the one hand, while on the other is intensified deprivation. The generally cold indifference of the one section to the condition of the other and the display of luxury aggravate this feeling of social disparity into one of active antagonism by the one class against the other.[71]

But Winnipeg labour leaders themselves came to accept the claim that the strike was a foreign-inspired aberration and became apologetic:

The Winnipeg Trades Council has fulfilled in no mean or small way the real function of a labor institution. Its deflection in 1919 was due to very unusual and abnormal circumstances. Made subversive to the propaganda, passion and prejudice arising out of a world war, its existence was for a time seriously threatened. It has however regained its poise, conscious by far of its greater mission in seeking to direct the thought of the workers into a more correct interpretation of those relations necessary between capital and labor in industry.[72]

Except for a few Jews who pioneered in organizing the garment workers, leadership in the trade union movement remained overwhelmingly British. In the 1920 provincial election, eleven Labour representatives, of whom ten were British, won seats in the legislature. Reorganized as the Independent Labour Party in 1921, the group included Fred Dixon as leader, several railway workers such as Arthur Moore, George Palmer and Charles Tanner, a teacher, William Bayley, and Albert Smith, a Methodist minister in Brandon. The strike made these labour representatives more wary of foreign support, which could clearly be used to discredit their movement. For the non-British, the strike's lesson was that whether they were agitators or not, aliens were the first target of reprisal. The threat of deportation became an effective deterrent. Thus the strike widened the ethnic division within the poorer class. With only a limited base of support, labour representation in the legislature by 1927 declined to three members.

Rural newspapers in the British southwest were virtually unanimous in condemning the strikers and in criticizing the provincial government for not taking sterner measures. All the jurors who convicted the strike leaders of seditious conspiracy were farmers.[73] Disgruntled also by declining post-war grain prices, and encouraged by farmers' political activity in Alberta and Ontario, a number of farmers entered as non-party candidates in the 1920 election and twelve won election. This cost Premier Norris his majority but he remained in office two more years. Political allegiances became confused, with former Liberals now sitting as Farmers and sitting Liberals continuing to desert Norris. One of the latter blamed him for the strike in fairly typical terms:

Unrest and discontent threaten the institutions and production of the country.

The recent general strike was nothing short of a revolution.

The policy of the Norris government . . . was to do nothing but sit and wait.[74]

On the alien question, W.R. Wood, secretary of the United Farmers of Manitoba, "forcibly emphasized the need of elevating the foreigner to the higher ideals of Canadian citizenship."[75] A Ukrainian elected in the northwest riding of Ethelbert as a Farmer candidate made a similar point defending "the foreigners" as "not inferior" but merely lacking opportunities, and stressed their loyalty to the Crown.[76]

House divisions generally saw the Farmers, under the leadership of William Robson, voting with the Conservatives, under Winnipeg lawyer John Haig, in urging economy and attacking alleged extravagance, while the Labour group generally supported the Norris government's program. One attitude shared by Farmers and Labour was a rejection of the old parties. Dixon was one of the first to express what later became a common theme in the legislature:

Increasing numbers of people consider this body nothing less than a glorified municipal council, and there is no more room for party politics in this house than in a municipal council, and the sooner we get that into our heads the better.[77]

To the Conservatives, this offered a way to escape the Roblin scandals. As for the Liberals, they had long solicited non-partisan support as a reform movement and since 1918 had identified themselves with the federal Unionists. But at a provincial convention in April of 1922, they narrowly voted to rejoin the Dominion Liberal party, and became vulnerable to charges of surrender to Ottawa and of "putting provincial interests in the back seat."[78] The delegates also split over the desirability of an "aggressive

[69]*Western Labour News* (Winnipeg), May 20, 22, 29 and June 4 and 7, 1919.

[70]*Manitoba Free Press* (Winnipeg), June 11, 1919.

[71]*Royal Commission to enquire into and report upon the causes and effects of the General Strike which recently existed in the city of Winnipeg*, H.A. Robson, K.C., Commissioner (Winnipeg: King's Printer, November, 1919), p. 27.

[72]*Winnipeg Trades and Labour Council Legislative Year Book, 1928*, p. 17.

[73]Masters, *op. cit.*, pp. 70-71 and 121; Cp. W.L. Morton, *The Progressive Party in Canada* (Toronto: University of Toronto Press, 1950), pp. 117-118 and 226-227.

[74]*Winnipeg Telegram*, February 3, 1920.

[75]*Manitoba Free Press* (Winnipeg), March 8, 1920.

[76]*Winnipeg Evening Tribune*, March 4, 1921.

[77]*Manitoba Free Press* (Winnipeg), March 22, 1921.

[78]*Ibid.*, April 28, 1922.

immigration policy" and the teaching of French in the public schools. A resolution on the latter issue produced stormy and prolonged debate:

D.R. MacLean said the resolution should be voted down, as he thought it meant the thin edge of bilingualism.

A Ruthenian delegate appealed for justice saying if the French people were entitled to recognition so were the Ruthenians who had done as much proportionally in the war as the French (Shouts of No! No!). F.L. Davis suggested this . . . would certainly mean the loss of some seats to the Liberal party. Many were now in doubt but if the resolution was passed they would be irretrievably lost.[79]

After the Norris government was defeated in the legislature in 1922, the United Farmers won a majority in the election. Party government was apparently ended. Yet the reality was little changed: the new ruling group was substantially the same as the old one — farmers of British origin from the southwest of the province supported by businessmen of British origin in south Winnipeg. This durable alliance now governed under a new name.

A new proportional system of representation in Winnipeg exploited the division within the lower class. Instead of marking a simple "X" on his ballot, the voter was now asked to number his choices on a long ballot listing 35 or 40 candidates for the 10 city seats. Among inexperienced voters, this created a confusion that as often as not worked to the disadvantage of Labour candidates.[80] In 1920, for example, the Liberals and Conservatives won six city seats with 44 per cent of the popular vote in the city, while Labour candidates, with 56 per cent of the city vote, won only four seats. Answering critics of the system, a *Free Press* editorial claimed that it helped keep Labour representation down:

Whatever is wrong with the old parties it is certain that Proportional Representation is not responsible for their woes. It is instead about the best friend they have got.[81]

Coalition was effective in other ridings, such as Brandon, where Albert Smith was defeated in 1922 by a "fusion" candidate, Dr. E.H. Edmison, supported by both Liberals and Conservatives. Also, a 1920 statutory ratio making each rural voter the equivalent of two city voters assured the over-representation of the British farming districts in the southwest. Thus the Farmers' majority in 1922 was based on only one-third of the popular vote.

After their victory, the farmers persuaded John Bracken to be premier. Like them, he was of Ontario British stock: his father's farm near Brockville, was reputed to be "one of the finest in Leeds County."[82] He came to Manitoba in 1906, and rose through agricultural extension work to head the Manitoba Agricultural College by 1920. Spartan by temperament, he probably remains the only premier to have swum in Hudson Bay and sprinted up and down the stony northern shoreline in September.[83] A visitor at a political meeting in a southwestern town compared him to "a Baptist preacher, perhaps because of his black tie and solemn expression" and was impressed that his dry exhortation on the need for disciplined economy "had the undivided attention of everyone in the hall."[84] Another observer commented:

He comes of Irish Presbyterian stock . . . who neither make jokes nor feel comfortable when they encounter wit. Incessant and laborious campaigns with the dry minutiae of provincial business have not exasperated his imagination, because he is not imaginative. He is an earnest young man . . . quite without frills.[85]

The basis of the Bracken government was the claim that good government was mainly a matter of careful administrative husbandry. That government should above all be firm, cautious, and conservative was the lesson drawn from the 1919 disorders. Both the prosperous business interests in Winnipeg and the farmers of the southwest shared the same goals: economy and stability.[86] Premier Bracken became custodian of the *status quo*. Remaining close to agriculture, he became also a prosperous landholder, owning by 1928 a 2,000-acre farm and after his retirement a 1,000-acre ranch estate in the Ottawa Valley.

Primary emphasis during the Bracken years was on the virtue of self-denial. The legislature became preoccupied with sin. Through the efforts of Mrs. Edith Rogers, wife of the president of the Crescent Creamery Company in Winnipeg and first woman elected to the legislature, smoking was prohibited in the legislature chamber.[87] Former suffragettes now scolded flappers and counselled that skirts should be longer. A newly-elected farmer expressed his view of the motion picture industry:

Personally, I would like to see the moving picture industry wiped out. One of the reasons for illegitimacy is that people are living so fast in these times.[88]

The government established a censorship board with extensive authority:

The board shall not approve any film or slide depicting scenes of an immoral or obscene nature, or which indicate or suggest lewdness or indecency, or marital infidelity, or showing the details of murder, robbery or criminal assault, or depicting criminals as heroic characters; and the board shall refuse to approve any other picture which it may consider injurious to public morals.[89]

Other issues stirring debate included the need for stringent limits on horse racing, whether evolution should be taught in the public schools, the need to arrest any child under sixteen found on city streets after 9 p.m., and reported orgies on Sunday excursion trains to Lake Winnipeg beaches. Liquor also roused spirited discussion, as when a provincial police commissioner claimed that 95 per cent of bootleggers were Jews engaged in a

---

[79]*Winnipeg Evening Tribune*, April 26, 1922.

[80]*Manitoba Free Press* (Winnipeg), July 20, 1922.

[81]*Ibid.*, July 25, 1922.

[82]A.G. Dexter, "A Professor in Politics," *Maclean's Magazine*, September 1, 1928, p. 16.

[83]W.J. Healy, "The Flying Prairie Premier," *Western Home Monthly*, December, 1926, p. 42.

[84]*Deloraine Times*, December 8, 1926.

[85]*Manitoba Free Press* (Winnipeg), January 7, 1927.

[86]W.L. Morton, *Manitoba, A History*, pp. 378-379.

[87]*Manitoba Free Press* (Winnipeg), February 10, 1921.

[88]*Winnipeg Evening Tribune*, March 3, 1921.

[89]*Statutes of Manitoba*, 1923, C. 1, Sec. 16-20, p. 8.

world-wide conspiracy to overthrow Christian values.[90] Total prohibition proved unworkable, since thousands of gallons of liquor were sold through drug store prescription; and after a referendum, the government permitted beer sales under careful regulation:

Every brewer who manufactures beer in the Province of Manitoba shall on every Wednesday make to the commission a return in writing showing in separate detail each and every sale of beer made by him during the successive six days terminating with the Saturday immediately preceding. Such return shall show (a) the name and address of each purchaser [etc.].[91]

Such questions of morality practically monopolized party politics, partly because the province's political system was securely in the control of the relatively prosperous class and other issues could not readily arise.

In a listing of about 700 prominent Manitoba citizens in 1925, the great majority were British.[92] Obituaries during the period show the same pattern. Alexander McLaren, proprietor of several hotels, came to Winnipeg in 1874 from Perth, Ontario. James Ashdown, a millionaire hardware merchant, came to Winnipeg in 1868 after working in his father's store in Weston, Ontario. William McMillan, a founder of the Dominion Elevator Company and the Winnipeg Grain Exchange, came to Winnipeg in 1875 from Pickering, Ontario. His brother, Daniel McMillan, accompanied the Wolseley expedition to expel Louis Riel and after serving as provincial treasurer in the Greenway government was knighted and appointed Lieutenant-Governor by the Laurier government. In a similar pattern, James Aikins, son of one of John A. Macdonald's cabinet ministers, came to Winnipeg in 1879 from Grahamsville, Ontario, became a major owner of downtown real estate, a director of Great West Life Assurance, the Imperial Bank of Canada, and other companies, and finally was appointed Lieutenant-Governor by the Borden government in 1916. Likewise, Theodore Burrows came to Winnipeg in 1875 from the Ottawa Valley, prospered with his uncle, the first Dominion land agent in Winnipeg, became head of numerous lumber and mortgage companies, and in 1926 was appointed Lieutenant-Governor to succeed Aikins. James Richardson, a director of numerous financial and grain companies, came to Winnipeg in 1912 after experience in the family business in Toronto. George Galt, nephew of Alexander Galt, another of John A. Macdonald's ministers, came to Winnipeg in 1882 from Toronto and within six years was president of the Winnipeg Board of Trade, as well as president or director of several financial and insurance enterprises. His view of politics was straight-forward:

If we in Canada would reflect more on our blessings and think less about our real or imaginary grievances, we would all be a happier and more self-reliant people.[93]

Of the same mind was Sir Augustus Nanton, son of a law partner of Alexander Galt in Toronto, who came to Winnipeg in 1883 and became a financial partner of Hugh Osler, son of Sir Edmund Osler of Toronto.

When Nanton was appointed president of the Dominion Bank of Canada in 1924, he delivered a characteristic warning:

In my opinion, the greatest peril which confronts Canada and especially this city is the teaching we hear of that is going on behind closed doors. This should be done away with. We welcome all good citizens from foreign lands but if they do not believe in the Christian religion, nor intend to keep our laws, they should be asked without delay to return from whence they came.[94] Most of these prominent citizens were members of Winnipeg's Manitoba Club, Canadian Club, and St. Charles Country Club, all clubs for successful persons of British origin. Hugh Robson, who succeeded Norris as Liberal leader in 1927 and was later appointed to the Manitoba Court of Appeal by the federal Liberal government of Mackenzie King, was a member of this group. So was the Conservative leader from 1922 to 1933, Fawcett Gowler Taylor, who in the latter year was appointed to the Manitoba Court of King's Bench by the federal Conservative government of R.B. Bennett. Former prominent politicians, such as Hugh John Macdonald, Clifford Sifton, and Robert Rogers, were also members, as were the province's leading jurists, such as Thomas Mathers and Daniel Macdonald. So were the province's two leading editors, John Dafoe of the *Free Press* and R.L. Richardson of the *Tribune,* both of whom, like most of this group, came to Winnipeg from Ontario. The *Free Press's* bitter attacks on the Winnipeg strike were, according to his biographer, to be expected from Dafoe, who "had joined the Winnipeg establishment and took some pride in the fact that the boy from the backwoods was now an accepted member of the Manitoba Club."[95] Several cabinet ministers, such as William Clubb and Richard Craig, the Attorney-General, were also members. The British group from Ontario thus comprised a ruling class, although it claimed that class politics was undesirable. Craig, for example, advised immigrants:

A government composed of one class is not democratic, but autocratic. Today we require a government of all the people, elected by the people and not by any one class.[96]

To the non-British, the attractiveness of this ruling class was a major incentive for Anglicization. The shame they felt in not being English is well expressed in a novel about Winnipeg in the 1920's by a writer of non-British origin. It tells of Sandor Hunyadi, the son of Hungarian immigrants, who tries to become an English businessman. At twelve, looking for a job as a gardener, he first visits the English neighborhood south of the Assiniboine River:

In a daze, he moved down the street. The boulevards ran wide and spacious to the very doors of the houses. And these houses were like palaces, great and stately, surrounded by their own private parks and gardens.
After securing a job from an English lady, he exults:

[90]*Winnipeg Evening Tribune,* February 22, 1922.
[91]*Statutes of Manitoba,* 1927, C. 32, Sec. 18A, p. 77.
[92]W. McRaye, ed. *Pioneers and Prominent People of Manitoba* (Winnipeg: Bulman Bros. Ltd., 1925).
[93]*Manitoba Free Press* (Winnipeg), April 16, 1928.
[94]*Ibid.,* December 17, 1924.
[95]M.S. Donnelly, *op. cit.,* p. 102.
[96]*Canadian Farmer* (Winnipeg), June 15, 1922. This newspaper was published in Ukrainian. The excerpts from it and other Ukrainian newspapers quoted herein were translated by Miss M. Pidhirnyj, whose assistance is gratefully acknowledged, as is the University of Manitoba's provision of funds to pay for the translation.

He was going to work for her, and so in a sense he belonged to her house and some of this high splendid arrogance of hers would be his too. This is the way it should be, he thought. This was how the rich English should act, this was the way they should look, dignified and cool-eyed and distant.[97]

After growing up, Sandor changes his name to Alex Hunter and tries to succeed as a rent collector. The novel's conclusion is gloomy: despite his effort to become like the English, "Hunter" fails in business and retreats into despair.

A primary concern of the British ruling group was to protect itself from taxation. Hence the provincial government pursued rigorous thrift, keeping annual expenditure to $10 million or less and producing budgetary surpluses year after year in the 1920's. Costs were held down particularly in the areas of health, education, and welfare. Of $5,000 appropriated for child welfare in 1921, for example, $420 was actually spent;[98] seven years later, the grant for two child welfare agencies was increased to $787.60.[99] On taking office, one of the Bracken government's first actions was to cut provincial allowances for widowed and deserted mothers, despite a mass protest meeting at Winnipeg's Grace Church.[100] Responding to briefs from the Winnipeg Board of Trade and a Taxpayers' Association protesting education costs, even though 104 schools closed for lack of funds in 1923, the government appointed a special commission to recommend further economies.[101] The school population increased by 15,000 between 1921 and 1928, but the provincial appropriation for education remained virtually constant and declined as a proportion of total expenditure.[102] In 1928, Miss Charlotte Whitton was appointed to appraise the administration of provincial welfare and her report stressed the adverse consequences of rigid cost reduction. Visiting a provincial charitable home for the infirm, she found 435 persons from under five to over seventy jammed into two inadequate buildings without any nursing staff.[103] The next year the provincial grant for the home was raised by $40, but three years later was reduced by $807.[104] After noting that the average monthly wage in Winnipeg in 1928 was $108.25, and that the minimum monthly subsistence budget for a family of four was $88.00, the Whitton report listed numerous case histories of families below this minimum, one example being "case no. 1937: father, 49, born in Poland, illiterate, incapacitated from osteoarthritis; mother, 44, illiterate; four children — girl, 16; girl, 11; girl, 8; boy, 5," who lived on a monthly income of $40.00.[105]

Regarding public health services, hospital directors repeatedly stressed the need for more financial support. The government's response, as in the 1927 Speech from the Throne, was to re-assert the necessity of "lessening the ever-increasing cost of public health activities."[106] That the poorer living conditions of the non-British immigrants were reflected in higher incidence of disease and early death received comment in both official and professional reports:

As persons of Ukrainian origin are usually regarded as robust, the rather high percentage of deaths of Ukrainian fathers at comparatively early ages may cause some concern as to whether hygienic and social conditions of their family life can be improved.[107]

Scandinavians [in Manitoba] appear to be susceptible to tuberculosis.

This is attributed partly to lower resistance and partly to poor housing conditions.

Manitoba's French-Canadians have a high death rate from diphtheria (22.2 deaths per 100,000 as against 9.8 per 100,000 for the whole province). Winter epidemics are common among them and the factors relating to these outbreaks are overcrowding in the homes and inadequate sanitation.

The typhoid morbidity rate among the [province's] Mennonites is 44.4 per 100,000 as against 16.0 per 100,000 for the province.[108]

In 1928, the Bracken government passed an Old Age Pensions Act, but it seemed that few of the poor survived long enough to qualify for it. It granted monthly pensions of $20 for persons over 70 years of age who had resided in Canada for at least twenty years. Both Liberals and Conservatives opposed the pension as too costly, since the province's share of the cost was to be raised by a supplementary property tax levy; but as one newspaper noted, the total cost involved was not great and the help it provided for the elderly was "better than nothing at all."[109]

The onset of the Depression in the fall of 1929 reinforced the government's determination to reduce public expenditure. When the stock market crashed, Premier Bracken was away on a European tour. He returned shortly and instituted a program of paring costs everywhere possible, to the extent of cutting the *per capita* daily bread allowance of mental patients from 11.99 to 11.68 oz.[110] In the province's northern territories, where the number of orphans whose other relatives could not assume responsiblity for them doubled between 1929 and 1930, the monthly allowance for each child was cut in half to ten dollars.[111] This policy held firm against requests for help from the increasing numbers of unemployed. On a winter afternoon during the 1931 session, for example, 4,000 assembled outside the legislative building

97John Marlyn, *Under the Ribs of Death* (Toronto: McClelland and Stewart, 1957), pp. 75-76. I am indebted to Professor Ed Rea of the University of Manitoba Department of History for drawing my attention to this novel.

98*Public Accounts of Manitoba,* 1921, pp. 27 and 114.

99*Ibid.,* 1928, p. 166.

100*Manitoba Free Press* (Winnipeg), March 23, 1923.

101J.C. Hopkins, ed., *Canadian Annual Review, 1924-1925* (Toronto: The Annual Review Publishing Company, 1925), pp. 402-404.

102*Public Accounts of Manitoba,* 1921, p. 31; and 1928, p. 12.

103*Report of the Special Commission of Inquiry into Welfare in Manitoba,* November 15, 1928 (Winnipeg: King's Printer, 1928), Part VI, pp. 7-10 [*Whitton Report*].

104*Journal of the Legislative Assembly of Manitoba,* 1929, p. 129; 1932, p. 168.

105*Whitton Report,* Part III, p. 51.

100*Journal of the Legislative Assembly of Manitoba,* 1927, p. 12.

107Manitoba, Department of Health and Public Welfare, *Annual Report, 1929* (Winnipeg: King's Printer, 1930), pp. 5-6.

108F.W. Jackson, "Racial Origin in Relation to Public Health Activities," *Canadian Public Health Journal,* 1931; cited by C.A. Dawson and E.R. Younge, *op. cit.,* pp. 272-273.

109*Winnipeg Tribune,* December 10, 1928.

110Manitoba, Department of Health and Public Welfare, *Annual Report, 1930* (Winnipeg: King's Printer, 1931), p. 69.

111*Ibid.,* pp. 11-12.

and their leaders conferred at length with the premier. Shortly after six, when it was already getting dark, he returned to the legislative chamber where the MLA's awaited him "amid a profound silence."[112] Other meetings sometimes became violent, as in the summer of 1935, when a number of unemployed seized and briefly occupied a soup kitchen.[113] With 25 per cent of its work force unemployed, Winnipeg by 1932 was reported as having the second highest urban *per capita* unemployment rate in Canada.[114] By 1937, the number of persons seeking relief in the province had reached 115,155, or a sixth of the population.[115] Since many were non-British, deportation was used to reduce relief costs. A reporter who lost his job in 1930 and had to apply for relief recorded the impact of this threat:

I came to appreciate for the first time the tremendous advantage it was to be a Canadian Anglo-Saxon in Winnipeg. And as time passed, the advantage widened when, as if racial intolerance was not enough, a new terror for the New Canadians began to stalk the land in the form of Immigration Officers with deportation orders in their hands.

The foreign born . . . sought more and more to melt into the background, say nothing, hear nothing. . . .

Ours was a society with a well-defined pecking order of prejudice. On the top were the race-proud Anglo-Saxons.[116]

Those eligible for relief earned it in such make-work projects as removing dandelions from the boulevards of south Winnipeg. In the city's north end, the housing of the unemployed was officially described in a 1939 report, which gave examples:

One house on Barber St. — no bath, no furnace, and not even a single sink — yet no less than twelve men are living in the basement, seventeen men, women and children are huddled in rooms on the first floor and eleven more persons are crowded in beneath the eaves on the second story.[117]

That some were worse off was indicated by reports through the decade of corpses found in various places, such as that of an unemployed man who died of starvation in the spring of 1939 in a freight car in the CPR yards.[118] Outside Winnipeg, the relatively poorer areas settled by non-British immigrants in the northwest, in the Interlake district, and to the southeast were dotted with abandoned homestead shacks and had the highest incidence of municipal disorganization, tax delinquency, and subsistence living standards.[119] Without much success, the Bracken government sought after 1932 to reduce urban unemployment by launching a back-to-the-land resettlement program sending relief families into these areas with monthly allowances from eight to fifteen dollars, depending on family size, payable for a maximum of 12 months, after which the families were to be self-supporting.[120] To cover the cost of these relief programs, the government imposed a flat 2 per cent wage tax, which a federal royal commission later termed "the heaviest income tax on low income groups in North America."[121] In contrast, the tax rate on the Winnipeg business community, according to an independent survey by Assessment Appraisers Ltd. of Toronto, was substantially lower than in other major Canadian cities.[122]

The poorer class provided little opposition to the Bracken government's policies. The French minority, preoccupied with preserving its religion and language, generally supported the government, and constituency contests were due more to the personal rivalry of candidates than to party differences. A form of quasi-seigneurial paternalism developed under the leadership of a small clique closely aligned with the French Catholic clergy and successively represented in the cabinet by Albert Préfontaine, Sauveur Marcoux, and Edmond Préfontaine. Only after 1936 did some French express an economic protest by voting Social Credit, largely because of the example of *Béret Blanc créditisme* in Quebec.[123] Associated with the French in the Roman Catholic church was the Polish community, so politically inactive that a recent history of it concludes simply that "Polish participation in the public life of Manitoba has been so far insignificant."[124] In 1932, a convention of citizens of Polish origin briefly considered running an independent "national" candidate to secure group recognition but, like the French, decided it would be better to be loyal to the government in office.[125] The more numerous Ukrainian community was divided into Greek Orthodox and Greek Catholic factions, which sometimes, as in 1927, promoted rival candidates.[126] A few Ukrainians were more radical: in 1932, when D.M. Elchesen, backed by a group of Conservative British businessmen, tried to address a north end meeting, he was shouted down with cries of "Traitor! You've gone over to the bosses!"[127] Generally, however, the Ukrainians tried to avoid offending the government: *Canadian Ukrainians do not have any influence. We are poor and need political help. Ukrainian farmers and workers depend for their livelihood on the more powerful. This forces us to support a politically influential party. Affiliation with small radical parties brings us Ukrainians only discredit and ruin.*[128]

[112]*Winnipeg Free Press,* February 26, 1931.

[113]James Gray, *The Winter Years* (Toronto: The Macmillan Company of Canada, 1966), pp. 157-159.

[114]*Winnipeg Free Press,* November 12, 1932.

[115]Manitoba Economic Survey Board, *Unemployment in Manitoba* (Winnipeg: King's Printer, 1938), pp. 31-32.

[116]J. Gray, *op. cit.,* pp. 131-132.

[117]Manitoba Economic Survey Board, *Interim Report and Findings* (Winnipeg: King's Printer, 1939), II, 325.

[118]*Winnipeg Free Press,* May 6, 1939.

[119]Manitoba Economic Survey Board, *Agricultural Income and Rural Municipal Government in Manitoba* (Winnipeg: King's Printer, 1939), pp. 80-90.

[120]*Winnipeg Free Press,* August 1, 1932.

[121]*Report of the Royal Commission on Dominion-Provincial Relations* (Ottawa: King's Printer, 1940), II, 98-99.

[122]*Canadian Annual Review, 1935–1936* (Toronto: The Annual Review Publishing Company, 1936), pp. 377-378.

[123]R. Turenne, *op. cit.,* pp. 117-129.

[124]V. Turek, *The Poles in Manitoba* (Toronto: Polish Alliance Press, 1967), p. 148.

[125]*Winnipeg Free Press,* May 25, 1932.

[126]*Canadian Farmer* (Winnipeg), June 25, 1927; *Ukrainian Voice* (Winnipeg), July 6, 1927.

[127]*Winnipeg Tribune,* June 10, 1932.

[128]*Canadian Farmer* (Winnipeg), June 8, 1932.

All signs show that the Bracken government will remain in power. This means that we have to elect candidates put forward by the governing party. . . . Candidates from parties making strange and impossible promises will bring us no advantage, only national dishonour.[129]

Like the French, the Ukrainians were primarily concerned with having one or two respectable national representatives on the government side. Serving in this capacity through the 1930's and after were a prosperous lumber and implement dealer, Nicholas Hryhorczuk, and a former police interpreter, Nicholas Bachynski. Again like the French, and like some Icelanders in the Interlake district, a few Ukrainians tried to protest by voting Social Credit in 1936, but with little effect.

Most vulnerable of these non-British groups was the German-speaking community. Circumspect since the First World War, it approached politics cautiously, and when it ventured to criticize the government, it was usually to request it to be true to its principles and to practice careful economy.[130] The group was divided into Catholics, Lutherans and Mennonites with the latter further split on their degree of orthodoxy. To escape Soviet collectivization, a new wave of relatively less conservative Mennonites came to the province during the late 1920's. They entered politics more readily than had their predecessors and Dr. C.W. Wiebe won election in 1932 as a Bracken supporter from the riding of Morden-Rhineland. By that time, Hitler's rise caused new divisions in the German community. A poem in a local German newspaper applauded his success:

Reach forth your hand to Adolf Hitler! Adolf! Let us grasp your hand![131]

Winnipeg was reported to be the "headquarters of the Canadian Union of Fascists," the German consul was claimed to be organizing Nazi cells, and brown-shirted Mennonites marched in the streets.[132] "Mysterious tappings" in the legislative building aroused fear of Nazi sabotage, but armed guards who searched "every nook and cranny" discovered that the sounds were being caused by maintenance carpenters.[133] Repeating the pattern of the First World War, such allegations of sedition obliged Manitobans of German origin to reaffirm their loyalty, as in an official statement issued by the local German-Canadian League:

Nazis constitute but a small minority. . . . German settlers here in the vast majority are loyal to Canada and to democracy.[134]

The rise of Naziism in the 1930's was comparable in its effect on Manitobans of German origin to that of the Bolshevik revolution on Manitobans of East European origin: both groups were obliged to be unobtrusive in provincial politics.

In 1932, under pressure from their federal leaders, the Liberals entered a coalition with the Bracken Progressives. After the election of that year sustained the government, two prominent Liberals, Ewan McPherson, a barrister, and J.S. McDiarmid, a south Winnipeg lumber merchant, joined the cabinet. The Conservatives remained outside the coalition but provided little opposition. The party was led from 1932 to 1936 by W. Sanford Evans, a wealthy Winnipeg publisher and grain merchant, who was succeeded in the latter year by Errick French Willis, a prosperous farmer in the southwest and son of the former Conservative leader R.G. Willis. Both Evans and Willis criticized the government primarily for not cutting expenditures and taxes further. On the latter's election as leader in 1936, for example, he declared that "technical advice had been obtained from an expert chartered accountant to show that a million dollars could be saved" by pruning government expenses.[135] The Conservatives publicly received testimonials of support from Winnipeg's business community, as in 1932 when 100 prominent businessmen published a statement pledging their support for the party,[136] and this enabled the Liberal-Progressives to distribute pamphlets to the ethnic groups declaring that the Conservative party "is not good for the poor people — it only helps those who are already rich."[137] But there was little real difference between prosperous farmers such as Willis and Bracken or between prosperous businessmen such as McDiarmid and Evans, and the two parties frequently voted together in the legislature. In 1936, it appeared that opposition would come from Social Credit, which unexpectedly won five seats in poor non-British districts in the north. When the movement's leader, Dr. Stanley Fox, joined the Bracken coalition after the election, some of his former supporters held meetings which expressed their sense of having been betrayed:

"Between 80 and 90 per cent of those who voted Social Credit voted, not for Social Credit, but as a protest against the Bracken government", Robert Gissing, Gimli delegate, complained. Cries of "Hear! Hear!" greeted his remark.[138]

After Dr. Fox became involved in court proceedings on a personal matter,[139] he was succeeded by non-British representatives such as Miss Salome Halldorson, J.M. Montagnon and William Lisowski. But as a protest movement, Social Credit failed to regain its original momentum.

Hence the only consistent opposition to the Bracken government came from the Independent Labour Party and its successor after 1933, the Manitoba Cooperative Commonwealth Federation.[140] Showing little change from election to election, the party platform regularly urged, as in 1932, increased relief, public health and unemployment insurance, public ownership of

129*Ukrainian Voice* (Winnipeg), July 22, 1936.

130*Der Nordwesten* (Winnipeg), June 15, 1927.

131*Ibid.*, March 1, 1933. I am indebted for the translation to Mr. A. Penner, a graduate student in political science at the University of Manitoba.

132*Winnipeg Free Press*, October 22, 1936; F. Epp, *Mennonite Exodus* (Altona, Manitoba: D.W. Friesen and Sons, 1962), p. 324.

133*Winnipeg Free Press*, April 12 and 13, 1939.

134*Ibid.*, April 21, 1939.

135*Ibid.*, July 25, 1936.

136*Winnipeg Tribune*, May 18, 1932.

137*Ibid.*, July 5, 1932.

138*Ibid.*, October 20, 1936.

139*Winnipeg Free Press*, May 25 and July 7, 1937.

140The Manitoba branch of the CCF was formed in 1933, but because of organizational difficulties in changing the official designation, candidates in the 1936 provincial election continued to be identified as running for the ILP.

natural resources and major industries, and increased taxes on higher incomes.[141] The party's predominantly British character gave it political legitimacy while reflecting the cultural conservatism that generally characterized labour politics in this period.[142] Most of its leaders — John Queen, Seymour Farmer, who succeeded Queen in 1935, James Woodsworth, and Stanley Knowles — were of British origin. Exceptions included Jews such as J.A. Cherniack, elected ILP treasurer in 1928, and Marcus Hyman, an Oxford-trained barrister, elected in Winnipeg in 1932 and 1936, and a Ukrainian, Joseph Wawrykow, elected for the ILP in Gimli in 1936 partly because he was the only Ukrainian candidate in the contest. Otherwise almost all ILP-CCF candidates in 1936, as well as those signing their nomination papers, were English. So also was an avowed independent socialist, Lewis St. George Stubbs, who topped the poll in Winnipeg's proportional representation list in 1936 and retained his seat until he retired in 1949. Most Communist candidates were also British: Leslie Morris, who ran unsuccessfully in 1932, was born in Somerset, England, in 1904, and came to Manitoba in 1920; James Litterick, who won a seat in 1936 and thus became the first Communist MLA in Manitoba, was born in Glasgow and came to Canada in 1925.[143] Remaining steady through the 1920's and the 1930's at about 5,000, the Communist vote was strongest in the city's north end. But it did not significantly increase in the non-British neighborhoods despite the party's emphasis after 1934 on cultural activities in ethnic associations.[144] Instead, among Ukrainians Stalin's purges and policies in the Ukraine caused splits and defections.

To the Comintern in Moscow in 1929, the Canadian Communist party's dependence on non-British support seemed a source of weakness.[145] But this could work two ways. The allegiance that the party received in Winnipeg from a few Ukrainians and Jews came mainly from immigrants who arrived in the 1920's and remained both apart from and an embarrassment to the older non-British group. By lending credibility to the 1919 charge that all foreigners were untrustworthy, their example widened the division between the British ILP-CCF and most of the non-British poor. As a survivor of the period later observed:

If you were British, you could be critical of society. But if you weren't, they blamed it on your background. You were a Communist. The Communists proved it. So it was best to keep quiet.[146]

Had there not been a Communist party, drawing publicized "foreign" support, more political cooperation might have developed between the British and the non-British lower class groups. In prejudicing such cooperation, the Communist party in effect assisted the supremacy of the Bracken government. Winnipeg's system of proportional representation in turn enabled a Communist candidate to get elected with a small scattered vote. This made the party a conspicuous if ineffective contender, and kept alive the 1919 spectre of alien revolution. The preoccupation of Communist spokesmen with international events similarly served the province's ruling group by seeming to confirm its claim that discontent with local economic conditions was inspired by sympathy for or allegiance to Russia and was therefore unpatriotic if not traitorous. A 1929 address by a Professor Scott Nearing was entitled "The Crumbling British Empire" and claimed that British imperialism would be replaced by American imperialism: "The United States will dominate, rule, exploit and rob the earth."[147] During the 1936 election, Tim Buck, the party's general secretary, spoke on the Spanish civil war, claiming that "in Manitoba, Ontario, Spain and France — the conflict is everywhere the same."[148] Similarly, Litterick's major addresses after his election were on such topics as Hitler's threat to Russia, the justification for the Moscow trials, the need for an embargo on exports to Fascist countries, and the dangers of Chamberlain's appeasement policy.[149] This compromised the party after the Nazi-Soviet Pact in 1939. Local Communists were interned under the Defence of Canada Act in 1940 and Litterick was disqualified from holding a seat in the legislature. His final speech was a defence of Soviet foreign policy and an attack on the Canadian war effort.[150] Few non-British voters could afford to share such views; more representative of their attitude was the advice given by Wasyl Swystun to a Ukrainian convention in Winnipeg in 1941, telling them to vote for the Liberal party in office because "we must all be good Canadians."[151]

Premier Bracken responded to the outbreak of war by calling for an all-party coalition, partly on the premise that in wartime political opposition was inappropriate. A similar case was made for the need to present a united front in negotiations with Ottawa, although there is little evidence that the government ever used or mentioned in later federal-provincial conferences the fact that it represented several political parties.[152] By absorbing the Liberals in 1932 and Social Credit in 1936, the coalition device had helped keep the Bracken government in office. It was also the fulfillment of Bracken's philosophy that government was merely a matter of administration, transcending class division and obviating class politics. As applied, however, the doctrine demonstrated itself to be a peculiarly unproductive form of conservatism. One of its first apparent effects was a sharp decline in voting. The turnout of registered voters dropped from 73 per cent in 1932 and 66 per cent in 1936 to 50 per cent in the 1941 election, 56 per cent in 1945 and 54 per cent in 1949.[153] There was a corresponding increase in acclamations:

141*Winnipeg Tribune,* May 17, 1932.

142M. Robin, *Radical Politics and Canadian Labour, 1880-1930* (Queen's University, Kingston, Ontario: Industrial Relations Centre, 1968), pp. 276-277.

143*Winnipeg Free Press,* July 30, 1936.

144D. Rowland, "Canadian Communism: The Post-Stalinist Phase" (M.A. Thesis, University of Manitoba, 1964), pp. 86-90.

145W. Rodney, *Soldiers of the International, A History of the Canadian Communist Party, 1921–1929* (Toronto: University of Toronto Press, 1968), pp. 152-153.

146Personal interview.

147*Manitoba Free Press* (Winnipeg), January 21, 1929.

148*Winnipeg Tribune,* July 24, 1936.

149*Ibid.,* April 6, 1938; *Winnipeg Free Press,* August 6, 1938 and March 21, 1939.

150*Ibid.,* December 18, 1940.

151*Ibid.,* March 31, 1941.

152M.S. Donnelly, *The Government of Manitoba* (Toronto: University of Toronto Press, 1963), p. 66.

153Compiled from the unpublished election reports on file in the office of Manitoba's Chief Electoral Officer, Legislative Building, Winnipeg.

6 in 1941, 7 in 1945, and 16 in 1949. In some ridings, such as those represented by Errick Willis, the Conservative leader in the coalition, and by Douglas Campbell, a cabinet minister and later premier, there were no elections for seventeen years; and in another, represented by William Morton, a coalition cabinet minister, there was no election for twenty-two years. After Bracken left Manitoba in 1943 to become national leader of the Progressive-Conservative party, he was succeeded by Stuart Garson, an Ontario-born farmer much like Bracken. When Garson joined the federal Liberal cabinet in 1948, he in turn was succeeded by Douglas Campbell, a prosperous farmer similar in background and temperament to Bracken and Garson. Statements by Campbell and Willis during the 1949 election expressed the philosophy with which the coalition justified itself:

The provincial government deals with the same matters as municipal councils. The present coalition has eliminated politics from the business of government and has made up for what it lacks in colour by gaining in efficiency. We aim to avoid wearying the electorate with partisan political speeches. All the brains do not rest in the heads of one party and therefore it seems logical that by using the process of coalition government, we should select the best men in both the Progressive-Conservative and Liberal parties. Where in the name of common sense is the need for party politics? Isn't it just a case of meeting together?[154]

Despite the coalition's claimed efficiency, however, its only major accomplishment was a rural electrification program. Its strength lay not in its legislative record but in the alliance of southwestern British farmers and south Winnipeg British businessmen that supported and financed it. This foundation was reinforced by appeals to ethnic groups, as in the address of a cabinet minister to the Polish Combatants' Association pledging the coalition's support for a "free Poland, undivided and independent."[155] Backed by a united dominant class and able to exploit cultural divisions in the lower class, the coalition seemed to have discovered the key to political immortality.

As a passive member of the coalition during the 1941 election, the CCF lost four of its seven seats in the legislature. But after withdrawing the next year, it received a surge of popular support comparable to CCF gains at the same time in Ontario and Saskatchewan. Its candidates, Berry Richards, a mining engineer, and Dr. Dwight Johnson, won two 1943 provincial by-elections in The Pas and Brandon respectively; party membership rose sharply from about 500 in 1942 to over 5,000 in 1944; and the annual budget approached $15,000, permitting the employment of two secretaries and two full-time organizers.[156] In the 1945 election, the party won 34 per cent of the popular vote; but with the system of representation that discriminated against both Winnipeg and the poorer northern ridings, this translated into only ten seats. From this high point, the party declined. As the Cold War began, a split occurred on the party's attitude toward the Soviet Union and on the advisability of collaboration with the local Communist Labour Progressive Party. Favouring cooperation, Richards and Johnson issued a joint statement:

Peace and progress will only be brought about by cooperation with, and understanding of, the Soviet Union, which involves the abandonment of anti-communism and the unity of all progressive forces.[157]

Both were ultimately obliged to withdraw from the party, and by 1949 both their seats were lost to the coalition. The controversy enabled the *Free Press* to claim that the CCF "has become a political bedlam in which the official views are opposed by a very large minority of Communists — the party is infiltrated today to the point where no one knows where it stands."[158] Such charges made the CCF more conservative. The Communist issue also cost the party what little support it had gained among non-British groups sensitive to charges of being disloyal. A Ukrainian newspaper commended the rejection of left-wing parties:

This time, just as in previous elections, many of our people either did not vote or, through ignorance, spoiled their ballots. This is inexcusable, for every vote is a vote for freedom and against communism. It is worth noting however that in our Ukrainian districts in the recent election there has appeared a marked deviation from socialist candidates. This is to be considered a healthy development.[159]

This attitude was reinforced by a numerically small but influential group of immigrants, mainly from the intellectual, business, and professional class, who were displaced by the Soviet occupation of Eastern Europe and brought bitter memories to Canada.[160] This ethnic hostility to Communism hurt the CCF despite its attempts to be respectable. With organizers such as Alistair Stewart and Donovan Swailes, and under the leadership successively of Edwin Hansford and Lloyd Stinson, it barely kept alive, retaining in the 1953 election only five seats with less than 17 per cent of the popular vote.

Another casualty of rising post-war anti-Communism was the Labour-Progressive Party member of the legislature, William Kardash. A veteran of the Mackenzie-Papineau battalion in the Spanish civil war, he won election in Winnipeg in 1941 with about 5,000 votes. After 1945, however, whenever critical international events occurred, his party was attacked. When headlines in 1949 reported a new defeat of Chiang Kai-shek and the charging of "top U.S. Communists" with conspiracy and espionage, demonstrators threw rocks at the LPP office and reduced a party meeting to a riot.[161] Even minor events sparked major reactions, as in 1953, when it was reported that twenty children were attending a Russian-Canadian Society evening class where they were exposed to Soviet textbooks. These allegedly contained poetry:

We sing songs about Stalin
We love our Stalin

154*Winnipeg Free Press*, September 30, October 11, 13 and 18, 1949.

155*Ibid.*, October 10, 1949.

156Provincial Secretary's Report to the 9th Annual Manitoba CCF Convention, October 24-26, 1944 (Mimeo.). This and subsequent CCF-NDP documents referred to below are in the files of the party at its provincial headquarters in Winnipeg. Permission to examine and use this material was given by the party's executive secretary, Mr. Donovan Swailes, and is gratefully acknowledged.

157*Winnipeg Free Press — Winnipeg Tribune,* December 10, 1945 (Joint edition put out during a typographers' strike).

158*Winnipeg Free Press,* September 13, 1949; Cp. W. Young, *The Anatomy of a Party: The National CCF, 1932–61* (Toronto: University of Toronto Press, 1969), pp. 201-205.

159*Canadian Farmer* (Winnipeg), November 23, 1949.

160P. Yuzyk, *op. cit.,* pp. 37-38.

161*Winnipeg Free Press,* October 14-17, 1949.

as well as the claim that a certain Ivan Polzunov invented the steam engine twenty years before James Watt.[162] Mrs. B. Dyma, president of the Ukrainian Catholic Women's League, called the teaching "vicious poisoning"; Slaw Rebchuk, a Liberal alderman, termed it "malicious propaganda"; and Metropolitan Ilarion Ohienko of the Ukrainian Greek Orthodox church condemned it as "Godless and evil."[163] Speaking for the government, the Conservative leader Errick Willis added:

We and the churches are the strongest fortresses against Communism.

Communism should be outlawed.[164]

When Kardash finally lost his seat in the 1958 election, he was probably right in attributing his defeat to ethnic and religious opposition. As the Communist vote declined and the Cold War appeared to abate somewhat, so did publicity on the threat of subversion or Communist infiltration. The CCF in turn could afford to be less defensive and began to attract more votes from the non-British lower class.

The first effective opposition to the coalition government, however, came from one of its traditional supporters, south Winnipeg's business community, increasingly concerned about the province's slow economic growth and the Campbell administration's evident preoccupation with rural matters. The attack on the coalition was initiated by a group of Conservatives led by Duff Roblin, grandson of Sir Rodmond P. Roblin. A Winnipeg automobile dealer associated with his family's business, he won a seat in south Winnipeg in 1949 as an Independent Conservative, and gathered support from other Winnipeg businessmen such as Gurney Evans, a son of the earlier Conservative leader Sanford Evans. This group helped extricate their party from the coalition in 1950, and four years later Roblin won the party leadership from Errick Willis. His victory in the provincial election that followed in 1958, shortly after John Diefenbaker's landslide federal victory, was almost a foregone conclusion. Ironically, one of the Campbell government's reforms helped defeat it: a 1957 redistribution of legislative seats, carried out by an independent boundaries commission, ended the system of proportional representation in Winnipeg and raised its number of seats in the legislature to twenty. Of these, the Liberals retained only St. Boniface, won by Roger Teillet with French Catholic support; while another was held by Winnipeg's Mayor Stephen Juba as an Independent. Otherwise the city polarized along class lines, with the poorer north end voting for the CCF and the wealthier south end voting Conservative.

That the whole province did not similarly polarize in 1958 was partly due to the Liberals' retention of their traditional ethnic appeal in some rural areas, such as the Mennonite district of Rhineland, won by Wallace Miller, the French and German districts of Carillon and La Vérendrye, won by Edmond Préfontaine and Stan Roberts, and the Slavic districts of Springfield, won by William Lucko, Emerson, won by John Tanchak, and Ethelbert Plains, won by Michael Hryhorczuk, son of Nicholas Hryhorczuk, the leading Ukrainian representative in the legislature during the 1920's and 1930's. All these districts, with the exception of Rhineland, where Mennonite farmers had prospered, were relatively poor and had been so since their original settlement. In these areas past ethnic traditions still served the Liberal party.

The first indication that they were declining came with two CCF victories in similarly poor rural non-British districts. Brokenhead was won by Edward Schreyer, and in the riding of Fisher Peter Wagner defeated Nicholas Bachynsky, who, like Nicholas Hryhorczuk, had been one of the leading Ukrainian Liberal-Progressive representatives and had been appointed Speaker of the legislature in 1950. Twenty years before the 1958 election, the prospect of having one of its members given such a position had been a potent symbol of ethnic recognition to a Ukrainian newspaper editor:

In English parliamentary bodies, the Speaker is called the President of the House, an extremely serious position, almost like a Minister. As their representative, our voters for the Ukrainian nation may be given an opportunity to have the first Ukrainian President of a legislature in the world.[165]

But it appeared by the late 1950's that the need for ethnic recognition was being replaced by class consciousness. The slow process toward political assimilation extended by degrees into remoter areas and made possible a polarization not only in Winnipeg but across the province.

The Roblin period was a transitional one, with the government containing both conservative and reform elements. Its progressive enterprise was substantially the achievement of the premier himself, assisted by representatives from poorer northern districts such as Dr. George Johnson of Gimli. Provincial expenditures on health, welfare, and education over the decade from 1956 to 1966 increased from $27.5 million to $136.7 million.[166] After overriding rural opposition, schools were consolidated and dramatically improved. The government established a Metropolitan Corporation to coordinate the municipal services in Greater Winnipeg, a Manitoba Development Fund and various advisory agencies to promote economic development, and a Housing and Urban Renewal Corporation. A major highway construction program was instituted and a massive water diversion channel constructed to prevent further Red River floods in Winnipeg. In the north, a new power development was launched and a new mining community established at Thompson. But the province's basic class structure appeared to be affected little by these reforms.

After showing almost no increase during the 1920's and 1930's, provincial income increased sharply in the post-war period. Average weekly wages rose from $41.06 in 1949 to $84.44 in 1967;[167] and *per capita* income in the province rose from $980.00 in 1948 to $2,317.00 in 1967.[168] These gains were partly cancelled by an approximate increase of 50 per cent in the cost

162*Winnipeg Tribune,* February 28, 1953.
163*Ibid.,* March 4, 1953.
164*Winnipeg Free Press,* March 27, 1953.
165*Ukrainian Voice* (Winnipeg), August 5, 1936.
166Manitoba Economic Consultative Board, *Fourth Annual Report* (Winnipeg: Queen's Printer, 1967), Appendix B, Table 12, p. 148.
167*Canada Year Book, 1952–1953,* p. 632; and *ibid., 1969,* p. 776.
168Canada, Dominion Bureau of Statistics, *National Accounts, Income and Expenditure, 1926–1956* (Ottawa: Queen's Printer, 1958), p. 65; and *ibid., 1967* (Ottawa: Queen's Printer, 1968), p. 36.

of living over the same period.[169] Average income figures, moreover, gave no indication of distribution, since a few large individual incomes could raise the average without any appreciable improvement of individual incomes at the bottom of the scale. Reported income tax statistics, by excluding the non-taxable returns of the poor and the non-monetary expense account and other benefits available to the upper income group, also tended to obscure or underestimate the gap between rich and poor.[170] But even within that limitation, they suggested that the range of income disparities from 1948 to 1968 remained virtually unchanged. In both years, the top 5 per cent of tax-payers reported receiving about 20 per cent of all income, the next 20 per cent received about 30 per cent of the income, while the bottom 75 per cent of taxpayers received the remaining 50 per cent of the income.[171] Taking into account the probably greater opportunities for tax avoidance and un-taxed capital appreciation available to the upper income group, it appeared that there was little or no economic class equalization in Manitoba during the post-war period.

The gleaming new Centennial Concert Hall, the new University build-ings, and the new luxury motor hotels built in Winnipeg during the Roblin period were remote from the lives of those on lower incomes. Following a tenement fire in which a three year old boy burned to death, a Metro state-ment reported that 5,000 residential buildings in the city deserved to be condemned and torn down.[172] Municipal Affairs Minister Thelma Forbes reported in 1967 that public housing was the "obvious answer" for the esti-mated 40,000 families in Greater Winnipeg who were unable to buy or rent privately built homes.[173] A slum-school principal tried throughout the period, without success, to persuade the government to locate a community centre for children in his neighborhood, and ended by taking a group of his pupils to the new Pan-American swimming pool in the city's south end to see "where the rich people live."[174] At the end of the Roblin years, there was still no hospital in the city's north end, although a public housing de-velopment was built alongside the railway tracks in the district. Illustrating the difficulties of those on welfare was the case of a deserted wife with three children who had her rent paid and received a monthly allowance of $95. When evicted by her landlord for complaining about unsanitary conditions, she appealed to city authorities:

"Why do I have to suffer this hell?" she shouted; "Why can't you help me?" she asked city aldermen, who sat with their eyes fixed on the table in front of them.[175]

Conditions had evidently changed little from 1946, when another deserted wife with three children was assigned by welfare officials to a cubicle in the city's old immigration building:

As we entered the front door our ears were assaulted by a splitting cacaphony of screams, cries, radios, wails and curses. Hordes of children ran yelling down the halls which were strewn with filth from overturned garbage cans. . . . Malodorous smells told of sour bodies, spilled wine, urine. . . .

In desperation, she too appealed to the city aldermen:

"I'm not going to be stuck in some lousy hole . . . with drunks and bums and filth! My children are not going to be stuck in some godforsaken hole where they don't have a chance."[176]

At the beginning of the 1960's, it was estimated that over 17,000 city families still lived in extreme poverty. Average annual family incomes ranged from about $3,000 to $5,000 in the central and north end city districts and from about $10,000 to $20,000 in the south end districts of River Heights and Tuxedo.[177] Outside the city, a similar class division obtained, as it had since 1901.[178] The average capital value of Manitoba farms in 1966 was about $45,000, with the districts to the southwest all well above this average and those to the northwest, northeast, and southeast of Winnipeg, where non-British immigrants had settled, all markedly lower.[179] A similar pattern applied in farm size, productivity, and income from sales. In one of the poorest northern areas, the Interlake district, a third of the farms had annual incomes of under $1,200, with correspondingly poor housing, education, and other public facilities.[180]

As families within such districts moved about in search of a better living the old cultural divisions disappeared.[181] The second and third generations of the non-British immigrants became less susceptible to ethnic appeals.[182] Among this younger group, in contrast to the "hesitant conservatism" of their elders, there was a greater drive toward improvement of their material circumstances as well as a skepticism that this could be achieved within the existing system.[183] The ethnic press, whose total circulation declined after

[169]*Canada Year Book, 1968*, p. 940.
[170]J. Porter, *The Vertical Mosaic* (Toronto: University of Toronto Press, 1965), pp. 104-112.
[171]Canada, Department of National Revenue, *Taxation Statistics, 1950* (Ottawa: King's Printer, 1950), p. 143; *ibid., 1970* (Ottawa: Queen's Printer, 1970), p. 113; Cp. H. Chorney, "The Political Economy of Economic Growth in Manitoba" (M.A. Thesis, University of Manitoba, 1970), pp. 131-133.
[172]*Winnipeg Free Press*, February 17, 1968.
[173]*Ibid.*, March 7, 1967.
[174]Personal interview.
[175]*Winnipeg Free Press*, November 22, 1968.
[176]From *Laugh Baby Laugh* by Ann Henry, reprinted by permission of the Canadian publishers, McClelland and Stewart Limited, Toronto.
[177]Metropolitan Winnipeg Social Service Audit, *Interim Report* (Winnipeg: Social Service Audit Committee, 1967), Vol. I, Table 10, p. 34; Cp. T.G. Nicholson and M.H. Yeates, "The Ecological and Spatial Structure of the Socio-Economic Characteristics of Winnipeg, 1961," *The Canadian Review of Sociology and Anthropology*, August, 1969, pp. 162-177.
[178]Canada, Dominion Bureau of Statistics, *Fourth Census*, 1901, Vol. II, Tables 4, 8, and 36; *Sixth Census*, 1921, Vol. V, Tables 79, 80, and 85; *1961 Census of Canada*, Bulletin 5.3-1, Tables 14-16 and 18.
[179]Canada, Dominion Bureau of Statistics, *1966 Census of Canada*, Vol. 5, *Agriculture Manitoba*, Table 22.
[180]D. Woodsworth, *et al., Rural Need in Canada, 1965; The Background of Rural Poverty in Four Selected Areas* (Ottawa: Canadian Welfare Council, 1966), pp. 12-19.
[181]*Ibid.*, p. 2.
[182]Cp. V. Kaye, "Political Integration of Ethnic Groups: The Ukrainians," *Revue de l'Université d'Ottawa*, 1957, pp. 460-470.
[183]M. Stancliff, et al., *A Comparative Study of Value Orientations among Three Ethnic Groups living in the Province of Manitoba*, A study conducted under the auspices of the Province of Manitoba Interdepartmental Committee for ARDA (Winnipeg: University of Manitoba, 1965), pp. 88-89 and 160-162.

1950, obliging rival newspapers to merge,[184] resisted this change yet admitted it, as for example in the 1959 election:

In Ethelbert Plains, the threat to the former Liberal minister, M.N. Hryhorczuk, was not from the Conservatives but from younger Ukrainians who supported the CCF.[185]

As the young were assimilated, moreover, many changed their names, so ethnic editors became less certain about the origin of candidates:

In the last legislature, there were members whose national origin was uncertain. Rumours claimed they were Ukrainian but it was impossible to determine this from their surnames.[186]

Had the province continued to attract as high a proportion of new immigrants after 1950 as it had in the period before and after the first war, these developments would have been offset by a continuing infusion of ethnic consciousness. But apart from a few hundred Philippine and Italian girls imported to work in the garment industry,[187] the province attracted relatively few immigrants: whereas before 1946, Winnipeg contained almost 9 per cent of all new immigrants in Canada, in the decade of the 1950's this proportion dropped to less than $4\frac{1}{2}$ per cent.[188] Intermarriage also blurred ethnic lines, most notably with the Icelandic group[189] but increasingly through the 1950's and 1960's among the others as well, although orthodox Mennonites and Jews retained high rates of endogamy.[190] Another factor assisting assimilation was the impact of television, extending even to long-isolated rural areas.[191] Rearguard action resisting these forces tended to be ineffective: under pressure from ethnic spokesmen, Ukrainian was introduced in 1963 into the Winnipeg school curriculum, but four years later, although there were in the school system approximately 6,000 children of Ukrainian descent, only 73 had been induced to study the language.[192]

In resisting the trend to assimilation and the political advantages accruing from it to a lower-class based party, there developed a more marked alliance between ethnic association leaders and the more conservative political parties. The political implications of even relatively minor ethnic questions were taken into account, as for example in his selection of entertainment for a Conservative convention, a program convenor reported that:

It might be advisable to have the Ukrainian choir and dancers, even if they cost more, for purely political reasons.[193]

Both the Liberals and Conservatives solicited the ethnic vote with speakers, patronage, and status symbols. After the federal Conservative victory in 1958, for example, Gunnar Thorvaldson, a wealthy lawyer of Icelandic origin, who had sat in the legislature from 1941 to 1949 as a Conservative, was appointed to the Senate, where he opposed government assistance to the Interlake area, saying he was shocked at its being considered "underprivileged."[194] A similar appointment, hailed by the Ukrainian press, was that of Professor Paul Yuzyk to the Senate in 1963 after he had long served the party by addressing Ukrainian Catholic meetings on its behalf. Other such Conservative speakers and former candidates included Maurice Arpin, a lawyer of French background, and Daniel Zaharia, a realtor, both of whom were appointed to the University of Manitoba board of governors, and Michael Baryluk, a lawyer and former candidate, supported strongly but unsuccessfully by the Ukrainian press, who was appointed a magistrate in 1968. Another Conservative candidate, Peter Okrainec, emphasized in his 1962 campaign that he had been head marshal of the dedication procession at the 1961 ceremonial unveiling on the legislative grounds of a statue of the Ukrainian poet, Taras Shevchenko.[195] The appeal of such devices was mainly to the middle-aged or elderly, who adhered to tradition despite what in many instances were bleak personal circumstances. An extreme example of this was a 68-year old Polish labourer and consistent Conservative voter who responded to a university questionnaire on his impression of political campaigns with a vivid statement of his difficulties:

Which campaign is the most effective for me I do not know. I have not radio no television no telephone. I never read newspaper. I live like rat in hole.[196]

Prominent Conservatives, such as the cabinet ministers, Harry Enns, a Mennonite rancher, and Sidney Spivak, a hotel and apartment owner, were in contrast relatively well-to-do, as was the prominent Liberal MLA and later MP, Mark Smerchanski, a geologist and businessman, who expressed firm conservative views throughout the 1960's, urging the need for lower public expenditures and taxes at a Liberal leadership convention in 1961, for example, and vehemently attacking a capital gains tax in 1969.[197] Smerchanski was descended from Ukrainian immigrants who came to Manitoba in 1903 and established a general store.[198] A statement by his father exemplified a central theme of ethnic allegiance in Manitoba's political history:

I became a Liberal in 1911. We have seven children and they are all like me good Liberals.[199]

The pattern appeared to be that those among the non-British groups who prospered or were co-opted into the Liberal or Conservative parties then served those parties by helping them exploit the ethnic traditions and divisions among those still in the lower class. In this way, ethnic leaders helped

---

[184]For example, the Winnipeg Icelandic newspapers *Heimskringla* and *Logberg* merged in 1959, as did *Der Nordwesten* and *Der Courier* in 1970.

[185]*Canadian Farmer* (Winnipeg), May 25, 1959.

[186]*Ukrainian Voice* (Winnipeg), December 5, 1962.

[187]*Winnipeg Tribune*, September 29, 1967; *Winnipeg Free Press*, November 12, 1968.

[188]Y. Kasahara, "A Profile of Canada's Metropolitan Centres," in B. Blishen, *et al.*, *Canadian Society* (Toronto: The Macmillan Company of Canada, 1965), p. 58.

[189]W. Kristjanson, *op. cit.*, pp. 505-508.

[190]*Report of the Royal Commission on Bilingualism and Biculturalism* (Ottawa: Queen's Printer, 1969), IV, 92-94 and 287.

[191]*Ibid.*, p. 135.

[192]*Winnipeg Tribune*, April 27, 1967.

[193]Party correspondence on program preparations for the 1964 annual meeting. This and subsequent references from the party files were located and examined with the permission of the party executive director, Dr. A. Schwartz, whose help is gratefully acknowledged.

[194]*Winnipeg Free Press*, March 11, 1967.

[195]*Ukrainian Voice* (Winnipeg), December 12, 1962.

[196]Personal letter.

[197]*Winnipeg Free Press*, April 15, 1961; *ibid.*, November 17, 1969.

[198]*Winnipeg Tribune*, November 15, 1967.

[199]*Ibid.*, April 20, 1961.

maintain the political hegemony of the predominantly British upper class which they joined or hoped to join. The gratification of lower class ethnic sentiment thus served as a tactical alternative to social and economic equalization.

In 1967, Roblin resigned the premiership and, after an unsuccessful attempt to enter federal politics, accepted an appointment as executive vice-president of Canadian Pacific Investments Ltd.[200] He was succeeded by Walter Weir, a funeral director from Minnedosa, who was first elected in 1959 and entered the cabinet in 1961. With Weir's accession, the government became markedly more conservative. One of his supporters, Gordon Lawson, an executive of James Richardson Ltd. and director of several companies, expressed the new administration's viewpoint:

The power to tax is the power to destroy. The lack of coordinated and controlled spending will result in an impossible burden on the taxpayer. I can't help but be staggered at the future costs of some of these programs.[201]

With this concern, the Liberal party was in full agreement. Its leader from 1961 to 1969, Gildas Molgat, a Winnipeg businessman of French descent, emphasized the need to restrain expenses:

The new premier of Manitoba has vowed that he will hold the line on taxes. I ask him to make sure his promise is not broken.[202]

As in the 1920's and 1930's, there was little difference between the two parties. Like the Conservatives, the Liberals drew much of their support from the business community of south Winnipeg. Molgat's nomination to the party leadership was by R.D. Turner, a Winnipeg airlines president, and it was seconded by Mark Smerchanski, a director of several mining firms. The party continued to include among its members many of Winnipeg's most prominent citizens: J. Elmer Woods, former chairman of the Canadian committee of the Hudson's Bay Co. and former president of the Monarch Life Assurance Co.; Peter Curry, chairman of the Greater Winnipeg Gas Co. and director of numerous companies; A.S. Leach, president of Searle Grain Co. and a director of the Bank of Montreal, Great West Life Assurance Co., Canadian Breweries Ltd. and other companies; James Ashdown, a director of the family hardware corporation and Canadian Indemnity Co.; George Heffelfinger, president of National Grain Co. and a director of the Winnipeg Grain Exchange; Rod McIsaac, president of Rodell Corp., who served as federal campaign chairman in the province in 1968 and later became provincial campaign chairman; and Brigadier R.S. Malone, publisher of the *Winnipeg Free Press* and president of the national newspaper chain, FP Publications Ltd.[203] Illustrating this Liberal group's favorable view of Weir's fiscal conservatism, Malone's newspaper repeatedly declared that Roblin's mantle "could not have fallen on a better man" and that "it will be a refreshing change to have a premier who is intent on keeping taxes down."[204] As in the 1920's and 1930's, most members of this group were members of the Manitoba Club, still symbolic of exclusive affluence in Winnipeg. The similarity between the two parties was further shown by federal-provincial voting patterns: south Winnipeg, which voted Liberal federally in 1968, voted Conservative provincially throughout the 1960's. Of the two parties, the Liberals received support from more senior corporate executives, particularly in the grain trade, probably because the Liberal federal government had more influence on their affairs. But this difference amounted to little in practice. In supporting the provincial Conservative government's policy of curbing taxation, the relatively wealthy in Winnipeg with few exceptions were united in a community of economic self-interest.

Notwithstanding this support, the Weir government began within a year of its formation to experience serious difficulties. When Weir reversed Roblin's decision and announced that Manitoba would remain out of the federal medicare program, widespread protest developed, particularly among those on low or average incomes confronted with a 25 per cent increase in the fee schedule of the Manitoba Medical Association. A statement from the Manitoba Association of Social Workers claimed that 200,000 persons in the province could afford no medical insurance whatsoever,[205] and a Manitoba Federation of Labour delegation led a protest demonstration to the legislature. The premier argued against the plan's projected cost and its compulsory nature,[206] but was finally obliged to negotiate the province's entry into the plan. Another difficulty arose after a Toronto consultant, Murray V. Jones and Associates Ltd., reported that living conditions in northern Manitoba were "among the most wretched in Canada."[207] Charging the government with indifference to these conditions, Gordon Beard, the Conservative MLA for Churchill, resigned from the legislature.

His action focused attention on the plight of the province's Indians and Métis. Since surrendering their land claims in the 1870's, they had come near extinction and still barely survived, a minority of about 60,000 that was proportionally larger in Manitoba than in any other province.[208] Their revenues from trapping and fishing were in decline and they were virtually excluded from employment in the new mining centres such as Thompson. With high rates of infant mortality, tuberculosis and malnutrition, their life expectancy was about 34 years. Provincial child care services were available to only about half of those who left their reservations.[209] An estimated 10,000 moved to Winnipeg between 1961 and 1966 and comprised a tenth of all welfare cases.[210] One of these, a forty-year old father of seven, reportedly living in a tenement "unfit for human habitation" asked: "Please can't you give me work? I can work hard," while officials noted that his son's arms were

200*Ibid.*, September 10, 1968.

201*Winnipeg Free Press,* May 11, 1967.

202*Ibid.*, December 5, 1967.

203Compiled from press reports, party membership lists and *The Canadian Who's Who,* 1967-1969 (Toronto: Who's Who Canadian Publications, 1969); Cp. E. Reed, "The Beautiful People of Winnipeg," *The Manitoban* (Winnipeg), March 3, 1970.

204*Winnipeg Free Press,* November 27, 1967; *ibid.,* March 8, 1968.

205*Winnipeg Tribune,* February 13, 1968.

206Legislative Assembly of Manitoba, *Debates and Proceedings,* March 19, 1968, p. 294.

207*Winnipeg Free Press,* April 20, 1968.

208H.B. Hawthorn, *et al., A Survey of the Contemporary Indians of Canada* (Ottawa: Queen's Printer, 1966), I, 376.

209*Ibid.*, pp. 156-158 and 328-329.

210*Winnipeg Free Press,* May 16, 1967; *Winnipeg Tribune,* October 9, 1967.

"covered with festering bug bites."[211] In the provincial penitentiary, over a quarter of the inmates were of Indian ancestry.[212] A visitor to a reservation southeast of Winnipeg in 1966 described the homes there:

Roseau, like many reserves, is situated on a swamp. . . . A house inadequate for a family of five holds 15 people . . . no insulation, no floor, no furniture, often no windows. . . . The homes are fetid, suffocating, den-like, full of humanity.[213]

A similar appraisal of northern Métis communities concluded:

The overcrowding and complete lack of facilities do not deserve by 20th century standards to be called substandard. They are subhuman.[214]

After the Weir government refused housing assistance on the grounds that no money was available, protest developed from the Manitoba Indian Brotherhood, headed by Dave Courchene, and from the Manitoba Métis Federation, one of whose spokesmen, Tom Eagle, declared:

We're going to make people aware of the power of the Indian and Métis vote. We could be the majority force in Churchill, The Pas, Rupertsland, Ste. Rose du Lac and we could swing the balance in a number of other places as well.[215]

Having been excluded from the franchise from 1885 to 1952, the province's Indians, like the Métis, were unused to voting or any political action. Those who did vote during the 1950's and early 1960's either supported the government or, in the case of some Catholic reservations, voted Liberal. But by 1968, the group's mood was clearly less pliable and more militant.

Similar dissatisfaction with the Weir government was expressed by Manitoba's French minority. Numbering about 80,000, this group remained mainly Liberal through the 1960's, partly because of tradition and partly because of Molgat's appeal, although in some poorer rural areas a few continued to express discontent with their economic circumstances by voting Social Credit.[216] Against this pattern of allegiance, Roblin could make little impression, even though he introduced a program whereby Catholic private schools could use some public school facilities and also allowed up to 50 per cent French language instruction in public schools in predominantly French districts. After Weir's accession, the government was less sympathetic toward the French and the premier repeatedly declared that in his list of priorities the question of language and cultural rights was far below the need for budgetary retrenchment. At the close of 1968, a French delegation to the cabinet departed publicly expressing its disappointment. Two weeks later, in an address to a Rotary luncheon, Weir declared his opposition to "special status" for Quebec and his belief in the need for "gradualism" on the question of language.[217] A St. Boniface newspaper responded: "il est inconcevable que le premier ministre du Manitoba, province où l'on s'est moqué de la Constitution et des droits culturels, puisse ignorer à ce point l'historique et avancer de telles idioties!"[218] In early 1969, Maurice Gauthier, president of the Franco-Manitoban Society, similarly attacked Weir for "retrogressive thinking":

It is not difficult to understand why such words as gradualism are extremely repulsive to Franco-Manitobans. It took 50 years to obtain a few crumbs of linguistic equality in Manitoba and the people are not prepared to wait another 50 years.[219]

After Weir reasserted his position at a federal-provincial conference in Ottawa, however, he obtained national publicity and enthusiasm, notably from the *Free Press*:

He went to Ottawa a relatively unknown provincial prairie politician and returned to Winnipeg a national political figure. Three times he challenged Prime Minister Pierre Trudeau. Twice he verbally fought the smooth-talking French-Canadian and forced him to back down.[220]

It appeared from this confrontation that the premier was to gain new political advantage from one of the oldest ethnic and religious antagonisms in the province. The government's victory in three out of four by-elections that shortly followed confirmed this impression, and after a poll survey by Elliott Research Corp. of Toronto reported that the time was now opportune, the premier called an election.

That his decision was based in part on the advice of a professional polling firm was indicative of the party's increasing use of techniques derived from advertising and commercial market research. This dated from the successful Conservative campaign of 1958, assisted professionally by Dalton Camp, who subsequently was awarded and retained through the 1960's the provincial government's tourism promotion account. After Camp's revolt against John Diefenbaker's leadership of the federal Conservative party, he was less favourably viewed by the conservative rural wing of the Manitoba party, and Walter Weir's campaign for the provincial party leadership in 1967 was managed by another advertising firm, McConnell-Eastman Ltd. of Toronto.[221] Advice on a continuing basis also came from a local firm, Foster Advertising. The approach to political campaigns provided by these two firms was illustrated by an advisory guide given to Conservative candidates:

An election campaign is first and foremost a selling campaign. It is designed to "sell" the candidate to the voters in the same manner that corporations sell a particular brand of automobile, soap or cigarette. The political organization must create a demand in the minds of the voters for their candidates, in exactly the same manner as the corporations create a demand for their particular brand of merchandise.[222]

Consistent with this philosophy of elections, the party's campaign in 1969 was directed by a public relations firm, which concentrated on newspaper and television advertising. It involved only relatively minor participation by

211*Winnipeg Free Press*, January 23, 1969.

212*Ibid.*, October 2, 1968.

213H. Robertson, *Reservations Are For Indians* (Toronto: James Lewis and Samuel, 1970), pp. 190-193.

214*Winnipeg Tribune*, March 10, 1967.

215*Ibid.*, November 24, 1967.

216R. Turenne, *op. cit.*, pp. 152-164.

217*Winnipeg Tribune*, November 13 and 27, 1968.

218*La Liberté et le Patriote* (St. Boniface), December 4, 1968.

219*Winnipeg Free Press*, February 14, 1969.

220*Ibid.*, February 13, 1969.

221*Winnipeg Tribune*, November 24, 1967.

222Manitoba Progressive-Conservative Party, *Campaign Advice to Candidates, 1966* (Quoted with the permission of party president, N. Nurgitz).

Premier Weir, who in the final two weeks of the campaign visited a number of rural centres but was otherwise inconspicuous. The theme of the advertising campaign was the need for Weir's continuing determination to restrain public spending, and this message was substantially conveyed by broadcast testimonials from average citizens who endorsed his firmness in resisting claims on the public treasury.

In contrast with the professionalism of the Conservative party and its access to public relations skills, the NDP organization appeared improvised and amateurish. Much of its public impact during the Roblin period was provided by its leader, Russell Paulley. A railway worker, Paulley was able at times to secure press headlines with blunt criticism of the government, but by 1968 he was handicapped by ill-health and a record of election disappointments. His party executive through the 1960's had to juggle deficits, and despite repeated emergency drives party membership remained low, amounting at the end of 1966 to 3,000, well below provincial CCF membership in 1945 and about a tenth of the party's 1966 membership in Saskatchewan.[223] The campaign manuals which belatedly appeared in 1967 retained much of the old CCF flavour:

Ideally, voters can inform themselves about the candidates and the issues. In practice, political parties must help provide this information. Canvassing is by and large a most interesting and pleasurable task. Ours is not to argue, but to meet and persuade.

Visitors always want to chat. No matter how pleasant this may be, the candidate must remember that he should be out winning votes, and not passing the time of day with old friends.

A good letters-to-the-editor campaign can be most effective, particularly if the local press is prepared to give you a fair break.

Billboards can be effective, but their cost virtually rules them out.[224]

Within the crisis-ridden context of the party's organization, this modest approach availed little; and the most encouraging gain during the 1960's was the gradual increase in the proportion of candidates, delegates and party members from the non-British minorities. An indication of this development was the 1968 candidacy of Sid Green, a Jewish labour lawyer, for the party leadership. Green lost to Paulley by a narrow margin, but it was more significant that for the first time in its history, the province's left-wing party was seriously considering someone of non-British origin as a prospective leader. To the NDP, as to increasing numbers among the younger descendants of non-British immigrants, questions of ethnic and religious background appeared to be of diminishing relevance in party politics. As ethnic and religious traditions exercised less effect in dividing lower class groups from one another, moreover, it became possible for them to coalesce politically in support of a party expressing dissatisfaction with existing inequalities. Even among those of non-British origin who had secured moderate prosperity through relatively accessible occupations such as teaching, the memory of past inequalities and obstacles endured by their parents was in some cases sufficient incentive to support a party committed to reforming the political and economic system.

This pattern provided part of the basis for the 1969 NDP leadership convention. Hastily moved up to June 7 after Premier Weir called the election for June 25, it was a contest between Sid Green and Edward Schreyer, MP for Selkirk. After they held a series of debates throughout the province in conjunction with nominating meetings, thus publicizing local candidates, there was little evident policy disagreement between the two contestants: in urging more help for northern areas and in arguing that programs such as medicare should be financed out of general revenues, in turn raised by higher taxes on the relatively more prosperous, both Schreyer and Green said little that had not been said before by earlier party spokesmen. Both emphasized the need for an ombudsman, an independent auditor of provincial expenditures, more low-cost housing, additional credit and marketing assistance for fishermen and poorer farmers, a further consolidation of municipal services in Metropolitan Winnipeg, and a continuation of the policy of transferring responsibility for paying for public education, health and welfare from the municipal to the provincial level. Such proposals had also long characterized the party's election campaigns and were in fact little different from the positions taken by the progressive wing of the Conservative party during the Roblin period. On the basis of their platform, therefore, there was little choice. At the convention, Schreyer won the leadership largely because of his successful record in politics and his expected ability to present an energetic alternative to Premier Weir. His German Catholic and rural origin was also expected to help attract those rural non-British groups already of increasing importance to the party. In the campaign he was assisted by a dozen party organizers from across Canada and by unprecedented NDP expenditures, later estimated by the party president at about $35,000.[225] But the result of the election was largely due to Schreyer's strenuous personal efforts and to the continuing process of change in Manitoba society.[226]

Just as Winnipeg polarized in 1958 so the whole province did in 1969: the poorer ridings in the north and east, whether predominantly Ukrainian, German, Icelandic, French, or Indian and Métis, voted for reform, while the older, mainly British ridings in the southwest voted for the *status quo*. The NDP representation in the legislature rose from twelve to twenty-eight seats, and its share of the popular vote increased from 23 to 38 per cent. Of the twenty-seven seats in Metro Winnipeg, the party won seventeen, mainly in the poorer north and central districts. Where it penetrated southward as in Crescentwood, won by University of Manitoba Professor Cyril Gonick, the division in poll results similarly reflected the division in the riding between a relatively wealthy neighborhood and one containing more modest

223Minutes of the Manitoba NDP Provincial Council meeting, December 10, 1966 (Quoted with the permission of party secretary, F. Petruic).
224Compiled from various mimeographed campaign guide sheets including *Why Canvass?* (August, 1967) and CCF-NDP *Organization Manual* (1968).
225*Winnipeg Tribune*, June 26, 1969.
226For a rather more detailed account of the campaign itself, see T. Peterson and P. Barber, "Some Factors in the 1969 NDP Victory in Manitoba," *Lakehead University Review*, Autumn, 1970, pp. 120-133; and T. Peterson, "Manitoba," in *Canadian Annual Review, 1969*, J. Saywell, ed. (Toronto: University of Toronto Press, 1970).

homes and lower-income households. Of the two ridings in the city of Brandon, likewise, the poorer one in the east was won by the NDP, while the relatively more prosperous one in the west was retained by the Conservative party. The NDP also won both of the northern mining towns, Flin Flon and Thompson, where better than average incomes were undermined by exceptional living costs and where union spokesmen repeatedly expressed local dissatisfaction with high rents and food prices. In the ridings of The Pas and Rupertsland, similar dissatisfaction in Indian and Métis communities assisted the NDP victory. In the fourteen northern and eastern ridings, generally, the NDP secured an average popular vote of 43 per cent; while in the same number of more prosperous ridings in the southwest, it secured only 19 per cent of the popular vote. Reversing this pattern of support, the Conservatives obtained 32 per cent of the vote in the north and east, but retained 47 per cent in the southwest.

This result did not appear to be an "ethnic revolt" in the sense that "ethnics" were "aroused" in seeking "the right they have now earned" to participate in the political process.[227] The ethnic associations, as in the past, were generally conservative in the campaign; some of their spokesmen, such as William Swystun, tried to exploit ethnic feeling on the issue of bilingualism.[228] After the election an ethnic press editor attacked socialism with customary vehemence:

Ed Schreyer, who knows a few words in Ukrainian because he grew up in a Ukrainian district, is assuring everyone that he will follow a so-called social-democratic course. Time will tell how far to the left the socialists will go and how far they will lead Manitoba into ruin.[229]

But the traditional ethnic appeals were now less effective; in the north-south polarization, the separate loyalties and rivalries of individual ethnic communities could no longer be identified. The NDP victory appeared to have been made possible by a decline in ethnic consciousness. Ironically, the major victim of this polarization was the Liberal party, which had served as a vehicle of assimilation for the non-British groups. It was debatable whether by voting according to class the non-British groups in 1969 were necessarily acting more rationally than their predecessors had in voting for the government in office and seeking in that way a measure of security from ethnic discrimination.[230] But the old Liberal party was no longer able to profit from immigrant need for acceptance. Campaigning under the leadership of Robert Bend, who succeeded Molgat as party leader six weeks before the election and resigned immediately after his defeat, the party presented the appearance of an elderly warrior, whose fatigue could scarcely be concealed by Dixieland bands and mini-skirted cheerleaders. Bend himself was a conservative survivor of the coalition period, and in neither style nor program did he distinguish himself from Premier Weir. Hence the electorate's polarization was assisted by its being presented with two clear alternatives: one conservative and expressed by Weir; and the other more progressive, expressed by Schreyer. A revived and vigorously reform-minded Liberal party could conceivably have secured the lower class vote, and might well have done so under Schreyer's leadership had he and others like him been attracted to it. With the Liberal failure to attract such leadership, however, the NDP became the party of reform for the relatively poorer class as well as for those generally unenthusiastic toward a government which showed little initiative beyond a repeated commitment to budgetary restraint.

When Larry Desjardins, elected as a Liberal in St. Boniface, announced he would sit as a Liberal Democrat and support the NDP, he gave it a one-vote majority in the legislature and the Schreyer government took office on July 15. Its first legislative session shifted medicare costs from premiums to income tax, raised the minimum wage and welfare allowances, increased credit for poorer farmers and fishermen, launched more public housing, and expanded grants and jobs for Indians and Métis. Finance Minister Saul Cherniack summarized the philosophy underlying this program:

There remain substantial numbers of individuals, and groups of individuals, within the provincial community who for one reason or another are barred from the abundance of good things this society has to offer. It may be that as individuals or groups they represent a minority of the population. The conscience of the community can rest no easier for this fact. The barriers that face these people are numerous — income levels, educational levels, geographic location, ethnic origin, and similar matters.

We hold firmly to the belief that a properly aroused community, acting intelligently and in concert, can remove these crude obstructions and open a new way to those who have previously known only disparity and discrimination.[231]

But not all legislative issues clearly related to class equalization. In 1970, the government became embroiled in a prolonged controversy over its plan to introduce public auto insurance. The next year it placed in receivership a pulp and paper complex at The Pas after the private firms involved were reported to be in default on government loans. These moves and the government's announcement that it was considering the establishment of a public agency to control the marketing of prescription drugs inspired business and opposition warnings that the threat of gradual nationalization of the economy would discourage private investment and curb the economic growth necessary to support its social reform program. A proposal to reorganize and integrate municipal institutions in Greater Winnipeg aroused further opposition from suburbs fearful of higher taxes. The cross-pressures of such questions could blur or divert the emerging class alignment. Despite its avowed commitment to equalization, moreover, the NDP could succumb to the institutionalized conservatism and caution of any government beleaguered by the myriad demands of every group that considered itself in

227D. Swainson, "Ethnic Revolt: Manitoba's Election," *Canadian Forum*, August, 1969, pp. 98-99.
228*Winnipeg Tribune*, June 23, 1969.
229*Canadian Farmer* (Winnipeg), July 5, 1969.
230Cp. A. Milnor, "The New Politics and Ethnic Revolt: 1929–1938," in *Politics in Saskatchewan*, N. Ward and D. Spafford, eds. (Don Mills, Ontario: Longmans Canada Ltd., 1968), p. 152.
231Legislative Assembly of Manitoba, *Debates and Proceedings*, September 18, 1969, p. 856.

some way disadvantaged. Increasingly image-conscious after assuming office, it hired a public relations agency, Dunsky Advertising of Montreal, which received part of the province's tourism promotion account in the same way that Dalton Camp had earlier been rewarded by Duff Roblin.[232] Nor did some party leaders seem as willing to tolerate the traditional degree of dissent and amateur participation in constituency associations and provincial council meetings. Except at nominations, constituency meetings were poorly attended and the party continued to lack the broad membership base of its counter-parts in Saskatchewan, British Columbia and Ontario. Because effective unionization included only about 20 per cent of the work force, little better than half the proportion in more industrial provinces, exceptional influence was wielded by a few strong unions such as the Steelworkers at Thompson and their leaders such as Len Stevens, president of the Manitoba Federation of Labour. Also, since the elected members, through their indemnity tithes, paid much of the party's expenses, and since the cabinet was able to reward its faithful party supporters with patronage appointments to over a hundred boards and commissions, there was little likelihood of the party's resisting control and direction from above. All this suggested that the NDP in office could become at least as oligarchic and professional as the Liberal and Con-servative parties. But whether it could do this and still be sensitive to its lower class constituency remained unclear.

Another factor crucial to its prospect was the possibility of a new Liberal-Conservative coalition. *Free Press* editorials repeatedly urged such a move and in 1969, the Liberal president Stan Roberts declared that if Liberal con-stituency associations "want to team up with the Tories, they can go ahead."[233] Old memories were revived as Liberal spokesmen also urged a return to non-partisanship. Before his appointment to the Senate, Gil Molgat, the former leader, pointed to economic development as an area where partisan divisions were inappropriate.

This question goes far above partisan considerations. And speaking on behalf of my party — of which I was then the leader — I said that we were prepared as a party to forget completely partisan considerations. . . . I think it is im-portant that we make it clear to all Manitobans that this indeed is not a partisan question. Now I'd like to suggest . . . that this would be a good com-mittee on which to start a completely non-partisan approach . . .[234]

A *Free Press* writer expressed a similar view:

If Manitoba is to remain true to its history . . . there should be a new non-partisan era ahead in our second century.[235]

In the bitter aftermath of defeat, however, the Conservatives rejected the Liberal party as an unwelcome ally. A *Winnipeg Tribune* editorial blamed Weir's defeat on the Liberal "establishment":

A significant reason has to be the blind partisan opposition of the Winnipeg Free Press *and the Liberal big business establishment which has wielded untold power here for years.*

The fact is the Liberal establishment is not liberal in the true sense at all. It represents reaction in its most regressive form.[236]

Addressing the party's annual meeting in 1969, Walter Weir reportedly "shook his fist and needed no sound amplifiers to make it known he would fight against socialism;" and an editorial commented:

Mr. Weir has made it crystal clear that he is striving for polarity in Manitoba politics. To Mr. Weir, the issue is simple — free enterprise versus socialism.[237]

Similarly, when he resigned as leader in 1971, Weir dismissed the possibility of coalition:

We have never been associated with those people, bloated with privilege and traditional status, who have come to think that the private enterprise system exists for their glorification and greater profit.[238]

The Liberals in return declared that their strategy would be "to portray both the NDP and the Conservatives as parties dominated by extremists" and thus provide "a middle-of-the-road option for the voters."[239] Equally committed to the struggle, the Conservatives exhorted their followers to exceptional effort:

For our country's sake — WE MUST WIN THE NEXT ELECTION![240]

Thus confronted, the NDP's future withstood conjecture.

Whatever the prospect, the pattern of provincial politics was fundamentally altered. Voting patterns were now such that the needs and wishes of the poorer class, irrespective of its members' ethnic origin, required more explicit recognition and accommodation by all political parties. The nature of immigration had long retarded this development. In provinces further west, where there was more immigration from the United States, the influence of American "radical" ideas was probably greater.[241] But Manitoba was occupied earlier and decisively by British immigrants from Ontario who became prosperous entrepreneurs in south Winnipeg and highly capitalized wheat growers in the province's southwest. Agrarian socialism did not attract them.[242] Their capacity, exemplified in the careers of such premiers as Norris, Bracken and Campbell, provided a firm base for the province's ruling class. Their advantages were manifold: command of the dominant language, preemption of much of the best land, greater political awareness and experience, more investment capital or access to it, better business and commercial

---

232*Winnipeg Free Press*, February 6, 1970.

233*Ibid.*, October 27, November 14 and 29, 1969.

234Legislative Assembly of Manitoba, *Debates and Proceedings*, October 7, 1969, pp. 1408-1409.

235*Winnipeg Free Press*, July 13, 1970.

236*Winnipeg Tribune*, June 26, 1969.

237*Ibid.*, November 26 and 27, 1969.

238*Ibid.*, February 27, 1971.

239*The Manitoba Liberal* (Winnipeg), January, 1971.

240Form letter to Progressive-Conservative members, February 12, 1970.

241D. Smith, "Prairie Revolt, Federalism and the Party System," in *Party Politics in Canada*, H. G. Thorburn, ed., 2nd ed. (Scarborough, Ontario: Prentice-Hall of Canada, Ltd., 1967), p. 191.

242Cp. H.M. Clokie, *Canadian Government and Politics* (Toronto: Longmans Canada Ltd., 1944), p. 94; S.M. Lipset, *Agrarian Socialism*, 2nd ed. (Garden City, New York: Anchor Books, 1968).

connections with Ontario, and perhaps most important, an invincible self-assurance. They constituted a sturdy "fragment" or off-shoot from mid-nineteenth century Ontario, intolerant and suspicious of later arrivals and increasingly confirmed in their sense of material and moral superiority.[243] Their political culture was a blunt conservative pragmatism as durable and enigmatic as a blank monument. Skill and tenacity gave them a remarkable political career. But like most ruling classes, they eventually wore out. From 1900 to the 1960's, their number declined from over 70 per cent to less than 40 per cent of the population. After Duff Roblin, few new leaders appeared. The old wealthy British families seemingly failed simply to reproduce themselves: in some cases the only survivors of a proud heritage were elderly widows or spinster daughters living alone in decaying mansions now over-shadowed by high-rise apartment blocks. The consolidation of farms in the southwest and the decline of Winnipeg as a business centre, beginning so gradually in the 1920's as to be unnoticed, encouraged the group's more vital and aggressive descendants to seek opportunity elsewhere, just as their grandfathers had sought it in Manitoba in the 1880's. Indeed the ruling group's ability to afford higher education for its children likely facilitated their departure. At the 1967 Conservative convention that chose Walter Weir, his supporters wore hard hats and appeared vigorously confident of retaining power yet another generation. But they proved unequal to the task and new leaders and spokesmen from the non-British groups emerged in their place. At their respective leadership conventions in 1970 and 1971, the Liberals chose I.H. Asper and the Conservatives chose Sidney Spivak and the transition from the old British group was evident: both Asper and Spivak were wealthy, articulate and aggressive Jewish lawyers from south Winnipeg, exemplifying the province's new, more culturally heterogeneous, upper class. On the rivalry between these new leaders and the NDP, questions about ethnic or religious identity had little bearing: British and non-British were mingled alike in both camps, mainly, though not exclusively, on the basis of their economic circumstances.

Had Manitoba been settled exclusively by British immigrants, it seems probable that party politics could earlier have reflected class divisions. Perhaps a left-wing party could have been more successful. But the non-British immigrants and the native peoples for decades remained relatively poor outsiders. When British working-class immigrants tried to redress their grievances, as in 1919, they had to go it alone without broad support, were disarmed by the racist charges of their opponents, and finally suppressed by force. In the Depression, while lower class protest was fragmented among the CCF, Social Credit, Communists and Independents, the government maintained itself with a beguiling doctrine of coalition that effaced election issues and with an electoral system that held down the representation of both Winnipeg and poorer northern areas. International developments — the two World Wars, the Russian Revolution, Stalinism and the Cold War — not only compromised or distracted left-wing reformers generally but recurrently smeared and intimidated German and Slavic immigrants. Religious divisions, conservatism and fear of intolerance also discouraged political activity, notably among Mennonites and French Catholics. Perhaps most important, basic economic need demanded a nearly total effort: a measure of material progress, provided by the period of post-war prosperity, was a prerequisite to political action. By long and prudent service to the ruling compact, the "national" representatives of the non-British groups slowly won respectability and legitimacy for their cultures. The need for defences against discrimination and deportation declined. Concern over the cultural and ethnic divisions in the province increasingly gave way to concern over the continuing disparities in income, living standards and opportunities. Having survived the vicissitudes of this process, Manitobans in their second century appeared ready for a more straight-forward competition between those disposed toward reform and equalization and those who expressed the need for restraint and stability.

243Cp. L. Hartz, *The Founding of New Societies* (Toronto: Longmans Canada Ltd., 1964).

* NEW BRUNSWICK *

The Politics of Pragmatism[1]

P. J. FITZPATRICK

Provincial politics in New Brunswick might best be described as parochial, stagnant, and anachronistic — reminiscent, in some ways, of politics in nineteenth-century Britain before the reform movement. The Liberal and Progressive Conservative parties dominate the political environment without fear of challenge or stimulation by third parties, sustained by gerrymandering,[2] patronage, and constituencies with hereditary political loyalties kept intact by ancient ethnic and religious antagonisms. Neither party is receptive to the idea, so fashionable elsewhere, of popular participation in government; party leadership is firmly of the opinion that it should lead.[3] But leadership in New Brunswick politics is not a matter of putting forth ideas or initiating well-defined policies. A visitor to the Legislative Assembly in Fredericton is more likely to hear a member advise the Assembly that maple syrup time has come to the Keswick than a debate on French Canada's role within Confederation. Question time in the Assembly is used not to challenge policy, but rather to query ministers about expenditures, in hopes of discovering patronage. Issues, when they are allowed to arise, interest government and opposition alike less on their own merits than as a means to score debating points, often using the most childish tactics.[4] In short, the Assembly functions less as a deliberative body than as an arena for partisan conflict.

Yet the electorate seems satisfied with this arrangement. If there were a felt need in the province for a more progressive or ideological mode of politics, then presumably viable alternatives to the two traditional parties would have arisen. But while the New Democratic Party, for example, may have the support of organized labour in other provinces, labour in New Brunswick seems to feel that it may best further its goals within the traditional two party system.[5] In fact, no third party Members have been elected provincially since 1920, when the United Farmers, contesting 26 of the 48 seats, elected 9 Members by taking 21 per cent of the popular vote.[6]

The NDP's ill success may be attributable largely to the failure of labour to become significantly aware of itself as an interest group, but it may also be

116

due in part to the timidity of the electorate. For although many voters grumble between elections about existing institutions, this discontent often fails to be articulated at the polls, where people feel obliged to obey social, ethnic, or religious rather than political imperatives.[7]

I. POLITICAL CULTURE

In no other province are the ethnic, religious, and geographic divisions quite so explicit or so closely balanced as in New Brunswick. The correspondence between these divisions and the distribution of political allegiance in the province is almost exact. 59.2 per cent of the population claims British origin, 34.2 per cent is of French extraction, while "others" account for only 6.6 per cent. Roman Catholicism has the adherence of 51.7 per cent of the population, the major Protestant denominations (Baptist, United Church, and Anglican) 40.6 per cent, and other denominations 6.6 per cent.[8] The Liberal party draws strong support from French Roman Catholics and significant support from Irish Catholics. The Conservative party commands the allegiance of most Protestants of British origin but receives only limited Catholic support.

One can draw an imaginary diagonal from Grand Falls in the northwest to Sackville in the southeast: north of this diagonal all districts are either

[1]Much of the material included here was gathered through discussions with party workers and through following Mr. Van Horne and Mr. Hatfield during the Conservative leadership race in 1966, the Restigouche by-election in 1967, and both Mr. Van Horne and Premier Robichaud during the 1967 general election.

[2]Successive premiers have promised reform of the distribution of Assembly seats since at least 1917. The most recent "redistribution" in 1967 added six new seats but was in essence a thinly veiled gerrymander. For example, the Milford-Randolph area, the only Liberal area of Saint John County, was added to the Saint John centre seats rather than to the new seat of Saint John West.

[3]As one Liberal put it, "They [the party leadership] stand on the mountain and throw it over — we are supposed to catch it."

[4]On one occasion the then leader of the opposition sent a dozen eggs, a bushel of apples, and a length of pulp wood to the government benches to prove a debating point.

[5]The NDP ran three candidates in 1967, capturing 1,247 votes in a four-member constituency out of 92,579 cast. In 1970, encouraged by their recent success in Nova Scotia, the New Democrats contested 32 seats, winning 3.4% of the popular vote.

[6]In 1944, the CCF ran 41 candidates, but despite capturing 68,248 votes, compared to the Liberals 282,367 votes (37 seats) and the Conservatives' 233,301 (11 seats), it did not return a single Member. The Left tried again in 1948 but took only one-half of its 1944 total vote and after a half-hearted attempt in 1952 disappeared from the provincial scene until the NDP contested Northumberland in 1967. The Social Credit party appeared once provincially, fielding candidates in 18 of 52 seats, took 9,490 votes and disappeared. Independent candidates have vanished as well — eight ran in 1948; by 1963 the field was down to one, with none in 1967. Drawn from Howard Scarrow, *Canada Votes* (New Orleans: Hauser Press, 1961), pp. 206-208.

[7]It is very common to think of oneself as belonging to a "Liberal family" or a "Conservative family" and to vote accordingly.

[8]Compiled from the Dominion Bureau of Statistics, *Census of Canada*, 1961.

TABLE I

New Brunswick Constituency Profile

Constituency	Seats	British	French	Other	Catholic	Major Protestant	Other	Party Supported 1967	% of Popular Vote 1967
			%			%			
Albert	2	83.3	3.2	13.5	9.2	84.5	6.3	Cons	59
Bathurst	1							Lib	66
Carleton	3	91.4	3.5	5.1	11.4	77.1	11.5	Cons	59
Campbellton	1							Cons	57
Charlotte	4	88.4	6.4	5.2	15.6	70.0	14.4	Cons	52
Edmundston	1							Lib	56
Fredericton	1							Cons	59
Gloucester	5	13.7	85.2	1.1	93.3	5.9	.6	Lib	65
Kent	3	14.6	82.0	3.4	90.5	6.0	3.5	Lib	63
Kings	3	87.2	3.5	9.3	14.1	79.9	7.0	Cons	62
Madawaska	3	5.2	93.8	1.0	97.6	2.1	.3	Lib	54
Moncton	3							Lib	52
Northumberland	5	63.5	31.4	5.1	59.6	34.4	6.6	Lib	60
Queens	2	83.1	8.5	8.4	14.1	75.9	10.0	Lib	49
								Cons	52
Restigouche	3	28.8	68.3	2.9	81.4	15.5	3.1	Lib	54
Greater Saint John Area	7	77.1	13.8	9.1	36.8	56.3	7.9	6 Cons	69
								1 Lib	48
Sunbury	2	71.3	17.3	11.4	33.3	59.9	7.8	Lib	57
Victoria	2	49.6	42.3	8.1	52.8	37.8	9.4	Cons	54
Westmorland	4	50.4	43.7	5.9	53.0	41.8	5.2	Lib	59
York	2	80.6	9.6	9.8	17.1	69.5	13.4	Cons	55

*Compiled from D.B.S. Catalogue No. 92-553, 92-554, 92-555, 92-556, 92-559, and Report, Chief Electoral Officer, Province of New Brunswick, 1967 General Election, pp. 6-10.

French or mixed, and all but two (one in 1967) Assembly seats are held by Liberals. South of the diagonal the population is predominantly English, and all but two (four in 1967) M.L.A.s are Conservative. Table I provides a breakdown of the electorate in each constituency by ethnic origin and religious affiliation and indicates the winning party in each riding in the 1967 election. The deviation from the Conservative norm in the English areas of Queen and Saint John can be explained by the personal popularity of the two Liberal candidates.[9] The Liberal victory in Sunbury is traceable to the strongly Liberal vote from servicemen stationed at CFB Gagetown.[10] Among the French constituencies only Campbellton City went Conservative.

This ethnic-religious pattern of voting behaviour is reflected in the party nominations and in the ethnic extraction of the Members of the 1967 Assembly. For the election of that year, the Liberals nominated thirty-seven candidates of British extraction and twenty-one of French extraction. The Liberals elected thirty-two M.L.A.s: all of the twenty-one French and eleven of the British candidates. The Conservatives nominated forty-two candidates of British and sixteen of French origin: twenty-six of the British candidates won, and none of the French.[11]

With the political parties so closely associated with particular patterns of ethnic and religious loyalty, political allegiance in New Brunswick is no casual matter. In certain other provinces, where this correspondence is not so close, a fickle electorate might feel free to cast its votes on the basis of issues and policies; but to a British Protestant New Brunswicker of United Empire Loyalist stock, for example, the idea of voting Liberal might well be unthinkable, an act of cultural treachery equivalent to conversion to Roman Catholicism. The comparative remoteness of government and a political apparatus that is visible to most of the electorate only around election time does much to ensure the unreliability of many voters in, say, Ontario; in New Brunswick, however, the relationship between the individual voter and his party is in many cases one of intimate reciprocity, a mutual loyalty sustained by, among other things, a wide distribution of "honest" patronage.

The New Brunswick public service has about 8,200 employees. But in the course of a year an equal number of casual employees are taken onto the public payroll. A loyal party worker is rewarded with a job on a road grader or in a garage, or given a few weeks work clearing highway shoulders. A casual employee may receive only about $1,000 from the government payroll in an average year, but in the New Brunswick employment context $1,000 is a lot of money. The patronage casual labour force is an institution in itself; the public service distinguishes between "regular" or "1960 casuals" and casuals *per se*. Of the approximately 8,100 casuals at least 900 may be classified as "1960 casuals," people who have been on the casual payroll since the present government took office — in effect, permanent public employees who have been saved the trouble of entering a civil service competition.[12] But unlike permanent employees this labour force is of course vulnerable to replacement by Conservative faithful when that party next forms a government.

Within a given constituency, the privilege of dispensing patronage rests primarily with the M.L.A., if of the government party, or the defeated candidate of this party, and with one or two members of the constituency committee. But the efficient operation of the patronage machine demands

---

[9]The Honourable Robert McCready, presently Speaker of the Assembly (plurality 123 votes), and the Honourable Robert Higgins, Minister of Economic Growth (plurality 21 votes), while extremely popular in their respective areas, had only narrow margins over their opponents. This may be a reflection of the tendency in the province to vote the ticket rather than to split one's vote. Mr. McCready was running in a two man riding, Mr. Higgins in a four member seat.

[10]Report of the Chief Electoral Officer, Twenty-Sixth General Election, 1967.

[11]Although at least two of the sitting Conservative members have mixed English and French parentage.

[12]These people have become such an institution that even though they are casual employees they now qualify for such fringe benefits as sick leave and vacations.

some degree of co-ordination and centralization. A small office exists in each constituency, manned by a "contact man" whose responsibility it is to receive calls requesting temporary help in the area, and to determine through the party system and the M.L.A. if a party worker is available. If so, this worker gets the job; if no party worker is available the job may well wait until one is. Patronage of this sort distributes the spoils of political victory to the lowest levels of the party in power and is the tangible reward for diligence and loyalty awaiting the rank and file of the party not in power. The voter is therefore encouraged to make his party affiliation explicit and the party is assured of a large core of active and loyal support. Since the electorate does gain something from this arrangement, there is little complaint against it.

This tolerance extends to patronage in the area of small government contracts and government purchases. During a Liberal administration, for example, a Conservative, finding his small company in danger of bankruptcy through the loss of government sales, might approach a Liberal friend, asking him to run the business at a 5 or 10 per cent commission while the Liberals are in office. Or, one partner in a firm will support the Liberals, the other, the Conservatives; if the Liberals are in office, the Liberal runs the firm and the Conservative partner is "silent." When the Conservatives are in, the roles are reversed. Needless to say, the parties make use of this system when campaign money is needed. The government party approaches the firm with a list of all purchases made from it and suggests an appropriate campaign contribution.

The party in office extends its ties to the electorate by making itself accessible. The citizen with a problem or grievance prefers to approach his M.L.A. or the defeated government candidate in his constituency rather than the more remote and less flexible civil service bureaucracy in Fredericton. He does not regard his M.L.A. as a quasi-ombudsman or as an errand boy for constituency complaints, but he knows that his mediator will solve the problem not by raising it with civil servants, but rather through a quiet chat with the appropriate minister. The M.L.A. is aided in this by provincial statutes giving the minister considerable discretion. Again, the citizen is both rewarded for and reinforced in his loyalty to the party.

When politicians lock horns in the Assembly or during a campaign, they are less likely to try to prevail over each other by reasoned arguments than by ridicule. This is, of course, in keeping with the emphasis within the political environment on partisan loyalty at the expense of issues and is completely tolerated by an electorate that perhaps feels closer to the political process because its legislators are unwilling to allow each other any dignity. Thus, during a 1970 budget debate, the Minister of Education could make parenthetical reference to Opposition Leader Hatfield's apparent reluctance to marry, implying some deficiency in the frontier virtues.[13]

There is a sense in which the vaudevillian element in political controversy serves a kind of diversionary function, offering the electorate the placebo of ferocious spectatorship in lieu of genuine political involvement. The concentration and insulation of power concomitant on this may be clearly seen in the structure of the party organizations.

II. PARTY ORGANIZATION

The rewards extended by a party to its faithful do not include a voice in party decisions. This prerogative is reserved for a select few. But as long as the party is faithful to its traditions and does not startle its constituents with heretical notions, and as long as patronage is forthcoming for loyal service, the rank and file does not resent this exclusion. Both parties hold annual provincial constituency meetings,[14] but usually all the decisions have been made in advance. The leadership decides if it will remain in office; if not, it chooses its successor. At the actual meeting, those present merely concur in the leadership decision, pass a motion of confidence in the provincial party leader, and adjourn.[15]

The New Brunswick Liberal Association,[16] the primary Liberal party organization in the province, consists of representatives from the constituency associations, the Liberal Women's Association, the Young Liberal Association, the university Liberal clubs, and the Liberal M.L.A.s. In all, about forty people are eligible to attend Association meetings, held four or five times a year. But even this inner circle is relatively powerless — or rather its members have power only insofar as it is delegated to them by the premier, who presides over the meetings. His presence and the members' awareness that their political fortunes are his to advance or retard ensure that Association meetings are free of any real activity whatsoever: policy suggestions are not raised, issues go undebated; instead representatives of the various constituency associations read invariably optimistic reports on Liberal strength in their districts, or fruitless squabbles arise between factions or individual representatives, which the premier smooths over. In short, party decisions are made not by the N.B. Liberal Association, but by the party leader. He may discuss matters with an informal group of advisors — mostly of the parliamentary party and a few of the extra-parliamentary party, some of whom may be in the Association — but the decision is his.

Among the prerogatives of leadership, in both parties, is the choice of candidates. While there is a degree of self-recruitment of candidates for federal elections, at the provincial level the recruitment process is centralized, heirarchial, and formalized — the party leader, abetted by his advisors, makes the final choices and the nominating conventions are arranged accordingly.[17]

---

[13]*The Daily Gleaner* (Fredericton), March 16, 1969.

[14]Also annual meetings of the Liberal Women's Association and Young Liberals, in constituencies where they exist.

[15]Periodically there may be a tempest in a tea-pot, as recently when students from the two universities in Fredericton appeared at the meeting of the Greater Fredericton Liberal Association and elected one of their student Liberal group as vice-president.

[16]The framework of the Progressive Conservative party is essentially the same. The Liberals are discussed here because the material was more readily available.

[17]A prime illustration of the leadership role was witnessed by the author as the Liberals held their nomination meeting for Saint John City in June 1960 in the old Mayfair theatre. After the meeting had been in progress for a while, the chairman made a statement to the effect, "We're not nominating to-night, two of our candidates

The leader's prerogative is limited only in that he must be careful not to offend the parochialism of a given constituency. Hence, it is rare that a candidate is "parachuted" into a safe seat, as the electorate would regard him as an "outsider" and his success would be doubtful.

On the other hand, a party worker who has earned the reward of office but who would not perform well in a single-member constituency may be smuggled into office, so to speak, by having him run in one of the multi-member ridings.[18] Both parties rationalize the existence of these constituencies by arguing that they make it possible for a candidate who is representative of a group in the minority in that area to gain office — for example, an Irish Catholic can in this way win election in an English Protestant area such as Saint John. More to the point, the parties know that the electorate rarely splits the ticket; one strong candidate in a given constituency can carry several weaker hopefuls to victory on his coat-tails.

Separate federal and provincial party organizations exist in the province only at the local level, but the frame of reference of the organizations is strictly provincial; only grudging efforts are made in federal campaigns. Ottawa is of interest to the parties mainly as a source of spoils — a senate seat for a member of the party leadership, for example. Or it may be necessary to tap the federal party's campaign chest for a provincial election campaign — especially if the provincial party is in opposition and cannot raise money locally.

As we have seen, the political landscape of New Brunswick has been portioned out more or less equally between the Liberal and Conservative parties, each of which, by identifying itself closely and almost exclusively with one of the province's two dominant ethnic and religious groups, has guaranteed itself a following of hereditary and apparently unshakable loyalty. The passive steadfastness of a substantial part of this electorate is warmed to active support of its party by a broad distribution of patronage or the promise of patronage. As many voters regard politics as a means by which they may express cultural loyalty rather than as merely an expedient means to obtain certain social ends, the politician in New Brunswick need not concern himself greatly with public issues or the formulation of broad policies. His constituents and the rank and file of his party are born into their political loyalties; there is no need for him to secure the loyalty of the former with reforms and social programs or the loyalty of the latter with a distribution of power downward through the party heirarchy. Politics in the province have therefore been characterized by both a freedom from substantial issues and an extremely narrow concentration of decision-making power at the top of the party organizations.

III. CONTEMPORARY POLITICAL SYSTEM

It is perhaps to be expected in a province whose politicians have had no reason to gain experience in the formulation of complex legislative programs that such a program, when it did come to New Brunswick, was proposed by a Royal Commission, given shape by hired experts from outside the province, and implemented by the Liberal government of Premier Louis Robichaud with an awkwardness that exacerbated to a novel degree the ethnic and religious tensions in the province.

In March, 1962, a Royal Commission on Finance and Municipal Taxation, commonly referred to as the Byrne Commission, after its chairman, G. Edward Byrne, Q.C., was appointed to "make findings and recommendations consistent with the public interest and the general welfare of the people of New Brunswick with respect to the whole field of relevent facts, issues and legislation relating to public or municipal fiscal matters within the Province of New Brunswick . . ."[19] The Commission's report and the resultant Programme of Equal Opportunity both threatened the province's ancient parochialism and gave that parochialism opportunity to find its fiercest expression.

The Byrne commission recognized that the system of municipal government in New Brunswick was out of date. The welter of parishes, counties, villages, and cities into which the province was divided was perhaps an adequate scheme of government in a society with an immobile population. But increasing urbanization and resultant displacements of people and capital had rendered the traditional institutions, particularly the county councils, obsolete. Commission studies revealed that while the counties had primary responsibility for education, health, welfare, and the administration of justice, most counties did not have financial resources equal to these responsibilities. The result, more often than not, was a tremendous imbalance in the level of services that the counties could provide. An urbanized county such as Saint John was able to spend $180.79 per capita on municipal expenditures, while a rural area such as Queens County could spend $53.24, a depressed area such as Restigouche only $19.06.[20]

The Byrne Commission stated that the solution to this problem was either to transfer adequate financial resources from the province to the municipalities or, as it recommended, to transfer the general service functions from the municipalities to the province. This recommendation, and its corollary that county councils be abolished, generated political passions the likes of which the province had not previously experienced. When the Liberal government moved to implement these recommendations in the form of the Programme of Equal Opportunity, it was faced with powerful opposition from at least three sources.

While Equal Opportunity was of value to all citizens, its impact as a plan of social change would be greatest in the depressed North Shore. This

are fogged in at Halifax." One naive party worker jumped to his feet and started to exclaim that he understood that it was to be an open convention, at which point the chairman bellowed, "I said we ain't nominating, now sit down and shaddup." End of dissention.

[18]There are two five-member, three four-member, six three-member, seven two-member, and only four single-member constituencies.

[19]Chapter 6, Acts of New Brunswick, 1961-62; also Order-in-Council 62-185, March 8, 1962.

[20]Report of the Royal Commission on Finance and Municipal Taxation (Fredericton, 1963) Table 7c, Appendix 07c.

area was solidly French, Roman Catholic, and Liberal (see Table I). On the other hand, the Programme would have the least impact in urbanized English-Protestant areas, such as Saint John and Fredericton. But these areas, under-assessed in the past, would carry the greater burden of taxation[21] under Equal Opportunity. Since many people had come to believe implicitly that the Liberal party was an Acadian party, it followed that in much of English New Brunswick the Programme of Equal Opportunity was regarded as a mani-festation of a French takeover. The argument that equal services should be available to all citizens regardless of where they lived or the fiscal capabilities of their municipalities fell on deaf ears. English New Brunswick, falling back upon its hereditary allegiance to the Conservative party, saw Equal Oppor-tunity as simply a plot on the part of the Liberals "to rob Peter and pay Pierre." This theme was elaborated upon, with much colour, all through Greater Saint John and the Saint John River Valley, the major areas of Conservative strength, and a latent but never absent hostility to French New Brunswick — and, by association, to the Liberal party — blossomed into virulence. In the midst of all this passion it occurred to almost no one that Equal Opportunity was a policy issue and as such could be constructively criticized.

Before considering other sources of opposition to Equal Opportunity, it may be profitable to examine some of the forms anti-French hostility in New Brunswick may take. The extreme fringe of Francophobia is occupied at present by the Canadian Loyalist Society,[22] an organization located in the Salisbury area.[23] As the Society is not without influence in the province, it is worth quoting one of its pamphlets in some detail:

The following letter has been sent to Louis Robichaud ....

"The Canadian Loyalist Association wish [sic] to congratulate you on the masterful manner in which you have deceived the people of New Bruns-wick and Canada by leading them to believe that New Brunswick has two official languages.

Your senseless, degenerate and ruinous official language act [sic] is one of the worst evils anyone ever tried to perpetuate [sic] on the citizens of this province."[24]

The pamphlet goes on to accuse the French of a complete takeover of govern-ment, an argument summarized in ten points for the faithful to memorize, and concludes with an attack on the federal leadership:

To-day, Canada is in the hands of three Frenchmen, i.e. Trudeau, John [sic] Marchand, and Gerald Pelletier (a hater of all English) and no English speak-ing person of consequence is attached to the Prime Minister's staff.

Trudeau, the legalizer of the sin of homosexuality, is trying to dissolve all ties with BRITAIN and the COMMONWEALTH in exchange for ties with France and Communist China. Trudeau has passed in Parliament Bill C-120 and has in effect by-passed the B.N.B. act [sic] and has imposed upon the country the French language. This bill [sic] is nothing short of LEGAL-IZED FRENCH COLONIZATION OF CANADA. [Emphasis in the original][25]

While these feelings may be openly expressed only by a fringe group, they may in fact be shared covertly by a significant number of English New Brunswickers.

The second major source of opposition confronting the Liberal party was the municipalities and county councils. The political leadership of the municipalities, realizing that a transfer of functions to the province would reduce their political power, were generally against Equal Opportunity.[26] They found an ally in the English press, notably the Fredericton *Daily Gleaner* and the *Atlantic Advocate,* which argued that Equal Opportunity would destroy local autonomy and lead to over-centralization.[27] This charge was leveled most strenuously against the decision to abolish county councils, despite the fact that the councils were anachronisms in most counties, without adequate financial resources, qualified staff, or effective leadership. But, given the patriarchal nature of local politics in the province, the councils were not without influence on public opinion. Sheer length of tenure gave many councillors strong positions in their communities; though in their sixties and seventies and perhaps out of touch with modern ideas of government, the inertia of thirty or forty years in office made them difficult to dislodge. The Liberal party underestimated their influence; the Conservatives capitalized on it.

The third source of major opposition to the Equal Opportunity proposals was the business establishment, most notably the Irving interests. The multi-million dollar empire of K.C. Irving of Saint John, Eastern Canada's most prominent businessman and industrialist, was, understandably, opposed to those provisions of the Programme which threatened the abolition of certain tax and assessment concessions.[28] But the Liberal party did not attract any popular support in the dispute between itself and the industrialist. If anything, it lost support, as a significant number of citizens look upon Mr. Irving as an economic saviour. The electorate did not consider the dispute a battle between its interests and those of the industrialist; their perception was that the man who brought industry to the province was being attacked.

In all its aspects, the Equal Opportunity debate reflected the parochialism of the electorate. The Liberal government hired a number of experts, former senior public servants from Saskatchewan and elsewhere, and created the Office of Government Organization to implement the Equal Opportunity Programme. These experts were denounced throughout the province as "outsiders," and OGO was seen as part of a Machiavellian conspiracy. This

21The province receives $1.50 per $100.00 assessment on all real property and property owners in urbanized areas have been complaining that their assessment has doubled and quadrupled within the past three years. Most are unwilling to admit that they were underassessed in the past.

22Formerly known as the Maritime Loyalist Association.

23This is an area where the Orange Lodge still exists in its nineteenth century context.

24Canadian Loyalist Association, *Bulletin,* n.p., n.d.

25*Ibid.*

26The mayors of two of the three major cities were Conservatives when Equal Opportunity was introduced. Mayor Jones of Moncton was mooted in both 1966 and 1969 as a possible leader of the Conservative party. Mayor Walker of Fredericton entered the 1969 Conservative leadership race four days after being defeated for re-election.

27*Atlantic Advocate* (Fredericton), October, 1966, p. 32.

28Report of the Royal Commission on Finance and Municipal Taxation (Fredericton, 1963) p. 16.

attitude was another manifestation of the political culture of the province — a hidebound intolerance of new ideas, a disdain, bordering upon abhorrence, of social and political change.[29]

But the debate also had the effect of making visible certain differences in ideology between the Liberal and Conservative parties. While neither party possesses issue-oriented politicians, nor is itself issue-oriented, the Liberals have demonstrated a responsiveness to change that, in effect, gives them a slightly left of centre ideology. The Liberals, once advised by the Royal Commission and the outside experts, were prepared to implement a programme with massive implications for social and political change. The idea of redistribution of wealth, accomplished through fair assessment of real property and equalization grants, was abhorrent to the Conservatives. Their feeling was that the depressed areas of the North Shore could improve their position through hard work and immigration, without government intervention. This was the attitude of the last Conservative administration, under Premier Fleming — which prided itself on having reduced the province's net debt by nine million dollars in eight years. In emphasizing such differences between the parties, the Equal Opportunity debate polarized the electorate even more than it had been polarized in the past. The Liberal party had its image as a French-Catholic party refined and the Conservative party became even more explicitly an English-Protestant party.

In the summer of 1966, a new element was added to this pattern of polarization and reciprocal hostility: the return to New Brunswick and New Brunswick politics, after an absence of six years, and the subsequent elevation to the leadership of the Conservative party of J. Charles Van Horne. During his fifteen months as Tory leader, Van Horne had a profound, if contradictory impact on the political system of the province. His rise to power illustrated that the establishment in the Conservative party could be thwarted; his successful by-election in Restigouche,[30] or more specifically his style of campaign, reduced even further his party's limited orientation to issues; his motions in the fifth session of the forty-fifth Assembly momentarily changed the nature of his party and at the same time made it easier for the Liberal government to introduce its language legislation; his campaign style during the 1967 general election introduced the ultimate wheeler-dealer, non-issue-oriented politician; his presence as party leader so split the Conservative party that this split was a factor in its 1967 defeat.

Van Horne projected the same messianic appeal in the rural areas that Diefenbaker possessed in the 1958 Federal campaign. His oratory was that of a prairie evangelist, but with northern New Brunswick colloquialisms.[31] He had the organizational skill of a Duplessis and attempted during the 1967 campaign to paint himself as a greater wheeler-dealer than W.A.C. Bennet, another native son. He was at various times an R.C.M.P. officer, a Canadian Army officer, a barrister, a businessman, a real estate developer, executive assistant to J.C. Irving, a federal Member of Parliament, party leader, and a Member of the Legislative Assembly. Yet even this wide range of occupations does not fully reflect his personality.

"Maverick" is the term most often applied to Van Horne by both the provincial and national press,[32] and the establishment of the Conservative party. He never exhibited the typical New Brunswick attitude, "my party right or wrong" — he criticized the Diefenbaker government on the floor of the Commons while a back bencher, supported the Liberal party against the Flemming government during the 1960 provincial election,[33] and opposed Hugh John Flemming in the Royal by-election in 1960, after Flemming had been appointed to the Diefenbaker cabinet. It would appear that Van Horne did not have a strong commitment to traditional party politics, that there was a populist strain in his political attitudes. While every politician attempts to convince the voters to cross party lines, with Van Horne this effort became a virtual fixation. He stressed that everywhere in the province traditional Liberals were casting aside their old political colours to join the Van Horne party, the peoples' party.[34] Likewise he had the ability to draw out the non-voter, no mean task in a province where there is substantial polarization between those who are deeply committed and those who are firmly apolitical.[35]

Van Horne was elected to the House of Commons in 1955 and re-elected in 1957 and 1958, but resigned in 1960 to work in real estate development in Canada and the United States. He returned from California in the summer of 1966,[36] and immediately upon his return the political scene took on an exciting new light.

There was considerable dissatisfaction among Conservatives with the somewhat dispassionate leadership of Cy Sherwood. Sherwood had been chosen party leader in 1962, after having served unofficially in this capacity since the defeat of the Flemming government in 1960, but many in the party felt that he was not sufficiently aggressive to confront in the Assembly, let alone defeat at the polls, the personality of Premier Robichaud. The dissatisfaction within the party grew, and after a party caucus in September 1966

29There was an identical response from some when Dr. Frankel recommended collective bargaining for New Brunswick public servants.

30The by-election on February 6, 1966, not his later by-election on November 4, 1968, which he also won.

31For example, his favourite remark that the Government seemed to be "dog dancing."

32E.g., *The Daily Gleaner* (Fredericton), November 25, 1966; *Star Weekly Magazine* (Toronto), October 17, 1966; and *The Globe and Mail* (Toronto), October 20 and 21, 1966.

33*The Daily Gleaner* (Fredericton), June 17 and 20, 1966.

34The Conservative slogan in the election campaign made no reference to the Conservative party, simply, "Van Horne for the People."

35In the 1963 provincial election, 15,958 voted in Restigouche, with a difference of only 360 votes between the Liberal who led the polls (three running) and the bottom Conservative (three running). In the February 1967 by-election, the Liberal candidate polled 7,000 votes, a drop of 646 votes from that polled by the top Liberal in 1963, yet Van Horne won by 2,673 votes, a net gain of over 2,000 votes, with no significant population increase in the riding. A few tombstones may have voted in 1967, but in essence Mr. Van Horne brought out 2,000 more votes than the 1963 Conservative candidates were able to do.

36It has been implied many times that Van Horne was brought back from California by the Irving interests, for whom he once worked, but no evidence is available to prove or disprove this allegation.

Sherwood resigned.[37] Richard Hatfield, a young Carleton County lawyer and businessman, scion of an old provincial family, was the first announced candidate for the vacant leadership. He was followed by Roger Pichette, a former minister in the Flemming government, and, in due course, by Van Horne.

The entry of both Hatfield and Van Horne into the leadership race was the beginning of a party split. Hatfield was the establishment choice, the man groomed by Sherwood and others for eventual leadership, the candidate of the "respectable Tories."[38] Van Horne, on the other hand, was the candidate of the frustrated, who had been chafing in opposition for six years, who felt Sherwood's leadership had been ineffective and that Hatfield was, like him, "too nice a guy."[39] But Van Horne's wheeler-dealer financial activities,[40] his support of the Liberals in the 1960 general election, his general "irresponsibility"[41] did not sit well with the traditional Conservatives, who attempted to secure the election of the more responsible Hatfield. The means by which Van Horne stifled this opposition is a classic study in political strategy and illustrates the difficulty that an opposition leadership has in keeping its troops in line without a partronage system at its disposal. Initially, a Conservative M.L.A. from Saint John, a St. Stephen businessman and former minister in the Flemming government, and two University of New Brunswick professors planned on marshalling opposition to Van Horne. He realized that the latter two had no following within the party and hence posed no threat; he went over the heads of the former two to the basis of their political support, swung the rank and file in their organizations, and forced them to capitulate. The Van Horne method of obtaining delegate support was straight-forward: if the local party leaders were sympathetic to him, he had them deliver the delegates; if the leadership was opposed, he went over their heads, got the grass roots support,[42] and in that way brought most of the local party leadership into his camp.

The outcome of the leadership convention was a foregone conclusion: Van Horne won handily.[43] But the party split, with the traditional Conservatives momentarily withdrawing as the Van Horne people moved into the ascendency. The attitude of one of the professors who had opposed him was indicative: "I am a man temporarily without a party."[44] There is evidence that these dissident Conservatives either did not work or expended only marginal effort during the 1967 campaign.

Van Horne's immediate concern after winning the leadership was to secure a seat in the Assembly. Due to the death of the Liberal Health Minister, a vacancy existed in Restigouche, and Van Horne received the party nomination for the February 6, 1967 by-election. His campaign in Restigouche was a microcosm of the campaign he conducted for the October 1967 general election. It was characterized by a total lack of policy discussion and an emphasis on bread and circuses — dances, socials, Ski-doo parties, white cowboy hats,[45] ball point pens, cigars, gimmicks galore — even George Hees riding on a fire engine with Van Horne. The Van Horne strategy was to get people to the public meetings so they could see what a fine fellow he was: a "swinger," a wheeler-dealer-manipulator, the guy who would get things done once he got to Fredericton. The Van Horne attitude toward issues and policies was that they were non-existent. Discussing campaign tactics in a television interview on March 8, 1967, his advice to his party was to:

Appoint a master of ceremonies, and have him rent the biggest hall he can find . . . provide some lively music to accomodate the spirit of the evening . . . if the rally begins at eight o'clock, start the music thirty minutes before that . . . speeches should be short, off the cuff, positive, and to the point . . . don't mention the name of your opponent or any other party . . . keep the length of the meeting to no more than ninety minutes . . . afterward, mingle with the crowd, shake hands, and have the musicians stick around . . . if the younger set wants to have a dance afterwards, let them.[46]

Van Horne won the by-election, sat as opposition leader for one session, and suffered personal defeat as the Conservative party was defeated in the October election. In one sense the epitome of the non-issue politician, in another sense he may have made a contribution to the lessening of racial tensions with his linguistic motion in the Assembly. Van Horne, while leader of the opposition, used a legislative tactic that Robichaud had used while opposition leader of presenting motions so wide-ranging in scope that it is next to impossible for the government to vote them down. The theory behind their usage, in an Assembly where private members bills and motions are very rarely introduced, was that a government that used its majority to vote down a motion that favoured motherhood and was against sin would receive adverse public reaction. By introducing a motion calling for the recognition of French and English as the two official languages, Van Horne created a

---

[37]The official version was that Sherwood called for a re-appraisal of the leadership, saying that he would take a few days to decide whether to re-offer. A credible version of what happened is that party dissidents, notably the president of the York Progressive Conservative Association, succeeded, over the objections of former Premier Flemming, in having Sherwood dropped.

[38]The Hatfield slogan, "Victory with Honour," suggests the kind of support he was trying to elicit.

[39]This was the standard refrain of delegates at the time of the leadership convention, particularly the day before the actual balloting.

[40]Star Weekly Magazine (Toronto) October 17, 1966.

[41]Tom Bell, Member of Parliament for the then riding of Saint John-Albert, nominated Van Horne at the leadership convention and when asked by the *Globe and Mail* why he had, is quoted as stating: "the mood of New Brunswick tends at the moment to be irresponsible . . . and Charlie is the guy who can fit that mood. He tends to be irresponsible . . ." *The Globe and Mail* (Toronto), February 4, 1967.

[42]Some such pressure may in fact have been brought to bear on Bell who, by temperament at least, was initially a Hatfield supporter.

[43]The official results of the balloting, although never announced, were as follows: Van Horne 458, Hatfield 135, Pichette 9.

[44]This was only one of a considerable number of defections from the party from among the ranks of the respectable Conservatives.

[45]This could probably be classed as the Van Horne trademark: white felt with a blue band, on which was printed "Pour le Peuple Van Horne for the People."

[46]Provincial Affairs Telecast, CHSJ-TV, March 8, 1967: *Telegraph Journal* March 9, 1967. Van Horne's final remark in relation to the young is of some interest, for while it is unusual to see younger people at political meetings, he attracted them in droves. In retrospect, it would seem that they were there not to be politicized but rather to socialize, as it was usual for Van Horne to hire a rock group whenever he held a meeting. During the general election the Conservatives hired Don Messer and the Islanders, who were allegedly not paid for performing, and the 1969 leadership convention, which chose Hatfield over Van Horne, had to do without live music.

climate of acceptability for the government's Official Languages Act when it was ultimately introduced. Although the Conservative Party and the WASP of the Saint John River Valley had virtually ignored the problems of the French in New Brunswick, the Van Horne motion demonstrated an awareness, on the part of some Conservatives, of the Acadian fact.

It is characteristic of New Brunswick's political climate that social inequalities have perpetuated themselves by circumscribing (through inadequate educational and other facilities) the political awareness of those who would most benefit from reform. Consequently, effective change must often be generated at the level of the party leadership and imposed "from above." Even Van Horne is no exception to this rule, since his grass roots support was largely cultivated, and he related to it more as choirmaster than as spokesman. But the principle is more clearly illustrated by the career of Premier Robichaud, who armed a personal belief in the social obligations of the state with the extensive powers of his office.

Robichaud's egalitarianism may have grown in part out of his own experience of ethnic and class barriers. Prohibited by lack of funds from attending the University of New Brunswick Law School, he articled in a small law office in Buctouche and eventually passed both the provincial and the U.N.B. law examinations, the second with high honours. Moreover, his studies at the Social Science School at Laval in the charged political atmosphere of the Duplessis regime doubtless reinforced his committment to social change.

Besides the Programme of Equal Opportunity, mentioned earlier, one of the Robichaud government's most significant reforms was the integration of Acadians into the economic and cultural life of the province. Through legislation and Orders-in-Council, Acadians received senior positions in the public service, a French-speaking Deputy Minister was appointed to the Department of Education, and L'Ecole Normale and L'Université de Moncton were structured to provide post-secondary education to Acadians in their own language. The Official Languages Act of 1968, though not completely proclaimed during the Robichaud administration, also establishes the right to use French in the courts, in the Assembly, and in dealing with the provincial bureaucracy.

Equally important, though perhaps more difficult to effect, were changes in the mechanics of the party system. In 1967, Robichaud introduced collective bargaining for public servants, including those who were hired on a casual-patronage basis. The upshot of this has been that when Conservative patronage committees have attempted to secure the dismissal of casuals appointed by the Liberals, the Canadian Union of Public Employees has stepped into the breech. CUPE has had about ninety per cent success in bringing cases of alleged political firings to arbitration. However, there has been considerable opposition to CUPE, both from local patronage committees and from much of the populace. The reaction of one Charlotte County MLA is perhaps typical.

. . . doing away with the patronage system — where those who work for you are favoured by you when you are in power — wouldn't that be doing away with the democratic system?[47]

The announcement by Premier Robichaud of a provincial election for October 26, 1970 was in one sense unexpected, but in another was fully predictable. While the calling of by-elections in Restigouche and Albert counties after the deaths of the sitting Members was interpreted by many as a sign of the premier's reluctance to risk a general contest, increased road construction and resurfacing provided one indication that this course was at least being considered. In fact, the Liberal caucus had discussed the possibility of a 1970 election as early as December, 1969 since, due to the slimness of his majority and the ill-health of several Members, the Premier feared defeat in the Spring Assembly session.

The Liberal campaign promised a continuation of programmes of social reform instituted during the past ten years, and the establishment of "pollution guidelines" and a guaranteed annual income. The Conservatives, whose campaign slogan was "It's time for a change," promised a Law Reform Commission, redistribution of multi-member constituencies, and general reform of the electoral system. They also promised to create 40,000 jobs by coordinating the efforts of various agencies to attract industry to the province.

The Conservative party secured electoral victory by taking a total of six seats from the Liberals: three in Moncton, two in Sunbury and one in Edmundston. Preliminary analysis shows that in Moncton, the Acadian elite and the working-class English were voting Conservative for diametrically opposite reasons. The Acadians felt that they had received all the redress they could expect from an Acadian Premier, and that in fact an English administration might be able to implement controversial sections of the Official Languages Act (to which both parties were by this time at least officially committed) with less opposition from the English electorate. It was felt too that in the formulation of policy, Hatfield's personal interest in Acadian problems would prove superior to the traditional sympathies of his party. The working-class English voter, on the other hand, saw in the Conservative party a potential source of relief from the language policies of both the federal and provincial governments.

The policies of the federal government were a factor as well in the Liberal defeat in Sunbury county. Canadian Forces Base, Gagetown is the only large-scale employer in the county, and the town of Oromocto is a direct result of the decision of the federal government in the 1950's to locate the largest military base in the Commonwealth in Sunbury. Preliminary analysis shows that many in the area, both civilian and military, were concerned about Ottawa's present and future defence policies. The civilians were apprehensive that, after the 1967 re-ordering of military priorities, further cutbacks would place the entire local economy in jeopardy. The military population apparently felt that government pay increases had been too late and too little. In both cases, discontent with the Federal party was expressed in a sense vicariously by a rather dramatic turn against the provincial Liberals. In

47 *Telegraph-Journal* (Saint John) March 31, 1971.

1967 the Liberal majority was approximately 1.7 to 1 in Oromocto and Base Gagetown; in 1970 it was 2 to 1 in favour of the Conservatives.[48]

In most areas the traditional ethnic identifications of the parties seem to have been strengthened in 1970. The Conservatives made gains in the English areas of Albert, Carleton, Charlotte, Fredericton, Kings, York, and Saint John West and stayed constant in Saint John Centre and Saint John East. Liberal support increased in the French counties, the areas of their traditional strength.

As shown in Table II, the percentage of the electorate voting was smaller than in the 1967 election.

TABLE II

	1970	1967
Provincial Turnout	81.9%	83.9%
English Areas (Average)	79.2%	81.6%
French Areas (Average)	85.1%	87.0%
Mixed Areas (Average)	81.5%	83.0%

Again, as in 1967 and 1963, the highest turnout was in the rural French areas such as Restigouche where 89.4% of the electorate voted (91.3% in 1967); the lowest turnout was in the English urban areas such as Saint John Centre where only 71% of the electorate voted (74.9% in 1967).

In general, voter turnout in the last three elections has been higher in rural than in urban, and in French than in English areas. One explanation for the former might be the parties' greater visibility in rural areas, as well as the close association of personal and political loyalties. In rural communities, elections are significant social events, often vitalized by inducements such as two-dollar bills, mickeys of rum, or boxes of chocolates. Along with these favours, which often have the status of obligations, gratuities may be paid to people working for the party on election day, with the effect of encouraging them to bring their extended families to the polls.

The higher voter turnout among Acadian than among English New Brunswickers could be a reflection of the Acadians' sense of exclusion from the economic and social elites in the province (there is an Acadian elite in Moncton but it is strictly localized). Consequently, Acadians may have a higher incidence of voter participation both because their interest is in changing rather than maintaining the status quo, and because their access to other forms of political leverage is restricted. In Bathurst and Edmundston, for example, where the only industry (pulp and paper) is English-controlled, the heavy Acadian vote may be an attempt to counter balance this power.

IV. CONCLUSION

Politics in New Brunswick have more colour than content. The politicians are less concerned with issues than with the parish pump; but this may be what the electorate wants. To an outsider, the patronage system may appear abusive; to the people it may seem to fulfill their needs more effectively than can institutionalized bureaucracies. To the democratic theorist, the imbalance between constituencies and the existence of multi-member ridings may appear unjust; to the people it may appear as the only way that an Irish-Catholic can get elected. To the urban dweller from Toronto, such election day activities as the sale or barter of votes may seem like something out of Tammany Hall; to the people, it's a few extra dollars and a lot of fun. To the urbane political scientist, the behaviour in the Assembly may appear infantile; to the people it's "the boys havin' a bit of fun." To the rest of the country, politics here may appear insupportably rustic; to the people of New Brunswick their style is preferable to the mass media politics that merchandise candidates like so much soap powder. But the electoral system and Assembly are still in need of reform, great families run the political affairs of some areas, non-issue-oriented politicians and a substantial patronage system prevail. Yet the people prefer their political system the way it is. Is there anything in democratic theory that implies that even when the people are wrong they are right?

---

[48]Compiled from the Report of the Chief Electoral Officer, Twenty-Sixth General Election, p. 19, and *Telegraph Journal* (Saint John) October 27, 1970. It might be suggested that the Liberal defeat in Sunbury was aggravated by the absence of a considerable number of officers and men on loan to civil authorities in Quebec during the "October crisis." The author's feeling is that if these troops had been home in time to vote, the Conservative majority would have been higher.

* NEWFOUNDLAND *

The Only Living
Father's Realm

SUSAN McCORQUODALE

In 1933 the report of a Royal Commission authorized to inquire into "the future of Newfoundland and in particular to report on the financial situation and prospects therein . . ." recommended among other things that the "country should be given a rest from party politics for a period of years."[1] The report recognized that Newfoundland was a small island caught in a worldwide depression, but nevertheless it reached the conclusion that much of the blame for the financial failure could be laid at the door of the extravagant political malpractices of successive governments during the years 1920—1931. The principal recommendations of the Amulree Commission were accepted, and between 1934 and 1949 party politics, at least in their most obvious manifestation, disappeared.[2]

The events of the 1930's stand in sharp contrast to those of the 1940's. In the latter period "politics" returned to the island when a new dynamic leader awoke the people to new political choices, culminating on March 31, 1949, when Newfoundland changed her constitutional status to become the tenth province in the Canadian federation. "Confederation" was thus doubly a new beginning: on the one hand the province turned her back on her history as an independent nation; on the other hand, after an interregnum of fifteen years the manifest garments of a modern, elected democracy were put on.

I. THE HISTORICAL BACKGROUND

Newfoundland has a present population of just over 500,000, nearly 40 per cent of which is concentrated on the Avalon Peninsula at the southeast corner of the island, furthest from the Canadian mainland.[3] There are few urban centres: St. John's has a population of 80,000 and Corner Brook, the next largest centre, has a population of 27,000. About 40 per cent of the people live in communities of under 1,000. The primary reason for this scattering of population is fish. Until the twentieth century, Newfoundland was regarded largely as a convenient way-station, far out in the Atlantic, useful for the "prosecution of the fishery." Today, while not as important economically — coming fourth in the Gross Provincial Product — the fishery is important socially. It employs about 15 per cent of the labour force and plays a role much like agriculture in developing countries: acting as a sponge to absorb a growing labour force for which other economic opportunities have not opened up.[4]

Economically, Newfoundland is a "have-not" province. The average unemployment rate (about 15 per cent) is the highest in Canada, about 30 per cent of rural families receive below $1,500 per annum while only 14 per cent of Newfoundland families receive $6,000 per annum, compared with upwards of 30 per cent for Canada as a whole. While still the lowest in Canada, income is improving. In 1965 the per capita income ($1,195) represented 60 per cent of the national average ($1,988) as compared with 51 per cent in 1950.[5]

Newfoundland's population is overwhelmingly British in ethnic origin — 93.7 per cent of her people are of Anglo-Saxon or Celtic stock, and 98.5 per cent are English-speaking only[6] Her divisions are not ethnic; they arise from religious and class antagonisms. Newfoundland has her share of battles between "Liberals" and "Conservatives," but tied into these divisions are folk images of old battles between Protestant "establishment" and Roman Catholic "reformers" in the nineteenth century, overlaid by liberal, largely Protestant movements in the twentieth century, and further complicated by the alleged anti-confederate attitudes of Roman Catholics.

A. The Early Years

While present-day orators like to claim that Newfoundland is "Britain's Oldest Colony," in point of fact the legal existence of a colony was not acknowledged by Britain until 1824. Before that successive English governments either ignored the settlers or actively sought to drive them off the island (while at the same time disputing the French claims to the fishery). The system of representative, but not responsible, government, tried out in 1824, was not a great success: tied in with the political defects were social conflicts, largely stemming from denominational antagonisms. In the early

---

[1]Great Britain, *Newfoundland Royal Commission,* 1933 (Lord Amulree chrm.), Cmnd. #4480.

[2]During this period the Commission of Government made efforts to informally sound out public opinion and municipal politics continued in St. John's.

[3]D.B.S., *Census of Newfoundland, 1966.* Total population of Newfoundland — 493,396; Total population Avalon Peninsula — 198,514.

[4]*Royal Commission on the Economic State and Prospects of Newfoundland and Labrador* (St. John's, 1967), pp. 16 and 179.

[5]D.B.S., *National Accounts, Income and Expenditures, 1967.*

[6]A Preliminary Report of the *Royal Commission on Bilingualism and Biculturalism* (Ottawa: Queen's Printer, 1965), pp. 192-196.

nineteenth century the population was approximately one-third Roman Catholic (for the most part Irish labourers brought over by the English fish merchants), one-third Anglican, and one-third non-conformist. But each denomination was not equally influential, and political struggles were coloured by this skewing of the influence patterns. The antagonism climaxed in the election campaign of 1861, when three men were killed and twenty wounded.[7] Expediency dictated a solution: religious representation in administrative appointments, in the personnel of the courts and, in fact, in all public offices.[8] This solution was later reinforced by the system of public education, which remains entirely denominational.

The twentieth century began for Newfoundland as a time of relative prosperity. Public interest in union with Canada was at a low ebb, having failed to arouse support both in the 1860's and the 1890's. The railway had been built, and by 1911 the age-old fishery disputes with France and the United States were settled. However, the beginning of World War I shattered hopes; before the end of the war, Newfoundland had seen over 5,000 of her men in arms and had added over $13 million to her public debt.[9]

The pre-war years had seen the rise of a new political force on the northwest coast of the island, the first genuine effort to unite fisherman into one great union. At its peak, the Newfoundland Fishermen's Protective Union had had about 20,000 members. Between 1908 and 1932 it was very important to the social, economic, and political life of the colony. It was the first such organization to stress to the fishermen that they were being robbed by the merchants and the government, that they should be proud of their calling, and that by organizing themselves into local, district, and national councils they could gain the political experience which, in the absence of local government, they lacked. The leader of the FPU was W.F. Coaker. In 1912 he made the decision to go into party politics by allying himself with the Liberals, at this time led by Sir Robert Bond, a former prime minister and a progressive who had looked beyond internal conflicts and had sought to bring Newfoundland into the international arena. Bond and Coaker lost the election in 1912, but clearly the new force was one to be reckoned with. The FPU ran eleven candidates and all of them won; five of the seven Liberals elected also won in "fishermen" districts.[10]

The election of 1919 saw the victory of the man who has been called the "political ancestor of J.R. Smallwood" — the new Liberal leader, Sir Richard Squires. Squires and Coaker fought and won the election as one political party, but in actual fact the bloc of fishermen's seats held the balance between the thirteen seats won by Squires and the twelve seats held by the opposition Conservatives. Coaker became Minister of Marine and Fisheries and introduced a new system of fish marketing (the "Coaker Regulations") which, at least in the beginning, stood a fair chance of winning merchant support and of organizing a chaotic situation. Unfortunately, the promises failed to materialize, the steam went out of the FPU, and when in 1924 scandal touched Squires, the government was forced to resign, only to return again in 1928.[11]

The economic dislocations of 1929 produced new political problems and by 1931 the twin pressures of a fall in the world price of fish and rising public debt at home were forcing Newfoundland into disaster. In 1929 the public debt stood at $87.7 million, by 1931 it was perilously close to $100 million and interest payments on the debt reached nearly 65 per cent of the average revenue over the preceding years.[12] Between 1931 and 1932 the value of exports fell from $33.5 million to $26.6 million.[13] The fishery failed in three successive years. One-quarter of the population was on relief. In spite of drastic cuts in expenditure, increased taxation, and desperate searches for alternative solutions, the government in 1933 was finally forced to request help from the United Kingdom.

B. The Commission of Government

The British Government promised in 1934 that when Newfoundland became self-supporting again responsible government would be restored on the request of the people. Economically, it was evident by 1945 that World War II had made Newfoundland "self-supporting"; she had in fact a financial surplus of $40.3 million when in 1949 she joined Canada.[14] Politically, as events turned out, it was to take four year and three elections for Newfoundland to decide on the future form of government and at the same time accept the leadership of the man who for the next twenty years would dominate the life of the new province.

First, in June 1946, delegates were elected to a National Convention called by the British Government to offer suggestions for a new form of government. Then came the first referendum vote on the choices put to the people. The results were:

Commission of Government — 14.3%
Confederation with Canada — 41.1%
Responsible Government   — 44.5%

It was necessary to hold a "run-off" referendum in July 1948, and the result was victory for Confederation.

[7]G.E. Gunn, *The Political History of Newfoundland 1832–1864* (Toronto: University of Toronto Press, 1966), p. 182.

[8]The phenomenon persists. In 1962 the Hon. J.L. Cheeseman, himself an Anglican, brought to the attention of the House of Assembly that out of six Senators in Ottawa not one was a member of the Church of England. "It is rather strange," he said, "when one-third of the population are Anglicans." ". . . it is generally considered here that seats will be proportionately distributed. The Anglicans of Newfoundland have no representative in the Senate." *Daily News* (St. John's), February 6, 1962.

[9]Great Britain, *Newfoundland Royal Commission,* p. 41.

[10]J.R. Smallwood, *Coaker of Newfoundland* (London: Labour Publishing Company, 1927), p. 35.

[11]In the election, Squires ran in Humber, a west coast district now "humming" as a result of an earlier decision to open a paper mill in the area. His personal victory was decisive (83 per cent of the vote) and his campaign manager was one Joseph R. Smallwood. G.O. Rothney, *Canada in One World* (Toronto: House of Grant [Canada], Ltd., 1966), p. 182.

[12]St. John Chadwick, *Newfoundland Island Into Province* (Cambridge: Cambridge University Press, 1967), p. 155.

[13]*Ibid.,* p. 155.

[14]*Royal Commission on the Economic State and Prospects of Newfoundland,* p. 419.

The delegates to the National Convention were instructed to "consider the financial state of Newfoundland and make recommendations on possible forms of future government." By the time the Convention first met in September 1946, the battle lines and the leading advocates of alternative courses had become clear: Joseph R. Smallwood, a populist politician and journalist who, after twenty-five years, had found the cause he had been searching for — Confederation of Newfoundland with Canada; Major Peter Cashin, a maverick member of the establishment who wished to see the island return to the proud tradition of four hundred years — independence and responsible government; and Chesley Crosbie, a respected member of the establishment who pleaded for the anti-confederate halfway house of economic union with the United States.

The British Government had made it a condition of election to the National Convention that the candidates had to reside in the districts they represented. This gesture towards grass-roots democracy went somewhat against the political traditions of Newfoundland, where outport constituencies were often but not invariably represented by men living in St. John's. Despite this attempt to broaden the base of politics, not one fisherman was elected. Only four of the delegates had had experience in the pre-1934 House of Assembly; two were lawyers and one a former magistrate, while many of the new men were co-operative field workers or teachers.[15] The Convention was able to put together a loose majority of anti-confederates out of those who favoured the return to full self-government and those who wished to see the Commission of Government retained, plus those few who held on to the hope of economic union with the United States. But it was not a "party" in the accepted sense; it lacked a leader and a clear sense of what it was for rather than what is was against. Smallwood, on the other hand, dominated his small group of confederate supporters and together they looked and acted more like a party.[16]

The debate over confederation revealed the peculiar regional, class, and religious nature of the battle. The centre of the anti-confederate movement was in St. John's; its dominant elements were merchants and Roman Catholics. Opposed were the residents of the 1,300 small and isolated communities around the island: fishermen and loggers who were largely Protestant. The roster of the key members of the Responsible Government League read like a "Who's Who" of the establishment.[17] The Roman Catholic Archbishop of St. John's was a known and implacable opponent of union with Canada, a position not shared by his fellow bishops in Grand Falls and Harbour Grace. But Archbishop Roche authorized a series of articles in a Catholic journal which succeeded in arousing a Protestant reaction. Jamieson records that sectarian bitterness was widespread and that "the greatest issue in the history of Newfoundland public life was dominated, in the dying days of the campaign [for the second referendum], by a full-fledged Catholic-Protestant feud."[18] The accepted mythology of the day, that somehow Confederation was a Protestant movement, ignored the facts that the vote cut across religious lines to a marked degree and that there were many Protestant communities virtually solid in their support for responsible government.[19]

Equally stressed in the accounts of the events from 1945 to 1949 is the emergence of the mass media, in those days primarily radio, as an instrument for reaching and creating public opinion. The communications pattern developed at that time was to carry Smallwood successfully through many future electoral campaigns. He was an experienced propagandist by 1945. Initially by means of radio, then via a lively, colourful newspaper and finally by well-publicized meetings in areas he knew to be "confederate," Smallwood projected himself and his cause successfully to an audience hitherto ignored and apathetic. The National Convention had almost defeated Smallwood in 1948 by the simple expedient of refusing twenty-eight to eighteen to put the choice "Confederation with Canada" on the ballot slips. But the daily proceedings of the Convention had been, for the full eighteen months preceding, broadcast over the government-owned radio network. Throughout the island, in homes, lodges, and halls, people had gathered to hear the broadcasts and thousands had become deeply and personally involved with the issues: for the first time they listened to *their* politicians talking about *their* country.[20] During this time Smallwood had directed almost his every word at the microphones and to the audience beyond. After the Convention's negative decision he tested the strength of his link with public opinion by reaching over the delegates' heads and calling upon the support of the people of Newfoundland. "Within days a blizzard of telegrams descended . . . on St. John's. These contained more than 50,000 signatures all asking for the inclusion of [the] Confederation [option] . . ."[21] The British government, responding to a plea it wished to hear, rejected the avowed function of the Convention and itself put the Confederation choice on the ballot. If we measure voter turnout alone, the campaign to awaken the people of Newfoundland was eminently successful. In 1946 only 20 per cent of those eligible had voted in the National Convention election.[22] By contrast 88 and 84 per cent respectively of the electorate participated in the referenda elections.

Another technique of persuasion that was to serve Smallwood well was initiated at this time — wavering supporters could be strengthened and opposition bought off with government appointments. On a train trip across the island with delegates to the National Convention aboard, Smallwood used this technique to such good effect that "at least three delegates disembarked convinced they were to become Minister of Finance, there were

[15]Hon. W. J. Browne, "The Case for the Restoration of Responsible Government," *The Book of Newfoundland* (1967), III, 127; and Richard Gwyn, *Smallwood, The Unlikely Revolutionary* (Toronto: McClelland and Stewart, Ltd., 1968), p. 80.

[16]Smallwood has himself said that the "dictator" charge so frequently laid at his door (unjustly) after he became premier, could have been attributed to him with greater truth during the referenda campaigns.

[17]D. Jamieson, "I Saw the Fight for Confederation," *The Book of Newfoundland*, III, 88.

[18]*Ibid.*, p. 103.

[19]*Ibid.*, p. 92.

[20]Gwyn, *Smallwood*, p. 84.

[21]Jamieson, "I Saw the Fight," p. 85.

[22]A.B. Perlin, *The Story of Newfoundland* (St. John's, 1959), p. 53.

also five potential chairmen of the Liquor Board and would-be Senators were as common as spruce trees."[23]

II. THE POLITICAL PARTIES, 1949-1968

The results of the first referendum had given the advocates of responsible government the idea that their cause was certain to win over confederation; they had led the poll 69,440 to 64,066. Support had come from St. John's, from the old business families, from the management of the largest papermill company — Bowaters of Corner Brook — and from the Roman Catholic Church. Their appeal had been to nationalism, conservatism, and fear of economic domination. These appeals had been successful in thwarting union with Canada in 1896. They were not destined to be so in 1949. The reasons for failure lay partly in the changed circumstances produced by Newfoundland's tentative steps into the twentieth century; partly in the opposition — a small band of dedicated followers with a clear cause, led by a man supreme in his skill as propagandist and organizer; and partly in the proponents of responsible government themselves — overconfident, they made too many assumptions. They were amateurs who ignored the fact that the confederation forces had breached many of the strongholds of the Responsible Government League on the Avalon Peninsula, and that overwhelming support in Roman Catholic Districts produced over-reaction in Protestant areas. Roman Catholics, after all, constituted only one-third of the island's population.

The Responsible Government League and the economic union activists made a clumsy joint effort against Smallwood in the seven weeks between the first and second referenda. But the businessmen and lawyers who surrounded Cashin and Crosbie were successful merely in discouraging the younger supporters of economic union, men like Jamieson and Stirling who perhaps alone were capable of an active, driving campaign. Moreover, opponents of confederation were running into a situation they were to face even more acutely in the future: the comparative lack of funds. The leading men on Water Street and the paper companies were unwilling to back their cause to the same extent that Liberals in Ottawa were backing theirs. Smallwood, billing himself as spokesman for the poor outporters, had had the use of a seaplane, motor transportation and cash for the traditional outlays for beer, rum, and votes. Gwyn suggests that the Confederate Association had amassed a fund of close to $150,000.[24] In the dying days of the Confederation battle, Smallwood fought hard to overcome the religious bigotry being aroused on all sides and he added respectibility and tone to the cause when the newspapers made it clear that several leading citizens had seen the light. The 22,000 voters who had voted for retention of the Commission of Government were wooed with the announcement that two of the Newfoundland Commissioners, Pottle and Quinton, were now working for the cause of Confederation.[25]

The result of the second referendum was just under a 7,000 vote majority for Confederation: 52.24 per cent in favour and 47.76 per cent against. Prime Minister King was agreeable to calling this an expression of the will of the people "clear and beyond all possibility of misunderstanding". In June 1948 negotiations over the Terms of Union proceeded in Ottawa and on March 31, 1949 Newfoundland joined Canada. Smallwood had virtually single-handedly changed the course of his island's history.

While the Ottawa talks proceeded, Smallwood was taking the steps through which the victorious Confederation Association became the Liberal party. In August Smallwood went to Toronto and dramatically introduced himself to the National Convention of the Liberals. In April of the next year he called a provincial convention where some 1,500 Newfoundland delegates were called together to achieve two purposes: to select Smallwood as leader of the Liberal party and to choose the candidates for the first provincial election. The first was unanimously achieved (and was the last time for twenty years that the party would officially express its confidence in him) and the second proceeded by a uniquely Smallwood method. The groups of delegates were supposedly free to elect the candidates for their respective districts. But one such nominee has recorded that Smallwood "had him down" for Bonavista South; that the delegates from the district were not all that keen on him and would have preferred a waiting "native son"; and that it was only after Smallwood met with the delegates and reminded them that they had chosen him to do an important job, and that he needed the right kind of men to help him, did they agree. Thus it was that Bonavista South — which in 1932 had defeated one J.R. Smallwood, the Squires' candidate — found its candidate and elected him with a 2,000 vote majority.[26]

By turning the Confederate Association into the Liberal party, Smallwood allied himself with a Canadian political party which had a national record of electoral success; he allied himself with his own pre-1934 party; and he provided years of campaign oratory to the effect that since all confederates were now Liberals, it followed that all Progressive Conservatives were anti-confederates. In a province where an ever increasing majority became persuaded of the benefits of Confederation, the Liberals thus assured themselves of years of electoral victories.

For the anti-confederates the choice was whether to remain a local party or to ally themselves with the national Progressive Conservatives. After the second referendum the diehards of the League for Responsible Government and economic union met in February 1949 with J.M. Macdonnell and Richard Bell. "Out of a crew of dissidents" the new Provincial Progressive Conservative party was born. The leader of the party, who within two years was out of Provincial politics and running for mayor of St. John's, has said that his party's defeat in 1949 was not so much by men as by cheques: Old Age Pension cheques and Family Allowance cheques which appeared as promised in the two months preceding the first provincial election.[27] The issue

[23]Gwyn, *Smallwood*, p. 79. Supported by Jamieson, "I Saw the Fight," p. 72.
[24]*Ibid.*, p. 99.
[25]Both these men joined the first provincial cabinet and one later became a senator.
[26]Ted Russell, "My Political Memoirs," *Evening Telegram* (St. John's), October 28, 1966.
[27]H.G.R. Mews, as quoted in the *Evening Telegram* (St. John's), January 1969.

in that first election, as it was to be for years, was personalized; voters either supported or were opposed to Smallwood. The Conservatives changed their leadership six times in sixteen years searching for an alternative personality. The first two elected leaders, J.G. Higgins and M. Hollett represented old, elite St. John's.[28] In 1959 J.J. Greene took over the leadership at the age of 31. He was son and grandson of politicians (his grandfather was prime minister in 1894) and remained leader until 1966. He resigned then in order to return to his law practice and the leadership fell to Dr. N. Murphy, who held it for only eight months. He had been elected in Humber East in 1962 and it was hoped that his accession to office meant a new electoral drive beyond the confines of the Avalon Peninsula. Unfortunately for the Progressive Conservatives the "big gun" of Smallwood himself was turned on their leader. As had been the case in 1959, when Hollett had been defeated in a direct fight with Smallwood, so in 1966 Smallwood and a young Corner Brook lawyer, Clyde Wells, running as a team in the two Humber seats defeated their respective Progressive Conservative and New Democratic Party opponents. The first full-time leader the Conservatives had had, Gerald Ottenheimer, was elected from St. John's East in 1966. Young, well educated (Ph.D in literature), and wealthy, Ottenheimer began a drive to bring new life to his party. A Leadership Convention held in May 1970 chose a federal M.P., Frank Moores, as the man who would lead the party in Smallwood's last election fight, called for October 28, 1971.

The Conservatives as they organized themselves in 1949 were aware of the disabilities of geography, class and religion they had inherited from the Responsible Government League. But as the leadership difficulties illustrate, for the first eight years of Confederation the party was bogged down in internecine squabbles; funds from national headquarters were spent unproductively and the Progressive Conservatives presented no real alternatives either in terms of policies or leadership.

In the two subsequent provincial elections after 1949 Smallwood easily gained victory. It is alleged that he scarcely bothered to campaign in 1956 and still won thirty-two out of thirty-six seats.[29] He quickly learned the techniques of parliamentary procedure and became the master of the House of Assembly. He began with a wave of reform legislation and created administrative machinery geared in many respects to the best models that either Ottawa or Toronto could provide. He invested heavily in education and medical care for children and those living in outports. He enthusiastically tackled the problems of economic development and industrialization. But many mistakes were made, and before the initial phase of the "revolution" was over Smallwood's chosen economist had been sentenced to four years in jail for fraud, some $30 million had been wasted, and Newfoundland was still backward and tied to the fishery.

Zest for the political battle and Smallwood victories in two more provincial elections came out of the federal Progressive Conservative victory in 1958. Diefenbaker and Smallwood clashed over two issues: the first arose out of the International Woodworkers of America strike against the Anglo-Newfoundland Development Company in western Newfoundland. In 1959 Smallwood enacted "the most punitive anti-labour legislation of any post-war

Canadian government other than that of Duplessis."[30] Violence resulted, and the RCMP's request for additional men to maintain order was refused by the federal cabinet. Federal-provincial relations were further strained that same year over "Term 29." This was one of the original Terms of Union negotiated in 1949 and dealt with a review of Newfoundland's fiscal position once Confederation had shaken down. A federal Royal Commission had recommended an annual grant of $8 million to Newfoundland in perpetuity, but Diefenbaker chose to make this grant only until 1962, when Newfoundland's position would be considered along with that of all other provinces. Smallwood denounced this as a violation of the Terms of Union. In August 1959 he called an election to gain a mandate and split the Conservatives over the issue of loyalty to Newfoundland versus loyalty to a national political party — an issue which attacked them at the very roots of their origin and support. The result was the defection of prominent Conservatives and the creation of the United Newfoundland Party. The party ran nine candidates in 1959 and won two St. John's seats. Their activities were condemned by the Progressive Conservatives as a ". . . three-way split of the anti-Smallwood forces which would guarantee the Liberals every seat."[31] In fact the Liberals elected one less candidate than in the previous election. By 1962 the United Newfoundland Party was dead. One of its leaders lamented that "had it been formed shortly after Confederation when local feelings for Newfoundland as a separate country still ran high, it probably would have had a much larger following. As it was by 1959 the intense local loyalists were beginning to fade and become vague under pressure of Confederation."[32]

The echoes of 1959 lingered into the 1962 federal and provincial elections. In the federal election Smallwood ran a personal campaign against W.J. Browne, the Solicitor-General in the Diefenbaker cabinet, as a representative of a government that had flouted the province's rights in the International Woodworkers of America and Term 29 disputes. This claim was symbolized by the appointment of United Newfoundland party member John O'Dea as campaign manager for the Liberal party's challenger in St. John's West.[33] A study of the voting during this election suggested two points which will be dealt with in this paper: the degree to which Roman Catholics vote Progressive Conservative and the inability or unwillingness of voters in Newfoundland to distinguish between federal and provincial politics.[34]

The provincial election which followed in November 1962 has generally been accepted as a "quiet" one. Smallwood had launched the election to gain support for a "great fishery programme, something special, something big

28Jamieson, "I Saw the Fight," p. 81.
29Gwyn, *Smallwood,* p. 126.
30*Ibid.,* p. 209.
31Statement of A.D. Pittman, Corner Brook President of the Progressive Conservative Association, quoted in *Daily News,* (St. John's) June 15, 1959.
32A.M. Duffy, quoted in *Canadian Annual Review* (1962), John T. Saywell, ed. (Toronto: Canadian Annual Review Publishing Co., Ltd. 1963), p. 47.
33George Perlin, "St. John's West," in J. Meisel, ed., *Papers on the 1962 Election.*
34*Ibid.,* pp. 12 and 14.

which must be done for our fisheries. I don't know what it is [yet] but I'm going to make a strong bid to find out."[35]

The result was the worst defeat Smallwood had yet suffered; one of his cabinet ministers was defeated and the Progressive Conservatives won seven seats, three of them off the Avalon Peninsula, and an Independent won in Labrador West thereby creating an opposition of eight, the largest yet faced by the Liberals.

In general the early 1960's were quiet years. More legislation was enacted to prevent strikes or lockouts in hospitals, but to balance such sanctions, the Newfoundland Federation of Labour was in 1963 permitted to present a brief to cabinet for the first time in seven years. The antagonisms of 1959 appeared to be lessening.

In 1963, when the Liberals returned to power in Ottawa, the earlier decision of Smallwood to pick J.W. Pickersgill from Manitoba as the member from Bonavista-Twillingate began to pay off. Massive hydro developments at Churchill Falls in Labrador and at Bay d'Espoir on the island were getting started, and the Trans-Canada Highway linking the island from east to west was paved. In addition, various Centennial projects were creating employment and once again a great fisheries programme was envisioned which would require an estimated $100 million over five years. Between 1963 and 1967 Newfoundland became Ottawa's favourite province. Pickersgill used his influence to dot the island with rural post-offices, authorized $14 million in improvements to the ferry links between the island and the mainland, provided subsidies to bail out Eastern Provincial Airways, and transferred responsibility for St. John's Harbour and its annual deficit to the National Harbours Board.[36]

The provincial election in 1966 climaxed the mood of prosperity. Smallwood fought "the first modern election campaign in Newfoundland's history" and spent an estimated $300,000 doing it.[37] He hired a Toronto advertising company and ran a campaign, based on motivational research, that stressed Labrador and hopes for the future rather than gratitude for Confederation. He fielded a younger team which injected needed vitality into the house and the cabinet, and wound up killing the Conservative hopes of the previous election and taking all but three seats.

This election has since been regarded as the beginning of the end of Smallwood's dominance; it is seen as an expression of gratitude to the Premier for past efforts, a last acknowledgement of the old style of demagogic politics before the onset of a younger, better educated, urban electorate searching for a more modern political style. Smallwood had set out to transform Newfoundland society, to bring material progress to his people and to encourage their participation in their own political future. But like Coaker before him, driven by frustration and impatience, he often took these new tasks into his own hands. Such "take-overs" were made of the co-operative movement, the fishermen's union, and municipal government. In building the province Smallwood has created a new economic elite apart altogether from the old Water Street establishment. The building contractors, the government supply firms, and a developing tertiary segment of the economy are tied closely with the Liberal party. New countervailing influence patterns in the economy are becoming apparent. In time economic diversification may generate political diversification. Traditional social forces have largely shaped Liberal party policy — for example Smallwood's excessive care vis-a-vis the churches on the question of denominational education and his willingness to entrench in the British North America Act the authority and privileges of the Pentecostal Assemblies. Paternalism, an element in pre-1934 Newfoundland society and politics, was encouraged in the post-1949 government. The Liberal Association of Newfoundland, for instance, existed only on paper. In reality Newfoundland was the personal fiefdom of the Premier, with all the lines of patronage and power running through his hands. In 1964, for instance, a group of Young Liberals met in Grand Falls and demanded a voice for their group in the Liberal party. Smallwood, the complete politician, absorbed their discontent by giving in and calling a meeting to reorganize. His choice for president of the youth group was Peter Cook, son of Senator Eric Cook, president of the senior Liberals. But the delegates elected Clyde Wells, a young Corner Brook lawyer. Smallwood and Wells fought as a team for the two Humber seats in the 1966 election, and it was Wells who joined John Crosbie in 1968 in their defection from cabinet.

The Conservatives regrouped themselves about their new leader, Ottenheimer, at a time when they were faced with either new life or death. One of the contributing factors in the almost complete victory of the Liberals in 1966 was the disarray of the Conservatives. Their leader, Dr. Murphy, had remained uncommunicative in Corner Brook and as always they had found it hard to find candidates. (One such has recorded that he was asked to run at 11 p.m. on the day before nominations closed and yet managed to come within 128 votes of winning.)[38] The Gander district became the one to watch in 1967. First, in a provincial by-election, the Progressive Conservatives turned an 1,100 vote defeat in the previous election into a 900 vote victory; the next month, in a federal by-election, the encouraged organization reduced the Liberal majority in Pickersgill's old seat from 6,400 votes to 1,700.

In June 1968 the tide for the Liberals ran out. Newfoundlanders, like all Canadians, had watched the election of two new national party leaders, but it appears that the decisive issues were local, not national. Smallwood's strategy since 1949 had been to fight federal elections as if they were provincial campaigns. This time it did not work to his benefit. After twenty years what local newspapers called the "inevitable reaction" occurred.[39] All over the island the opinion was expressed that it was time for a change. A tough budget, a cutback in capital expenditures, the discrediting of Smallwood's administration in a report on the province's economic prospects, the defection of

[35] J.R. Smallwood, quoted in *Canadian Annual Review* (1962) p. 47.
[36] Gwyn, *Smallwood*, p. 287.
[37] *Ibid.*, p. 281.
[38] R. Penny, "The Progressive Conservative Party of Newfoundland—An Exploratory Study," (unpublished term paper, Memorial University of Newfoundland, 1968), p. 35.
[39] Editorial, *Evening Telegram* (St. John's), June 27, 1968.

two prominent Liberal cabinet ministers, Smallwood's questionable tactics during the election — all contributed to the Liberal defeat, aided by a resurgent Progressive Conservative party fielding aggressive candidates backed by good organization.[40] Smallwood was severely shaken by the upset, but bounced back with an effort to establish a "new" Liberal party with an elaborate grass roots organization, and promised in a qualified manner to resign the leadership of the party at a nomination convention to be called late in 1969.

The history and achievements of the CCF-NDP in Newfoundland can be briefly told. One CCF candidate ran in St. John's East in the first federal election of 1949. Of the 18,170 votes cast, he won 197 (1 per cent). In all, the party contested fourteen times for federal seats between 1949 and 1965. Its largest overall share of the vote, which it received in 1962, was 4.9 per cent. The party's difficulty in obtaining candidates and maintaining an organization between elections can be seen when it is noted that only four of the nine candidates ran in more than one election. In St. John's East there was no Federal NDP candidate between 1949 and 1962.

The story at the provincial level is much the same. The party's initial thrust came in 1956 when ten candidates were fielded under the label of the Newfoundland Democratic Party. A total of thirteen districts have been contested during various elections, but in only five of them was a campaign mounted more than once. During the 1962 and 1966 elections a deal was apparently made between the NDP and the Progressive Conservatives in which the Conservatives agreed to contest only Humber East and to leave Humber West to the NDP. The result was an upsurge in NDP voting in Humber West. Ed Finn, leader of the party, came within 240 votes of defeating the Liberal cabinet minister and won 48 per cent of the vote. But in 1966, the NDP's candidate was opposed by Smallwood himself and its share of the vote fell to 33 per cent. In general terms, the NDP suffers from being too orientated to the "mainland" in leadership and policy. Moreover, in the context of the Newfoundland political culture there is no place for a mass party with a progressive philosophy; to many outport voters, at least until very recent years, it was almost presumptuous to question what the "big fellows" were doing. The tradition lingers on: political battles are fought between Liberals and Tories; third parties are regarded as intruders.

III. THE ELECTORAL SYSTEM

This study will now turn to an analysis of provincial voting results and outline some information on the size and religious composition of the constituencies. Tentative conclusions will be drawn with regard to the voting patterns.

Smallwood and the Liberal party have dominated Newfoundland electoral results since 1949, and this has been true since the original referenda campaigns. Out of twenty-seven electorial districts, nine voted for Responsible Government in the first referendum. At the second referendum only seven districts maintained their anti-Smallwood position, and in the first provincial election in May 1949, only four of the original nine gave their support to the Progressive Conservatives — successively lost were Bonavista South, Carbonear, Port de Grave, Harbour Grace, and St. John's West (the latter four all on the Avalon Peninsula). Electorally the Liberals have continued to dominate, and their dominance has held also at the federal level — that is, until the June 1968 election.

TABLE I

Newfoundland Provincial Elections 1949—1966

	Per cent Turnout*	Total Seats	Accla- mation	Liberal Seats (% total vote)	Conservative Seats (% total vote)	Others
May/49	76	28	0	22 (65%)	5 (33)	1
Nov/51	58	28	5	24 (63)	4 (35)	0
Oct/56	59	36	5	32 (66)	4 (31)	0
Aug/59	68	36	1	31 (58)	3 (25)	2
Nov/62	57	42	2	34 (58)	7 (36)	1
Sep/66	64	42	3	39 (61)	3 (34)	0

TABLE II

Newfoundland Federal Elections 1949—1968

	Per cent Turnout*	Liberal Seats (% total vote)	Conservative Seats (% total vote)
June/49	58	5 (72%)	2 (28)
Aug/53	57	5 (67)	2 (28)
June/57	52	5 (62)	2 (38)
Mar/58	74	5 (54)	2 (45)
June/62	72	7 (59)	8 (36)
Apr/63	69	7 (64)	0 (30)
Nov/65	66	7 (64)	0 (32)
June/68	66.3	1 (43)	6 (53)

*These voter turnouts are the lowest in Canada.

40*Ibid.*

Conservative voting strength has been concentrated on the Avalon Peninsula. The geographical strength of the party can be demonstrated as follows:

TABLE III

Median Percentage (rounded) of Conservative Constituency
Vote in Provincial Elections 1949—1966

Year	Avalon Peninsula	Non-Avalon Peninsula
1949	51	20
1951	37	14
1956	41	24
1959	34	29
1962	45	33
1966	31	27

The total vote for the Liberal party's candidates in provincial elections across the province has thus never been less than 58 percent. In the seventeen years between 1949 and 1966 they have never had less than 80 per cent of the seats in the Legislative Assembly. In terms of Schlesinger's definition of party systems, Newfoundland is clearly the only Canadian provincial example of a one-party system.[41] At the federal level the picture, until 1968, was no less decisive. The Liberals had averaged about 60 per cent of the vote and in three of the seven pre-1968 elections had won all the seats. The only conclusion we can draw in view of the reversals of June 1968 is that significantly the break came first at the national level — if in fact a definite swing away from the Liberals has occurred. In both the United States and the Canadian national scenes, the federal party has tended to be more competitive than the respective state or provincial ones.[42]

The individual provincial districts vary considerably in the number of registered voters. After the 1962 redistribution they ranged in size from the 1,109 eligible voters in Labrador West to 9,902 in St. John's South. Over the five provincial elections from 1949 to 1962 the median size of a district was 5,850 registered voters.[43] Accepting any size either 25 per cent over or under this median as an "average-sized" district, it is calculated that of the forty-six districts named between 1949 and 1962 some twenty-three (50 per cent) fall within the average category — leaving seven districts "too large" and sixteen districts "too small". The Progressive Conservative vote in these districts is shown in Table IV.

These figures suggest that St. John's is considerably under-represented. The median number of voters is 56,800 for the city districts (leaving out the essentially "urban" voters in surrounding districts). Given the provincial median of 5,580 voters, St. John's should on the principle of strict equity be entitled to about ten seats, where it actually has six. Redistributions in 1956 and 1962 did not materially affect the positions of either the government or the opposition in the St. John's area (see Table V).

TABLE IV

Median Vote of Progressive Conservative Party
Provincial Elections 1956–1966 (rounded)

Districts over 7,312 voters in size	Progressive Conservative Vote (%)
Humber East	43
Humber West	29
St. John's East	57
St. John's North	39
St. John's West	40
St. John's South	54
St. John's Centre	55

Districts under 4,388 voters in size	Progressive Conservative Vote (%)
Bay de Verde (1962 election only)	42
Ferryland	53
Hermitage (acclamation 1962)	0
Labrador North	20
Labrador West (Independent elected 1962, joined Progressive Conservatives)	55
St. Mary's	37
St. Barbe North (1962 election only)	10
St. Barbe South	50
St. George's	30
White Bay North	17

TABLE V

Election Results — St. John's

Victories	1949-1951	1956-1959	1962-1966
Liberals	3	3	3
Progressive Conservative	5	5	7
UNP*	0	2	0

*United Newfoundland Party — a splinter Progressive Conservative group which fought only the 1959 election.

41 J. Schlesinger, "A Two-Dimensional Scheme for Classifying the States According to Degree of Inter-party Competition," *American Political Science Review*, XLIX (December 1955), 1120-1128.

42 J. Rasmussen, "A Research Note on Canadian Party Systems," *Canadian Journal of Economics and Political Science*, XXXIII, No. I (February, 1967), 98-106.

43 These and the following figures are based on a compilation of *Federal and Provincial Election Statistics for Newfoundland* by David Day, Staff Writer for the St. John's Evening Telegram, St. John's, 1966.

On the other hand, Labrador is considerably over-represented. In 1962 it had a total of 5,588 registered voters, "entitling" them to one member (using our median) when in point of fact it returned three, two Liberals and one independent (the latter turned Conservative in 1966).

The drawing of constituency boundaries in Newfoundland has traditionally been governed not by population or geography but by religious denomination. It was the pre-1932 practice to attempt to draw boundaries so that each district would have a majority of its members adherent to one religious denomination and that the total in the House of Assembly would bear a near proportion to the overall religious balance of the island. By 1935 this practice was running into difficulties because of population shifts, and in fact 44 per cent of the members represented constituencies in which there was no denominational majority.[44] When Smallwood took over in 1949 he continued with the districts as drawn by the Commission of Government. His first opportunity to redraw boundaries came in 1955 and the result was a new version of the denominational balance in the House. In the first place, the formula was changed to a "one-third, one-third, one-third" rule which was "wrong" on two counts: the population breakdown in 1961 was Roman Catholics 35.7 per cent; Anglicans 28.5 per cent; United Church 21.4 per cent and other 14 per cent; and, secondly, the traditional rule was representation strictly according to population. This meant that as the House was increased to thirty-six seats in 1955 the Anglicans were "entitled" to eleven seats, not the twelve seats allotted to them under the "one-third" rule, the United Church to nine, the Salvation Army three and the Pentecostals one.[45]

Even if the new version of the rule were accepted, some peculiar things happened to at least one Roman Catholic seat. In the original draft of the bill, Harbour Main in the Conception Bay area of the Avalon Peninsula was destined to end its life as the last dual riding in the province. But during the course of the debate the government announced that a twelfth Roman Catholic district was needed and that the choice had fallen on Harbour Main. The opposition pointed out that there were 9,500, 8,900 and 8,800 registered voters respectively in St. John's Centre, East, and South. Why should the 6,000 voters in Harbour Main be given the extra seat? Could the reason be an anticipation of the results of the election, since only 41 per cent of the St. John's voters chose the Liberal party, while in Harbour Main the Liberal vote was 55 per cent. Equally, asked the opposition, why divide St. Mary's and Placentia East, giving each new constituency a member, when together they did not have the population of any of the three new districts in St. John's?[46]

In 1962 when redistribution increased the House to forty-two members, Mr. Smallwood congratulated himself that the balance was now 14-14-14 when in point of fact what he achieved was the under-representation of urban areas that just happened to have a tradition of Conservative voting. It should be added here that however "unfair" the boundaries, at least one geographic fact is taken into consideration. The Avalon Peninsula contains about 40 per cent of the population of the island and with a total of seventeen seats it accounts for about 40 per cent of the seats in the House. The trouble is that urban St. John's loses out to rural Bay de Verde, St. Mary's, and Ferryland.

TABLE VI

Percentage of Roman Catholics
(1961 census) and Liberal Vote in Provincial Districts *

DISTRICT	% of Population Roman Catholic	% of Vote Liberal — 1956		% of Vote Liberal — 1959	
St. Mary's	99.5	Bonavista N	92	White Bay N.	90
Ferryland	97.6	Trinity N	90	Labrador	84
Port au Port	92.4	White Bay N	89	White Bay S	80
Placentia E	82.7	Labrador (2)	86	Twillingate	80
St. George's	67.7	Twillingate	85	Grand Falls	80
Bell Island	57.6	Fortune	84	Burin	80
Placentia W (2)	56.3	Burin	82	Bonavista N	80
Harbour Main	53.1	White Bay S	82	Carbonear	79
St. John's (5)	49.9	St. Barbe	80	Burgeo	77
Burin	36.6	Green Bay	80	Fogo	76
Grand Falls	36.4	Trinity S	80	Fortune	76
Fortune	35.0	Placentia E	75	Bonavista S	72
Humber W	33.5	Port de Grave	74	Trinity N	70
Labrador (2)	27.4	Gander	74	Gander	70
Humber E	26.8	Bonavista S	71	Placentia W	70
White Bay S	26.5	Port au Port	70	Harbour Grace	69
Carbonear	26.0	St. Mary's	70	Port de Grave	65
Harbour Grace	22.5	Carbonear	70	St. Barbe	65
Port de Grave	22.5	Ferryland	68	St. George's	63
Gander	20.8	Humber W	67	Green Bay	61
St. Barbe	17.4	Burgeo	66	St. John's (5)	61
White Bay N	15.5	Bell Island	60	Port au Port	60
Fogo	12.58	Humber	60	Ferryland	60
Bonavista S	12.4	St. George's	60	Humber W	55
Bonavista N	10.5	Harbour Grace	60	Placentia E	55
Trinity S	10.2	Grand Falls	56	St. Mary's	55
Trinity N	5.4	Harbour Main	55	Humber E	54
Green Bay	5.1	St. John's (5)	41	Harbour Main	50
Twillingate	3.0			Bell Island	40
Burgeo-LaPoile	2.1				

*Data on religious breakdown of the individual constituencies was supplied by Mr. Michael Staveley, Department of Geography, Memorial University of Newfoundland.

With constituency boundaries drawn according to religious considerations, it is useful to discover the precise strength of the various denominations in each provincial constituency and to relate this to Liberal voting to
determine the extent of the correlation. Data from the 1961 census was applied

[44] G.O. Rothney, "The Denomination Basis of Representation in the Newfoundland
Assembly, 1919—1962," *Canadian Journal of Economics and Political Science*, XXVIII
(1962), 562.
[45] *Ibid.*, p. 566.
[46] *Ibid.*, p. 567.

to the boundaries used for the 1956 and 1959 elections. The analysis could not be carried into the 1962 and 1966 elections because of the 1962 redistribution. The hypothesis being tested was whether there was a correlation between Roman Catholicism and Conservative voting.

A statistical test using Pearson's Product Moment Correlation Co-efficient[47] indicates that there is no significant relationship between the percentage of Roman Catholics in a district and the percentage of Liberal voting. The strength of the relationship is simply a reduction of 11.2 per cent. In other words, there is a very weak correlation between Roman Catholicism and Liberal voting when we consider the island as a whole. The assumption that Liberal voting can be predicted on the basis of religion cannot be statistically substantiated. On the other hand, in St. John's there is apparently an overall correlation, which might be related to other factors, such as traditional anti-outport attitudes, differing economic bases, etc.

A study of Newfoundland's political parties is a study in virgin territory. The principal research efforts of the author are reported on in the following section. There are gaps — virtually nothing is said about party finances, mass attitude sets in the electorate, linkages between the provincial and national party organizations, or the policy postures of the parties — but a start has been made.

IV. THE NEWFOUNDLAND HOUSE OF ASSEMBLY

During 1968 a study was undertaken of the current membership of the Newfoundland House of Assembly. This took the form of structured interviews with all but six of the forty-two members. Biographical data were obtained for all members and where appropriate will be included. The interview schedule was adapted from that used by Kornberg in his 1962 survey of the Canadian House of Commons.[48] This survey research information is rare as regards the province of Newfoundland.

In terms of legislative experience, the Newfoundland House of Assembly has a very high turnover rate. In Newfoundland the life of a parliament has averaged 3.8 years and nearly 75 per cent of the members elected serve less than two terms.

TABLE VII (a)

Members of the Nfld. House of Assembly,
Turnover 1949–1968 (%)

Served one term	45
two terms	29
three terms	10
four terms	16
five terms	4
six terms	5
	(N = 100)

Of the 9 per cent who have served at least seventeen years all but one (P.J. Canning) have also served as cabinet ministers. The men recruited are generally (41 per cent) between 40 and 49. The age at entry into the House is as follows:

TABLE VII (b)

Nfld. House of Assembly — Age at Entry (%)

20–29	7
30–39	25
40–49	41
50–59	17
60–69	8
Over 70	1
	(N = 100)

So transient a membership in a legislature sponsors weakness on the part of government backbench and opposition members alike. Power and influence flow to the cabinet.

A. The Cabinet

In size the Newfoundland cabinet has grown from eleven during the interim government of April and May 1949 to eighteen as of July 1968. Of that interim cabinet, three did not appear in the first elected cabinet of May 29, 1949. Two apparently chose not to run again and the third ran and lost in Placentia-St. Mary's, thus becoming the first of only three cabinet ministers to suffer defeat at the hands of the Newfoundland electorate.[49] From May 1949 to April 1967, some twenty-eight men had served in the cabinet and, while it is difficult to be wholly accurate, they appear to have served as shown in Table VII(c).

Table VII(d) shows that from 1949 to 1962 the median age of the cabinet steadily advanced. During the 1966 election, Smallwood made an effort to bring younger men into his cabinet and the median age took a sharp downward shift to 51.5 years as of January 1967.

[47]Pearson's Product Moment Correleation Coefficient is

$$r = \frac{NE\,XY - (EX)\,(EY)}{[NE\,X^2 - (EX)^2]\,[NE\,Y^2 - EY^2]}$$

The regression equation is $y = a + bx$. For further descriptions see Hubert M. Blalock, Jr., *Social Statistics* (New York: McGraw-Hill Book Company, 1960), ch. 1.

[48]Allan Kornberg, *Canadian Legislative Behavior: A Study of the 25th Parliament* (New York: Holt, Rinehart & Winston, Inc., 1967).

[49]M. Sinnott, Placentia-St. Mary's, lost by 144 votes in 1949; A. Johnson, St. John's West, lost by 1,395 votes in 1952; and C.M. Lane, St. Barbe South, lost by 173 votes in 1962.

TABLE VII (c)

Newfoundland Cabinet — Years in Cabinet

3 yrs. or less	2
4–7 yrs.	7
8–11 yrs.	3
12–15 yrs.	6
Over 16 yrs.	6

TABLE VII (d)

Year	Median Age of Cabinet
1949	48.5
1956	53.5
1960	57.5
1963	59.5

The size of the cabinet has raised questions, especially after an increase in July 1968. If we exclude the four members of the opposition and Mr. Speaker, it means that of the thirty-seven voting Liberals, eighteen are in the cabinet. Newfoundland has one of the largest provincial cabinets in Canada, and the only one where the cabinet nearly outnumbers the government backbenchers.

TABLE VII (e)

Size of Provincial Cabinets
(Parliamentary Guide 1967)

Province	Size of Cabinet	Seats in House	Govt : Opposition
Alberta	16	63	58 : 5
B.C.	15	55	33 : 22
Manitoba	12	57	31 : 26
N.B.	14	52	31 : 21
N.S.	14	43	39 : 4
Nfld.	18	42	38 : 4*
Ont.	23	108	78 : 30
P.E.I.	10	32	17 : 15
Que.	21	108	56 : 52
Sask.	13	59	32 : 27

*Figures as of July 1968.

B. The Cabinet Ministers

A study of the career patterns of the Newfoundland cabinet ministers shows that nearly all of them entered cabinet directly from private life, few had previous political experience, and almost none had had experience as back-benchers.[50] Of the twenty-eight men who have served between 1949 and 1967, ten (45 per cent) brought to cabinet a "political" background, having been members of the National Convention in 1946, early converts to the confederate cause, members of the Squires government, etc. The next largest group (nine cases) were either businessmen (contractors, owners of fish plants, etc.) or lawyers in private practice. The third category was a miscellaneous group of exdeputy ministers and magistrates (eight cases), nearly all of whom entered public life during the days of the reform-minded Commission of Government.

In social background the ministers are well educated, often coming from "political" families that have traditionally sent a son into politics. Formal education is as follows:

TABLE VII (f)

Newfoundland Cabinet — Educational
Levels Ministers Serving 1949-1967

University degree	11	(three Ph.D.s; four LL.B.s)
Professional or technical training	10	(six normal school)
Grade 11	6	
Unknown	1	
	(N = 28)	

Newfoundland's division are those of religion and class rather than ethnic origin. Uniformly the cabinet ministers are either English or Irish — even the one bilingual member born on the French island of St. Pierre comes of English stock. The religious breakdown for the whole sample is as follows: Roman Catholics, nine; Anglican, twelve; United Church, seven. Individual cabinets, however, demonstrate clearly that one of the characteristics of any Newfoundland cabinet will be its religious balance:

TABLE VII (g)

Cabinet of	1949	1956	1957	1963	1967
Roman Catholic	2(20%)	4	5	5	5(30%)
Anglican	5(40%)	4	5	5	6(35%)
United Church	4(40%)	3	4	4	6(35%)
	11	11	14	14	17

In addition, 70 per cent of the cabinet ministers were born in outports, a fact to be expected in view of their ages, but also something that links government and voters.

Kornberg in his study of the 25th Parliament notes that 46 per cent of M.P.s were elected to public office prior to their election to Parliament, that 73 per cent had held an office in their political party, and that only 18 per cent were complete amateurs. Of the members of the Newfoundland cabinet only 33 per cent (nine cases) had held elected office, 22 per cent had held an office in the Liberal party (six cases), another 20 per cent had gained "political"

50The exceptions being the seven ministers (not in our survey) who were promoted to cabinet in July 1968.

experience as activists in local interest groups (unions of teachers, fishermen, etc.) and some 25 per cent apparently came to office as amateurs. The category "office in their political party" tells us something about the state of organization of the Liberal party. Two of the ministers had been active in the Young Liberals, an organization founded only in 1964. Another was unofficially the "local rep" of the party in the district where he did business. He had in fact carried the Liberal campaign for seven federal elections. This unofficial, latent type of organization of men who can be counted on to conduct campaigns in districts where they are well known was the operational rule in party life. We can test this statement with reference to answers given to questions such as: "Have you ever held an office in your party?" or "How did you first become interested in politics?" and "Was there any particular person or group that encouraged you to enter politics?" Although the data for cabinet ministers is weak because our sample covers the whole period rather than the 1968 office holders only, it still is apparent that if we exclude the four or five ministers who joined the government in 1949, we have only one instance of a "self-starting" minister (who conforms in other respects to characteristics noted by Kornberg: "high class origins, early interest in politics, superior education and prestigious occupation").[51] In all other cases political recruitment occurred "because J.R.S. invited me," or "invited to run by J.R.S," or "J.R.S. asked if I wanted to do something for Newfoundland." Recruitment appears to lie at the invitation of Premier as head of the party rather than in the party as a differentiated organization.

As to the future expectations of the ministers, only five expressed a clear political intention: three claimed that they would not run for any other political office in the future; and two that they were clearly (and publicly) committed to being candidates for the leadership of the party after Mr. Smallwood's retirement. As for other ministers, none expressed an interest in public offices, judgeships, seats in the Canadian Parliament, or municipal politics.

In many respects the Newfoundland cabinet is an elite body in comparison with the society from which it comes. The members are generally better educated, have high status occupations, and more often than not come from relatively high socio-economic backgrounds. They have, presumably, been chosen to present a balanced religious face to Newfoundland society, fully as much as they have been chosen to bring ability, professional acumen or regional representation to cabinet discussions. In terms of their previous political experience, they apparently fall into two groups: the early converts to the Confederate cause who fought the campaigns with Smallwood and who add to the Cabinet an element of stability and personal acquaintance with the "good old days"; and the newer, younger men, better educated, ambitious, less particularistic in outlook, and eager to set themselves, their party, and the province in the mainstream of Canadian political life.

C. The Backbenchers

Our sample for the social-educational-political background of the House of Assembly numbers seventy-two. Of these we have data from interviews with all of the 1968 members of the House (twenty-six) and standard biographic data for the forty-six members who served between 1949 and 1965.

TABLE VIII (a)

Principal Occupations and Level of Education
Members of the Newfoundland House of Assembly 1949–1968

Occupation			Canadian M.P.s (%)§
Professionals*	27	(37%)	51%
Proprietor-Managers	26	(36%)	25%
Teachers†	8	(11%)	
Low status‡	11	(15%)	12%
	72		
Education			
University degree	25	(35%)	72%
Post Grade 11 training	17	(24%)	
Grade 11	19	(26%)	
Grade 10	2		
Unknown	9	(12%)	

*Includes master mariners, magistrates, and journalists as well as lawyers and doctors.
†Includes two policemen.
‡Includes one dairy farmer.
§Kornberg, *Canadian Legislative Behaviour,* p. 45.

As is true for the national scene, so it is in Newfoundland: members of the legislature tend to be members of a profession, usually law. The data for the province is insufficient to establish whether or not, as is true in Ottawa, the *proportion* of lawyers in the legislature has declined since confederation. The "over-representation" of lawyers is striking in a province where educational attainment for the population as a whole is the lowest in Canada; and even more striking is the fact that so high a proportion of the M.H.A.s are either the owners or managers of business concerns, when less than 8 per cent of the provincial labour force are classified by DBS as being in "managerial occupations."[52] At the other end of the occupation scale it is noteworthy that there have been through the years a fair number of members (six to eight) who rose to office as union organizers. Smallwood, as a self-proclaimed "socialist," apparently made an effort to attract a few "left-wingers" as counterweights to the heavy conservative bias in social background among Liberal legislators. In Newfoundland, largely associated with fishing in the public mind, in 1968 no member of the House listed his occupation as fisherman.

Class origin as determined by the status of the father is available only for the 1968 backbenchers. They are nearly equally divided (eight to nine cases respectively) between fishermen fathers and fathers whose occupation is variously listed as "clerical," "electrician," "carpenter," or "railway worker." Together these two categories make up 64 per cent of the sample, indicating that the members generally come from humble backgrounds. Of the remaining 36 per cent of the House, by stretching the definition of "professional", we have six fathers in this group (cabinet ministers, ships' captains, etc.) and three who were "businessmen" (lumbermen, coopers, etc.)

[51]Kornberg, *Canadian Legislative Behavior,* p. 52.
[52]D.B.S. 1961 Census, Series 3.1, Labour Force.

TABLE VIII (b)

Religious Affiliation of Newfoundland House of Assembly

	Liberal		Progressive Cons.		Ind. or UNP
Roman Catholic	11	(26%)	17*	(80%)	2
Anglican	17	(35%)	1		1
Salvation Army	1				
United Church	19	(39%)	1		
Unknown	0		2		
	48		21		3 (Total 72)

*Includes two men who began political life as PCs but subsequently ran for other parties.

TABLE VIII (c)

Birthplace of Members of Newfoundland House of Assembly

	Liberal		Progressive Cons.		Ind.	Totals	
St. John's	9	(19%)	11	(50%)	1	21	(30%)
Outports	34	(71%)	6	(28%)	1	41	(57%)
Foreign (including Canada)	4		6		0	4	(6%)
Unknown	1		5		0	6	(8%)
	48		22		2	72	

Tables VIII (b) and VIII (c) demonstrate the overwhelming proportion of Progressive Conservatives who are both Roman Catholic and "townies" (local jargon which expresses the traditional distrust between outporters and the residents of St. John's). On the other hand, the Liberals present a much more balanced position, although their religious balance by no means reflects that of the provincial population (for 1961 populations, see page 151, above).

The data indicates that overwhelmingly, Liberal members of the House were born in outports; and that over 40 per cent of the 1967 members of the House were born and lived in the districts they represented. Adding those born elsewhere but with family or business associations with the district and currently living there raises the figure to 50 per cent of members (both Liberals and Conservatives). A less "direct" representative role falls to another 27 per cent of the House because in this case, while there is a family or business connection with the district, the member lives in St. John's. Only 20 per cent (six cases) of the members have no personal or professional connection with their districts and do not live there. (This observation is not of course meant to imply that they are any less able as district representatives). But when we note that three of these six are young men first elected in 1966, it may be that Newfoundland is beginning to accept a less traditional political system of representation, and beginning perhaps to accept the idea that it is party label that counts fully as much as personal knowledge of the candidates. However valid this assumption may prove to be for the future, it remains the present rule that one of the qualifications any aspirant to political office in Newfoundland should have is personal connection with the district he wishes to represent. There is strong evidence to show the presence in Newfoundland of what might be termed "political families." Dealing only with the twenty-six backbench members currently in the House, ten come from politically active families — having fathers who were campaign managers for Squires, or were members of the National Convention — two are the sons of present-day cabinet ministers, and two the sons of former members of the House.

D. Political Experience and Recruitment

It would appear that in Newfoundland, participation in local government is a recognized avenue of access to legislative office. Although the percentage of members bringing political experience with them is considerably less than at the national level (36 per cent as compared with 48 per cent), this experience has been gained mostly as municipal councillor or mayor (nineteen out of twenty-six cases). This is all the more remarkable because the establishment of local government has been an uphill battle by the provincial government against massive resistance or indifference. This trend has become particularly noticeable since 1960 and it appears to be equally true for both sides of the House.

As for holding office in their party, nearly 50 per cent of the members (22 per cent of cabinet) report that they have been "associated" with the party, although not necessarily by way of formal office. Such association has consisted principally of acting as campaign manager for individual candidates in the local district, but has included such things as chairing political meetings, general activity during the Confederation battle, or membership in the youth organizations of the party. Very often the only formal link with the Liberal party has been as director or member of the executive of the Laurier Club, a St. John's social organization. Nevertheless, about 23 per cent of the present members entered the House as complete amateurs in the sense that they have never held either public or party office prior to becoming M.H.A.s.

Political recruitment presents a slightly different picture at the backbencher than at the cabinet level: the invitation by Smallwood is critically important to Liberals, but apparently there are more "self-starters" as well, approximately 20 per cent. In one case the member, having served several years as an organizer with the Liberals, went into a St. John's seat and for two years "nursed" the constituency. In another district the Liberal member, who came from a high status "political" family, busied himself in affairs of church, school, hospital and local government to such an extent that when he said he was willing to run, the party gladly accepted. In two cases we apparently have prominent men of the district recommending to Smallwood who the next candidate should be. We also have some evidence that the Premier consults with the "senior member of the district" as to the choice of candidate, and at least one member believes his name was picked at a meeting between J.R.S. and a prominent clergyman in his district. Finally, we have the four Progressive Conservative members of the House, obviously not chosen by J.R.S.

and just as obviously claiming to have been recruited through the normal nominating choice of party conventions, supplemented by invitations or encouragement from prominent leaders.

Between 1949 and 1968 there are at least five instances of men changing party labels in order to win a seat in the House of Assembly. A present-day member of the Supreme Court, for example began his political life as a Progressive Conservative, left the fold in 1959 over the Term 29 issue, ran and won in St. John's East under the United Newfoundland Party, and swept the full political spectrum when in 1962 he ran and lost in St. John's as a Liberal.

The combination of the relatively loose or informal affiliation with a political party added to a very clear dependence on the Premier, at least insofar as Liberal members are concerned, has implications for the Newfoundland political system. It suggests that members may not be intensely partisan and committed to the political party that recruited them into public office, as their counterparts at the federal level are reported to be. In Newfoundland partisan feeling and loyalty tend rather to focus on Mr. Smallwood. Access to office lies less in local prominence in and connection with a district and more in acceptability to the Premier. Support for this conclusion is found in answer to the question: "Do you think there are fundamental differences between the two major parties in Newfoundland? If so, what?" In the opinion of 65 per cent of the backbenchers the answer is "no." For those who feel differently on the matter the detected inter-party variation is thought to be produced by different approaches to "economic development" or by hazy partisan stereotypes, as when Liberals are seen as being "genuinely interested in the people" and the Tories, by contrast, are depicted as the "merchant party." But for the greater number party difference is simply a matter of "personality" or "leadership" (or, more cynically: "money"; "out-promise the other guy"). For most Liberal members the party is not separated from the current leader of that party.

Asked if they had future expectations in politics, 60 per cent of the backbenchers answered "yes" (seven of them were appointed to cabinet in July 1968). In one sense M.H.A.s in Newfoundland appear more ambitious than their counterparts in Ottawa, 75 per cent of whom have expressed themselves as satisfied with their present position).[53] The explanation probably is that at the provincial level there is ample room for political advancement, while in federal politics the greater range of theoretic options is counter-balanced by keener competition among M.P.s. In any case, the challenge and prestige associated with membership in the House of Commons is of a higher order than those commonly experienced in a provincial legislative role.

In social characteristics Newfoundland M.H.A.s represent an elite group although not to the same extent as M.P.s. In comparison with this latter group, fewer have professional occupations, more are businessmen, and fewer are the holders of university degrees. To a marked degree the M.H.A.s come from relatively high status homes, a fact all the more remarkable in comparison with the low economic level of the province as a whole. But perhaps their most striking group characteristics is the overwhelming degree to which they represent their districts as delegates from a cohesive traditional society. This point will be dealt with again in the section which follows. As for the avenue into politics, the interviews bring out the importance of an invitation from the Premier rather than the self-recruitment one might expect from such an elite group. Finally, entry to the House appears to most of the members to be the next step up from local politics and hopefully will eventually lead either to a cabinet appointment or office at the federal level.

E. Candidacy and Goals

The decision to "go into politics" in Newfoundland is apparently based on three motives: for about 55 per cent of the House (backbenchers and cabinet ministers alike) the most important thing was the invitation from the Premier to run. Some of the members mentioned a citizens group which called them to office, but for the majority the call came from Smallwood, who assigned them to a district. Kornberg found a similar but smaller group at the national level (22 per cent). He termed this an "unmotivated group" of legislators who were generally responding to local pressures.[54]

A second group of Newfoundland legislators share a motive with their Canadian counterparts, the apparent simple and powerful personal desire to become M.P.s; the size of the two groups is about the same, 35 per cent. This personal predisposition was expressed in terms of the "challenge" of the job, the desire to "gamble" or to be "where the action is." In other words, they enjoyed politics and wanted in.

A third motive expressed by the legislators is termed "policy-service" and means that for 10 per cent of the respondents (23 per cent at the national level) their desire to run sprang from a wish to do something either for the province as a whole or specifically for their districts. (The above should not be taken as mutually exclusive categories. The data record only the first response to a question about the decision to run for office in the first place.)

In the Kornberg survey, 47 per cent of M.P.s replied to the question "What are the most important things you want to accomplish?" in terms of national goals. This is a somewhat surprising response in view of the well-known limitations of backbencher influence in policy areas. When asked the same question Newfoundland M.H.A.s overwhelmingly (65 per cent) orientated themselves first towards their constituencies. The most important verbalized goals were expressed in terms of paved roads, hospitals, and employment opportunities. The following comments are typical:

Act as liaison between the district and the government. No delusions about policy.

Obtain services for my district, leave it with reasonable roads, power, and health.

One of the main reasons I ran was to obtain modern facilities. The settlements were isolated, now roads are there.

[53]Kornberg, *Canadian Legislative Behavior,* p. 55.
[54]*Ibid.,* p. 69.

For the remaining 35 per cent the goals were for the "country," i.e., Newfoundland, and provincial progress. Typical comments were:

I have strong feelings about Newfoundland, how difficult things have been for it, the need for industrial development. As a province we have to make a contribution to Canada.

I have a greater duty to Newfoundland. This is the province I love and I must do something for it.

Things are wrong here, I want to change things, improve education, economic opportunity, the involvement of our people.

It seems clear that for most of the provincial members, the focus of their representation is towards the constituency, towards a specific geographic area.

The next step was to ascertain how members carry out their representational roles. At the national level Kornberg arranged responses on a continuum.[55] First, at one extreme, were those who felt that they were required neither to consult with nor perform services for their constituents (a very small 15 per cent of "trustees"). Second, there was a larger group which tried to span the chasm between independent thinking and constituency influence (36 per cent of "politicos"). Finally, there was a third and largest group (49 per cent termed "delegate-servants"), who felt required to consult with the constituency and perform services as requested. In Newfoundland the responses do not quite correspond to these categories. In the first place only one member took the "trustee" role; "They elected *me*. I do what I think best." The balance struck in the rest of the sample was not between independent thinking and the constituency; rather it was between the district first or the province first. The initial response of 20 per cent of the House was to put the district first: "My first obligation is to the people who sent me." But for the largest single group (40 per cent), the first obligation was to the larger unit: "Province as a whole comes first, feel this way even as a backbencher." Only one Newfoundlander expressed any Canadian goals or responsibilities. These opinions do not appear to be influenced by political party, the age of the respondent, or by whether or not he represents a rural or urban district.

It seems reasonable to assume that provincial M.H.A.s, much like their counterparts in Ottawa, campaign on a province-wide ("national") platform and the member, pledged to support the policies of his leader, sees his first responsibility here. But considering the size of Newfoundland and the close personal ties that most members have with their districts, it is not unreasonable to expect that they will also find the role of "delegate-servant" congenial. When asked what they would miss most if they had to give up politics, 45 per cent mentioned "being around the district and meeting people."[56] For the 30 per cent who would miss policy involvement, the category includes those who enjoy "The sense of being part of it," those who value having the House as a forum from which to express their views, or those who express satisfaction in the work and relish the feeling that "J.R.S. can call on me."

The role of delegate-servant-ombudsmen can be measured in another way. Newfoundlanders write to or telephone their members a great deal. Twenty-eight per cent of the sample replied that the most frequent way their constituents got in touch with them was by telephone. Letter-writing seems almost equally heavy.

TABLE VIII (d)

Correspondence Per Week, Newfoundland M.H.A.s

Between 40 and 50 letters per week	17%
Between 20 and 30 ,, ,, ,,	17%
Between 10 and 20 ,, ,, ,,	17%
	51%

For 70 per cent of the members it is clear that what their constituents want are jobs, help with welfare problems and, occasionally, "reasonable" requests for municipal incorporation, hospital services, and so on. M.H.A.s like the personal satisfaction of helping people, but some also see it as a weakness in Newfoundland that the people look upon the member as an agent in St. John's; "inordinate" numbers rely overmuch on the member for service — "They think I am God Almighty" — and are too little concerned about personal responsibility. For the remaining 30 per cent the outlook is "broader" than the constituency, either because the respondents are cabinet ministers or part of the small opposition group, or because they are ambitious younger men, better educated and uneasy with "old-style politics."

When asked whether they thought that most of the time they knew how the rank-and-file in the district felt on major issues, 70 per cent of our sample replied with a straightforward "yes." What is equally interesting is the manner in which the members read public opinion. Nearly one-half the respondents claimed that they understand their districts. There is no need to *ask* about local opinion; they live in their districts and *know* the direction and intensity of collective opinion. In a second category (about 40 per cent) are those who, while they feel they are aware of local opinion, report that they find out what the district is thinking through talking to certain key people[57] who are "inherited" when a new member moves into the district. Members were specifically asked to rank certain groups from the stand-point of their usefulness to the members in providing good advice or information. Three points were assigned for a first choice, two points for a second, and one point for a third choice. The results were:

Personal friends and neighbours	56	points
Business Leaders	35	″
Party Leaders	33	″
Clergy	32	″

[55]*Ibid.*, p. 106.

[56]It is not easy to make the comparison on this question with the Kornberg study. At the federal level 31 per cent of the M.P.s combined "policy" satisfaction with constituency service, while 43 per cent expressed the psychological satisfaction of being "where the action is," where crucial national decisions were being made.

[57]This category has been quite strictly defined in that the term "key people" or "contacts" had to be used. The inference is that this is *more* than a mere sample testing of opinion. It denotes the deliberate effort to find personnel, a reliance on them and, as will appear in the next section, these men are in fact the "latent" organ of the Liberal party.

Only two members mentioned Union Leaders and "other" was listed as civil servants, visitors from the district, or other M.H.A.s.

It does not appear possible to relate these differential approaches to public opinion to variations in type of districts. Each opinion response category, for instance, includes some urban St. John's districts, some small island fishing districts, and at least one Labrador unit. Neither do the differential member responses to local opinion correlate strongly with the religious characteristics of districts, the political party of the member, differences in party affiliation, or variations in the educational, occupational, and experience of the members. At the national level it appears possible, for example, to assert that, ". . . in general, the better educated and those who had been in the business world or were members of a profession tended to select the less parochial roles."[58] This conclusion is not possible in Newfoundland. One is left only to speculate that differences in representational goals and style relate either to the social and historical character of districts or to the idio-syncratic preferences of sitting members.

F. Party Organization and Campaigns

When asked "How important was your party organization in determining the outcome of the last election?" some 80 per cent of Canadian M.P.s felt that parties were crucial to their success. In Newfoundland, by contrast, only about 40 per cent responded in this manner while another 40 per cent felt that the party was of no importance in their success. Indeed, in some cases formal party organization in the district was in fact unwelcome. The term "party," however, must not be taken too literally. Operationally speaking, what Newfoundland Liberals and Progressive Conservatives mean by party is a type of latent organization that becomes activated during elections. The party campaign workers are considered by members to be experienced and able. In some urban centres they are capable of running sophisticated campaigns.

On the other hand there are members who not only had no local organization, but often did not *want* one. A typical comment: "I'd rather be clear of them (i.e., party workers). My wife and I did it alone." The reasoning of this group is that while organization is necessary in larger centres, in rural areas the member ought to be able to do the job himself if he is any good. This is not to suggest that these members do not campaign with vigour — they do — nor that they are not glad to wear the political label "Liberal" and be known as "Joey's man."

The pattern of association between member attitudes toward party organization or campaign technique and variables such as party affiliation, rural-urban district characteristics and religion, is suggested below. Members favouring the old political style tend to be Liberal, Protestant, and representatives of rural districts.

In order to test party loyalty the Liberals only in our sample were asked whether they thought they could win in their districts as Progressive Conservative candidates. Rather more than 55 per cent felt that party image was the main determinant of their victory. For another 20 per cent of the Liberal respondents there is a mixed assessment: either they weigh equally the elec-

TABLE IX

	Party Organization Important	Party Organization Not Important
Political party		
Liberals	11	14
PC's	4	0
	15 cases	14 cases
Constituency		
Rural	3	12
Urban*	12	2
	15 cases	14 cases
Constituency religion		
Roman Catholic	6	2
Mixed	4	4
Protestant	5	8
	15 cases	14 cases

*Includes three districts which serve largely as "dormatory" suburbs for St. John's.

toral influence of party and candidate, or speculate they could win depending on who ran against them — whether for example they would have to face both a "J.R.S. Liberal" *and* a Conservative, or whether they would be allowed to run as an Independent. Finally, just over 15 per cent of the Liberals thought they could win their districts as Progressive Conservatives.

G. The Party in the House of Assembly

Formal organization of the legislature in the Province of Newfoundland seems minimal. At each annual session, several standing committees are set up and members appointed to them: Library and Standing Orders, Municipal Affairs, Privileges, and Elections. In general however, the work load is light, business tends to be transacted informally, and formal reports are seldom issued. Internal party organization appears even weaker. For the four Conservatives any meeting over coffee can be termed a caucus: among the Liberals there does not appear to be agreement on how often the party held a caucus during the 1968 session. About 50 per cent of the members set the figure at two meetings; another 25 per cent thought they met three or four times; and the rest alternatively set the figure at five, six or eight times, or some variant of "not very often". It appears that a caucus is held at the opening of the session — "Joe talks the whole time" — whose purpose is to inform the backbenchers, to "acquaint the members with the thinking of the Government." Then during the session members are free to ask for a caucus as needed: presumably these meetings will be more specific in terms, dealing with a cabinet crisis, the budget, denominational education, and so on. Backbenchers believe that there

[58]Kornberg, *Canadian Legislative Behavior,* p. 117.

have been occasions when their influence has been brought to bear on decision-making. A case in point was the withdrawal of a divorce bill in 1967 because public opinion in Newfoundland was not quite ready for it. The bill has since been enacted. Finally, government backbenchers, both individually and as groups, have informal access to ministers and the Premier in order to complain about and to suggest improvements in relation to public programmes.

This brings us to the question of the party leadership roles in the House. If a member had a problem, with whom would he discuss it, through whom would he approach the Premier? The members were asked, "Who are the party leaders on your side of the House? What would you say are the main reasons for their influence?" In scoring this question, it was taken for granted that Premier Smallwood held first place. What we were interested in discovering was the structure beneath him of informal influentials and intermediaries. First choices were awarded three points, second choices two points, and so on. Results (as of July, 1968) were:

T.A. Hickman, (Minister of Justice)	41	points*
L.A. Curtis, (President of the Council)	31	"
F.R. Rowe, (Minister of Education)	27	"
E. Roberts, (Minister of Welfare)	16	"

* Hickman joined the Progressive Conservative Party in February 1970.

This rating reflects both the younger and the older elements of the cabinet: Curtis and Rowe are older in years and in experience, Hickman and Roberts are younger men and were first elected in 1966. The basis of these ministers' influence is undoubtedly their relationship with Smallwood. Rowe has been his personal friend for twenty-three years, he has served in six different cabinet posts and is considered an able administrator, experienced with politics and the civil service. Hickman is bright, an able lawyer, active in church affairs before joining the government, and is considered honest and not tainted with politics. Curtis reaches back to the Squires days, and brings tremendous experience into discussions. He is also close to Smallwood. Roberts is the youngest and has been close to the Premier and the mainland Liberal party for six or seven years, first as National President of the University Liberals and then as Smallwood's Executive Assistant.

Another avenue of influence was explored with a question about the influence of the local party organization on M.H.A.s. When a similar question was put to national legislators their replies showed the importance to them of local opinion leaders as reference groups and that not only did such influence occur, but that it *ought* to.[59] Almost without exception the provincial legislators took another meaning from the question: no persuasion group would be allowed to use them. The local key men were judged not to be interested in the legislature, although they probably had a fair amount of influence on the Premier. The Premier had his cronies, whom he probably met out at Roche's Line (the Premier's home in the country). He was thought to rely heavily on local contacts during an election, and throughout the year they feed information to the Premier. Clearly it is at this level that important contact takes place. This result is not surprising in view of the dominant role of Smallwood as premier and Liberal leader; it is in his office that the decisions are taken. Secondly, the result is expected in view of the attitude of most of the M.H.A.s that they intuitively know their districts and that local opinion can best be ascertained by them in person. Interaction with non-party influentials is thus regarded by many as unnecessary and is not welcomed by a few.

A similar sort of misunderstanding occurred in connection with a question about pressure groups and their relations with members. They were often regarded as sinister organizations, groups to be avoided by an independent member. Many felt that external bodies could not use them as channels of influence: "My United Church never asked for a thing." On the other hand, once it was made clear that municipal councils could be considered as pressure groups, then nearly one-third of the members replied that they listened to and encouraged the development of municipal government, local improvement committees, and road boards. These encompass just about all the formal governmental organization there is on the island. It was the opinion of the members that the churches in recent years have exercised diminished influence and that the Federation of Newfoundland Fishermen either does not exist in their area or if it does, it is weak. None of the members from the industrial centres of Grand Falls or Corner Brook mentioned contacts with organizations, which may imply union leadership's assessment of the relative political strength of Newfoundland backbenchers. Often the contact between member and constituent is in a face-to-face setting. Either a fisherman will come alone, or a small group of men, often accompanied by their clergyman, will come to town to see the member and perhaps "Joey" himself. On the whole the community is considered "too rural" for organization although it is changing and "people are beginning to speak up a little more now."

When asked about their *own* membership in organizations, either professional, civic, or fraternal, the members indicated their attachment to at least one traditional Newfoundland association: 60 per cent of them are members of either the Masonic Lodge or the Knights of Columbus. Other than that memberships are scattered through the Bar Association, inactive (generally) membership in service clubs, athletic and sports clubs, or church committees.

In conclusion, political parties in Newfoundland during the last twenty years have lacked stable organizational structures. The Liberal party has been little differentiated from the leader of that party, and Conservatives until recently have had an organizational structure characterized by internecine warfare. In the House of Assembly the data have revealed the elite characteristics of the members, their relatively high socio-economic status, education, and occupations. Their roles have been shown to be largely traditional and they exhibit a remarkably close association with their constituencies. Local party organization viewed from their prospective varies from non-existent to sophisticated, generally informal in nature. Demands on the political system are apparently rarely articulated through formal interest groups. The functional effectiveness of the House is uncertain because of the size of the Liberal majority and the high turnover rate of the members. The immediate future of Newfoundland will be critical.

59*Ibid.*, p. 136.

The Party System in Nova Scotia: Tradition and Conservatism

J. MURRAY BECK

Nova Scotian parties did not emerge Minerva-like from the province's rocky base. They were the products of various forces acting and reacting on each other to produce syntheses that in turn became subject to the same process of change. The analysis that follows attempts to relate the Nova Scotian party system to the broader milieus of the political and social systems, using a rough approximation of David Easton's concept of inputs and outputs.[1] First, there will be an examination of the factors — the inputs — which have gone into the shaping of the parties: then there will be a treatment of the outputs of the parties, especially as they provide political leadership and public policies.

I. HOW NOVA SCOTIAN PARTIES CAME TO BE WHAT THEY ARE

A. The Historical Roots

A useful technique for bringing comprehension and order into the early period of Nova Scotia's politics is the functional approach of E.E. Schatt-schneider.[2] It contends that the nature of the politics and parties of a country or region is largely determined by the objectives of the dominant politicians of the day. From the granting of representative institutions in 1758 almost up to the winning of responsible government in 1848 the character of Nova Scotian politics was determined by a Halifax Compact more closely inter-connected by family relationships than the Family Compact of Upper Canada. Until the close of the American Revolution a mercantile group headed by distillery merchant Joshua Mauger possessed more power than it needed to ward off the challenges of an immature assembly and to dominate the colony's politics for its own ends.[3] With the coming of the Loyalists it appeared as if something akin to parties might develop from the cleavage between Loyalists and pre-Loyalists. But once it became clear, as it did under their patron John Wentworth, governor from 1792 to 1808, that the Loyalists "were not to be denied a reasonable share of the patronage, constitutional agitation lost much of its old charm. The cleavage between Loyalists and pre-Loyalists in the Assembly melted away never to be revived."[4]

Nova Scotia continued to be dominated by an oligarchical clique of merchants and officials centred in the Council of Twelve who, in their executive capacity, held the governor in fief and, in their legislative capacity, checkmated the Assembly. Shortly after 1800, William Cottnam Tonge sought to unite the Assemblymen from outside Halifax — the country members — in support of such measures as the taxation of landlords and higher customs duties, thereby challenging the oligarchy in its possession of the major privileges that it was using to maintain its hold on government. However, Tonge's "country party" was hardly a disciplined grouping and on several occasions the Assembly adopted a middle course in preference to his extreme proposals.

The Assembly had become a much more robust body after it obtained sessional indemnities for itself in 1781 and thereby ensured the attendance of non-Halifax members on a regular basis. It even won from the prerogative-conscious Wentworth a deviation from the British practice that left later colonial secretaries aghast. The Nova Scotian financial procedure came to be that, after the essential expenses of government were met, the Assembly usurped the normal role of the executive by dividing the remaining revenues, obtained principally from customs duties, among the counties for roads and bridges, and by appointing commissioners to spend the moneys. Reluctantly the Council acquiesced in this practice, which did not interfere with the oligarchy's own interests, because the alternative would have brought the entire business of government to a halt. The result was to provide the services that the assemblymen and their constituents most valued in the manner they wanted them — without resort to direct taxation. It was no wonder that relative peace descended on the Nova Scotian scene for more than two decades and that parties did not take shape until late in the 1830's, long after their appearance in the Canadas.

In the 1820's protests were directed against the political, economic, and ecclesiastical power that was concentrated in the Council of Twelve. They were sporadic assaults in areas of special concern to a few leading assemblymen, however, and not full-fledged attacks on a totally irresponsible system. By 1830 the first demands for genuine parties were being heard. They were

[1]See, for example, David Easton, *A Systems Analysis of Political Life* (New York: John Wiley & Sons, Inc., 1965).

[2]See E.E. Schattschneider, "United States: The Functional Approach to Party Government," in *Modern Political Parties,* Sigmund Neumann, ed. (Chicago: The University of Chicago Press, 1956), pp. 194-198.

[3]For a full treatment of early Nova Scotian parties, see M. Gene Morison, "The Evolution of Political Parties in Nova Scotia: 1758—1848" (M.A. thesis, Dalhousie University, 1949).

[4]J. Murray Beck, *The Government of Nova Scotia* (Toronto: University of Toronto Press, 1957), p. 29.

an outgrowth of the politico-ecclesiastical radicalism of Principal Thomas McCulloch of Pictou Academy, and were made vocal by the Pictou Scribblers, especially Jotham Blanchard, in the *Colonial Patriot*. The Scribblers argued that, although the Canadas had well-developed parties to withstand misgovernment, there was "yet no *organized party against misrule* in Nova Scotia, and therefore the regularly *organized party* on its side had easy times. It is only to form themselves into a phalanx, when anyone has the effrontery to attack, and the individual assailants are soon wearied of insulated efforts."[5]

Before the struggle against the entrenched oligarchy was to be united, Joseph Howe had to become as convinced as the Scribblers of the need for a disciplined reform party, and that took thirteen years to come about. Starting adult life as a "mild Tory," he is purported to have said that "the Pictou Scribblers . . . have converted me from the error of my ways"; yet in late 1830 he was still equating party with faction, and insisting that "the party to which we belong is the *Province of Nova Scotia*."[6] Five years' experience and a celebrated libel suit convinced him that the Halifax oligarchy had extended its tentacles into every nook and cranny of Nova Scotian society and intended to keep them there. No reforms were possible, he concluded, "without a majority pledged to the people, and kept in salutary awe of them in the Assembly."[7] However, he was not advocating party in the normal sense: fearing that parties would be no more than selfish factions, he was proposing a rally of the Nova Scotian people, whose representatives in the Assembly would keep a strict surveillance over the governor's advisers and the provincial bureaucracy. Largely because of Howe, the Assembly to which he was himself elected in 1836, contained, in addition to a number of "loose fish," two nascent parties — a larger one which supported his condemnation of the oligarchy and a smaller one which sustained the Council. Such was the genesis of the Reform and Tory parties of Nova Scotia.

Although Howe accepted the Durham Report as soon as he read it, he did not yet favour the disciplined parties that were needed to make Durham's major recommendations effective. In contrast, Herbert Huntington of Yarmouth — the Robert Baldwin of Nova Scotia — contended that, since there were two sides to all the major public questions in the province and since the political opinions of every public man were as well known as in England, parties ought to function in Nova Scotia much as they did in Britain. Because Howe still had no clear concept of what he expected of a party, Governor-General Charles Poulett Thomson (the later Lord Sydenham) had no difficulty in persuading him to enter into a coalition with the moderate Tory J.W. Johnston in 1840. Apparently Howe took the view that men of moderate opinions from the *two existing parties* could work together harmoniously for rational, responsible government, thereby frustrating radicals and reactionaries alike. He soon discovered that to make a strong administration something more was required

. . . than nine men treating each other courteously at a round table. There is the assurance of good faith — towards each other — of common sentiments, and kindly feelings, propagated through the friends of each, in Society, in the Legislature and in the Press, until a great Party is formed . . . which secures a steady working majority to sustain their policy and carry their measures.[8]

Thus, step by step, Howe had been "induced almost against his will to don all the trappings of the typical colonial reformer of his day,"[9] including a recognition of the need for disciplined parties.

The inevitable outcome was the breakdown of the coalition in December 1843. Thereafter the great political debate hinged on the applicability of party government to the colonial sphere. The Tories would "admit of no principles or issues in colonial politics which could in any way justify two clearly defined political parties such as existed in England";[10] the Reformers conceded that the issues in Nova Scotia politics could not possess the same absolute significance as those in Britain, yet they insisted that these issues were just as important to colonials as those agitating the larger sphere were to Britons. Accordingly Howe devoted all his great energy to creating the strictly disciplined following that was needed to beat the Tories. In the election of August 5, 1847 the voters could clearly distinguish between Tory and Reform candidates in every county, and the election was largely a plebiscite on responsible government. The Reformers' majority was only 7, but the new Assembly contained none of the "loose fish" who had been accustomed to swim in any pool that chanced to be full. Parties had been needed to secure responsible government; in turn, responsible government helped to rivet party government on the province.

B. The Social Milieu

Charles Dickens watched the proceedings of the Nova Scotia Legislature in 1841 and said "it was like looking at Westminster through the wrong end of a telescope."[11] However, it was by no means certain that British institutions would ever be completely at home in their new environment. Joseph Howe, it is true, had prophesied that

... 'little things are great to little men,' and to little Provinces, and I could point to a dozen [past] questions of internal policy ... and to a dozen [future] ... that were or will be of just as much importance to the people of Nova Scotia, as were the questions upon which ministers [in England] have come in and gone out ... since 1688. It cannot be otherwise in the very nature of things.[12]

Despite Howe's optimism, few issues of substance appeared during the 1850's, and by 1855 one-time advocates of party government such as the *Acadian*

5*Colonial Patriot* (Pictou), February 20, 1830 (italics in original).
6*Novascotian* (Halifax), October 28, 1830 (italics in original).
7Howe to Blanchard, October 26, 1835, quoted in J. Murray Beck, "Joseph Howe: Mild Tory to Reforming Assemblyman," *Dalhousie Review*, XLIV (Spring 1964), 52.
8Howe to Falkland, April 3, 1843, Howe Papers, Public Archives of Canada, VI, 39.
9Beck, "Howe: Mild Tory," p. 56.
10Beck, *Government of Nova Scotia*, p. 80.
11Charles Dickens, *American Notes and Pictures from Italy* (London: Macmillan and Company, 1903), p. 18.
12J. A. Chisholm, *The Speeches and Public Letters of Joseph Howe* (Halifax: The Chronicle Publishing Company, 1909), I, 361.

Recorder were saying that "at the present juncture . . . it would nonplus the shrewdest politician to invent any cogent reason for the division of the representatives of Nova Scotia into two parties, regularly organized for the annihilation of each other, in the halls of our Legislature. We are not aware of a single public question, of the least consequence to any class, being in suspense. . . ."[13]

The split of the Assembly along religious lines in 1857 and the "disputed election" of 1859 — the outcome of which depended on whether half a dozen Liberals were legally entitled to sit in the Assembly — led to several years of bitter, partisan maneuvering. These events also caused the *Sun* to lament that "the game of politics is becoming a pretty expensive one, and so long as parties remain constituted as they now are, Bluenose must expect to pay for it";[14] and the lieutenant-governor, the Earl of Mulgrave, to observe that "no great political question . . . divides [the parties] . . . which should keep them in perpetual antagonism to one another. The matter in dispute is now simply one of men, not measures."[15]

Nova Scotian politics of the early 1860's was by no means moving towards the impasse of the Canadas, however; the short-term religious split bore no resemblance to the differences arising from race and religion in Canada. "The Nova Scotian parties and groups all accepted the existing social order, and agreed both upon the role to be played by government and upon the specific means calculated to provide good government. The most suitable designations for the administration and its opposition had become the Ins and the Outs; the struggle between the two was one for place, power, and the spoils of office."[16]

For a few years the question of Confederation did provide an issue that permitted a meaningful cleavage of the electorate along party lines. But Confederation also served to restrict the province's legislative field, attenuate its financial power, and reduce the possibility of provincial initiative, thereby lessening the likelihood that the parties would be clearly divided on issues in the future. As early as 1876, the *Acadian Recorder* concluded:

There is not, nor can there ever be, any policy dividing the people as far as local matters are concerned. The policy of the opposition will be to struggle by every means . . . to reach the treasury benches, and the policy of the Government will be to checkmate them, and retain the place and power they hold. A change of government in Nova Scotia now-a-days, would only mean changing the officials in some four or five heads of departments. . . . Hereafter the local elections will turn on purely local matters.[17]

Prophetically, most subsequent elections hinged on the performance of one specific function: the management of the day-to-day business of government. So it has remained to this day. By 1970 however, that business was of the order of $350 million annually, and its management had itself become a meaningful issue.

Issues or the lack of them have a distinct bearing on party ideology; in turn, it is closely related to the intangible complex of beliefs, emotions, and values that comprise the political culture of Nova Scotian society. Highly pertinent to the Nova Scotian political culture is Walter Bagehot's "cake of custom," or the idea that "it is the dull traditional habit of mankind that guides most men's actions, and it is the steady frame in which each new artist must set the picture that he paints."[18] Although Bagehot had England in mind, the point he made is no less applicable to Nova Scotia.

By Confederation the general shape of the provincial community had taken form. Pre-Loyalists and Loyalists, Acadians, English, German, Scottish, and Irish had taken up their abode, and no great influx of settlers was to follow. The development of the coal and steel communities was still to come; the smaller settlements were to blossom into larger towns; but the shape of rural Nova Scotia has remained much the same to this day. An unusually large proportion of the society agreed upon a basic stock of attitudes and values. Highly significant was the antipathy towards direct taxation, especially on property. This feeling was all the more intense because the Nova Scotians' major demands on government had for so long been met through the seemingly painless imposition of customs duties.

The attitude of the public towards direct taxation was significant in engendering the Assembly's excessive caution. This explains why in the 1850's the counties and districts were permitted to decide for themselves whether to incorporate for purposes of local government. In the end none of them did; their attitude was that of the newspaper correspondent who urged that "the clarions of war should be sounded, and Taxation, Taxation, Taxation proclaimed throughout the county."[19] Even in areas settled by people whose forebears had governed themselves through the New England town meeting the antipathy was no less strong. Paradoxically, the province that was the first to gain responsible government had to have local self-government forced on it. The Conservative government of Simon Holmes imposed local self-government in 1879 to alleviate serious financial difficulties, but paid the price with defeat in the next election.

The Nova Scotians' dislike for direct taxation long prevented the adoption of a free education system through compulsory assessment. Joseph Howe advocated free education in the 1840's, but it was the Conservative government of Charles Tupper which summoned up enough courage to implement it in 1865. If newspaper correspondence is any indication, the school question might have brought about Tupper's defeat if the Confederation issue had not altogether submerged it in the election of 1867. As for the Confederation question itself, the threat of increased taxation under the new order was an important, although not the dominant, issue. Also significant was the fear of a rush into the unknown: the caution in accepting any innovation that might lead to additional taxation had grown into a suspicion of innovation itself.

13*Acadian Recorder* (Halifax), January 20, 1855.

14*Sun* (Halifax), April 17, 1861.

15Mulgrave to Newcastle, April 3, 1862, *Journals of the Nova Scotia House of Assembly, 1863,* Appendix 11, Civil List, p. 6.

16Beck, *Government of Nova Scotia,* p. 111.

17*Acadian Recorder* (Halifax), May 9, 1876.

18Walter Bagehot, *The English Constitution* (London: Oxford University Press, 1928), p. 8.

19*Novascotian* (Halifax), October 6, 1856.

This suspicion was shared by the provincial politicians. Thus Charles Tupper refused to accede to the demands of Archbishop Connolly of Halifax that Nova Scotian Catholics be accorded the same guarantee in education as those of Ontario were to enjoy. The problem was resolved in a typically Nova Scotian manner of refusing to meet the problem head-on. By convention the local authorities — first in Halifax and later in some Cape Breton communities and the larger mainland towns — would give recognition to Catholic schools within the public school system. For the politician this device had the pleasing result of completely removing a vexed question from the provincial arena.

The conservative nature of the society has caused some undesirable political practices to endure; this is particularly true of patronage. Prior to 1848, vacant offices invariably went to the hangers-on of the Family Compact and its cliques in the county towns; for a time thereafter the Reform ministry resisted the pressures to supplant the incumbents with its own partisans, but by the mid-1850's it had bowed to the clamours of its supporters for jobs. Subsequently both parties unabashedly resorted to the spoils system.

Even after Angus L. Macdonald's government set up the Nova Scotia Civil Service Commission in 1935, the situation remained much the same; the Commission served as a front behind which a Liberal administration could follow the old procedures and escape criticism. R. MacGregor Dawson said in 1945 that *"so long as the Civil Service Act is applied and interpreted as it is to-day, there is no reason to expect anything but an outburst of dismissals following a change of Government."*[20] Fortunately a trend developed after World War II towards strengthening the Commission, adding to the categories of personnel over which it had the jurisdiction, and making it more the kind of body it was alleged to be. This development took place not because public attitudes demanded it, but because partisans were less attracted to low-paid provincial offices in the ensuing period of prosperity.

In other areas patronage survives, although also in a less offensive manner than previously. For many decades politics in the rural districts was highway politics; the first — and often the only — condition for securing work on the highways for oneself or for one's team of horses or truck was support of the party in power. More recently the vast increase in highway expenditures has permitted — indeed, almost obliged — the government of the day to let its political opponents share in the benefits. In the matter of government purchases the friends of the party in office still appear to have a preference, but only under regulations that ensure the protection of the public interest.

The mores of the society are also tolerant of the evils associated with the electoral process. For many years the Liberals manipulated the electoral rolls to their own advantage, but never so brazenly as to incur the wrath of an easy-going public. Nova Scotians will tolerate only so much of this kind of thing, however, and when the Conservative party, not nearly so skilled in gauging the public attitudes, appeared to be using similar methods flagrantly to steal an election, their tactics back-fired. Certainly the Great Franchise Scandal played a part in the Conservative defeat of 1933.

Electoral bribery and corruption was being practised on an extensive scale as far back as the election of 1830. As in the other Atlantic provinces it is difficult to overcome the tradition that anything goes in politics. One observer stated as late as 1933 that the electoral process "drags . . . many of our leading citizens down to the level of gangsters."[21] Even today, "no matter how high-intentioned a candidate may be he is forced to fall in line with a system which operates on the principle that elections are not won by prayers."[22] Yet, when a prominent Conservative admitted as much during the provincial campaign of 1967, the Toronto *Daily Star* acted as if it had made a discovery; not so the people of Nova Scotia, who appeared neither surprised nor shocked. To all appearances, however, the practice of buying votes is not quite so prevalent as it once was.

The agencies of political communication have done little to break down the conservatism and caution, the tendency to cling to things of the past — even if undesirable. Rather, they have operated to maintain things as they are. It is a sad commentary on the press that it has retrogressed steadily since the 1840's when an extraordinary variety of newspapers agitated the issues of the day. So long as the Liberal Halifax *Chronicle* confronted the Conservative Halifax *Herald,* the public at least had access to province-wide newspapers that expressed the views of the major parties. Since 1949 the public has had to be content with the Halifax *Chronicle-Herald,* whose publishers express their Conservative views obliquely and seldom take stands on anything that might alienate their readers or advertisers. Its predecessor, the Halifax *Herald,* went to incredible lengths in its pro-British, anti-American stance, especially in the federal elections of 1891 and 1911; the present paper has not served the cause of national unity by its catering to the Anglo-Saxon backlash against French Canada that is all too prevalent in Nova Scotia.

The province's pressure groups normally do not work through the political parties or their members as such; they present their requests to the cabinet, in some cases through annual briefs. Sometimes the opposition takes its cue from the government's failure to meet an interest group's demands, but since the membership of these groups usually cuts across party lines, they are often reluctant to have their interests adopted by any one party. Over the years the Union of Nova Scotia Municipalities has tried so hard to maintain its nonpartisan character that it has suffered in effectiveness. The exception to the general rule is trade unionism, which has been largely responsible for any success that the Independent Labour Party, the CCF, and the NDP may have had. However, the unionists, too, are pragmatic Nova Scotians, and they support the old parties when their interests seem to warrant it. Thus Nova Scotian pressure groups barely disturb the even tenor of the party system.

[20]R. MacGregor Dawson, *Report on the Civil Service,* No. XVIII of the *Report of the Royal Commission on Provincial Development and Rehabilitation,* Section 15 (italics in original).

[21]See speech of R.H. Murray as reported in the *Chronicle* (Halifax), September 27, 1933.

[22]Beck, *Government of Nova Scotia,* p. 265.

The people who have provided the formal and informal leadership of the community further contribute to the conservative character of Nova Scotian politics and government. Much as John Porter has shown it to be applicable to all Canada in *The Vertical Mosaic*,[23] so in Nova Scotia an upper and upper-middle income elite, principally composed of lawyers and businessmen, has left a deep impression on the politics and parties of the province. On the two occasions in which the minority Conservative party was in such dire distress that its survival seemed in doubt, a few of these notables (to use Max Weber's term) nursed it back to health and thereby preserved an institution that the elite found congenial. The business elite has also helped to keep in office for long periods Liberal premiers whose administrations were to its liking.

Clearly this is not an environment in which the major parties are likely to espouse a meaningful ideology. "Not a Conservative leader since Confederation has, in fact, pretended to be the exponent of a conservative creed or sought inspiration from English or American conservatives, and those Liberal leaders who have attributed their own success and the province's well-being to their acting in consonance with liberal tenets were treating the intelligence of the electorate with scant respect."[24] Both the Liberals and the Conservatives are pragmatic parties that take stands on specific issues more on grounds of expediency than principle. They have often reversed the roles expected of parties bearing their names. The Liberals long resisted the introduction of universal suffrage because it could do them no good politically; the Conservatives favoured it as a means of preventing the dominant Liberals from manipulating a property franchise in their own interest. Again, the Conservatives tried for more than fifty years to have a second chamber of dubious merit abolished; the Liberals tolerated it as a means of strengthening their own position.

There is also no difference between the parties in their attitudes towards social legislation. Because the Liberals were almost always in power, they enacted all the early legislation of this kind, but after the Conservatives assumed office in 1956 their record on social legislation compared favourably with that of their opponents.

Both the Liberals and Conservatives emphasize, however, that too much can be expected of governments and that paternal legislation is not the remedy for economic and political ills. Both hold that the duty of a government is simply to "create conditions under which its citizens can work out their own destiny." This, in fact, is the closest that either comes to having a philosophy. But although the statement appears vague and platitudinous, it is at least flexible enough to permit a government to meet the needs and desires of a small community which is not characterized by a sharp conflict of interests.[25] Understandably there is much to sustain the existing party system — characterized as it is by two major parties competing for public support — and little to challenge it. In David Easton's model one kind of input — demands — places a political or party system under stress, while a second type of input — supports — maintains it. In Nova Scotia there is an abundance of diffuse support fed into the system as a result of the strong ties of loyalty to the old-line parties. Because the population was static and the influx of new people small, and because caution and conservatism were the prevailing attitudes, the process of political socialization — especially as the family contributed to it — led to the state of affairs that Attorney General J.W. Longley described in 1894:

Under the party system whole families maintain with a sort of proud tradition an unbroken history as partisans for generations. . . . A party convention will muster the same men and especially the same families it did twenty years before. Political issues may have changed, leaders may have changed and the party may have gone utterly wrong in the interval, it matters not. The old party traditions have gone on and its adherents have remained serenely blind.[26]

The situation remained much the same until the end of World War II. Since that time — although there are no surveys to measure it quantitatively — the percentage of Nova Scotians who identify themselves as party adherents and the intensity of party identification have diminished somewhat, as knowledgable party workers will readily attest. To a high percentage of Nova Scotians, however — especially those living in areas least subject to change — the old parties continue to be endowed with a sense of legitimacy: they can still be counted on to promote the general welfare of Nova Scotians.

Rarely has the party system been confronted with demands of such an intensity, variety, and volume as to overload it, cause output failure, and threaten its collapse. The most serious threat occurred in the provincial election of July 27, 1920, when twenty-nine Farmer-Labour candidates polled 32.3 per cent of the popular vote compared to the Conservatives' 23.3 per cent, and when eleven Farmer-Labour candidates were elected to the Conservatives' three.

For this phenomenon to have occurred in tradition-oriented Nova Scotia, a series of factors had to be operating to the same end.[27] The first was a political vacuum: the Liberals, after thirty-eight uninterrupted years in office, were hardly a party of initiative and vision, even in a tradition-oriented province; the Conservatives, suffering from the bad image of the Unionist administration at Ottawa, had fallen into disarray.

The economic situation made such distasteful alternatives seem even more repellent. Much of the province's industry and union activity had become concentrated in the coal and steel areas of Pictou, Cumberland, and especially Cape Breton counties. After the stimulus of the wartime boom was over, the loss of the Quebec coal market, the decline in railway construction and hence in the demand for steel, and the increase in freight rates seriously affected the province's heavy industry. A worsening situation was

23John Porter, *The Vertical Mosaic: An Analysis of Social Class and Power In Canada* (Toronto: University of Toronto Press, 1965), especially ch. 13.
24Beck, *Government of Nova Scotia*, p. 156.
25*Ibid.*, p. 157.
26*The Week*, XI (January 5, 1894), 126-127.
27Some of the material on the Farmer-Labour groups came from the papers of A.A. MacKenzie and D.A. Sutherland written for the seminar in Nova Scotian politics and government at Dalhousie University.

magnified by a steep rise in the cost of mining coal (much more pronounced than in the United States), the long, expensive haul to central and western Canadian markets, and the lack of capital resources to cope with technological changes. The Independent Labour Party of Cape Breton had been established in November 1917; later the closing of war industries and a serious wage-price squeeze in an already unfavourable economic context led to the founding of the Independent Labour Party of Nova Scotia in April 1920.

It is perhaps not surprising that labour would take concerted political action. It occurred in the heavily unionized areas — particularly Cape Breton County — where the population had not been static but had become increasingly concentrated during the preceding three decades, where there had been some immigration, and where the tenets of British trade unionism, including that of intervention in politics, were strong. However, it does come as a surprise that the United Farmers of Nova Scotia came into being barely a week later. In 1919 the Nova Scotia Farmers' Association had 269 locals in fourteen of the eighteen counties; fruit growers, dairymen, and poultrymen had associations of their own; the number of co-operative societies had risen to eighty-seven; and all these organizations had given the farmer a sense of affiliation and joint action. Still, there was nothing in these associations to indicate that a static rural population of mixed farmers with widely divergent interests could be induced to take concerted political action.

However, the same factors were operating among the farmers as among the industrial workers: a definite political vacuum, serious economic difficulties, and especially a pronounced wage-price squeeze. One of them stated the farmers' case thus:

The farmers of this province, fed up with doing the drudgery of production while the politicians, forgetful of their election promises, have been enjoying the high lights of social life at Ottawa and Halifax, have at length decided to withdraw their allegiance from the old party standards, to do their own thinking, their own organizing, and when they get into power, to do their own legislating for the benefit of a country which, in the last analysis, is mainly agricultural.[28]

Further impelling the Nova Scotian farmers into action were the United Farmer organizations in the other provinces — particularly in neighbouring New Brunswick — and their recent electoral triumph in Ontario.

The Farmer-Labour group might have elected more than eleven members in 1920, but for two reasons. The first was the failure of farmers and unionists to co-operate effectively. While they did present a combined slate of candidates in three counties, the relationship between them is typified by the farmers' reaction to the delegation of unionists that appeared before the founding convention of the United Farmers of Nova Scotia: "before they had a chance to talk they were told to work longer hours."[29] The more significant factor, however, was the tactics used against the Farmer-Labour group. Before either group could get properly organized, Premier George Murray had the Assembly dissolved on June 28 and an election called for July 27. The *Morning Chronicle*, after denouncing the Farmer-Labourites as socialistic agitators, said that Nova Scotians were sensible people who had no use for alien radical ideas;[30] the Antigonish *Casket* feared that "these blockheads may persuade the people to give their quack-medicine a trial and put the clock back three thousand years";[31] and the Pictou *Advocate* warned that "the boys whose sacrifices in the war and whose bodies lie in France did not give up their lives there in order that Canada should be handed over to Socialists and Bolshevists."[32]

As quickly as the Farmer-Labour movement had mushroomed, so it collapsed. Its members made a poor showing in the legislature, and the Conservatives, who have a habit of rising Phoenix-like from the ashes whenever their position as a second party is threatened, recovered quickly to become the spokesman for all discontented Nova Scotians during the early 1920's.

In contrast with the Farmer-Labour group, the CCF did not get properly organized in Nova Scotia until some years after its founding. In the federal election of 1935 the Reconstruction candidates of H.H. Stevens garnered the votes of protest and reform. They captured 13.9 per cent of the popular vote (mostly in eastern Nova Scotia and especially in industrial Cape Breton and Pictou counties), their best showing in all Canada. It was perhaps revealing of the Nova Scotian character that the radicalism the province chose to support was the mildest imaginable.

The CCF did not make a genuine start in Nova Scotia until 1937, when District 26 of the United Mine Workers of America affiliated with it; thereupon the Nova Scotian section of the CCF was organized. In 1941 it polled 7 per cent of the vote and elected three members to the legislature, all from Cape Breton County. Four years later, as a result of the disillusionment prevailing generally throughout Canada, the CCF raised its share of the popular vote to 13.6 per cent, but lost one of its seats. This was its peak, for although it (or the NDP) retained two Cape Breton County seats up to 1956 and one up to 1963, its popular vote plummeted, reaching a low of 3 per cent in 1956. Federally, Cape Breton South returned a CCF member between 1940 and 1953, and an NDP member in 1962. For the same reasons that led Cape Breton County to elect Labour candidates in 1920, it has been the only part of the province to accord significant support to the CCF and the NDP. Beginning in 1956, however, its coal miners and steel workers turned in large numbers to Robert Stanfield and the Conservatives. Thus even the members of the strongest unions in the province display the same pragmatic attitudes as Nova Scotians generally. It ought not to be surprising, therefore, that the limited success of a third party has been largely confined to one of the eighteen counties. Where industrial concentration does not exist and where few outsiders have been introduced into a long established population, the hold of the old parties has not been challenged. The nature of the economy and the social structure tend to reinforce this state of affairs.

[28]*Herald* (Halifax), January 30, 1920.
[29]*Morning Chronicle* (Halifax), April 15, 1920.
[30]*Ibid.*, July 3, 1920.
[31]*Casket* (Antigonish), July 8, 1920.
[32]*Advocate* (Pictou), July 23, 1920.

The economic development of the province up to now has not been such as to evoke any pronounced feelings of class consciousness, and divisions based upon class have therefore no real significance. Furthermore, there is no substantial economic group which, in the manner of the grain growers of Western Canada, is able to maintain a cohesive political existence by attributing the insecurity of its material position to dependence upon outside financial interests. For while the Nova Scotian primary producers may subsist in what Professor Macpherson describes as a state of "quasi-colonialism,"[33] their problems are so diffuse that combined action to improve their lot is rendered extraordinarily difficult.[34]

In the provincial election of 1970 the NDP fared somewhat better, polling 6.7 per cent of the popular vote and electing two members in Cape Breton County, but as yet there is no evidence that this improvement in the party's fortunes is likely to continue.

C. The Political Milieu

The British parliamentary system, the federal system, and the electoral system have all left their marks on Nova Scotian parties. The first has had its usual results on party discipline. In the 1850's a few assemblymen defected from their parties on the railway and the religious issues; in the 1860's a few more left because of retrenchment and Confederation; but since 1867 defections have been almost nonexistent. Straight party votes in the Assembly became normal at an early date, and Nova Scotian party leaders have seldom been confronted with even a hint of rebellion in the party caucus.

In contrast, federalism has affected the Nova Scotian parties much more than those of most provinces. The act of union itself produced a rearrangement of the existing parties, and in the grand shuffle of supporters the anti-Confederates or Liberals fared much the better. The Confederates immediately incorporated themselves into the federal Conservative party, and like the latter assumed the name Liberal-Conservative, the designation of the Conservatives in the United Province of Canada since the 1850's. Because the Confederates could not win elective office in anti-Confederate Nova Scotia they prevailed upon Sir John Macdonald to ensconce them in lucrative federal offices.[35]

For the anti-Confederates the problem was not nearly so simple. They soon had to face the serious difficulty confronting any party that cannot fulfill a basic promise — in this case repeal of the Union. Their inability or unwillingness to adopt strong measures for the "liberation" of the province alienated their extremist followers; at the same time the Confederates were trying their best to wean away the lukewarm supporters of repeal.[36] After the anti-Confederates lost a dozen seats in the provincial election of 1871, they realized they could no longer continue to win elections simply by blaming their opponents for the fact of Confederation.

Their position in federal politics was even more difficult. To expect their members at Ottawa to remain in splendid isolation was indeed a forlorn hope. "Going up to Ottawa as red-hot Antis," complained the *Morning Chronicle*, "they have been successively wheedled, with four or five sturdy and honorable exceptions, into giving an almost unbroken support to a Government which includes Howe and Tupper."[37] Prior to the federal election of 1872, the anti-Confederate newspapers anxiously deliberated which of two courses their M.P.s should follow in the next Parliament. They agreed that, if their M.P.s were to join in any alliance at all, it would have to be with the Blake and Mackenzie party in preference to the "designing [Macdonald] faction . . . now . . . denying us an honest, vigorous and economical government."[38] But the Nova Scotian M.P.s might also maintain their independence, get all the federal moneys they could for local services, and refuse to enter into alliances until questions of principle had superseded the struggle for power in the Dominion.

Seemingly the second alternative was decided upon; apparently, too, the federal election of 1874, fought as it was on the Pacific Scandal and a return to honest government, provided the principles that were needed to seal an alliance. The eighteen anti-Confederate (or Liberal) members that Nova Scotia returned in 1874 all became faithful supporters of Alexander Mackenzie's government, and two of them entered the cabinet. The result was to complete the integration of the Nova Scotian parties into the national parties and to submerge the one issue that permitted the meaningful cleavage of the electorate along party lines.

Indirectly, however, Confederation continued to affect the parties. Because it left the Liberals with a larger core of supporters than their opponents, they entered every contest with a decided advantage over the Conservatives. The failure of federal Conservative governments until 1896 to show much concern for their provincial counterparts also assisted the Liberals substantially. Above all, Nova Scotian Conservatives had to take the blame for the unpopular fiscal and tariff policies of the national government.

Macdonald's cavalier treatment of W.S. Fielding's Liberal government led to a provincial election on the repeal of Confederation in 1886. It is difficult to determine how much a secessionist Fielding was; undoubtedly he accepted the repeal plank partly as a means of placating the extremists within his own ranks and partly as a means of putting pressure on Macdonald for additional financial assistance. How much his overwhelming victory was due to his government's record and how much to the repeal argument is impossible to tell; the federal Conservatives carried the province decisively in opposing repeal less than a year later and thereby laid the matter to rest.

33C.B. Macpherson, *Democracy in Alberta* (Toronto: University of Toronto Press, 1953), pp. 245-247.
34Beck, *Government of Nova Scotia*, p. 169.
35*Ibid.*, p. 154.
36*Ibid.*
37*Morning Chronicle* (Halifax), July 8, 1872.
38*Ibid.*, January 8, 1872.

Prior to the provincial election of 1890, however, the Conservative organizer, C.H. Cahan, was again bewailing the federal government's failure to consider the provincials:

... if Mr. [Charles Hibbert] Tupper [the Minister of Marine and Fisheries] had set himself to work to destroy the liberal-conservative party in local politics he could not have adopted methods more likely to effect his purpose than those he has pursued in his treatment of the saw-dust and lobster questions....

We are really fighting a federal contest without the aid of federal leaders, federal patronage, and federal rallying cries. We have in every county the odium which the Dominion government may perchance have incurred.[39]

Factors such as these helped to keep the provincial Liberals in power (except for the recession election of 1878) during the first part of their lengthy tenure of office extending from 1867 to 1925. Yet the margin between the parties was not such as to prevent the Macdonald federal government from winning decisively in Nova Scotia in four general elections between 1878 and 1891. This was partly due to the desire of a have-not province to support the party that it felt was likely to win a federal election, and hence assure itself of federal beneficence. Until recently at least Nova Scotia has been one of the country's more accurate bell-wethers. The existing state of affairs — Liberal at Halifax and Conservative at Ottawa — was perpetuated because, not unnaturally, the abler Liberal politicians remained in provincial politics, while the abler Conservative ones were drawn to Ottawa. Much of the Conservative success federally was due to Charles Tupper, who could always be counted on to rescue the Macdonald government from its difficulties in Nova Scotia. Yet Tupper's presence was a drawback to the provincial party, for as long as he dominated Nova Scotia Conservatism, "the [provincial] party had a 'leader' of sorts and thus it could afford, or so it thought, to accept inferior leadership on the provincial scene while it waited for the emergence of another Tupper."[40]

Ironically Tupper could do more for Macdonald in Nova Scotia than he could for himself in Nova Scotia as prime minister in 1896. It was also unusual that Fielding, as Laurier's minister of finance, could use the national policies of Macdonald, which he had previously condemned, to promote one of the country's greatest booms. Nova Scotia shared in the prosperity and responded to it by reinforcing Liberal supremacy both provincially and federally in the first decade of the century. To Fielding's chagrin, however, he could not convince his compatriots of the merits of reciprocity in 1911, even though it was specially calculated to serve their interests: the Halifax *Herald* urged them not to truck or trade with the Yankees, and latent pro-British sentiment did its work.

The character of federal — Nova Scotian relations and the nature of federal-provincial party relationships changed substantially after World War 1. Not only did Nova Scotia, like the other Maritime provinces, fail to recover from the post-war recession as quickly as the rest of Canada, but its slow rate of growth compared with central and western Canada became obvious for the first time. Since then there has been continual jockeying between the old parties to have themselves recognized as the better spokesman for the provincial interest. Sometimes it has been difficult to determine whether the party or the provincial interest is foremost in their thinking.

During the early 1920's the Conservatives took over a newly formed Maritime Rights movement and used it as one vehicle, among others, to win decisive victories federally and provincially in Nova Scotia during the later years of the decade. Under the Conservatives, the movement took a peculiar twist. The Duncan Commission, a federal royal commission investigating the province's disabilities, altogether ignored the major ill, the incidence of the protective tariff, allegedly at the insistence of a Conservative government at Ottawa. For that reason a Liberal premier, Angus L. Macdonald, later appointed his own agency — the Jones Commission — to remedy the defect.

The province's most successful politicians in recent decades, Angus L. Macdonald and Robert Stanfield, sought especially to create for themselves the image of provincial defender against unfavourable federal policies. Macdonald even demanded that a federal government of his own party get out of the lesser tax fields if it expected the provinces to abandon the major ones. Stanfield, who came to be regarded as the builder of a new Nova Scotia, got credit — much to the Liberals' indignation — for the assistance provided by the Pearson government for provincial development, even though he capitalized politically on his criticism of the same administration.

Federal party leaders normally think it desirable to have governments of their own party in power in the provinces; Nova Scotian (and other) premiers are of two minds on this issue. Undoubtedly they find it more congenial to deal with a prime minister of the same political persuasion at Ottawa; but such a situation inhibits them in using the federal government as a scape-goat for provincial ills. Robert Stanfield found the Pearson government at Ottawa much less sympathetic than the Diefenbaker one, but the change at Ottawa had its compensations: it permitted him to add to his image of champion of the provincial interest. In the federal election of 1965 he was the chief Conservative campaigner in Nova Scotia, denouncing the Pearson government's treatment of off-shore mineral rights and the government's application of a tight-money policy equally throughout Canada. There was more than a little truth to the lament of the Liberal national campaign director that "the Stanfield machine creamed us."[41]

How much the provincial interest has suffered in the efforts to maintain harmony between the federal and provincial sections of the old parties is not calculable. It is pertinent to wonder, however, whether Nova Scotian M.P.s and M.L.A.s have been too concerned with maintaining over-all party solidarity at the cost of safeguarding provincial interests; whether their representatives at Ottawa have been content with little more than temporary sops; and whether it would have been to the advantage of Nova Scotia to

[39]C.H. Cahan to John S.D. Thompson, March 28, 1890, Thompson Papers, Public Archives of Canada, Item 12017.

[40]Peter C. Aucoin, "The Conservative Leader in Nova Scotia: Selection and Position in a Minority Party" (M.A. thesis, Dalhousie University, 1966), p. 64.

[41]For details of the campaign see J.M. Beck, "The Electoral Behaviour of Nova Scotia in 1965," Dalhousie Review, XLVI (Spring 1966), 29-38.

have followed the course of the Prairie provinces by returning third-party representation in strength to both the federal and provincial parliaments.

The electoral system has affected Nova Scotian parties even more than has the federal system. That effect can be seen more easily if some sort of order is brought into Nova Scotian elections through a classificatory scheme (see Table I). Perhaps most useful is the technique used by Professor Angus Campbell in classifying American presidential elections.[42] Campbell assumes that the vote cast by the electorate (or specific groups within the electorate) may be split into two parts: the normal vote division to be expected, other things being equal, and the current deviation from that norm. While at any one time there is a majority party and a minority one, short-term forces may produce large enough fluctuations from the normal vote to elect the candidate of the minority party without disturbing the basic division of party loyalties: such is a deviating election. If the fluctuations are not large enough to defeat the majority party, the election is a maintaining one. Occasionally the popular feeling is so intense that enough voters change their basic commitments and produce a new majority party: that is a realigning election.

The Nova Scotian election of 1836 — the first one in which there was anything resembling party divisions — must be regarded as a realigning one since, not only did it lead a substantial portion of the electorate to align itself in support of reforming principles, but it also returned a majority of assemblymen who favoured reform. Although any attempt to reconstruct the party bases must be largely conjectural, Joseph Howe had good ground for boasting that much of his support came from the sturdy agriculturalist who had won his farm from the wilderness and who objected to maintaining a top-heavy, irresponsible, governmental establishment. It it no less clear that the Tories did best in the shire towns and bigger communities where the local compacts of merchants, officials, and lawyers were closely tied in with the larger compact at Halifax; the Tories' consistently better showing in the township ridings as compared with the county ones serves to confirm it. It is equally evident that, while the Tories could count on a preponderant share of the Church of England vote, the Reformers more than made up for it by the strong support they received from the Protestant Dissenters and Roman Catholics, two groups for which Howe had always shown a great deal of sympathy. The exception was the Baptists; Howe alienated this group in 1843 by his determined opposition to government grants to sectarian colleges.

On the basis of support of this kind the Reformers — in the 1850's they came more and more to be called Liberals — remained the majority party until 1867, but not decisively so. Thus the Tories, by catching their opponents unprepared in a surprise election in 1843, emerged as the larger element in a two-party coalition. Even the responsible government election of 1847 was a nip-and-tuck contest, as were the subsequent ones of 1851, 1855, and 1859. The two parties became still more closely matched as a result of Howe's break with the Catholics in 1857 and their wholesale desertion to the Tories. The Conservatives won the most decisive election of the pre-Confederation period in 1863 when the Liberal government collapsed from old age and lack of leadership. But like the election of 1843, it was a deviating election, since there was no substantial change in basic voter commitment.

TABLE I

Classification of Nova Scotian Elections:
1836–1967

Maintaining Elections	Deviating Elections	Realigning Elections
		1836
1840		
	1843	
1847		
1851		
1855		
1859		
	1863	
		1867
1871		
1874		
	1878	
1882		
1886		
1890		
1894		
1897		
1901		
1906		
1911		
1916		
1920		
	1925	
	1928	
1933		
1937		
1941		
1945		
1949		
1953		
		1956(?)*
1960		
1963		
1967		

*The election of 1956 is shown questionably as a realigning one, since it can be argued that the realignment of political forces under Robert Stanfield was not completed until the election of 1963.

In contrast, the election of 1867 in which Nova Scotians divided for and against Confederation was a realigning one. "For the moment even the old shibboleths of Conservative and Liberal were discarded in favour of

42Angus Campbell, *et al.*, *Elections and the Political Order* (New York: John Wiley & Sons, Inc., 1966), ch. 4.

Confederate and anti-Confederate, and while the nucleus of the Confederates was Conservative just as that of the anti-Confederates was Liberal, the break in party ties was on such a scale as to create new parties in fact as in name."[43] The realignment occurred within all groups, and the net shift in the voters' party identification was sufficient to make the Liberals a much stronger majority party than they had been between 1836 and 1867. It took until 1874 or thereabouts for the situation to stabilize itself, but the Conservatives were still substantially in the minority. They remained so until Robert Stanfield's success in 1956, since their victories in 1878, 1925, and 1928 were short-lived ones resulting from recession and financial difficulties.

This is the context in which the electoral system has operated in Nova Scotia. Recently Professor Alan Cairns has suggested that in Canada's federal elections the electoral system has tended to stimulate the politics of sectionalism and has thereby contributed significantly to the evolution of the party system. Because the party leaders realize they can reap rich dividends in seats — altogether out of proportion to their parties' votes — from specific regions, they deliberately cater to such areas. The result, Cairns suggests, has been "a politics of opportunism based on sectional appeals and conditioned by one-party bastions where the opposition is tempted to give up the battle and pursue success in more promising areas."[44]

In the small community of Nova Scotia this brand of politics is hardly possible. None the less, the first-past-the-post electoral system by which a candidate with a plurality is elected has had almost as drastic results because of its usual propensity to give the winning party a disproportionately large share of the seats and the second party a disproportionately small share (see Table II). In the twenty-two elections between 1867 and 1953 the Liberals received only 49.8 per cent of the votes, but got 68.1 per cent of the seats; the Conservatives gained 44.2 per cent of the votes, but only 29.2 per cent of the seats. In eleven of these elections the Conservatives won eight seats or less and in only one election did they elect sufficient assemblymen of ability to conduct an efficient opposition and look like a credible alternative to the ruling Liberals.

Despite their overwhelming predominance, the Liberals' share of the popular vote never exceeded 52.9 per cent after 1911, and despite the Conservatives' minority position their popular vote fell below 38.5 per cent only twice since Confederation. The Conservatives suffered severely because their vote was quite evenly distributed across the province and because they could count no seat as safely theirs. For them the result was to produce a chronic instability of leadership such as seldom befalls a major party.

Sometimes, indeed, the Conservative leaders appeared to be playing a game of musical chairs, although not of their own will. Dr. William MacKay was Conservative House leader in the Twenty-ninth General Assembly (1886—1890), but gave way to C. H. Cahan when he was defeated in his own riding; he resumed the leadership in the Thirty-first Assembly (1894—1897) when Cahan was rejected by his own constituents. John F. Stairs, the first elected leader of the provincial party, in contrast with the House leaders of pre-1897 days, never became a member of the Assembly although he tried to in 1897 and 1901.

TABLE II* (a)

Results of Nova Scotian Provincial Elections : 1867–1970

Year	Popular Vote			Percentage of Popular Vote		
	Liberal	Conservative	Other	Liberal	Conser-vative	Other
1867	44,339	29,095	2,182	58.6	38.5	2.9
1871	39,213	32,808	3,128	52.2	43.7	4.2
1874	37,169	29,492	921	55.0	43.6	1.4
1878	45,672	52,311	3,268	45.1	51.7	3.2
1882	49,945	45,247	1,205	51.8	46.9	1.3
1886	61,822	49,216	1,943	54.7	43.6	1.7
1890	71,202	63,720	1,407	52.2	46.7	1.1
1894	75,121	68,455	1,073	51.9	47.3	0.7
1897	84,000	67,779	968	55.0	44.4	0.6
1901	78,375	57,689	2,147	56.7	41.7	1.6
1906	84,359	66,638	7,423	53.2	42.1	4.7
1911	99,192	88,114	6,851	51.1	45.4	3.5
1916	136,315	131,844	2,215	50.4	48.8	0.8
1920	154,627	81,044	112,283	44.4	23.3	32.3
1925	161,158	270,544	12,260	36.3	60.9	2.8
1928	209,380	218,974	4,862	48.3	50.5	1.1
1933	166,170	145,107	4,805	52.6	45.9	1.5
1937	165,397	143,670	3,396	52.9	46.0	1.1
1941	138,915	106,133	18,583	52.7	40.3	7.0
1945	153,513	97,774	40,271	52.7	33.5	13.8
1949	174,604	134,312	33,618	51.0	39.2	9.8
1953	169,921	149,973	25,765	49.1	43.4	7.5
1956	159,656	160,996	10,690	48.2	48.6	3.2
1960	147,946	168,023	31,686	42.6	48.3	9.1
1963	134,873	191,128	14,076	39.7	56.2	4.1
1967	142,945	180,948	18,371	41.8	52.8	5.4
1970	174,943	177,986	26,724	46.1	46.9	7.0

Perhaps the story of Charles E. Tanner best illustrates the oscillating fortunes of a Conservative leader in Nova Scotia. First elected to the Assembly in 1901, he assumed the House leadership of a contingent of two, and was later proclaimed leader of the provincial party. He was re-elected to the Assembly in 1906, thereby becoming the first Conservative leader since 1886 to retain his seat. He found his position as leader so unrewarding, however, that he ran federally in 1908. He failed to get elected and then could not win back his provincial seat. The election of 1911 returned him to the Assembly with ten followers; five years later he gave the Liberals a good fight, but — as was almost to be expected — he lost out personally. He had had enough;

[43]Beck, *Government of Nova Scotia,* p. 154.
[44]Alan C. Cairns, "The Electoral System and the Party System in Canada," *Canadian Journal of Political Science,* I (March 1968), 75.

shortly afterwards he accepted a more secure resting place in the Senate. His successor, W.L. Hall, suffered an even more unkind fate: he lost his seat in 1920 and was deposed as leader just before the great Conservative triumph of 1925.

After eight years on the government benches, the Conservatives went through a similar, although shorter cycle. Their leader, Gordon S. Harrington, lost his seat in 1937, and his successor, L.W. Fraser, could not get elected in either 1941 or 1945. On the latter occasion the Conservatives, for the first time, won no seats at all. "I can no longer lead this party hopefully," said Fraser, "and that leaves me only one course to follow."[45] For such sentiments, which might have been echoed by most of his predecessors, the electoral system was substantially responsible. By returning to the legislature only a corporal's guard of members from a party that normally polled at least two-fifths of the vote, that party was left lacking in leadership, low in morale, and deficient in organization. Only a deep-seated tradition of party identification enabled it to survive at all.

More recently the Liberals have been administered a milder dose of the same medicine. Their leader was defeated in 1960 and 1963, and while Gerald Regan won his seat in 1967, his party's 41.8 per cent of the vote gave it only 13 per cent of the seats. Under these circumstances the Liberals were having the same difficulties that the Conservatives once experienced in maintaining morale and rebuilding their organization. Obviously the electoral system has had a potent effect on both the working of the legislature and the nature of the parties and provincial politics.

II. HOW NOVA SCOTIAN POLITICAL PARTIES HAVE AFFECTED THE POLITICAL AND SOCIAL SYSTEMS

A political system must, above all, provide leadership and make decisions for the society, and political parties play a key role in performing both functions. Since the Nova Scotia House of Assembly has — indirectly at least — been a major decision-maker on the provincial level, its composition is of special significance. Of 1043 assemblymen elected between 1867 and 1970, two were Independents, eleven were Farmer-Labourites, thirteen were CCF, and the rest were members of the old parties — 626 Liberals and 391 Conservatives. The practices that the parties use to nominate their candidates are therefore crucial and are closely connected with party organization per se.

The conversion of the casual party meetings of the 1840's into organized conventions took place in stages and by no means uniformly throughout the province. During the 1860's, shortly after dissolution the unofficial party leaders in the shiretowns would send circulars regarding a nomination meeting to their friends in the outlying districts. In 1871 the Conservatives of Pictou introduced a significant innovation: "All those in attendance at the nomination meeting from a specific polling district chose one person from among themselves — a *delegate* so-called — to sit on the committee which proposed the candidates."[46] In the federal and provincial elections of 1874 the

TABLE II* (b)

Results of Nova Scotian Provincial Elections: 1867—1970

	Seats			Percentage of Seats		
	Liberal	Conservative	Other	Liberal	Conservative	Other
1867	36	2		94.7	5.3	
1871	25	13		65.8	34.2	
1874	24	14		63.2	36.8	
1878	8	30		21.1	78.9	
1882	24	14		63.2	36.8	
1886	29	8	1	76.3	21.1	2.6
1890	28	10		73.7	26.3	
1894	25	13		65.8	34.2	
1897	35	3		92.1	7.9	
1901	36	2		94.7	5.3	
1906	32	5	1	84.2	13.2	2.6
1911	27	11		71.1	28.9	
1916	30	13		69.8	30.2	
1920	29	3	11	67.4	7.0	25.6
1925	3	40		7.0	93.0	
1928	20	23		46.5	53.5	
1933	22	8		73.3	26.7	
1937	25	5		83.3	16.7	
1941	23	4	3	76.7	13.3	10.0
1945	28		2	93.3		6.7
1949	28	7	2	75.7	18.9	5.4
1953	23	12	2	62.2	32.4	5.4
1956	18	24	1	41.9	55.8	2.3
1960	15	27	1	34.9	62.8	2.3
1963	4	39		9.3	90.7	
1967	6	40		13.0	87.0	
1970	23	21	2	50.0	45.7	4.3

*Sources: Up to 1886, newspaper election reports; since 1886, appendices to *Journals of the Nova Scotia House of Assembly* and *Returns of General Election for the House of Assembly,* (Halifax: Queen's Printer).

practice was extended to other counties and in 1878 it was a commonplace. The election of 1871 was also noteworthy for an occasional reference to the nomination gatherings as *conventions*. By 1878 this term — an American importation — was in common use and by 1882 it was employed almost exclusively. However, bona fide conventions would be largely a myth as long as the parties had no organization until just before an election.

February 4, 1878 was therefore a red-letter day for party organization. On that date the Liberals established the Reform Association of Halifax and

[45]*Chronicle* (Halifax), February 22, 1946.
[46]J.M. Beck, "The Nomination of Candidates to Nova Scotia," *Dalhousie Review* XXXVI (Winter 1957), 365.

organized themselves on a permanent basis, not only at the county level, but also at the ward and polling district levels. This permitted them to introduce another significant innovation in August 1878: "a convention consisting solely of delegates accredited by the organization in the wards and polling districts selected the party's candidates in an inner room, while the members of the Reform Association and their friends gathered in a larger outer room to await their determination."[47] Perhaps it was understandable that the Liberals contrasted these procedures with the undemocratic ones used by the Tories in the same county: "The wire pullers get together in some garret in the city and cook up their ticket. Then . . . as a matter of form, they invite gentlemen to come in from the rural districts. . . . What a farce!"[48]

Actually the Conservatives of Halifax had set up a Liberal-Conservative Association in July 1874 in response to Charles Tupper's argument that a party without organization tended to be a multitude of scattered atoms. The Association did little to build up an organization at the grass roots, however, and it was not until 1882 that it could hold a convention similar to that convened by its Liberal counterpart in 1878. Before similar conventions could be held outside Halifax, the county and local organizations had to be established on a firmer basis, a development that took place spasmodically over the next decade or two. In the case of the Liberals a great spurt of organizational activity followed Laurier's visit to Halifax and the founding of the Nova Scotia Liberal Association in December 1890; within two months county organizations were set up in Richmond and Guysborough for the first time.

The county and local organizations of the Conservatives – a weak and dispirited party – came into being more slowly. As late as July 1896, the Halifax *Herald* declared them "not fit even to choose delegates to a general convention," and Peter Aucoin has written of the party:

. . . it was such a nebulous thing that it is questionable if it should be called a party at all. It had no provincial organization and no rules regulating party membership, the nomination of candidates, the selection of a party leader, or anything else for that matter. . . . In essence, the party was the loosest association between notables in Halifax and in the other counties.[49]

Accordingly, under the urging of their national leader, Sir Charles Tupper, the Conservatives took steps in October 1896 to "reconstruct, remodel, re-equip and infuse some hurrah into the party."[50] Borrowing the designation of their English counterpart, the National Union, they established the Liberal-Conservative Union of Nova Scotia and thereby equipped themselves with an extra-parliamentary apparatus similar to that of the Liberals.

In both parties the relationship between the parliamentary parties and their mass organizations has varied over time and it is hardly true to say – as R.T. McKenzie states of British parties – that a healthy balance has existed between the two, ensuring all the more that the parties have been highly useful adjuncts of liberal democracy. During the long tenures of Liberal premiers George Murray and Angus L. Macdonald, which included most of the period between 1896 and 1954, these two figures dominated the extra-parliamentary organization as much as they liked; indeed, there is more than a suspicion that Macdonald let the organization decay in his later years. Nevertheless, the Liberal party workers attributed their almost continuous success to superior organization on both the provincial and county levels, and, because the lower echelons of the party helped to allocate the local patronage, the Liberals had no trouble in maintaining a coherent organization at the polling district level.

Normally the Conservatives had nothing comparable to this. Between elections their only activity was the annual meetings of the provincial and constituency associations; their organization at the polling district level was nonexistent, or at least quiescent in most counties.

Yet, when an election [was] called, they [were] usually able to enlist a sufficient number of the old faithful to provide at least the semblance of a contest in every constituency. Generally their only solace after the counting of the ballots on election night [was] to register surprise at the size of their popular vote despite the strength of the contending forces.[51]

Twice, in 1920 and in 1945, the Conservatives lost their position as second party in the legislature, and it took a few notables to save the party and effect a resurrection; undoubtedly the fear that the Conservatives might be supplanted by a radical alternative spurred them into activity. On the second occasion it was Robert Stanfield, President of the Young People's Conservatives, who directed the re-organization of the party that made him its leader two years later. By maintaining that organization in fighting trim, he was ready to take over the province when the opportunity arose in 1956. Normally, however, the experience has been that strength in party organization has been more effect than cause, that nothing succeeds like success, and that a party in opposition experiences a loss of morale and weakened organization. Yet, when the scent of victory is in the air, there is no dearth of volunteers to fight the opposition party's election battles. Generally the organization of the Liberals and Conservatives can be said to be democratic in the sense that no one who wishes to participate in their affairs is likely to be denied the opportunity.

Such is the organizational apparatus that chooses the old parties' candidates for the Legislature and the premiership. When Conservative Premier E.N. Rhodes and Liberal Premier Angus L. Macdonald entered the federal cabinet in 1930 and 1940, the party rank and file did not participate in the choice of their successors. However, these were exceptional circumstances; it seems certain that neither party will in future choose a leader through means other than its provincial association assembled in a leadership convention. Of the seven such conventions held by the Conservatives, only the one that chose Robert Stanfield in 1948 involved a contest for the leadership. In contrast, four of the five Liberal conventions — all held since 1930 — have had contests. The one held in 1954 was too much of an exercise in democracy, for it produced a religious cleavage and left wounds that took a long time to heal.

47*Ibid.*, pp. 365-366.
48*Acadian Recorder* (Halifax), August 20, 1878.
49Aucoin, "Conservative Leader," p. 66.
50*Morning Chronicle* (Halifax), October 16, 1896.
51Beck, *Government of Nova Scotia*, p. 161.

Both parties have had difficulties — although of a different kind — in maintaining an appropriate relationship between the "brass" and the "grass." As recently as 1964, there have been spirited contests for election to the executive of the Nova Scotia Liberal Association; in that year a young "ginger group" demanded more aggressive direction of the party's affairs. For the Conservatives the problem has been to secure greater involvement of the rank and file in party concerns. To that end in recent years they have had the members of the provincial cabinet — the directors of the corporation — subjected to questioning by the ordinary membership — the shareholders of the corporation — at the annual meeting of the provincial association.

At the constituency level the Conservative party organization was so weak prior to the 1950's that in many constituencies it was impossible to convene a delegate convention. In the rare case in which a nomination was contested, the party ran the risk of having an unsuitable candidate foisted on it by an open convention. Since the revitalization of the Conservatives neither of the old parties has had to run that risk. Although contested nominations are by no means the rule, they have become much more common since the mid-1950's.

Whom do the conventions nominate as possible assemblymen and potential political leaders? Anyone who seeks to establish that one party's conventions select candidates who are different from those of the other party in philosophy or in any other respect is pursuing a will-o'-the-wisp. To the onlooker in the Legislature's public galleries, the elected candidates, like members of other provincial assemblies, appear to be a rather mediocre lot; however, their lack of oratorical ability often conceals their good common sense. Almost invariably they are local men: the candidature of an outsider is likely to raise questions, and the parties have seldom resorted to carpetbaggers except in the absence of a suitable local candidate. From the earliest days of the Assembly one-fifth to one-third of its members have been lawyers, and in recent Assemblies the proportion is tending to be even larger. In earlier years the number of general merchants often rivalled that of the lawyers, but today the non-lawyers among the assemblymen are of diverse occupations — farming, lumbering, contracting, medicine, journalism, manufacturing, finance, and insurance. As in the Parliament of Canada, trade unionism is poorly represented. On the whole the members come largely from the middle and upper-middle income groups, but none the less they reflect — perhaps too accurately — the tradition-oriented political culture.

From the assemblymen come most of the true decision makers, the premiers and cabinet ministers. In Nova Scotia the premiers have had an even greater influence than is normal, simply because four of them — William Stevens Fielding, George H. Murray, Angus L. Macdonald, and Robert L. Stanfield — held the premiership for sixty-six of the eighty-three years between 1884 and 1967. (It would have been seventy-one years if Macdonald had not entered the federal cabinet during World War II.) Each stamped something of himself on the character of his administration.[52]

Contrary to the ways of British political parties — especially the Conservative party, in which the leader and prime minister normally "emerge" after proving their mettle in the Commons — these four Nova Scotians took over the party leadership, and sometimes the government, almost sight unseen. Fielding had been an assemblyman and executive councillor for less than two years before he became premier; Murray had made three unsuccessful attempts to be elected to the Commons or Assembly before he took over the premiership and at the time he formed his government he was serving in the cabinet as a member of the Legislative Council; Macdonald assumed the premiership months before he sat in the Assembly; and Stanfield became Conservative leader the year before he was elected to the legislature.

Each of the four provided a different type of leadership, although it may be stretching a point to call it leadership in the case of Murray. By his own admission, he "refused to place himself in the vanguard of public opinion and to persuade it to accept policies which he conceived to be conducive to the provincial interest."[53] As he put it, "new ideas cropped up from time to time, and it was the duty of the government to discern the wishes of the public and to meet these wishes as occasion demanded."[54] To innovation of any kind, he put his inevitable question: Has it been tried elsewhere and with what success? "Under him the Ontario statute book became the utmost limit to which Nova Scotia might hope to aspire in many matters."[55] This philosophy pervaded Nova Scotian government for 27 years (1897–1923); it left the statute book deficient in legislation appropriate to the nascent positive state and left the administrative machinery obsolescent.

In contrast, Fielding, Macdonald, and Stanfield sought, in different contexts, to ensure that the climate was favourable for provincial development to take place. Although Fielding's premiership (1884–1896) fell within the period of laissez-faire government, his was the first Nova Scotian administration to assume "the initiative in all the most important measures of the session."[56] With some truth he could be credited with "waking-up [Nova Scotia] from a Rip van Winkle sleep"[57] for he undertook, among other things, an extensive programme of building roads and bridges as capital projects, and induced outside interests to develop the provincial coal resources.

Under Angus L. Macdonald "the Liberals secured once more the Fielding type of leadership."[58] In the early years of his premiership, at least , he insisted that no government ought to be content with the mere routine of administration and that all its departments should give real leadership in their respective spheres. On his assumption of office in 1933, despite the impoverishment of the provincial finances, he proclaimed the Old Age Pensions Act, which his Conservative predecessors had left dormant on the statute book, and initiated

---

[52]Some of the material on the four premiers comes from the papers of Mary Ellen Clancey, Allan Dunlop, David Flemming, Frank Hennessey, A.A. MacKenzie, and J.W. O'Brien written for the seminar in Nova Scotia politics and government at Dalhousie University.

[53]Beck, *Government of Nova Scotia*, p. 161.

[54]*Debates and Proceedings of the Nova Scotia House of Assembly*, 1906, p. 114.

[55]Beck, *Government of Nova Scotia*, p. 201.

[56]*Acadian Recorder* (Halifax), April 27, 1885.

[57]*Ibid.*, March 9, 1894.

[58]Beck, *Government of Nova Scotia*, p. 162.

an ambitious programme of hard-surfacing the main highways. While the Macdonald of post-1945 days was more reluctant to assume new initiatives, he had already acquired the image of willing innovator.

The philosophy of Robert L. Stanfield was that Nova Scotians should forget the days when they were content to attribute all their ills to sinister forces in central Canada and seek to raise themselves by their own bootstraps. It was a basic function of government, he contended, to provide the climate and incentives needed to promote economic development. Despite his reputation for caution, his administration advanced $200 million for the establishment of secondary industries and the name "Stanfield" became inseparably associated with "the new Nova Scotia."

How are the four premiers' long tenures of office to be explained? Obviously Murray's is the most difficult. In part it is to be accounted for by the attitude of his Conservative opponents, whose philosophy differed little from his and who concentrated all too much on destructive criticism to oust him from office. But it was due much more to Murray himself: in him were combined a pleasing affability that made him personally attractive and the political subtlety of a Mackenzie King. While the performance of the brokerage function is much less exacting in Nova Scotia than it is on the national level, Murray did have to moderate class interests at a time when the province was first experiencing serious clashes between capital and labour. His maxims were infinite caution and political expediency. On the platform he abstractly espoused the interests of labour and the masses, but he candidly admitted that his policy was to secure the greatest possible development of the province by making the burden on capital as light as possible. By going into social legislation as little as possible and by accepting the protective tariff he convinced the corporate world that nothing was to be gained by upsetting his government. The outcome was that he managed to avoid alienating the labour vote until 1920, while enlisting the tacit support of even Conservative businessmen.[59]

The success of the other leaders stems in part from their concept of leadership, but there were other factors as well. Fielding inherited the government when the opposition was in disarray, and he quickly and solidly established himself and his party in a position of pre-eminence. Perhaps his goatee did "cover the closest mouth in politics,"[60] but his facility with a trenchant phrase, his logical and incisive speech, his ability to reduce financial complexities to a single formula understandable to the layman, and the impression he created of fairness and integrity all won him public respect. His defence of Nova Scotian interests against the brusque treatment of John A. Macdonald and his success in promoting provincial development served further to create the attractive image that withstood all his opponents' attacks.

Macdonald and Stanfield riveted themselves on the province for many of the same reasons, but not with the same facility. The former took over a party in good health and within three years used recession and the Great Franchise Scandal of 1933 to gain power. Stanfield had more formidable difficulties to overcome, especially in reorganizing a party devoid of representation in the legislature and in eroding the support of such a majestic father figure as Angus L. Macdonald. The latter's death in 1954 accelerated his progress towards victory. The convention to choose Macdonald's successor split along religious lines and the new premier, Henry Hicks, followed a courageous, if politically unwise, course in proceeding with far-reaching changes for the financing of education that substantially increased municipal taxation. Both factors affected the election of 1956: the first caused the Liberals serious losses among the Catholic voters in eastern Nova Scotia, but the second may have tipped the balance in a close election by producing Conservative majorities in western Nova Scotia. It is perhaps true that "Stanfield grows on one," because it took three elections to produce the massive realignment of voters that ensured his political domination of the province.[61]

By 1963 Stanfield, like Macdonald, had inspired the trust and confidence of the people — indeed had created a rapport with them — and had won the good opinion of the business community. Both men succeeded in impressing themselves on the public mind as defenders of the provincial interest against unwarranted or unreasonable federal action; both were regarded as vigorous proponents of a better Nova Scotia; both were strong partisans, yet managed to create the impression that they stood above politics; both performed the leadership function without riding roughshod over deeply implanted tradition or imposing heavy additional taxation. However, their relations with their parties were different, Macdonald, who relied more on his personal strength maintained a distance between himself and his party; under him Liberal slogans proclaimed that "All's well with Angus L." In contrast, Stanfield, the party man, led a team and Conservative advertisements referred to "A Stanfield Government" or "The Stanfield Team." Personal qualities also became part of the public image of both men. In Macdonald's case it was sentimentality—the poor boy who worked his way through college and ultimately became premier—his Scottish name and ancestry: "it was when he 'put on his kilt' that one rich facet of his personality was revealed. Then we could expect the felicitous phrase, the reverent communing with the bards."[62] In Stanfield's case it was his humility: the rich man who drove an unostentatious Volvo and who walked two miles to work from his home in the south end of Halifax.

Is there something in the Nova Scotian character that makes the people feel more secure when they have a father figure presiding over their destinies? Other provinces, especially Quebec and Ontario, have similarly experienced long tenures of office, although not extending over such protracted periods as Nova Scotia. It seems likely, therefore, than an accidental coincidence of personalities and circumstances, rather than peculiarities of the provincial character, account for the Nova Scotian phenomenon. Because the major parties have not differed markedly in ideology, the voter has tended all the more to emphasize the leader. David Easton might say: the outputs from Nova

---

[59]*Ibid.*, pp. 166 and 167.

[60]Joseph Schull, *Laurier* (Toronto: The Macmillan Company of Canada, Ltd., 1966), p. 188.

[61]See Peter Aucoin, "The Stanfield Era: A Political Analysis," *Dalhousie Review,* XLVII (Autumn 1967), 400-409.

[62]*Casket* (Antigonish), April 22, 1954.

Scotian parties — through their impact on society generally — have contributed to the emergence of new inputs, especially in the form of diffuse support (leaders with attractive images and the like), that tend not only to maintain the party system as it is, but also to preserve the existing balance of the major parties over long periods.

The major Nova Scotian parties, as performers of functions, display little out of the ordinary. As connectors they bridge the gap between the people in society and their political and governmental systems. Their raison d'être is the expectation that they will be called on to perform the function of manager-operator of the government. To that end they act as nominators — in modern Nova Scotia no candidate who is not the nominee of a political party has a hope of being elected; as broker-mediators — in a province where ethnic, religious, and class differences are not pronounced the task of reconciling interests is much less exacting than at the national level; and as organizers — like their national counterparts the old-line parties in Nova Scotia do more to organize the electorate for victory at the polls than to organize support for coherent schemes of public policy.[63]

A substantial, though decreasing, number of Nova Scotians have a high sense of party identification; for them a party has considerable capacity to influence their behaviour simply because it exists, no matter what is done in its name by the leadership. By the process of perceptual distortion they simply ignore or explain away what is objectionable in party activity; thus the parties' *"being* as well as *acting* as important."[64] The tendency of a father figure to become the symbol of the party reinforced the phenomenon.

If the Engelmann and Schwartz typology of parties[65] is applied to Nova Scotia, the Liberals and Conservatives are broad-based, cadre parties of electoral success with governmental experience. More explicitly, they have a wide measure of support across ethnic, religious, and class lines; their local associations do not have "the populist notion of possessing the right to direct the destinies of the party";[66] they are highly pragmatic and oriented to political success rather than to principles; they have governed the province and have provided leadership and decisions on a day-to-day basis, although the Conservatives have acquired most of their experience since 1956. In contrast, the CCF/NDP — the only other party that has had more than a transient existence — falls into the type of "mass" party of principle with a restricted base and no governmental experience.

It can be argued that Nova Scotians would have benefited from experimenting further with a party of the second type. However, the point is surely academic, since the political culture of Nova Scotia almost guarantees that the conditions necessary to bring such a party to power would have to be altogether catastrophic in nature. The existing parties may be a case of Tweedle-Dum and Tweedle-Dee, but nothing yet in the offing challenges their existence. As Lord Bryce said of their American counterparts, they "continue to exist, because they have existed. The mill has been constructed and its machinery goes on turning, even when there is no grist to grind."[67]

The events of the 1960's continued to demonstrate the meaninglessness of party ideology. During these years the Conservative governments of Robert Stanfield and G.I. Smith used $200 million of public money to promote industrial development, and, although they had not intended it, the province found itself the owner of a heavy water plant, a steel mill, and a stereo-television factory. Gerald Regan, the Liberal leader, could say that "Premier Smith is too much of a socialist for me," and the management (or, as the Liberals alleged, the mismanagement) of provincially-owned and provincially-assisted industries had become a major political issue. In fact, it was a prime factor in undermining the Smith government and in bringing the Liberals to power in October 1970. All in all, however, the only significant change in decades in the working of the parties has been that, with the renascence of Conservatism, a one-and-a-half party system has been converted into a genuine two-party system.

[63] See the functions of parties as outlined in Neil A. McDonald, *The Study of Political Parties* (New York: Doubleday & Company, Inc., 1955), pp. 22-26.

[64] *Ibid.*, pp. 21 and 22.

[65] See F.C. Engelmann and M.A. Schwartz, *Political Parties and the Canadian Social Structure* (Toronto: Prentice-Hall of Canada, Ltd., 1967), pp. 3-14.

[66] *Ibid.*, p. 243.

[67] James Bryce, *The American Commonwealth* (New York: Macmillan Co., 1907), II, 24.

* ONTARIO *

A Three-Party System in Transition

JOHN WILSON AND DAVID HOFFMAN

It is a commonplace of Canadian political life that in the provinces, as well as at Ottawa, it has been customary for political parties to enjoy extraordinarily long periods of power. In the early years after Confederation, while the Conservatives were generally much stronger than the Liberals in national elections, both parties developed particular bases of strength at the local level which allowed each of them to remain the leading political group in different provinces until at least the turn of the century. Since that time, however, the Liberals have been conspicuously more successful than other parties in dominating both levels of government in Canada. On the face of it, therefore, the most striking characteristic of the Ontario party system is not simply the continued strength of one party but the fact that it has been the Conservatives who have governed the province almost without interruption throughout the modern period.

Since 1905 they have been out of office only twice: during the brief, four-year term of the UFO-Labor coalition after World War I, and again between 1934 and 1943, when the Liberals last controlled the legislature at Queen's Park. By any standard this is a remarkable achievement, and yet, more fundamentally, the dominance of the Conservative party is probably not the most important aspect of the contemporary party system in Ontario.

Viewed in a very general way there are two contrasting patterns in the development of party competition in modern democratic political systems. In Western Europe, which is often taken as the paradigm case, industrialization significantly altered — even completely destroyed — the structure of nineteenth century politics. Middle-class liberal parties withered in the crush between rising working-class parties on their left and conservative (but often remarkably flexible) parties on their right. In North America, on the other hand, the appearance of an urban working class has not destroyed the pre-industrial party system. Here liberal parties have been able to survive — and even to dominate the politics of both Canada and the United States — by successfully directing their appeal to a heterogeneous collection of electors including industrial workers, farmers, and professional groups. At the same time parties oriented primarily to organized labour have generally been confined to the periphery of the political system.

It is true, of course, that this has not everywhere been the case. But the rise to prominence of the CCF/NDP in Western Canada, while often depending to a greater extent on the support of farmers than might be expected with a party of the left, has *always* occurred at the expense of at least one of the traditional middle-class parties, suggesting that the alternative to the customary North American pattern is indeed the kind of party competition which has evolved in Western Europe. In this sense the most intriguing feature of politics in Ontario is less the obvious success of the Conservative party than the fact that the contemporary party system conforms to *neither* of the usual patterns. Instead, there has been a very considerable growth in the strength of the CCF/NDP — drawn largely from the industrial working class — while, at the same time, *neither* of the older parties has disappeared. Nor is this a reflection of some temporary fit of irritation on the part of the electorate. The fact is that for nearly thirty years, beginning with the election of 1943, the system in Ontario has been characterized by competition between three electorally strong parties, and it has now developed to a stage where any one of them might reasonably expect to take power at the next election. It is, in short, a pure three-party system.

But while there can be little doubt that this is the most important fact of political life in Ontario, and that the future of the province ultimately depends upon the direction in which the forces which have created and maintained the existing pattern of party competition move, it is nonetheless a comparatively recent phenomenon when viewed in the light of an active political history which spans nearly a century and a half. In fact, it seems likely that the peculiar structure of the party system in the modern period arises out of the circumstances of the province's development in its formative years. To understand contemporary Ontario politics it is therefore necessary to go back to the beginning.

I. THE ONTARIO POLITICAL TRADITION

The pattern of party competition in Ontario since 1943 is obviously different from everything that has gone before.[1] But while the system was dominated almost without exception from its beginning until World War II by the contest between the two older parties, the contrast between the two periods disguises another division which is equally striking. The strength of the Conservative party in modern times makes it difficult to believe that Ontario was once "by large odds a Reform and not a Conservative Province."[2]

[1]The distinction between the two periods, as well as the persistence of the three-party system since 1943, may easily be seen in the columns relating to the share of votes cast for the parties in Table I, pp. 204-205.

[2]"The Ontario Elections," *Canadian Monthly and National Review*, September, 1879, p. 225.

In fact, however, the Liberals were the leading political group in the province for the better part of the nineteenth century, and continuously from the introduction of responsible government in 1848 to the collapse of the Ross government in 1905.[3]

In the very early days Reformers often constituted a majority of the Legislative Assembly of Upper Canada, although their strength was generally irrelevant in any contest with the executive council. And while Conservative administrations frequently controlled the legislature after the union of Upper and Lower Canada in 1840, the Tories were unable to win a majority of the seats in Canada West in any general election between 1844 and Confederation.[4] After 1867, with the single exception of Sandfield Macdonald's Conservative-dominated coalition, which lasted only until 1871, the Liberals governed Ontario without interruption for over thirty years.

But their command of the system never led them to seek a radical alteration of the province's traditional social and political order. It seems probable that the explanation of the peculiar conservatism of post-Confederation Liberal administrations lies in their experience of the Union legislature between 1841 and 1867. The principal element in the early Reform programme had been the demand for responsible government. After this was achieved there was little in the way of serious social and political reform which the leadership of the party was prepared to consider, and in the circumstances which the difficulties of maintaining stable government in the Union legislature presented there was hardly any opportunity for the promotion of major change. The dominant sentiment among Reformers therefore came to be one which simply favoured sound administration of the province's affairs.

It is true, of course, that the party harboured within its ranks in the early 1850's a radical element which espoused ideas often described as American-inspired and republican in character.[5] For the Clear Grits nothing less than the wholesale transformation of Canadian political institutions would do. Critical of the benefits of responsible government, and totally discontented with the more moderate liberalism which had dominated the Reform movement since the rebellion of 1837, they sought an end to "the pageantry of an aristocratical government." In their combination of a suspicion of financial and railway interests with a demand for political and economic equality of opportunity they may be seen as forerunners of the agrarian protest movements of the early twentieth century.[6]

In fact, however, the Clear Grits never had a significant influence on the Reform party. By the mid-1850's, as the alignments which were to mark the post-Confederation years began to take shape, many of them could find less cause for dissatisfaction with the direction in which the party was moving and gradually the distinctions between the two wings became blurred. Thus, although in many ways they represented an Upper Canadian version of Jacksonian democracy, the Clear Grits offered little more than a minor counterpoint to what has been characterized as the dominant theme of the political culture of British North America. If "ascriptive," "elitist," "hierarchical," "stable," "cautious," and "restrained"[7] cannot easily be extended to describe the values of the whole of Canada, there is no doubt that they apply to the vast majority of the politically effective and articulate residents

3A comparison of the seats won by the Liberals, as shown in Table I, in the years before and after 1905 makes it clear that the election of that year must also be regarded as a watershed in Ontario's political history. The data we present in Table I are in conflict before 1934 with the only other published record of the province's electoral history which we have seen: M.C. Urquhart and K.A.H. Buckley, eds., *Historical Statistics of Canada* (Toronto: The Macmillan Co. of Canada, Ltd., 1965), series W288-298, p. 631. Although there remains some uncertainty about the party affiliation of some candidates until the 1880's, after checking the official sources very carefully we are satisfied that the data in Table I provide the most accurate account of Ontario electoral history that can be given. We have relied mainly on the record in Lewis to establish party affiliation, because it is based on the returning officer's report in the case of each constituency. Where necessary, however, we have adjusted this to take account of an elected member's own statement in the *Canadian Parliamentary Companion* and the *Canadian Parliamentary Guide*.

Only three elections present any significant problem: 1867, 1894, and 1919. Properly speaking, only about 28 members of the first legislature can be clearly identified as part of what would become a coherent Liberal opposition party, according to Paul G. Cornell, "The Genesis of Ontario Politics in the Province of Canada (1838—1871)," in *Profiles of a Province: Studies in the History of Ontario* (Toronto: Ontario Historical Society, 1967), p. 71. But these were supplemented from time to time by a number of independent members, many of whom had contested the 1867 election under the Liberal label while open supporters of the Sandfield Macdonald coalition. Four of the members we have shown as Liberals were among the "Nine Martyrs" who, although elected on an anti-coalition platform, had gone over to Macdonald by the beginning of the second session. If these four are added to the Conservative side in Table I the government would have had 45 members to the opposition's 37 — which was the actual division of strength in 1868, according to James Young, *Public Men and Public Life in Canada* (Toronto: William Briggs, 1912), II, 52. Lewis shows the other five members of the group as Conservatives.

In 1894 the difficulty is created by confusion over the number of members elected by the Patrons of Industry. In this case we have accepted the claims made by Louis A. Wood, *A History of Farmers' Movements in Canada* (Toronto: The Ryerson Press, 1924), pp. 140-141, since most other historians appear to agree with his count.

There is no agreement in any of the known sources as to the number of members elected for each party in 1919. However, we believe our figures to be correct, based as they are on the record in Lewis matched with the members' own entries in the *Canadian Parliamentary Guide* for 1920.

4Paul G. Cornell, *The Alignment of Political Groups in Canada 1841—1867* (Toronto: University of Toronto Press, 1962), p. 85. Canada West was the name used in the Union period for what is now Ontario.

5We are indebted to Professor Leo Johnson of the University of Waterloo for drawing to our attention a number of sources which indicate that the intellectual origins of the Clear Grits are to be found in British, rather than American, radical movements of the day. Indeed, many of the points in the Clear Grit platform bear a strong resemblance to the principal demands of the People's Charter in Great Britain. One of the most influential people in the development of Clear Grittism, Charles Clarke, had emigrated from England in 1844 and had carried with him something of the Chartist upbringing he had experienced at the hands of his schoolteacher, the old Chartist leader Thomas Cooper. See Charles Clarke, *Sixty Years in Upper Canada* (Toronto: William Briggs, 1908), Chap. II and III.

6The Clear Grit platform, which first appeared in William Macdougall's paper *The North American* on February 14, 1851, is reproduced in Clarke, *Sixty Years*, pp. 65-66.

7Seymour Martin Lipset, *The First New Nation: The United States in Historical and Comparative Perspective* (London: Heinemann, 1964), pp. 250-268, *passim*. See also his "Revolution and Counter-Revolution: The United States and Canada," reprinted in Orest M. Kruhlak *et al.*, eds., *The Canadian Political Process: A Reader* (Toronto: Holt, Rinehart and Winston of Canada, Ltd., 1970), pp. 13-38. For a recent study of some aspects of the Ontario political culture see E. J. Heubel, "Michigan and Ontario Legislators: Perspectives on the Federal System," *Canadian Journal of Economics and Political Science*, XXXII, No. 4 (1966), 443-454.

of Ontario in the nineteenth century.[8] Nor does support for the generalization come solely from the extreme: John Graves Simcoe or, later, the High Tory members of the so-called Family Compact. The best evidence comes from the political left; from the success of George Brown, Edward Blake, and finally Sir Oliver Mowat in binding the elements of radical agrarian protest to the cause of moderate reform.

The foundations for the future development of Ontario liberalism were laid in the dying years of the Union period. By the late 1850's Brown's disenchantment with the moderate Reform leadership had brought him closer to the radicals, and after the Toronto *Globe* became the central organ of the gospel of political reform in Canada West, the tone of the whole movement changed.

Brown's accession tended to shift the inspiration [of Grittism] in the British direction. Brown himself became more and more sentimentally British as he grew older. Moreover, as publisher of the Globe, *he was a business man on the make, and Toronto was a growing business centre. As Toronto grew, and as the* Globe *grew, the original frontier agrarianism of the Grits was imperceptibly changed into something subtly different.*[9]

These changes put the seal on the fate of the Liberal party. By 1867 its leadership rested principally with Toronto businessmen, financiers, and lawyers; but the bedrock of its electoral support remained concentrated in the farming communities of the southwestern part of the province – in precisely those counties settled by that "most yeasty and unsafe of populations"[10] which had supported the principles of Clear Grittism. In the twentieth century they were to serve as a solid core of Liberal strength in an otherwise rather hostile province, but in the nineteenth century they formed the bridgehead from which the party captured and kept control of the legislature.

The pattern of post-Confederation politics in Ontario was therefore largely determined by forces generated before 1867. The government which took office after the formal proclamation of the British North America Act was in fact a coalition born of the difficult final years leading up to Confederation. The new premier, John Sandfield Macdonald, shared the view of his federal namesake that a no-party administration was the most appropriate kind for the formative years of the province. And although Brown opposed such an arrangement vigorously (on the ground that it would lead to "corruption, extravagance and the abandonment of principle") Macdonald was nonetheless able to form a government after the September elections which drew support from moderate Reformers as well as Conservatives. Brown, defeated in his own riding and bitter at what seemed to him the failure of the party, resigned the Reform leadership and never ran for election again.

At the beginning of the session he was replaced by Archibald McKellar, who in turn passed the leadership to Edward Blake early in 1870. But by this time the opposition's attack upon the government had managed to detach sufficient of the "loose fish" to undermine the coalition's strength, and when the result of the 1871 election temporarily deprived the government of its majority (through the controversion of the election of several Conservative supporters) Sandfield Macdonald was compelled to resign following defeat in the Legislative Assembly on a vote of confidence. Blake thus became the first Liberal premier of Ontario. In 1872, however, legislation was passed abolishing dual representation and — having opted to keep his seat in the federal parliament — he too was obliged to give up the provincial leadership. The mantle now fell upon Oliver Mowat, who had been persuaded by Blake to leave the bench (where he had gone after participating as a Canadian delegate in the Quebec Conference in 1864) and to return to politics by taking on the premiership. Thus, within the space of five years the Reformers had served under four leaders. It was a curious omen of trouble ahead, as yet many years removed.

But in Oliver Mowat — the Grand Old Man of Ontario[11] — they had found that combination of energetic leadership and canny judgement which was to be the hallmark of the period of Liberal dominance. In these years it was the Conservatives who were driven to shuffling leaders and platforms after every two or three electoral defeats in a desperate search for the key to the government's weakness.[12] In fact, however, despite the often quite substantial Liberal majorities in the assembly, the margin between the two parties in the electorate was never very great: in the six elections between 1872 and 1896 which the Liberals fought under Mowat's leadership the gap between them in the percentage share of votes cast only once exceeded 3 per cent. Clearly the Liberal victories owed a good deal to the over-representation of the rural constituencies where the party found its main support.[13]

[8]See S.F. Wise and Robert Craig Brown, *Canada Views the United States: Nineteenth-Century Political Attitudes* (Toronto: Macmillan Co. of Canada, Ltd., 1967), p. 94.

[9]Frank H. Underhill, "Some Reflections on the Liberal Tradition in Canada," in his *In Search of Canadian Liberalism* (Toronto: Macmillan Co. of Canada, Ltd., 1960), pp. 14 and 15. See also Fred Landon, *Western Ontario and the American Frontier* (Toronto: McClelland & Stewart, Ltd., 1967), pp. xiii-xvi, 217-237.

[10]Sir John Macdonald's description of the Scottish and American settlers who dominated the southwestern region. In the 1871 census people of Scottish and American origin constituted nearly a third of the population of the Lake Huron and Southwestern Ontario districts.

[11]Mowat is perhaps best known for his vigorous defence of the interests of Ontario in the development of the Judicial Committee's interpretative scheme for the British North America Act. See J.C. Morrison, "Oliver Mowat and the Development of Provincial Rights in Ontario: A Study in Dominion-Provincial Relations, 1867–1896," in *Three History Theses* (Toronto: Ontario Department of Public Records and Archives, 1961), separately paginated. See also A. Margaret Evans, "The Mowat Era, 1872–1896: Stability and Progress," in *Profiles of a Province: Studies in the History of Ontario* (Toronto: Ontario Historical Society, 1967), pp. 97-106.

[12]Sandfield Macdonald resigned the Tory leadership in 1872. During the period of Liberal dominance the Conservatives had four more leaders: M.C. Cameron (1872–1879), William R. Meredith (1879–1894), George F. Marter (1894–1896), and after 1896 James Whitney.

[13]Rural strength helped the Liberals in another way. In the general election of 1883, to take one example, they won all eight seats in the Grand Valley with an aggregate of 55 per cent of the vote. But in the six leading towns in the area — Berlin (now Kitchener), Brantford, Galt, Guelph, Preston, and Waterloo — the Conservatives won 53 per cent of the vote. A careful analysis will show that through the better part of the period of Liberal ascendancy the Conservatives invariably won a majority in the towns whose electoral strength was lost in the heart of dominantly rural, and Liberal, ridings.

TABLE I

Electoral History of Ontario 1867–1967

Year	Registered Electorate	Per cent Turnout	Share of votes cast (%)					Number of seats won					Total Seats	Number of candidates as a percentage of total seats				
			Con.	Lib.	NDPa	Farm	Other	Con.	Lib.	NDPa	Farm	Other		Con.	Lib.	NDPa	Farm	Other
1867	214,742	74	49	49			2	41	41			2	82	94	98			13
1871	203,496	64	46	51			3	38	44				82	89	90			11
1875	283,856	67	47	48	*		5	36	49	1			88	88	94	1		23
1879	389,441	64	47	48			5	29	58			1	88	97	91			27
1883	388,223	67	47	48	2		3	38	49			1	88	92	95	3		19
1886	465,385	68	47	48	4		1	32	58				90	91	96	6		10
1890	507,856	64	46	49			5	35	55			1	91	93	93			18
1894	539,352	69	35	41		15b	9c	28	46		17b	3d	94	72	85	1	37b	26e
1898	564,735	76	48	47	*		5	43	51				94	96	97	1		20
1902	596,649	73	50	48	*		2	48	50				98	100	96	13		11
1905	614,914	72	53	45	*		2	69	28			1	98	99	98	6		10
1908	623,497	72	55	40	2		3	86	19	1			106	99	86	20		14
1911	655,655	56	55	39	3		3	83	22	1			106	100	74	13		8
1914	734,489	68	54	38	2		6	84	25	1		1	111	98	82	14		23
1919	1,580,099	74	33	26	10	24f	7	25	28	11	45f	2	111	94	59	23	65f	19
1923	1,712,031	56	50	21	5	22f	2	75	14	4	17f	1	111	92	70	20	66f	15

Year	Total vote																
1926	1,802,187	64	56	22	1	11g	10	74	21	1	16g	112	99	56	3	25g	32
1929	1,804,862	56	57	32	1	5g	5	92	13	1	6g	112	100	75	4	13g	20
1934	2,130,420	73	40	50	7	1h	2	17	70	1	1h	90	100	97	41	4h	48
1937	2,228,030	71	40	51	5	1h	3	23	66		1h	90	100	99	43	8h	46
1943	2,269,895	58	36	31	32		1	38	16	34		90	100	100	96		18
1945	2,469,960	71	44	30	22		4	66	14	8	2i	90	100	98	99		56
1948	2,623,281	68	41	30	27		2	53	14	21	2i	90	100	100	90		27
1951	2,750,709	64	48	32	19		1	79	8	2	2i	90	100	100	86		16
1955	2,905,760	60	49	33	17		1	84	11	3	1i	98	100	98	83		40
1959	3,196,801	59	46	37	17		*	71	22	5		98	100	100	83		19
1963	3,427,620	63	48	35	16		1	77	24	7		108	100	100	90		22
1967	3,676,523	66	42	32	26		*	69	28	20		117	100	100	100		13

*Less than half of 1 per cent.
aBefore 1934 these columns include only Labour and Socialist candidates, from 1934 to 1959 only CCF candidates.
bPatrons of Industry.
cIncludes 4 per cent cast for candidates of the Protestant Protective Association.
dIncludes two elected PPA members.
eExclusively PPA candidates contested 12 per cent of the total seats.
fUnited Farmers of Ontario.
gProgressives.
hAll farmer candidates. The elected member called himself UFO.
iCommunists.

Sources: *Sessional Papers of the Province of Ontario, 1868-1920; Return From the Records of the General Election* (Toronto: Queen's Printer, 1924-1968); Roderick Lewis, comp., *Centennial Edition of a History of the Electoral Districts, Legislatures and Ministries of the Province of Ontario 1867-1968* (Toronto: Queen's Printer, 1968); *Canadian Parliamentary Companion, 1868-1897; Canadian Parliamentary Guide, 1898-1968.*

The Liberals also owed something to the patronage system which Mowat created, organized, and trusted. When traditional party loyalties are weak and when the number of electors is manageably small, patronage constitutes a crucial lubricant in the system of party government. This Mowat fully appreciated[14] and cleverly exploited, without leaving himself open to successful attack from the Conservatives. Nor did Sir Oliver ignore the party gains to be had from a judicious allocation of electoral boundaries: he was easily able, as Sir John Willison put it, to "redistribute constituencies with Christian humility and partisan ingenuity."[15]

Irish Catholic voters, especially in the towns, were another source of Liberal strength. Although the link between Brown's anti-papist *Globe* and the Reform party must have been an embarrassment to Liberals seeking such support, the relationship appears not to have had serious electoral consequences for the party. It is true that in federal elections Macdonald managed to hold the support of the Catholic hierarchy as well as that of the Catholic electors of Ontario, which he had won from the Reformers in 1854,[16] but in provincial elections Mowat's resistance to pressure from the Ontario Tories to abolish the separate school system counted for rather more. It kept the Catholic bishops and their flock for the most part tied to the provincial Liberal party.[17] Mowat's success in this endeavour often drove the opposition to extremes. In 1883 William Meredith, the Conservative leader, had made an open bid for the Irish Catholic vote and, although there had been no shift in the total share of the votes cast going to the two parties, the Tories had recovered a number of seats. Despite this modest success, in the next three provincial elections they returned to an anti-Catholic position — but with no better result, for the party appeared unable to win enough Protestant support to counterbalance the French and Irish Catholic support which was lost. Moreover, the growth of the Protestant Protective Association and its entry into the 1894 campaign (although never formally endorsed by the Conservatives) created an image for the opposition which was skillfully turned to the government's advantage.[18] Behind the call of the *Catholic Register* for "every lover of justice and right" to defeat both the Conservative party and the PPA, the faithful fell into line and, in voting for the Presbyterian Mowat, contributed to the worst Tory defeat in Ontario since Confederation.

The 1894 election was the last for both leaders. Meredith had tried everything to dislodge the Liberals: in addition to taking both sides in the Catholic controversy he had made a genuine attempt to overtake the government with reform policies similar to those espoused by the Tory democrats in England. But Mowat was not easily outflanked. The tradition of reform was the property of the Liberal party, and while its leader "was not a Radical, nor a Liberal, nor even a Whig . . . [but] a Tory in social instinct and in political practice and outlook"[19] he was nonetheless responsive to pressures for social and political change. Secured by their strength in the rural southwest, the Liberals could seek support in other directions: from manufacturers in the towns through general acceptance of a policy of tariff protection, and from Catholics through the preservation and even improvement of their educational rights.

The policy which Mowat had evolved in the years before 1894 and on which the government . . . based its arguments was so broad in its scope and at the same time so pragmatically fitted to the needs of the province that only the title, The Ontario System, seems inclusive enough. In the same way that Macdonald's policy became the National Policy and its author the nation-builder par excellence, Mowat's grasp of Ontario development made his policy the system for the province, and himself its great builder.[20]

He had developed a superb political coalition: sustained by patronage, by a high degree of cabinet cohesion, by an aggressive defence of provincial rights, and by sound financial management which even the Conservatives were bound to admire.

Mowat's record was indeed "a model of conservative reform,"[21] and yet the splendid edifice could not stand forever. Notwithstanding the rash of labour legislation prior to the 1894 election — most working men now had the vote[22] — there was considerable truth in Meredith's claim that the world had moved faster than the Liberals. Mowat had never been much interested

[14]See Sir John Willison, *Reminiscences: Political and Personal* (Toronto: McClelland & Stewart, Ltd., 1919), p. 96.

[15]*Ibid.*, p. 101.

[16]See Joseph Wearing, "Pressure Group Politics in Canada West Before Confederation," *Historical Papers Presented at the Annual Meeting of the Canadian Historical Association, Ottawa, 1967*, pp. 75-94.

[17]See Paul Douglas Stevens, "Laurier and the Liberal Party in Ontario" (Ph.D. thesis, University of Toronto, 1966), p. 164.

[18]Although we show only two elected members for the PPA in Table 1, there is considerable evidence that at least fourteen members of the Association, most of them running as straight Conservatives, actually were elected to the legislature in 1894. For the details see James T. Watt, "Anti-Catholicism in Ontario Politics: The Role of the Protestant Protective Association in the 1894 Election," *Ontario History*, LIX, No. 2 (1967), 57-67. The Conservatives did not contest the election at all in North Oxford, where Mowat was opposed by a PPA candidate.

[19]Willison, *Reminiscences*, p. 101. See also W.S. Wallace, "Political History: 1867—1912," in *Canada and Its Provinces* (Edinburgh edition), Adam Shortt and Arthur G. Doughty, eds. (Toronto: Publishers Association of Canada, Ltd., 1914), XVII, 138.

[20]Janet B. Kerr, "Sir Oliver Mowat and the Campaign of 1894," *Ontario History*, LV, No. 1 (1963), 3.

[21]Wallace, "Political History," p. 177.

[22]The Manhood Suffrage Act of 1888 extended the vote to all adult males, abolishing all earlier property qualifications with one or two minor exceptions. The Ontario Franchise Act of 1917, which gave the vote to all adult women, provided for basically the suffrage enjoyed in the province since that time. However, towards the end of the 1971 session legislation was passed lowering the legal age of majority to 18, which of course lowers the voting age for all future provincial elections. Many other changes in the province's election law were recommended in the first four reports of the legislature's Select Committee on Election Laws, and some of these were incorporated in a revised Election Act, passed in 1969 and amended in 1971. For a review of all aspects of Ontario election law see T.H. Qualter, *The Election Process in Canada* (Toronto: McGraw-Hill Co. of Canada Limited, 1970), *passim*.

in questions of economic inequality. Once the basic pattern of federal-provincial relations had been established by judicial decision the chief concerns of the party seemed increasingly irrelevant to the society growing about it, and when, in 1896, Sir Oliver exchanged his premiership for the position of Attorney General in Laurier's first cabinet the framework of power he had so patiently fashioned began to disintegrate.

Neither A.S. Hardy nor George Ross, who followed him in quick succession,[23] could maintain the dominant position which the Ontario Liberals had enjoyed since Confederation. Although they survived in office through two further elections, what has been called the inexorable logic of Canadian federalism now began to work against them. With Laurier in power at Ottawa federal policies unpopular at a time of rising nationalist and imperialist sentiment in Ontario had a damaging effect on the appeal of the Ross government. At the same time, the organizational benefits which it might have been hoped national success would bring to the provincial party failed to materialize. Laurier could not find able Ontario lieutenants to give the attention to the province that now had become essential. For the harsh fact was that Mowat had left the Ontario party organization in a severely weakened state — in fact in a condition from which it has never recovered.[24]

Thus, in order to preserve their slender margin in the legislature, the Liberals were driven to corruption. In a series of by-elections ballot-stuffing, personation, and intimidation became common Liberal practices,[25] and, although a Royal Commission never proved it, there was widespread suspicion that they had tried to bribe a Conservative member, Robert Gamey, to support the government.[26] Laurier advised Ross to resign rather than seek to continue in office through the use of such tactics but the Ontario premier apparently thought that the Conservatives could not win with Whitney as their leader. In Willison's opinion, had Ross stepped down "in deference to wholesome public sentiment he would have protected his own reputation and dignity, and the restoration of the Liberal party in Ontario would have been a far less onerous undertaking for his successors."[27] But Ross chose instead to call a general election for January 25, 1905. It was a disaster for his party.

For their complicity in patently dishonest electoral practices and for their timidity on the issue of prohibition (which Mowat had managed to keep out of provincial politics), the Grits were punished by those same upright, God-fearing farmers of Ontario who had always served as the bedrock of their electoral strength. In the rural southwest alone their representation was cut in half. At the same time the Liberals began to feel the effect of their failure to respond to Ontario's rapid urbanization. Charles Humphries has described the forces which were working to alter the face of the province's politics:

The first decade of the twentieth century witnessed a critical and apparently unalterable change in the nature of Ontario society. In 1901, 42.9 per cent of the population of the province lived in incorporated places; by 1911 that figure had risen to 52.5 per cent. In the space of these ten years Ontario became, quite literally, urbanized, most notably in the south-central region. Agriculture yielded its prime position in the province's economy to manufacturing and business. The Conservatives observed the change and acted;

the Liberals, with a few exceptions, failed to appreciate the altered circumstances and, consequently, were unmoved by them. At the century's turn, the Conservatives increasingly represented the new interests of the growing cities and towns and they were rewarded for their perception; the Liberals remained tied to a declining rural population — in some instances the decline was real and, in others, relative — and they were penalized for their insensitivity.[28]

The 1905 election marked the end of Liberal dominance in Ontario. For the first time since Confederation the Conservatives polled a substantial majority of the votes cast and reduced Grit representation to less than a third of the seats in the Legislative Assembly. There thus began a stranglehold on Ontario politics that has since been interrupted only twice.

If Mowat's administrations had not been radical, Whitney's new government was not especially conservative. In some ways Liberal policies were merely continued — in, for example, the defence of provincial rights and the development of the North. But in several other respects, in education policy, in labour legislation, and in the promotion of the public ownership of utilities — most obviously in the establishment of the Ontario Hydro-Electric Power Commission in 1906 — Whitney was a good deal more willing to innovate.[29] He showed as well an appropriate concern for the well-being of Catholic electors by appointing two leading members of that faith to his first cabinet (Mowat had had only one Catholic in his cabinets) and he took especial pains to improve the party's machinery in the constituencies. At the same time stiffer penalties for electoral corruption were enacted.

In the face of this strategy the Liberal party slipped even further into the morass. In the years after 1905 Conservative power at Queen's Park was much strengthened by the progressive decay of the Liberal organization. By 1911, to take one aspect of the problem, the Grits could find candidates for

[23]Hardy became premier upon Mowat's resignation. Ross replaced him in 1899 and continued to lead the party after his government's defeat until he was appointed to the Senate in 1907. He was followed by G.P. Graham who resigned later that year to join Laurier's cabinet. The leadership then fell to Alexander MacKay.

[24]See Stevens, "Laurier and the Liberal Party in Ontario," pp. 222, 301, and 305.

[25]Willison, *Reminiscences,* p. 321.

[26]See Charles W. Humphries, "The Gamey Affair," *Ontario History,* LIX, No. 2 (1967), 101-109; and Willison, *Reminiscences,* p. 329.

[27]Willison, *Reminiscences,* p. 325.

[28]Charles W. Humphries, "The Sources of Ontario 'Progressive' Conservatism, 1900—1914," *Historical Papers Presented at the Annual Meeting of the Canadian Historical Association, Ottawa, 1967,* p. 119.

[29]The Workmen's Compensation Act of 1914 made the employer responsible in all cases of injury to employees, a departure from previous policy which must have added to urban Conservative strength in these years. The extent to which direct government intervention has been used to foster the development of Ontario's economy must have significantly affected the dominant ideas and attitudes of the people of the province, by legitimizing a modern and collectivist approach to political problems. For an account of the pattern of government intervention in the earlier years see Harold A. Innis, "An Introduction to the Economic History of Ontario From Outpost to Empire," in his *Essays in Canadian Economic History,* Mary Q. Innis, ed. (Toronto: University of Toronto Press, 1956), pp. 108-122.

only three-quarters of the seats in the legislature.[30] Earlier in that year the federal election had reduced their representation from Ontario to a mere rump at Ottawa and party spirits throughout the province were at their lowest ebb. In addition to that Alexander MacKay, the second leader to follow Ross, had resigned a short time before the election and the relatively unknown and inexperienced Newton Rowell was compelled to lead a party not only torn in rivalry between its Toronto and rural wings but which, he said, "had neither organization, literature, nor the funds to provide for even the most necessary arrangements."[31] The overwhelming Conservative majority of 1908 was therefore hardly reduced at all.

The election of 1911 also introduced a new and divisive issue into Ontario politics. Although the Conservatives had been publicly opposed to the use of any language other than English in the schools of the province, they had not made an election issue of the regulations implemented in 1890 allowing French or German to be used in those districts where there was a demand (provided that English remained the language of general instruction). Now, reacting to pressure from the newly-formed French Canadian Educational Association of Ontario for equal rights for the French language, several Conservatives called for completely unilingual instruction. The situation created tensions in the Ontario Catholic community as well as internal difficulties in the two political parties.

During the first three decades after Confederation the proportion of Catholics in the Ontario population remained at roughly 17 per cent. But by the census of 1911, while the percentage had increased only slightly, the composition of the Catholic population had changed rather dramatically. The bulk of Roman Catholics in 1867 had been of Irish origin — people who came to Canada in the great wave of immigration after 1840. After the turn of the century it was French-speaking people from Quebec, moving into the upper Ottawa Valley and northern Ontario, who added substantially to the growth of the province's Catholic population. Indeed, it was in large measure the rapid growth of Ontario's French-speaking community which so alarmed members of the Protestant faiths. In the minds of many of them the separate school issue and the French language issue were inextricably fused — with great cost to the interests of English-speaking Catholics whose bishops were now beginning to establish some kind of understanding with the Conservative government over the matter of financial support for elementary schools.[32]

The election itself did not provide an open party fight; nor was there a precise division between Catholics and Protestants. But the Liberals were able to appear less committed to either side of the issue and succeeded in offsetting their otherwise unimposing performance by gaining two seats in ridings in which the French-speaking vote may have been significant.[33]

Their position was no more more precise in 1914. In fact Rowell's tactic was to avoid the bilingual schools question by arguing that the implementation of prohibition — as the keystone of social reform — was the foremost issue of the campaign. The Conservatives, on the other hand, placed themselves squarely behind the policy which had led in 1912 to the Department of Education's controversial Regulation 17[34] — a policy which, incidentally, received the wholehearted support of the Irish Catholic clergy of the province. In the heat of the campaign party positions became blurred. *Le Droit* advised French-speaking Ontarians to vote Liberal to protect their language rights; *Le Temps* suggested an altogether different course: ". . . as between two evils we must choose the less, we prefer to remain with Mr. Whitney. . . . Mr. Rowell's attitude is disastrous for the future of the French language in Ontario."[35] To add to the confusion, a former editor of the Orange paper, the *Sentinel,* outraged by what he regarded as government concessions in the 1913 revisions to Regulation 17, called on English-speaking voters to support the Liberal party as the best guardian of their language.

The extent to which religious and language factors entered into the result remains unclear. The state of Liberal organization was still sufficiently weak to prevent them from contesting much more than four-fifths of the seats and their stress upon prohibition undoubtedly served to diminish their appeal to the urban working class. Still, it appears that they benefited from the French-speaking vote in such ridings as Essex North, Ottawa East, Sturgeon Falls, and Russell — defeating two French-speaking Conservatives in the process. But over the entire province, with the bulk of Protestant and Irish Catholic opinion on the government side in the bilingual schools question, the Liberal share of the vote was less than it had been in 1911. Against Whitney's progressive Conservatism the Grits — still tied to their rural supporters — were unable to develop a winning alternative.

As Ontario entered the war years it thus appeared that the Tories had acquired a permanent hold on the government at Queen's Park. But by the middle of 1919 it was clear that they were in trouble. Principally, they had fallen victim to those circumstances of the federal system which dictate that in times of national crisis attention will be focussed on the central government. The Hearst administration's record, because it was noticed less, appeared considerably less impressive than the legislative achievements which had characterized Whitney's period of leadership.[36] At the same time, the immediate postwar years — when demands for social reform have been generally most pronounced — offered the Liberals the very opportunity they

[30]For an account of the internal divisions which hampered the Liberals in this period see P.D. Stevens, "Laurier, Aylesworth, and the Decline of the Liberal Party in Ontario," *Historical Papers 1968: A Selection From the Papers Presented at the Annual Meeting of the Canadian Historical Association, Calgary, 1968,* pp. 94-113.

[31]Quoted in the *Canadian Annual Review,* J. Castell Hopkins, ed. (Toronto: Annual Review Publishing Company, Ltd., 1911), p. 477.

[32]See Margaret Prang, "Clerics, Politicians, and the Bilingual Schools Issue in Ontario, 1910—1917," *Canadian Historical Review,* XLI, No. 4 (1960), 282.

[33]*Ibid.,* p. 286.

[34]The regulation in its original form limited the use of French as a language of instruction to the first two years of schooling. A slight revision in 1913 permitted some flexibility in the local application of this rule at the discretion of the Minister of Education. For further details of the controversy see Prang, *Canadian Historical Review,* XLI, 289-307.

[35]Quoted in the *Canadian Annual Review,* J. Castell Hopkins, ed. (Toronto: Annual Review Publishing Company, Ltd., 1914), p. 448.

[36]William Hearst had become premier in October, 1914, following Whitney's death.

sought for the recovery of political power. But the formation of the Union Government in 1917, which had effectively crippled the national party, had left the Ontario organization in a state of thorough disarray. Rowell had resigned the leadership to join Sir Robert Borden's cabinet, taking with him much of the structure he had built up in the province after 1911.[37] Moreover, the bitter struggle between conscriptionist and Laurier Liberals in the constituencies had made it difficult to prepare the ground for the general provincial election due in the autumn of 1919. The Liberals were therefore able to contest only three fifths of the seats — grim testimony to the sorry state of the once great party of Reform.[38]

For all that, organizational weaknesses were by no means the principal contributing element in the Liberals' inability to take advantage of the discontent in the countryside. Nor can the defeat of the Conservative government properly be described — for rural voters at least — as the explicit rejection of the provincial Tories. The result of the 1919 election was, strictly speaking, a revolt against *both* older parties, but a revolt which had its roots mainly in criticism of the conscription policy of the Union Government and its effect upon the already dwindling rural population.[39] As the war had progressed, both farmer and labour organizations had expressed increasing concern that their members should not bear the brunt of the war effort — equality demanded a conscription of wealth as well as men. When Borden went back on his promise of the 1917 national campaign not to conscript farm help the effect on farmers' movements throughout the country was electric. In Ontario a special convention of the United Farmers Organization meeting in June, 1918 endorsed a resolution calling for independent political action: if satisfaction could no longer be gained at the hands of the traditional parties the farmer must "go into politics or out of farming."

No one was more surprised than the leaders of the farm organization when the UFO emerged from the election as the largest single group in the Assembly. Nevertheless, although they had contested barely two-thirds of the seats, the farmers accepted the opportunity to take power. In co-operation with the Independent Labor Party (which had elected a sufficient number of members in the towns to give the two groups together a majority in the legislature) they provided Ontario with its only experience of "third party" government. The success of the farmer-labour coalition derived mainly from frustration — felt by many farmers and working men alike — with the inadequate representative capacity of the traditional parties. Their solution was direct class representation in the legislature through members of their own organizations. Thus, the subsequent "broadening out controversy,"[40] and in particular the idea of fusion with the Liberal party, was, in the eyes of many of the government's supporters, tantamount to subversion of the principle of independence that had inspired the original entry of the two groups into provincial politics. For others the 1919 election had represented a sharp break with family loyalties which needed the special conditions of social unrest to sustain it. The immediate postwar period had provided the occasion when that break — if it was ever to come — could be established. But once those special circumstances no longer existed most Ontario electors returned to their earlier allegiance.

However, the process did not take place in all cases with equal speed. Most urban Conservatives were drawn back almost immediately in Howard Ferguson's 1923 sweep of the province. In the rural areas, on the other hand, there is some evidence — based on a township by township analysis — that the Tory vote hardly changed at all between 1919 and 1923, and that the party owed its success to a general decline in the UFO vote which appears to have been caused by an extraordinarily high degree of abstention among farmers. Many Liberals — still faced with their party's inability to find a satisfactory leader[41] — evidently either did not bother to vote at all (in 1923 the Liberal share of the vote dropped to its lowest level at any time since Confederation: 21 per cent) or turned to the Tories in disgust. Thus, while the United Farmers were able to hold just under half their seats in 1923, they ceased to exist as a coherent legislative group after the general election of 1926. In their place a number of Progressive and Liberal-Progressive farmer candidates appeared who were eventually to join the Liberal party.

The 1920's were lean years indeed for the Grits. With yet another leader — William Sinclair — they passed their time in a luckless crusade against the demon rum and, at the end of the election of 1929, found themselves with a mere thirteen seats in the Assembly. Not once did they contest more than three-quarters of the province's constituencies. The party had become "not much more than a rural Protestant splinter group, narrowly based on a dozen predominantly dry ridings, its policies bankrupt, its leadership pathetically weak."[42] The Conservatives, on the other hand, had succeeded in putting together an urban-rural power base more impressive even than that which the Liberals had enjoyed under Mowat. Ferguson's interest in the problems of agriculture had won him nearly two-thirds of the rural districts; his moderate "wet" policy along with the generally prosperous conditions of the late twenties made him friends among the growing number of city electors. His "under the table" support of separate schools even won him the normally Liberal Catholic vote. Only the province's French-Canadians, "still leery of

[37]Peter Regenstreif, "The Liberal Party of Canada: A Political Analysis" (Ph.D. thesis, Cornell University, 1963), p. 129.

[38]Some of this weakness may have been due to Mackenzie King's attempt to persuade the Ontario party to follow his own strategy of avoiding open contests with the farmers. See R. MacGregor Dawson, *William Lyon Mackenzie King: A Political Biography, 1874—1923* (Toronto: University of Toronto Press, 1958), pp. 315-316.

[39]In the cities, on the other hand, the vote for the ILP reflected both a general protest against the older parties and a criticism of the Hearst government's unwillingness to pass legislation providing for a 44-hour week and for collective bargaining. The ILP won eleven seats, one of them being Hearst's own riding of Sault Ste. Marie. For a brief account of the campaign see Brian D. Tennyson, "The Ontario General Election of 1919: The Beginnings of Agrarian Revolt," *Journal of Canadian Studies*, IV, No. 1 (1969), 26-36.

[40]For an account of the role of the intra-party dispute in the collapse of the UFO see David Hoffman, "Intra-Party Democracy: A Case Study," *Canadian Journal of Economics and Political Science*, XXVII, No. 2 (1961), 223-235.

[41]The Liberals had tried three different leaders after Rowell's resignation in 1917: William Proudfoot (1918—1919), Hartley Dewart (1919—1922), and F. Wellington Hay (1922—1923).

[42]Neil McKenty, *Mitch Hepburn* (Toronto: McClelland & Stewart, Ltd., 1967), p. 31.

[his] Orange-dominated Party,"[43] remained outside the fold. Ontario seemed perilously close to a one-party system when Ferguson handed over the premiership to George Henry on December 15, 1930. Two days later, however, the Liberals chose as their leader a man who was to reverse dramatically the tide of the party's fortune.

To say that Mitchell Hepburn saved the Liberal party in Ontario is both an exaggeration and an understatement. In the furious election campaign of 1934 in which he managed to extricate it from the tiresome liquor question and to implicate the Tories in charges of corruption, Hepburn *was* the Liberal party. Fighting without adequate funds or organization he turned what might have been a comfortable victory for the Conservatives into an absolute rout. The depressed economic conditions of the early thirties provided the setting; his flaming oratory was the instrument. At the end of it all the Liberals had converted the largest Conservative majority in Ontario's history into a Grit sweep so thorough that they won every seat in the province west of Toronto, to say nothing of the North. It was an incredible electoral upset.

But because the victory of 1934 was so completely his own achievement, Hepburn's success did little to restore the Liberal party as a major force in the province. No annual meetings were held after 1932; no special effort was made to re-establish the party machinery in the constituencies; no consistent programme of social reform was developed. Guided by a few close business and mining friends and the province's senior civil servant, Chester Walters, Hepburn did not so much evolve a legislative programme as react instinctively to events. He never understood the importance which the economic changes of the interwar years had for the future development of Ontario. One of his political contemporaries, E.B. Jolliffe, later recalled this weakness:

I did feel very strongly about what I thought to be his indifference — and. antagonism — towards people who were victims of a depression they had not created. . . . I first met him in the summer of 1935 . . . in his office, when he had just cut all the single unemployed men off relief — because as one who had been a hard-working farmer, he just didn't believe there was any reason at all why a single man should be without a job. . . . He was extraordinarily insensitive to what was happening to the people in the cities and towns, very sensitive to the complaints of his farmers.[44]

Thus, under Mitchell Hepburn's leadership the Liberals were unable to make the break with their past which was necessary if they were to recapture the commanding position they had lost in 1905. Still, the magnetism of his style was sufficient to carry the party through one more election, through his hysterical campaign against the growth of industrial unionism in the province,[45] and into the political upheaval brought on by the war.

The 1937 election was the zenith of Hepburn's career. From then until his sudden resignation from the premiership in 1942 he grew progressively less interested in the day-to-day affairs of government and more obsessed by his bitter feud with Mackenzie King.[46] The party itself, which had depended heavily for its cohesion upon Hepburn's domination of the legislature, quickly "began to fly apart into disparate factions"[47] when he was replaced by Gordon Conant. But the disintegration wrought by the split between the federal and provincial wings had gone so far that even the substitution of Harry Nixon for Conant in the spring of 1943 could not stem the tide.[48] In the electoral disaster of the summer the party's representation was cut to a bare sixteen seats from the sixty-six it had won in 1937. In its place the CCF became the official opposition facing a minority Conservative government led by George Drew.

The 1943 election was probably the most important in Ontario's history. For one thing it represented the beginning of the serious three-party system which has now become the hallmark of the province's politics. Although the provincial CCF had been in existence since 1932 it had never managed to make a significant impression on the Ontario electorate. In the early days it had been wracked by internal disputes which had sapped its organizational strength and its miserable performance in the province in the federal election of 1940 seemed to have demonstrated its irrelevance.[49] But as the war continued the mood of people everywhere in Canada changed. In rapidly industrializing Ontario the growth of trade unions, an increasing disposition not to fear the consequences of national planning, and a general acceptance of the need to build a new and better postwar world fostered the growth of support for the party. And in the vacuum created by the Liberal government's failure under Hepburn to adjust to the new economic circumstances of the province it was comparatively easy for the CCF to overcome the traditional two-party dominance of the system. Caught in the crush of a rising labour vote in the cities and in the North on the one hand and Conservative gains in the countryside on the other, the Liberals, although polling nearly as many votes as the CCF, were necessarily decimated.

At the same time, the fact that the Conservatives formed the government in 1943 now appears crucial. Of course, given the CCF's weak organizational base and the magnitude of the task which lay before it, in a sense it may be claimed that it was sheer good fortune for it to have done as well as it did.

---

[43]*Ibid.*

[44]From a CBC radio broadcast, November 15, 1967. See also Neil McKenty, "That Tory Hepburn," in *Profiles of a Province: Studies in the History of Ontario* (Toronto: Ontario Historical Society, 1967), pp. 137-141. Mr. Jolliffe was leader of the Ontario CCF from 1942 to 1953.

[45]For details of Hepburn's reaction to the 1937 Oshawa strike see McKenty, *Mitch Hepburn*, pp. 104-118.

[46]Richard M. H. Alway, "Hepburn, King, and the Rowell-Sirois Commission," *Canadian Historical Review*, XLVIII, No. 2 (1967), 113-141.

[47]McKenty, *Mitch Hepburn*, p. 258.

[48]The choice of Nixon was designed to heal the breach with Ottawa. Mackenzie King had favoured him for several years and no less than eight federal cabinet ministers were present at the convention to assure his success: McKenty, *Mitch Hepburn*, pp. 265 and 266.

[49]The party was established in November, 1932 as a federation of the Ontario Labour Conference, the Associated CCF Clubs, and what remained of the UFO. But in 1934, after the dispute with the UFO had practically destroyed the movement's structure, it was reorganized on the basis which is broadly preserved today. For details of this period see Gerald L. Caplan, "The Failure of Canadian Socialism: The Ontario Experience, 1932—1945," *Canadian Historical Review*, XLIV, No. 2 (1963), 93-121.

On the other hand the UFO before it — certainly no better organized — had managed to win a plurality of seats and there was therefore no special reason for supposing that another third party could not manage the same. Moreover, it might have been expected that the social composition of the CCF vote would have been sufficiently stable to allow the party to escape being confined to the one term of office which had destroyed the UFO. But forming the administration, even for a brief period, would have been important for other reasons in 1943. The Liberals and the Conservatives, prodded by the need for unity during the war, might very well have joined forces to defeat a minority CCF government: in at least one other province they had been willing in the same period to form a coalition government to keep the CCF from power.[50] Had they done so in Ontario they would have run the risk of thereby admitting that there was — as the CCF claimed — no real difference between them, and they might equally have alienated those who were disposed to see the new men given a chance. In any case it can hardly be doubted that the CCF would have been able to produce an efficient and competent government and time — perhaps no more than a year while the wartime mood prevailed — might have been enough to convert the "Communist-CIO-CCF" dictatorship of the propagandists' imagination into a group of respectable administrators of a prosperous and expanding economy.[51]

But it was not the CCF which was to lead Ontario into the postwar world. Having lost the confidence of the legislature in the spring of 1945, Drew went to the country in June and the first of a since uninterrupted series of overwhelming Conservative majorities was the result.[52] The province's three-party system has nonetheless been preserved. Although the CCF was able to form the official opposition only once — in 1948 — it and its successor (the New Democratic Party) have continued to command a moderately satisfactory level of support. At the same time the Liberals, while too strong to be replaced by the NDP, have rarely attracted more than a third of the vote. The possibility of a serious threat to the government must therefore lie beyond a resolution of the struggle between the two opposition parties.

II. THE CONTEMPORARY PARTY SYSTEM

It is clear that the continued dominance of the Conservative party in Ontario politics depends primarily upon the inability of either the Liberals or the New Democrats to establish themselves as the obvious alternative to the government. But the forces which prevent the one opposition party from destroying the other are less easy to discover.[53]

The weakness of the Liberals is particularly striking when compared with the success of the federal party in the province in the modern period. Since 1935 they have, almost without exception, won considerably greater support in Ontario in federal elections than the Conservatives — both in terms of seats and votes — and yet they have been unable to keep that support in provincial campaigns. No one explanation gives a thorough account of this phenomenon, but generally it appears to be due to the lower salience which provincial politics may have for the kind of people who vote Liberal federally, together with the destructive effect which national success has on the personnel and organizational capacity of the Ontario party — and therefore on its ability to mount an appealing provincial campaign.[54] Whether these circumstances can be altered remains, of course, a matter for speculation.

Of more importance, however, is the emerging relevance of social class as an influence on the party vote in Ontario. Although it has been fashionable with the older parties in Canada to seek to avoid the growth of a pattern of party competition based primarily on considerations of economic and social position, it has always been the case that where the conditions of particular provinces lent themselves to such a development the argument against it was much less persuasive than it was nationally. The multitude of conflicting interests — which it has been claimed requires a successful national party to be no more than "a loosely-knit representative collection of voters from all groups"[55] — is rarely reproduced in its entirety in each provincial system. Farmers' parties, for example, managed to stay in office in the Prairie provinces long after the Progressives had ceased to be of consequence in the House of Commons. In British Columbia the CCF/NDP, although never able to form a government, has nonetheless remained a significant element in the provincial party system for over thirty years through a direct appeal to the

---

[50]Hepburn had considered coalition with the Tories in 1937 to deal with labour unrest in the province. See McKenty, *Mitch Hepburn*, pp. 119-124.

[51]For an account of some of the problems facing the CCF at the end of the war see Gerald L. Caplan, "The Ontario 'Gestapo' Affair, 1943—1945," *Canadian Journal of Economics and Political Science*, XXX, No. 3 (1964), 343—359. For a general survey of voting in the period see Dennis H. Wrong, "Ontario Provincial Elections, 1934—55: A Preliminary Survey of Voting," *Canadian Journal of Economics and Political Science*, XXIII, No. 3 (1957), 395-403.

[52]An extremely interesting account of the postwar period may be found in Jack Cahill, "The Tory Years," *Toronto Daily Star*, February 14, 15, 16, and 17, 1968. See also Peter Silcox, "Some Problems of Opposition Leadership in Ontario Provincial Politics" (paper delivered to the annual meeting of the Canadian Political Science Association, Calgary, 1968).

[53]One of the principal contributing factors to the weak Liberal image must be the frequent changes in leadership the party has undergone since the end of the Second World War. After Hepburn (who had been chosen House leader during the 1944 session) was personally defeated in Elgin in 1945 Farquhar Oliver became leader. Since then there have been six further changes. This is in sharp contrast to the CCF/NDP which has had — until Donald MacDonald was replaced by Stephen Lewis at the October, 1970 convention of the party — only two leaders since the office was established in 1942. Before that time the party was headed by its chief administrative officer — the Provincial Secretary — who was not always the same person. See Leo Zakuta, *A Protest Movement Becalmed: A Study of Change in the CCF* (Toronto: University of Toronto Press, 1964), p. 63.

[54]For a more extensive analysis of this aspect of Liberal weakness see our "The Liberal Party in Contemporary Ontario Politics," *Canadian Journal of Political Science*, III, No. 2 (1970), 177-204. The federal and provincial electoral data we examine there make it quite clear that the customary explanation of the phenomenon — that the electorate deliberately seeks a balance of power between the two levels of government — cannot be sustained.

[55]F.H. Underhill, "Concerning Mr. King," *Canadian Forum*, September, 1950, p. 125.

industrial working-class.[56] In Ontario there is now some evidence that electors are more willing than in the past to regard their social class as a satisfactory basis for choosing between the parties.[57] The position of the Liberals is made the more difficult in this development by the fact that the Ontario NDP enjoys an especially clear image as a party which is sensitive to the problems of the workingman. Survey data indicate that nearly half of those who can name something they find attractive about the NDP mention its attitude to labour. In contrast, the Conservatives are seen primarily as an efficient party while the Liberals have no clearly defined identity at all.[58]

It is generally the case that the dominant image of a party is a reflection of the principal characteristics of its supporters. Nowhere is this more evident than in the socio-economic characteristics of those electors who identify with the NDP.[59] Compared to the population of the province as a whole (or to the sample) the party's support is clearly more heavily concentrated in the younger age groups, among men, among skilled workers and particularly members of trade unions, and among people who describe themselves as members of the working class. In religious affiliation, as would be expected of a party that owes its strength to its appeal to labour, NDP supporters exhibit a distribution which is almost identical to that of the province itself. They appear as well to be somewhat more inclined to regard themselves simply as Canadians rather than as members of distinct ethnic groups.

On the other hand Liberal supporters mirror nearly every characteristic of the electorate, apart from a superior strength among those aged 35 to 49 and the customary dependence upon adherents of the Roman Catholic faith and people of non-British origin. In the transitional phase of a party system such a pattern of support — drawn more or less equally from all groups in the population — is not only typical for a party of the centre but is likely to help it maintain its competitive position. But if, as seems likely, economic status becomes an even greater influence on the vote in the future, the fact that the Liberal party does not depend upon any special economic group may ultimately be a source of weakness.[60] Moreover, since it does draw disproportionate support from Roman Catholics and people who continue to claim a distinct ethnic identification other than English, it is possible that much of the party's current working-class strength comes from those who put these considerations before their economic status. But the pressures of urbanization tend to destroy such identifications and it may therefore be the case that in Ontario at least the Liberals will not be able to keep these people with them in the future.

The party's difficulty is made even more acute by the fact that the Conservatives are already attracting electors whose interests are broadly opposed to those of NDP supporters. Quite apart from a greater dependence upon the older age groups, people who prefer to call themselves English-Canadians, and adherents of the major Protestant faiths, the most striking aspect of Conservative support is its dominantly middle-class character. Compared to the sample as a whole the party's strength is more heavily concentrated in the higher socio-economic groups: nearly three-quarters of its supporters live in non-union households and over half of them describe themselves as middle-class.[61] Of the three parties then, only the Conservatives and the New Democrats are clearly rooted in distinct sectors of the electorate.

The character of a party may also be revealed by the kinds of candidates it chooses to represent its cause. As a general rule, of course, it would not be expected that the most politically active members of a society would reflect with any precision the occupational structure of the general population. But while Ontario is much the same as other representative systems in this respect there were nonetheless differences in the backgrounds of the candidates who contested the 1967 election which are related both to the parties' images and to the characteristics of their supporters.[62]

[56]See Martin Robin, "The Social Bases of Party Politics in British Columbia," *Queen's Quarterly*, LXXII, No. 4 (1965—66), 675-690.

[57]See, for example, Wallace Gagne and Peter Regenstreif, "Some Aspects of New Democratic Party Urban Support in 1965," *Canadian Journal of Economics and Political Science*, XXXIII, No. 4 (1967), 529-550; and John Wilson, "Politics and Social Class in Canada: The Case of Waterloo South," *Canadian Journal of Political Science*, I, No. 3 (1968), 288-309. Alford reported that Ontario had "the highest level of class voting in six of the ten surveys" used in his study. See Robert R. Alford, *Party and Society: The Anglo-American Democracies* (Chicago: Rand McNally & Co., 1963), p. 263. That this development is part of the ongoing process of industrialization is by now well-established. See Robert E. Lane, "The Politics of Consensus in an Age of Affluence," *American Political Science Review*, LIX, No. 4 (1965), 874-895.

[58]These observations are based on data collected in a representative survey of the Ontario electorate conducted early in 1967. Respondents were asked: "What are all the things you like about the provincial _____ party here in Ontario?" Some three-quarters of the sample could name something they liked about at least one of the parties; the remainder had no opinion at all. Of those mentioning anything they liked about the NDP 47 per cent referred to its attitude to labour, while 35 per cent of those who gave a reason for liking the Conservatives mentioned their efficiency. The largest group amongst those who expressed an opinion about the Liberals were the 21 per cent who had merely a "general liking" for the party. Further details of the survey may be obtained from the Data Bank of the Institute for Behavioural Research at York University, where the data deck and codebook have been lodged.

[59]The data in Table II represent the distribution of a number of socio-economic variables among respondents who identified with or felt "closer to" one of the three parties. Five Social Credit supporters are excluded as are 178 respondents who were either independents or did not know which party they identified with.

[60]The Liberals, of course, regard this as an advantage. Speaking to a party meeting in London the Ontario leader, Robert Nixon, claimed that both the Conservatives and the NDP were hampered by being too closely identified with single interests. "The Liberals aren't in the pockets of big business and we are not in the pockets of labor unions," he said. "We are for the individual and if we can convince people of that, we will form the next government of Ontario." *Kitchener-Waterloo Record*, June 29, 1970.

[61]The strongly middle-class character of the provincial Conservative vote depends to a considerable extent upon the support of people who persistently vote Liberal federally but who switch parties in provincial elections. See Wilson and Hoffman, "The Liberal Party" 190, 194-196.

[62]Data relating to a wide range of characteristics for the candidates of the three parties in 1967 were collected by the authors through a mail questionnaire, supplemented by direct contact to complete the canvass. Of the 351 candidates considered only five refused to answer and the relevant data for each of these were available from the *Canadian Parliamentary Guide*. Such data as we present in Tables III, IV, and V are therefore reported in absolute figures. The right hand column in Tables IV and V shows the number of candidates which would have been expected in each category if the parties were precisely representative of the provincial distributions in the 1961 census. Fifteen other candidates in 1967 are not considered here, including seven for the Social Credit party and two Communists.

TABLE II

Socio-economic Characteristics of Party Supporters in Ontario in 1967

| | | Con.[a] | Lib.[a] | NDP[a] | Province[b] |
		%	%	%	%
Sex	Male	52	51	58	50
	Female	48	49	42	50
Age Groups	21 - 34	25	28	35	32
	35 - 49	33	43	41	33
	50 - 64	22	19	15	21
	65 and over	20	10	9	14
Religious	Anglican	23	12	17	18
Affiliation	Baptist	7	4	2	4
	Jewish	1	2	1	2
	Presbyterian	12	4	6	8
	Roman Catholic	13	44	25	30
	United Church	32	21	26	26
	Other	11	10	14	} 12
	None	1	3	9	
Ethnic	Canadian	39	40	50	42
Identification[c]	English Canadian	53	39	38	43
	French Canadian	3	7	2	5
	German	1	2	2	2
	Italian	1	5	1	3
	Other	3	7	7	5
Union	No one belongs	74	65	46	63
Households	Only head belongs	22	31	44	31
	Others belong	4	4	10	6
Subjective	Upper class	2	2	2	2
Social Class	Middle class	52	42	30	40
	Working class	46	56	68	58

[a]Number of cases: Conservative, 309; Liberal, 343; NDP, 208.

[b]The first three distributions are compared to 1961 census data for Ontario. The others are compared to the distribution in the whole sample since appropriate census data were not available.

[c]Respondents were asked: "To what ethnic group do you consider that you belong? English Canadian, French Canadian, or another ethnic group?" The answer "Canadian" was accepted, which makes a comparison with census data impossible.

Although the New Democratic Party contributed along with the Liberals and the Conservatives to the great excess of middle-class candidates, it came considerably closer than either of the other parties to including a representative number of people in skilled and semi-skilled manual occupations. Both the measures of socio-economic status which are presented here show how limited were the cases of working-class candidatures with the two older parties, irrespective of the support they received from that quarter.[63] There are, however, other differences between them which may have a bearing on the image they present to the electorate. The Conservatives were most obviously a party of small businessmen, while the Liberals appeared to be

TABLE III

Objective Social Class of Candidates in Ontario, 1967

	Con.	Lib.	NDP
Professional	34	48	54
Managerial and Executive	19	12	15
Small Managers and Supervisors	61	48	21
Other White Collar		2	1
Skilled Workers	2	7	17
Semi-skilled Workers	1		8
Unskilled Workers			1
Total	117	117	117

TABLE IV

Occupations of Candidates in Ontario, 1967

	Con.	Lib.	NDP	Male Labour Force
Lawyers	16	31	7	1
Teachers	7	11	29	2
Other Professional	8	9	23	7
Small Business Owners	30	16	4	} 13
Other Managerial	22	18	9	
Insurance	8	3		1
Farmers and Farm Workers	12	12	10	11
Service and Recreation, Transport and Communication	3	4	5	19
Craftsmen, Production Process	3	5	14	} 45
Union Representatives			4	
Others	8	8	12	18
Total	117	117	117	117

especially attractive to lawyers. But it was the New Democrats, in addition to including more workingmen in their ranks, who had the largest number of candidates in professional occupations — drawn mainly from among teachers and social workers. NDP candidates were also the youngest, with the briefest length of party membership and the shortest period of residence in their constituencies; and they were rather more likely to report that the 1967 campaign was their first attempt at any public office.[64]

[63]Table IV lists the most prominent occupations of the candidates and compares them to 1961 census data for the male labour force in Ontario. Table III arranges these data on the basis of objective social class. For further details of the classification scheme used in Table III see Wilson, "Politics and Social Class in Canada," p. 299, n. 34.

[64]Only seven Conservatives had not previously been candidates for any level of public office, whereas thirty-nine Liberals and sixty-six New Democrats had never run before. At the same time, nineteen New Democrats, eight Liberals, and only four Conservatives had never lived in the constituency they were contesting.

In ethnic origin and religious affiliation candidates for the three parties were somewhat more representative of the population as a whole. Generally speaking, those members of Ontario society who are of neither British nor French origin were under-represented when all the candidates are taken together, but this is primarily due to their relative absence from the ranks of the Conservative party. Within the NDP and especially the Liberal party their numbers were almost as great as would be expected on the basis of their strength in the total population. Among candidates of British origin there were intriguing differences which look back to the nineteenth century: the Conservatives had many more with English ancestors than would be expected if the party were perfectly representative of Ontario society, while the Liberals had a greater number of Scots. On the other hand, each of the three parties had the same number of French Canadian candidates, and in almost precisely the proportion called for by the provincial distribution. The extent to which all candidates reflected the social composition of their party's support is most obvious in the case of religious affiliation. The Conservatives, whose typical candidate appeared to be the small businessman of English origin, found over two-thirds of their people among adherents of the Anglican and United Churches. At the same time, only among Liberal candidates were Roman Catholics prominently represented, although their numbers were not inconsiderable with the NDP. The outstanding characteristic of NDP candidates, however, was the inordinately large number of those who professed no religion at all, which mirrors a somewhat less noticeable condition among the party's supporters. Whether these data indicate a weakening of the influence of religion in Ontario politics is unclear, but the fact that the United Church — evidently the home of the more politically active — was over-represented among the candidates of all three parties suggests that these lines of division may be less significant than they have been in the past.

It may be argued, of course, that a party's image is more affected by the performance of its group in the Legislative Assembly than by the kinds of candidates it chooses in every part of the province. At the same time, since it is the elected members who are noticed by the general public, the extent to which a party is regarded as representative of a particular set of interests may depend more upon the socio-economic characteristics of the people who speak for it in the legislature than anything else. Equally, if it were to be found that all of a party's women candidates, for example, appeared in constituencies which the party had no hope of winning, something would thereby have been suggested about the assumptions made by local associations in assessing the nature of the contest in their area.[65] In any case a closer examination of the party caucuses will prevent unwarranted conclusions being drawn on the basis of the attributes of the candidates alone.[66]

In fact, while there are some differences which require comment, there are no dramatic variations between the collective characteristics of any party's elected members and those of its candidates taken all together. The disparities in objective social class which were observed between the Liberals and the Conservatives on the one hand and the NDP on the other are maintained in the legislature, but within the middle class the sharp contrasts which existed among candidates are somewhat diminished. While the Liberals still have

TABLE V

Ethnic Origin and Religious Affiliation
of Candidates in Ontario, 1967

	Con.	Lib.	NDP	Province
English	51	29	39	36
Irish	17	14	19	16
Scottish	23	30	20	16
Other British	1	3		1
French	11	11	11	12
German	5	5	9	8
Italian		5	2	5
Scandinavian	2	1	3	2
Slavic	5	11	8	8
Other	2	8	6	13
Anglican	38	21	13	21
Baptist	3	2	3	5
Jewish	2	4	7	2
Lutheran	2	2	2	4
Presbyterian	13	9	8	9
Roman Catholic	14	35	21	35
Unitarian		3	5	—
United Church	42	35	33	31
Other	3	5	2	} 10
None		1	23	
Totals	117	117	117	117

a proportionately greater number of lawyers the Conservatives are now rather closer to them in this respect, although continuing to be dominated by representatives from the commercial world. And the New Democrats are less dependent upon teachers while remaining the party with the largest percentage of members in professional occupations. Indeed, the fact that nearly two-thirds of the NDP caucus is middle-class would suggest that the party is in reality no different from the others in the interests it seeks to serve. Elsewhere in Canada, however, the party's elected members exhibit broadly the same distribution of occupational backgrounds.[67] Moreover, the pattern is fairly common among social democratic parties: only about a third of the

65Fifteen women contested the 1967 election, three each for the Conservatives and the Liberals, and nine for the NDP. Two were elected: one Conservative and one New Democrat, both in urban ridings.

66The data in Tables VI and VII are drawn from the survey mentioned in footnote 62. Since the parties have different numbers of seats in the legislature all distributions are shown as percentages and may not add to 100 per cent because of rounding.

67In the Manitoba, Saskatchewan, and British Columbia NDP caucuses members with professional occupations considerably outnumbered those with working-class backgrounds in 1970, as they did in the House of Commons. This has not however, always been the case in British Columbia. See Martin Robin, "A Profile of the B.C. Legislature," Canadian Dimension, January-February 1966, pp. 26-28.

parliamentary members of the British Labour party, for example, come from the working class, and among its professional members more than half are teachers.[68] It therefore seems probable that the Ontario New Democrats are as distinct from the Liberals and the Conservatives as it is reasonable to expect them to be.

In most other areas the differences which were observed between candidates are preserved in the legislature. The Liberal and NDP caucuses have almost identical average ages while Conservative members tend to be rather older.[69] The dominant position of the United Church in all three parties is also maintained, but beyond that elected Liberals are the most Catholic and elected Conservatives the most Anglican.[70] With ethnic origin as well, broadly the same distinctions noticed among candidates reappear in the party caucuses, although here the Liberals are more obviously a party favoured by people who are of neither British nor French ancestry. Only about a quarter of their candidates came from outside the "charter groups"; a third of their elected members do so. Finally, while it is no doubt the case that the greater representation of French Canadians among Conservative members is linked to the difficulty which the Liberals have in holding on to their federal supporters in provincial elections, the fact that the Conservatives are able to show this kind of representation at all must contribute to the maintenance of that difficulty.[71]

Of course, it is also true that an inclination on the part of French Canadians to support the traditional governing party in Ontario may be at the heart of this difference between the Conservatives and the Liberals. Whether or not that can be shown to be the case it is a fact that since 1957 they have received in the cabinet itself due recognition of their importance in the province through the appointment of two ministers of French origin.[72] It is unclear to what extent this arrangement has been deliberate, but in any case it is not very surprising. With the increasing growth of government activity the role of the legislature in the making of crucial decisions affecting the social and economic life of the province has diminished. In Ontario, as elsewhere, the effective centre of power and responsibility has now become the cabinet and as a consequence the function of representation has increasingly been removed from the legislature to the executive council. At the national level in Canada it is well understood that the process of selecting a cabinet has, since Confederation, served the additional purpose of providing a formal mechanism for the preservation of national unity. But even in Ontario it may be argued that the extent to which the cabinet is representative of the principal sectors of the province may be a measure of the degree to which it is capable of responding to the demands of the society. Its composition can equally be taken as a rough indication of the government's ordering of political priorities and interests, at least as they are perceived by the prime minister.

Of course an Ontario premier, like any other, is limited in the task of constructing a cabinet to the material he has available in his caucus. It would therefore be wrong to conclude that because the present cabinet contains no members with backgrounds in manual occupations the government is unconcerned with the problems of the workingman. There may be areas where

TABLE VI

Occupations of Members Elected
to the Ontario Legislature in 1967

	Con. %	Lib. %	NDP %
Lawyers	20	29	10
Teachers	4	11	10
Other Professional	9	7	35
Small Business Owners	28	18	
Other Managerial	17	7	10
Insurance	4		
Farmers and Farm Workers	14	14	
Service and Recreation, Transport and Communication		4	5
Craftsmen, Production Process		4	10
Union Representatives			5
Others	3	7	15
N	69	28	20

the presence of an appropriate labour voice in the council room would add materially to the government's deliberations, but there is no special reason to believe that its views on such questions as the use of *ex parte* injunctions in labour disputes would be much altered by such an addition. For in fact Mr. Robarts' 1967 cabinet was, if anything, more middle-class than the caucus

68See D.E. Butler and Anthony King, *The British General Election of 1966* (London: Macmillan & Co., Ltd., 1966), pp. 208 and 209.

69The average age in 1967 of Conservative, Liberal, and NDP candidates was, respectively, 49.9, 42.8, and 40.0. As might be expected, elected members were older: in the same order, 50.6, 43.3, and 43.0.

70It is difficult to trace the religious affiliation of elected members before 1911 because few of them reported the matter in the *Canadian Parliamentary Guide* or the *Canadian Parliamentary Companion*. However, an examination of the data for 1919 and 1943 suggests that the proportion of Anglicans in the Conservative party and of Roman Catholics in the Liberal party has remained much the same.

71French Canadian candidates generally run in dominantly French constituencies, of which there are at least eight in Ontario (depending on the criterion for dominance). In these ridings the Conservatives draw significantly greater support provincially than they do in federal elections. In rural areas this appears to be due to shifts between the two older parties while in heavily French sections of the cities, and especially in areas of working-class concentration, federal Liberal voters seem more inclined to abstain in provincial elections. See Wilson and Hoffman, "The Liberal Party," pp. 187-189.

72Early in 1971 the reconstructed cabinet had three ministers of French origin. The first French Canadian member of an Ontario cabinet was F.E.A. Evanturel, who served as Minister without Portfolio in the last months of the Ross government in 1904. J.O. Réaume was Minister of Public Works in the Whitney administration until his defeat in 1914. Since 1930 there has always been at least one French Canadian member of the provincial cabinet with the single exception of the Drew ministry from 1943 to 1948.

TABLE VII

*Ethnic Origin and Religious
Affiliation of Members Elected to the
Ontario Legislature in 1967*

	Con. %	Lib. %	NDP %
English	42	21	35
Irish	16	11	20
Scottish	20	25	20
Other British		7	
French	10	4	5
German	6	7	
Italian		4	
Scandinavian	1		5
Slavic	3	11	10
Other	1	11	5
Anglican	38	11	15
Baptist	3	4	5
Jewish	1	4	10
Lutheran	1	4	
Presbyterian	7	11	
Roman Catholic	12	21	15
Unitarian		4	10
United Church	35	36	40
Other	2	7	
None			5
N	69	28	20

from which it was drawn.[73] Nearly half of the ministers were businessmen and the rest virtually all lawyers; only three farmers and a doctor added some variety.[74]

This distribution is, of course, not the least bit representative of the Ontario population as a whole. But what is intriguing about the occupational structure of the 1967 cabinet is that — apart from the excessive number of lawyers — it fairly accurately reflected the backgrounds of Conservative members. Together with the near perfect match which existed between cabinet and caucus with respect to ethnic origin this suggests that there may have been some attempt to take account of particular interests among government backbenchers. Roman Catholics, for example, received a degree of representation in the executive council roughly equivalent to their strength in the caucus. On the other hand, while Anglicans were as numerous as adherents of the United Church among elected Conservative members, they were outnumbered in the cabinet. But the Tory *vote*, as suggested by Table II, depends more upon United Church supporters than any other religious group. Equally, while the number of Roman Catholics in the cabinet grossly underrepresents their strength in the Ontario population as a whole, it *does* reflect the weight of their contribution to Conservative electoral success.

TABLE VIII

Socio-economic Characteristics of the Ontario Cabinet, 1967

Occupations (%)		Religious Affiliation (%)		Ethnic Origin (%)	
Doctor	4	Anglican	28	English	45
Lawyers	36	Presbyterian	9	Irish	14
Small Businessmen	23	Roman Catholic	9	Scottish	23
Other Managerial	23	United Church	45	French	9
Farmers	14	Other	9	Other	9
N	22		22		22

The possibility that somewhat more subtle political considerations were the determining factor when the prime minister selected his cabinet — rather than the structure of the caucus or the composition of the province's population — appears to be confirmed by the pattern of regional representation which existed among ministers appointed after the 1967 election. The most rigid convention in respect of representation in the federal cabinet is the one which dictates that each province must have at least one member where possible, and that Ontario and Quebec, because they are larger, must each have no less than four. If this example were followed in Ontario — based on the population strength of each region — a cabinet of twenty-two members would be expected to have four from eastern Ontario, seven from the Toronto region, nine from the western region and two from the North. In fact, however, the 1967 cabinet contained five ministers from eastern Ontario, evidently at the expense of the western region. But eastern Ontario is the strongest Conservative area in the province. If Mr. Robarts' cabinet had been chosen on the basis of the number of votes cast for the government in each of the four regions, its actual composition in 1967 would have precisely reflected the balance of Tory electoral strength throughout Ontario.[75]

The fact that the executive council has now largely replaced the assembly in performing the function of representing what are thought to be important interests in the province is not simply the product of increasing government

---

[73]The data in Table VIII are based on the twenty-two member cabinet appointed following the 1967 election.

[74]This was broadly the case in 1963 as well. See Fred Schindeler, "The Ontario Cabinet: Definition, Size, and Representative Nature," *Canadian Public Administration,* IX, No. 3 (1966), 344.

[75]Changes in the cabinet since 1967 have not significantly altered these aspects of representation in the executive council. The addition of a third minister from the North to the larger, twenty-four member cabinet chosen in 1971 by the new premier would be expected — both on the basis of population strength and the distribution of the Conservative vote. But eastern Ontario remains over-represented with five ministers, now apparently at the expense of Toronto. It should be noticed that the attempt to recognize the dominant interests of areas within provinces — which is often seen in the construction of federal cabinets through the assignment of particular portfolios to particular regions — appears also to occur in Ontario. For examples of this kind of representation see *Ibid.,* pp. 339-341.

activity. Until very recently the rules of the Ontario legislature gave the executive an influence considerably in excess of what would be expected in a parliamentary system modelled after Westminster. Ministers were not required to answer questions, nor to produce a satisfactory reason for refusing, and more often than not such answers as were forthcoming were given long after any purpose the question might have served had disappeared. Even the opportunity to introduce private members' bills was severely curtailed. These arrangements, which existed without major alteration from the time of the first session of the legislature following Confederation, not only limited the influence of the opposition but promoted the personal authority of the prime minister who, as leader of the House, controlled all its business.[76]

Inevitably, there have been direct political consequences of this experience which the recent adoption of much more democratic rules of procedure cannot be expected to alter immediately. The most obvious is that the special qualities of the party leaders become the focus of political attention while ideological debate tends to be suppressed. Even the New Democratic Party has been forced to adopt a campaign style which makes the leader the real issue in an election. In 1967, the party's principal poster consisted of a rather large head and shoulders photograph of its chief, with the caption: "MacDonald — the Man for Ontario." In other respects as well the NDP appears to have accepted the established rules of the modern political game in the province. Electoral strategy, for example, is now devised in much the same fashion as in the older parties. Direction of the campaign rests with a committee chosen less for its representativeness of all opinions in the party than for its expertise, and decisions are more and more influenced by the evidence which can be extracted from specially-commissioned public opinion polls.

Indeed, contrary to the customary view, the similarities in the organizational styles of the three Ontario parties are more striking than the differences. Both the Liberals and the NDP give considerable authority in the making of policy to a convention of the constituency membership,[77] although the regular biennial meeting of the New Democrats is probably more representative of grass roots opinion in the party.[78] Both also hold their leaders accountable to the rank and file.[79] Even the Conservatives, traditionally the least concerned with this problem, have recently adopted a set of rules designed to place some constraint upon the freedom of action of the party leadership.[80] The New Democrats, of course, like most social democratic parties, claim far greater influence for their mass membership than either of the older parties, but at the constituency level there is some evidence that decision-making rests as much in the hands of the local executive as is the case in the classical form of the cadre party and that the distinguishing elements among the three are less to be found in organizational differences than in general sentiments and attitudes of mind.[81]

The fact that the NDP is willing to abide by the conditions in which party competition occurs in Ontario and, indeed, to take full advantage of them,[82] makes the possibility of an eventual Liberal revival even more remote. For despite their attempts to develop a participatory membership the Liberals continue to suffer organizational problems. Before their 1969 convention in Hamilton an article in the party newspaper drew attention to a series of weaknesses in the party machinery in constituencies outside the Toronto area. The

76For an account of the manner in which the rules have favoured the government see F.F. Schindeler, *Responsible Government in Ontario* (Toronto: University of Toronto Press, 1969), especially chaps. 5 and 6. In the autumn of 1969 extensive changes were recommended which would significantly add to the opposition's ability to question the ministry and to raise their own issues through private members' bills. See Ontario, Legislative Assembly, Select Committee on Rules and Procedures, *Report* (Toronto: mimeo., 1969). Most of the reforms suggested by the committee were adopted in the spring of 1970 in a revised version of the legislature's Standing Orders. See *Journals of the Legislative Assembly of the Province of Ontario*, CIV, 3rd Session, 28th Legislature, April 22, 1970, pp. 92-113.

77The Liberal party's arrangements here are less clear than the NDP's. In May, 1966 the Liberals adopted amendments to their constitution which provide for a measure of accountability by the parliamentary caucus to the rank and file membership. Article VII, section 5 of the new constitution states that "at each annual meeting and policy rally [which must be held at least once every two years] a member of the caucus appointed by the leader and when the party forms the Government a member of the Cabinet appointed by the leader shall attend and report to the rally upon the consideration given, the decisions made and the reasoning therefor regarding resolutions passed and submitted at the previous policy rally and/or Annual Meeting, which decisions shall be ratified unless there is a contrary decision by the meeting or rally." By contrast, the NDP constitution asserts in Article 6, section 2, that "the provincial convention shall be the governing body of the provincial party, and shall have final authority in all matters of principles, policies, constitution and program."

78Delegates to NDP conventions are chosen on a basis which reflects the different membership strength of the various constituency associations and affiliated organizations. Liberal conventions, on the other hand, give equal weight to each constituency and have as well a large number of delegates who participate as a consequence of their being officers (often appointed) in one of the party's regional associations, or who represent the women's, young people's, and university organizations of the party. Conservative conventions are broadly similar in composition to those of the Liberal party.

79Although the NDP constitution (like the CCF before it) requires the election of the leader at each biennial convention — providing a mechanism for his removal should the necessity arise — until quite recently this avenue of expression for membership protest had fallen into disuse. Mr. Jolliffe was challenged between the elections of 1945 and 1948, but after a new leader was chosen when he stepped down following his personal defeat in York South in the 1951 election no further contests occurred until 1968. In that year the party's deputy leader in the legislature mounted what initially appeared to be a strong challenge, only to be soundly defeated by Mr. MacDonald — with considerable help from the loyal trade union leaders amongst whom Mr. Renwick had failed to develop any significant support. In 1970 the circumstances were somewhat different. For an account of the events leading up to Donald MacDonald's resignation, and the subsequent contest between Stephen Lewis and Walter Pitman for the party leadership (as well as the role played by the trade unions in the change which took place) see Harold Greer, "NDP Palace Coup is Bared," *Kitchener-Waterloo Record*, October 7, 1970. In the Liberal party leadership conventions may be called at the discretion of the Executive Board but Article VI, section 2 of the party's constitution requires that a convention must be called in any event within two years after a provincial general election. At the 1969 Hamilton conference of the party Mr. Nixon was confirmed as leader.

80At their 1969 annual meeting the Conservative party approved a constitutional amendment to permit the calling of a leadership convention *at any time* when the party is in opposition. When it is in power, however, such a convention may only be called if the leader dies or retires. Early in 1971, after Mr. Robarts had indicated his intention to resign, a special convention of the party chose William Davis — the Minister of Education and the man who had always been expected to follow Mr. Robarts — as its new leader. The contest was, however, extremely close, with Mr. Davis winning only on the fourth ballot and then only by the small margin of 44 votes out of 1,580 cast.

almost total absence of local offices, organizers, and members for provincial purposes was contrasted with the organizational strength which the Liberals are able to muster for federal elections. Without very extensive improvement in these circumstances, it was claimed, there could be little expectation that the fortunes of the provincial party would ever improve.[83] Part of this difficulty is due to the separation of the federal and provincial Liberal organizations at the local level. Often the directing executives have no links at all, and even on occasion work against each other. The Conservatives also maintain a dual structure of constituency associations, but because they are in power at Queen's Park the effect on their provincial membership is negligible.[84] The NDP avoids this problem altogether by being organized entirely on the basis of provincial ridings, and developing committees from the executives of the appropriate associations for managing federal campaigns.[85]

But even the ability to repair its organization may not be enough to restore the Liberal party's former strength. For it now appears to be indisputable that the social and economic forces which have been at work since before the Second World War have put an irretrievable stamp on the face of Ontario's politics, and that the final stage of a transitional phase in the development of the provincial party system has begun.

III. THE FUTURE OF ONTARIO POLITICS

Both the 1905 and 1943 elections have been seen as the benchmarks of Ontario's political history. The one brought to an end over thirty years of Liberal dominance in a largely pre-industrial society, and ushered in the modern era. The other marked the beginning of serious three-party competition in the province and the possibility of a new kind of challenge to the strength of the Conservative party. Now, nearly thirty years later, it seems probable that this third period in the development of the Ontario party system is drawing to a close. The evidence lies mainly in the result of the 1967 provincial election and what it suggests when compared to what has gone before.

No one, of course, imagined that the Conservatives could be defeated in 1967. And yet, observers were equally clear after the fact that it was the New Democrats who had had the greatest impact. "In my opinion," wrote Scott Young, "their showing opens the door to a profound political change in this province — a trend that is the most important in the party's history anywhere in Canada, except when they first won in Saskatchewan."[86] But while the NDP improved its performance all across Ontario in 1967, even the most superficial examination of the results makes it clear that its greatest support came from those areas where the forces of urbanization and industrialization have been at work for the longest time.[87]

If winning a quarter of the popular vote is arbitrarily regarded as putting a party significantly in the running in any one area, then in 1963 the NDP was a serious competitor only in Toronto and Hamilton. In fact, in 1963 nearly half of all the votes cast for it came from Metropolitan Toronto alone, when only about a quarter of the provincial electorate was to be found there. In 1967, on the other hand, a three-party system could clearly be seen in operation in every major industrial area of the province: in the larger cities of Toronto, Hamilton, and Windsor; in the Grand Valley — which is dominated by the smaller cities of Brantford, Galt, Guelph, Kitchener, and Waterloo; in the Niagara-Burlington-Mississauga region where the greatest population growth has occurred; and in the North. What is intriguing about this development is that it was balanced by a growth in NDP support in the less industrialized regions sufficient to reduce the party's dependence on the largest cities and to make it a serious competitor across Ontario as a whole.[88] Still, even in these areas its strength was to be found mainly in centres of urban growth such as Peterborough — concealed in the gross result for the Central Ontario

[81]Local NDP executive members are more likely than others to express some concern about the need to consult the membership, but in practice this does not often occur. See Ronald F. Freeman, "Ontario Party Organization: The Myth and the Reality of the Classification of Parties" (M.A. thesis, University of Waterloo, 1969), ch. 5.

[82]An important contributing factor in the recent success of the party has been its willing adoption, wherever in the province it promised victory, of techniques of electoral organization first developed in Toronto's east end ridings. The most authoritative description of the method may be found in Desmond Morton, *With Your Help: An Election Manual* (Ottawa: The New Democratic Party, 1966). See also *The Riverdale Story: A By-election Campaign* (Toronto: The New Democratic Party of Ontario, 1964) for an account of what party strategists regard as an almost perfect application of the technique of saturation campaigning. An attempt is made to evaluate the method in Desmond Morton, "The Effectiveness of Political Campaigning: The NDP in the 1967 Ontario Election," *Journal of Canadian Studies,* IV, No. 3 (1969), 21-33.

[83]See "View From the Outside: The Grass Roots Need Shaking," *Liberal Action* (Toronto), March, 1969.

[84]Individuals who join either the Liberals or the Conservatives at the local level need not join both the federal and provincial associations. If they do join both there are separate, and frequently different, membership fees. See Freeman, "Ontario Party Organization," Chap. 5.

[85]All members of the provincial party who live in a particular federal riding are eligible to nominate candidates for federal elections and choose delegates to national conventions. The 1970–71 Ontario membership of the NDP, used to establish constituency delegate strength at the 1971 federal convention, was 24,707. Ontario Conservative headquarters give a comparable figure of 91,000 for their provincial membership, while it is estimated that some 50,000 individuals hold either a provincial or a combined federal and provincial membership in the Liberal party.

[86]"History Books Will Show the NDP Has Just Made Its Second Advance," *The Globe and Mail,* October 19, 1967.

[87]Although there was a very extensive redistribution in 1966 the data in Table IX are for identical areas in each election. The results in individual polling subdivisions in 1963 were reaggregated on the basis of the new constituencies, which were in turn combined to create the regions which are used in Table IX.

[88]In this respect the NDP may be said to have "come of age" in the 1967 election. In contrast to 1963 only a third of all votes cast for the party came from Metropolitan Toronto, another third from other city ridings, and the rest from mainly rural ridings. This compares to the distribution of the electorate in 1967 in these same groups of constituencies: respectively, 26, 28, and 46 per cent.

TABLE IX

Results of the Ontario General Elections of 1963 and 1967 by Region
(horizontal percentages)

	Conservatives			Liberals			New Democrats			Other		
	1963	1967	Change	1963	1967	Change	1963	1967	Change	1963	1967	Change
Metropolitan Toronto	45	38	−7	30	29	−1	25	33	+ 8	*	*	none
Hamilton	35	33	− 2	30	24	−6	35	43	+ 8	*	*	none
Ottawa	48	48	none	42	38	−4	5	14	+ 9	5		−5
Windsor	35	27	− 8	45	37	−8	20	36	+16			none
London	66	49	−17	25	31	+6	9	20	+11			none
Niagara − Burlington − Mississauga	52	46	− 6	37	28	−9	11	26	+15	*		none

Region												
Southwestern Ontario	51	44	− 7	45	44	−1	4	11	+ 7	*	1	+1
Lake Huron	55	48	− 7	43	41	−2	2	11	+ 9	*	*	none
Grand Valley	45	36	− 9	42	35	−7	13	28	+15	*	1	+1
Central Ontario	57	50	− 7	34	29	−5	9	21	+12	*		none
Eastern Ontario	62	59	− 3	33	30	−3	5	11	+ 6			none
Ottawa Valley	59	56	− 3	37	35	−2	3	9	+ 6	1		−1
Northern Ontario	43	39	− 4	34	29	−5	22	32	+10	1	*	−1

*Less than half of 1 per cent.

region. In contrast to this the Conservatives and Liberals lost ground in almost every part of the province, although it is worth noticing that the Liberals were least affected in those regions which have always provided them with the most reliable support: Southwestern Ontario and the Lake Huron district.

The 1967 result belies the claim that a party which seeks mainly to articulate the interests of the industrial working class cannot hope for significant electoral success. For the fact that the NDP made startling gains in some urban constituencies and only minor ones in others — a pattern of change which also appears in the regional data — conceals the real nature of the transition which is taking place in the Ontario party system. On the face of things these very different individual results suggest an entirely erratic pattern due, perhaps, to the superior quality of local campaigns in particular areas. In fact, however, the largest increases in the party's vote appeared in those dominantly working-class constituencies where it had not already achieved the level of support which would be expected for a successful labour party. The pattern of change in 1967 therefore points to the development of a much firmer relationship between NDP strength and working-class concentration — wherever it occurs in the province — than at any time since 1943, and suggests as well that the party is attracting a much higher proportion of the working-class vote than it has ever managed before.

In ridings such as York South, Oshawa, and Hamilton East the CCF/NDP vote has steadily increased in proportion since the end of the Second World War. In these cases the party's position may be said to be stabilized at a level high enough for such seats to be regarded as safe in almost any circumstance. In a very large number of other constituencies, however — such as Brantford, Kitchener, Welland, and the three Windsor area ridings — where the developing labour vote ought to have solidified very quickly after 1943, the party's support has until lately been comparatively insignificant. The fact that these smaller cities in southern Ontario — to say nothing of the North — began in 1967 to produce a pattern of voting broadly similar to that which had already become established in most parts of the Metropolitan Toronto area and in Hamilton appears to be the single most important aspect of the election.[89] Even in the city of Toronto itself there is evidence that the most important changes were of this character. A careful analysis shows that the most prominent increases in the NDP vote occurred mainly in areas of working-class concentration and that the variation in the size of the increase in these cases was almost entirely accounted for by those which were previously weak drawing level in 1967 with those where the party had already established a commanding position.[90] As urbanization, industrialization, and union organization extend further throughout Ontario, destroying the more traditional influences on the vote of religious affiliation and ethnic origin, this pattern of change may be expected to occur with greater frequency, pointing to a much stronger competitive position for the NDP across the province in the future.

At the same time, it may be significant that there was a clear tendency in 1967 for the Liberals to gain at the expense of the Conservatives in middle-class areas — in Toronto at least. If this kind of change were to be repeated in all the urban centres of the province the Liberal party's dilemma might be

ONTARIO

TABLE X

Change Between 1963 and 1967 in Selected Areas of Toronto

Area	Percent of Male Labour Force in Manual Occupations	Percentage Point Change			
		Con.	Lib.	NDP	Other
Tract 145	74	− 9	− 9	+21	−3
Tract 298	73	− 9	− 6	+15	
Tract 102	70	− 8	−16	+27	−3
Tract 174	66	− 5	− 6	+12	−1
Tract 273	64	− 6	− 6	+12	
Tract 187	57	−11	− 5	+15	+1
Tract 272	48	−11	− 5	+16	
Tract 132	36	− 1	− 7	+ 8	
Tract 150	18	+ 8	− 1	− 6	−1
Tract 196	17	− 8	+ 9	− 2	+1
Tract 206	15	+ 1	− 3	+ 2	
Tract 153	13	+ 2	+ 1	− 3	
Tract 92	10	−15	+13	+ 2	

somewhat less severe than it now appears, even if such a change could do little more than maintain for them their present position in the legislature. On the other hand, there are a number of reasons for doubting whether the Liberals would be able to take advantage of a general improvement in their potential electoral support.[91] The most important of these was bluntly stated

[89]In some of these cases, of course, the change may have been due to changes in the political character of the labour movement over the past few years. For details of the origin of the party's difficulties with organized labour in the Windsor area, for example, see Ian MacPherson, "The 1945 Collapse of the C.C.F. in Windsor," *Ontario History*, LXI, No. 4 (1969), 197-212.

[90]This interpretation of the changes which took place between 1963 and 1967 is supported by an analysis of a purposive sample of 28 census tracts in Toronto — half mainly middle class and half mainly working class — designed to contrast the effect of social class on the vote. For 1963 the relationship between the level of the NDP vote and the size of the manual labour force in these areas is given by $r = + 0.73$ ($t = 5.48$ with 28 observations, $p < .001$). For the same areas in 1967 the relationship was much stronger: $r = + 0.91$ ($t = 10.94$ with 28 observations, $p < .001$). The data in Table X are taken from this sample.

[91]For a more extensive discussion of this point see Wilson and Hoffman, "The Liberal Party," 202-204.

by Mr. Robarts himself in a rather angry debate in the Legislative Assembly towards the end of 1969:

It has been the great tragedy of the Liberal Party in this province — since Mitch Hepburn's day really — that they have always been in the pocket of the federal government — the federal party. Their policies are simply an adjunct to what their party wants federally. They come here and when we stand up on this side of the House for the rights of the people of Ontario, they stand against us.[92]

And as if to emphasize the extent of the polarization which is taking place in the province the Prime Minister turned, and pointing to the NDP benches said: "I can only say that I know where the enemy is and I will fight."[93]

But while such a view of the irrelevance of the Liberals to Ontario politics may be too harsh, there is still no evidence that their electoral support has increased to the point where they might successfully challenge the government.[94] Equally, there are no convincing grounds for supposing that they will necessarily benefit from the new strength of the federal party in Ontario. Although Liberal gains in the 1968 federal election were made largely at the expense of the Conservatives it is unlikely that a similar shift will occur at the provincial level, since there is no reason to believe that the many federal Liberal middle-class voters who switch to the provincial Tories will not for the most part continue to do so. Nor is there any evidence in the federal result that the NDP may be in trouble. In fact, the pattern of support for the party which appeared throughout the province in 1968 in areas of heavy working-class concentration precisely mirrored the changes which had taken place only a few months earlier in the provincial election, again irrespective of the previous electoral history of the community.[95] There is therefore some reason to believe that the NDP will continue to flourish, as will the Conservatives with their superior strength in most of the rural regions of the province. But there is equally no prospect of an immediate Liberal decline, if only because there is no prospect of the immediate disappearance of the combination of forces which promotes the party's survival. What, then, is the likely future development of the Ontario political system?

Such a question cannot possibly be answered without a much clearer perception of the mechanics of the pure three-party system.[96] It has often been assumed that where the system of government is essentially of the parliamentary type, based on the British model, the existence of a three-party system marks a period of transition in the character of the society itself. Generally speaking, the changes which are assumed to be taking place in such a situation are those which typically accompany the shift from a pre-industrial to a fully-developed industrial society depending almost entirely on manufacturing and the kinds of economic activity which always go with it. Because the successful operation of the parliamentary form of government is held to demand no more than two dominant parties — or at the very least a government with a clear majority — it is usually assumed that the three-party system which has been generated by changes in the society must eventually be replaced through the gradual disappearance of the least effective political group.

But the demands which are said to be characteristic of parliamentary government, and which dictate the need for two rather than three parties, are entirely legislative. It is quite possible for the society to support three parties with sufficient *electoral* strength to maintain themselves while the distribution of partisan loyalty which is required for stability in the legislature remains; that is to say, most of the time one party will have a working majority. In fact this is nearly always the case where the division of opinion in the electorate gives much greater weight to one of the three competing parties, as it customarily does.[97] The other two divide more or less equally (it would hardly be a three-party system if they did not) and are on that account significantly weaker than the leading party. When all three parties contest every seat in these circumstances the result is very often an overwhelming majority for the strongest party with the other two being grossly under-represented. It is therefore important to distinguish between a three-party system which appears *only* in the electorate and one which appears in the legislature as well.

The distinction affords some insight, perhaps, into the likely development of Ontario politics. For while it is clear that the province has had an *electoral* three-party system since 1943 it is only with the 1967 election that this distribution has begun to be reflected to any extent in the Legislative Assembly. Although the government retains a comfortable working majority at Queen's Park, its margin over the combined strength of the opposition parties

[92]Ontario, Legislative Assembly, *Debates*, 28th Legislature, 2nd Session, 1969, pt. 9: 9858.

[93]*Ibid*. There is a good deal of evidence that Conservative strategy is now directed towards a campaign based on this perception of the political situation in the province. See, for example, Frances Russell, "Tories Need an Issue, Don't Plan an Election Before 1972," *The Globe and Mail*, June 1, 1970.

[94]Indeed it may even have declined since 1967. In a provincial by-election in Middlesex South in September, 1969 the NDP won a striking victory over the Conservatives in part by capturing nearly two-thirds of the vote in the working-class east end of London but also by driving the Liberals into third place in many of the rural townships which take up some two-fifths of the riding's population. For an analysis of the by-election based on an extensive survey of voter opinion see Joachim E. Surich, "The Nature of Political Change: The Case of Middlesex South" (M.A. thesis, University of Waterloo, 1970).

[95]Examples of this pattern may be found in constituencies in Windsor, London, Welland, and Brantford, where neither the CCF nor the NDP had ever won significant federal support. The likelihood that the party's position has improved substantially in some of these areas since 1968 is suggested by the result of the federal by-election in Brant in May of 1971. The federal riding contains not only the provincial constituency of Brantford but more than half of the constituency of the Ontario Liberal leader as well.

[96]For a discussion of some aspects of the question see J. Blondel, "Party Systems and Patterns of Government in Western Democracies," *Canadian Journal of Political Science*, I, No. 2 (1968), 180-203.

[97]This observation led Blondel to conclude that "it may be permissible to add, after considering the evolution of party systems, particularly in the early part of the twentieth century, that genuine three-party systems do not normally occur because they are essentially transitional, thus unstable, forms of party systems." See *Canadian Journal of Political Science*, I, 185.

has been substantially reduced in size for the first time since 1948, and it may therefore be said that the province is clearly moving into the critical stage of the transition. It could be argued, of course, that the pattern of the results since 1948 undermines this view. The election of that year was, as it happens, similar in almost every respect to 1967 and yet it began a trend away from rather than towards a fully-developed three-party system. On the other hand, it is quite possible that both the 1943 and 1948 elections were merely the result of the initial shocks to the political system of the transition to an industrial society which has now gone very much further in Ontario than was the case at the end of the Second World War. If that is true, and if the current trend to a pure three-party system in the electorate were to be maintained — that is to say, if the parties were to become more nearly equal in the electorate — it might be expected that the result would be a period of minority government with no guarantee as to which of the parties would be the strongest in the legislature. In time, if the British model is to be taken as an example, such a situation would have to be resolved because it would directly confront the demands of the parliamentary system of government. In short, the electorate would eventually have to either settle on a new combination of the two leading parties or determine to preserve the older pattern.[98] The third party could then be expected to decline in strength until at least a legislative two-party system had been re-establishd.

The manner in which such a transformation might take place in Ontario is, of course, very seriously affected by a whole range of factors. It seems clear, for example, that either the Liberals or the New Democrats could come to power simply as a consequence of the cumulative effect of three-party contests in individual constituencies with widely varying socio-economic characteristics, and that through a similar collection of accidents they could be driven from office at the following election.[99] Other influences, such as sharp differences in the size of electoral districts, have a powerful effect on the nature of party competition during the transitional period, by distorting the extent to which the distribution of party support in the legislature is a faithful reflection of the electorate's opinion.[100] Moreover, when the electoral system regularly produces such results it has other effects. Since the view which the voter has of the relative strength of the parties appears to be based on his perception of their position in the legislature, any inclination to shift may be weakened by the fear of "losing" his vote. On top of all this, changes in the leadership of any of the parties — and both the Conservatives and the NDP have made significant changes here since 1967 — must seriously affect the pattern established at previous elections, especially in a system where the leader is as important as he is in Ontario in determining the voter's loyalty. Few of these factors are finally within the control of any one party and yet each can be decisive in the delicate balance which a three-party system represents.

In these circumstances no one could be expected to forecast even the immediate future. It nonetheless seems probable that the province has entered the transitional phase — where both the electorate and the legislature reflect a more nearly equal division of opinion — which suggests that before very long there must be an end to the pattern of competition which has persisted since the end of the Second World War. One thing, however, is certain. The character of Ontario politics will not be seriously changed until one of the opposition parties has taken power from the Conservatives and kept it for more than two terms. No one has managed *that* for nearly seventy years.

98That is to say, the electorate would have to opt either for the Western European or the North American pattern of party competition.

99In 1967, as some measure of the extent of the three-party system in the electorate, nearly two-thirds of the 117 seats were won with less than 50 percent of the votes cast. In every other provincial general election since 1948 (when nearly 70 percent of the seats were won on minority votes) less than half of the ridings have produced this kind of result.

100It seems clear that the present distribution of seats strongly favours the Conservative party. The redistribution which preceded the 1967 election was the first by an even nominally independent commission and yet its recommendations resulted in nearly half of the new constituencies having electorates which exceeded a 25 percent tolerance above or below the average electorate for all ridings in the province. This is due to a very substantial over-representation of the rural areas, where Conservative support is much greater than in the cities. For the terms of reference of the redistribution commission see *Journals of the Legislative Assembly of the Province of Ontario*, XCVI, 3rd Session, 26th Legislature, April 18, 1962, p. 171. In 1970, however, the Select Committee on Election Laws recommended a more uniform pattern for the distribution of provincial electoral districts, involving a quota based on the current population of the province with provision for a variation of no more than 25 percent above or below the quota in the case of individual constituencies. See Ontario, Legislative Assembly, Select Committee on Election Laws, *Third Report* (Toronto: Queen's Printer, 1970), pp. 35-38.

ONTARIO

* PRINCE EDWARD ISLAND *
Big Engine, Little Body

FRANK MacKINNON

Prince Edward Island has one of the largest governments in the world and this fact determines the nature of its party politics. The province is 140 miles long and from 3 to 35 miles wide, and its population is 109,000. Yet it has a lieutenant-governor, a premier, a cabinet of ten, a legislature of thirty-two, a chief justice and three other supreme court justices and three county court judges, and all the fashionable government departments, boards, and commissions. The number of politicians and civil servants per population, per square mile, and per dollar earned or spent is immense.

In this sense the Island reflects Canada as a whole, for the nation has eleven sets of governmental institutions to handle the affairs of only twenty-two million people. In some parts of the world governments of similar size would be sufficient for several hundred million people.

Prince Edward Island is the smallest partner in a huge federation, and, like Tasmania in Australia and Rhode Island in the United States, it is relatively so small that it is easy to question whether or not it should be a separate province. Size is not the major issue, however, in assessing political, economic, and social units, especially when the unit concerned is a distinct geographic entity with a tradition of its own. There is no evidence that man has been any happier or life more fruitful in very large units than in very small ones. And little places have their own role to play and their own characteristics to develop among the varied international, national, and local political organizations designed to administer the affairs of man. The politics of Prince Edward Island illustrates, not so much public life in miniature, as the staging of a large production in a tiny theatre. It has played for two centuries and, if the plot is complicated and the price high, both participants and spectators have had a grand time.[1]

I. THE DEVELOPMENT OF PARTIES

Prince Edward Island's politics have been lively since its government was established in 1769. The first party activities were the result of personal and group rivalry in government, church, and militia. The population was only

271 when the government was set up, yet right from the start officials vied for what little power and influence there was. Churches struggled for ascendancy over each other, and the militia sought glory in an establishment where a shot was never fired in anger. The families of officials wanted to translate favourable connections in the mother country or politicial position in the colony into social prestige and dynastic distinction. People soon sorted themselves into political, denominational and social categories, and, because these categories were too numerous for a small and isolated colony, they exaggerated their own importance and quarrelled bitterly. The resulting turmoil threatened the very existence of the colony.

Another source of party politics was the land question. The British government, when it took over the Island from the French in 1763, had no definite plans for its administration. After much discussion and a survey, the authorities divided the Island into sixty-seven lots and distributed them to persons who had some claim on the Crown. These landlords were expected to bring out settlers and develop their holdings: in return they would receive "quit rents" from the settlers. This scheme hampered the Island's development for a century. Most absentee land proprietors were unwilling or unable to do much for their distant holdings; the settlers were not secure on land they did not own and often were unable to pay rent for it or unwilling to improve it. The settlers had all the problems of homesteading without the stimulus of ownership. As a result the Islanders early developed the habit of looking to distant authorities for action and money.

By 1800 group rivalries and land problems were the source of most political activity. The first organized political party, called the Club of Loyal Electors, appeared in 1810. Led by J.B. Palmer, who held several political offices, and joined by a number of American Loyalists, it was organized to oppose the proprietors and gain control of the Assembly at election time. The party had branches throughout the colony and held meetings to rally supporters and promote discussion on public issues, particularly the land question. Palmer was a friend of Governor J.F.W. DesBarres and was therefore able to exercise influence. Some officials were suspicious of the group, however, and, as a result, DesBarres instructed Attorney General Charles Stewart to make a report on it. Stewart reported that the group was a "self-created permanent political body . . . for the purpose of controlling the representation of the people in the House of Assembly, as well as the appointment of public officers. . . . This same society have had the temerity of more than insinuating that they could procure a dissolution of the General Assembly of the Island, whenever it suited their views." Stewart concluded that a group with such revolutionary ideas "is highly illegal and unconstitutional and . . . ought to be discountenanced and suppressed."[2] The Loyal Electors stirred up considerable interest, but lost much of their effectiveness when DesBarres retired in 1813.

[1]For a general description of Prince Edward Island government and politics see Frank MacKinnon, *The Government of Prince Edward Island* (Toronto: University of Toronto Press, 1951).
[2]Charles Stewart to J.F.W. DesBarres, Oct. 18, 1811, Prince Edward Island Papers, Public Archives of Canada, A25, p. 247.

Governor C.D. Smith would not tolerate them and they were forced to work secretly. The party then became just another faction, unorganized and with shifting platforms and personnel.

The conflicts involved in the relations between governor, Executive Council, Legislative Council, Legislative Assembly and courts which were common to all the colonies were in full operation in Prince Edward Island during the struggle for responsible government from 1830 to 1851. The Assembly was kept in the background in its early years, partly because the other institutions wished to retain their powers and partly because the Assembly took a long time to attract enough able members to exert any influence. Organized party activity in the Assembly, as distinct from early temporary liaisons centered around current grievances, developed after 1832 when the Assembly advocated separation of the Executive and Legislative Councils, inclusion of members of the Assembly in the Executive Council, regular sessions of the Assembly (which had been called together only at the will of the lieutenant-governor), and respect from other institutions for the traditional rights and privileges essential to any parliament. These reforms were encouraged by the Colonial Office, but several governors and the family compacts kept delaying their enforcement. After the two Councils were separated in 1839 and two members of the Assembly were appointed for the first time to the Executive Council, reform leaders proceeded to the real issue of responsible government — the ultimate control of public affairs, especially finance, by elected members of the Assembly instead of the governor and his advisers.

The alignment of politicians into conservative and liberal or reform parties took place in much the same way as in the other colonies. There was no outright rebellion, but each year the sessions of both houses became increasingly bitter as each side became organized. Local officials spared no accusations or strong language in reporting the activities of their opponents to the Colonial Office. Even the governor was rebuked by Gladstone for using "sarcastic and contemptuous language," instead of "that calm and measured tone" necessary to official business.[3] Deadlock between executive and legislature, the refusal of supply, and rising public support for the reformers, together with instructions to the governor from the Colonial Office which ordered reform, led to the implementing of responsible government in 1851 and the assumption of office by the Liberals under George Coles. This was the first government to take office because it had the confidence of the Assembly.

Prince Edward Island got responsible government later than the other colonies because her government and legislature did not include a sufficient number of able men. This lack was evident in both the Executive and Legislative Councils where family connections and denominational representation were obvious determinants in appointments. Governor Ready had reported in 1827 that there was no one of wealth, talent, respectability, weight, or consequence in the upper chamber. There was little improvement by 1845 when Governor Huntley showed open contempt for members of the Assembly and their capacity for public affairs.[4] Nevertheless reform could not be prevented and the decisive factor in granting it to the Island was the example of reform in the other colonies.

Events soon proved, however, that even in 1851 the Island was not ready

PRINCE EDWARD ISLAND

for responsible government. Political turmoil, legislative chaos, and bad management resulted in incredible governmental spectacles from 1851 to 1873. In that period there were no less than twelve governments, and the province was in a continuous state of electioneering. Public careers were brief, so brief that, because the title of "honourable" was then given for life to cabinet members, the number of citizens with that title reached scandalous proportions. Competent men were discouraged from entering politics by the upheaval, while the main cause of it was the lack of able leaders.

The issues were also a major contribution to the political troubles. Denominational struggles were the chief problem because they introduced so much bitterness into politics. The control of the schools by churches and clergy, the allocation of public funds to denominational institutions, the teaching of the Bible in the classroom, the incorporation of the Orange Lodge, and clerical interference in political matters were regular subjects of legislative wrangling and public discussion. As a result of the acrimony involved, they were the main issues that toppled governments, ended political friendships, and ruined personal careers. Less emotional, but still troublesome, were discussions of land reform, especially proposals for the confiscation of proprietors' estates. The rights of both landlord and tenant were vigorously championed and riots and raids were common. As Confederation approached, questions of union and independence kept the political pot boiling furiously. There were controversial issues in all the colonies, of course, but within the narrow confines of Prince Edward Island they were particularly intense.

These problems clearly affected the party system. When responsible government first began public men were divided for a short while into "liberals" and "conservatives." There was an opportunity to develop these groups into alternating governments and oppositions formed on teamwork and personal associations. But disputes over denominationalism, land reform, and union cut through party lines to such an extent and in such varying ways that it was impossible for any leader to hold enough of his colleagues together long enough to form a workable party. Both sides were loose and shifting associations of interest groups based on weak and temporary compromises. In this period when most colonies were developing industry and communications Prince Edward Island was instead over-occupied with politics. The resulting bad government hampered the growth of the province for decades and was a legacy which future administrations never overcame and which many of them simply continued.

Church politics and union issues became so severe in 1870 that a one-party government could not be formed because there were no stable parties. J.C. Pope finally put together a coalition by getting its members to sign a pledge to drop these issues; in addition he focussed official and public attention on an interesting diversion — a railroad. The Prince Edward Island Railroad

3Gladstone to Governor Henry Vere Huntley, June 30, 1846, Prince Edward Island Papers, Public Archives of Canada, G16, p. 459.

4Ready to Lord Bathurst, June 12, 1827, Prince Edward Island Papers, Public Archives of Canada, A44, p. 97; Huntley to Lord Stanley, April 22, 1845, Prince Edward Island Papers, G48, p. 204; and Huntley to Gladstone, April 17, 1846, Prince Edward Island Papers, G48, p. 284.

was supported with enthusiasm and it was built on a grand and expensive scale with extensions, branch lines, and patronage to please everyone. This escape was an illusion, however, because the Island could not afford a railway. Money ran out, debentures were unsaleable, and the Island went bankrupt. The old issues were soon revived, temporary political associations dissolved, and government disintegrated. The only alternative was Confederation.

When the Island entered Confederation in 1873 its "liberal" and "conservative" parties were little more than temporary debating teams with convenient names. Various attempts were made to organize them; John A. Macdonald personally contacted his local friends and Alexander Mackenzie was able to attract all the new province's M.P.s to his side during the Pacific Scandal crisis. It appeared that federal politics would stimulate local party stability. Fresh controversy broke out in 1876, however, when the school question split the legislature in two: Protestants formed a coalition government, and Roman Catholics formed the opposition. Politicians soon realized that this alignment was a source of chaos; after the passing of the Public School Act of 1877 they drifted back once more into liberal and conservative groupings.

From this point the firm development of modern political parties on Prince Edward Island began. Two of the disrupting issues had been settled; union by Confederation, the land question by the Land Purchase Act of 1875 and accompanying arbitrations and federal financial assistance. Denominational problems were eased temporarily by the Public School Act and by the simple expedient of covering them up. Larger issues appeared as Island politicians participated in national affairs. Provincial Liberal and Conservative parties soon realized that with the many diversities in the electorate, they could not rigidly reflect one viewpoint but would have to represent the varying viewpoints of those whose votes they sought. They also wanted close associations with federal politicians in order to obtain concessions and patronage. Consequently, the development of local parties followed closely the growth of their federal counterparts. This association with federal parties has had one remarkable result: the Island has always elected governments of the same political allegiance as the government in Ottawa.

II. THE POLITICAL SETTING

Prince Edward Island parties function within a gigantic governmental structure and relatively small constituencies. The legislature consists of thirty-two members (increased from thirty in 1965), representing sixteen two-member constituencies. The cabinet comprises ten members (increased from nine in 1966). Thus almost a third of the legislative branch is made up of executive members — a large portion by any standard of administration. If the party in power were to have a bare majority, cabinet ministers would comprise no less than ten-sixteenths of the government side of the house. The cabinet therefore dominates both the caucus and the legislature, and a larger than normal amout of debate and decision-making takes place, in fact if not in form, in the cabinet rather than in the legislature. Each opposition party has complained bitterly about this fact and the consequent lack of information and discussion — for example, the disputes about developing industry in Georgetown from 1965 to 1968 and economic improvement plans in 1968 and 1969.

The sixteen constituencies, necessarily small in area, vary in the number of voters — from 5,851 in fifth Queens to 1,421 in fifth Kings in the 1966 election. This arrangement encourages highly localized contests and concentration on minutiae which would go unnoticed in larger areas. The paving of an extra mile of road, the giving of some benefit to a family, or the recognition of the services of a party worker — always factors anywhere — can easily become important issues in a tiny constituency. The pressures of his voters on a candidate are very great, and without question they limit his perspective both when he is a candidate and when he holds office.

Politics is carried on, therefore, with a high degree of informality and politicians are much closer to the people than are their counterparts elsewhere. It is not difficult for members of the legislature to maintain a substantial acquaintance among the voters. They are never more than a short drive from their constituencies and can attend local functions readily. House members who are lawyers, doctors, and merchants maintain political contact through their professional occupations because politics on the Island is generaly only a part-time occupation — even for the premier and his ministers. It is difficult to attend many functions on the Island without seeing at least one member, and the attendance of cabinet ministers is common.

In Prince Edward Island there is great interest and participation in the activities of party organizations. Everyone knows everyone else in a given area and the voters are labeled house by house and one by one. With few exceptions all citizens are interested and most of them know, or have met or seen, the candidates and the party officials. This intimacy affects party workers and supporters in three ways. Some view party activities as a normal adjunct to the business of government; these people keep Island politics going because they understand the significance of what they are doing. Others regard politics as great sport. It is their hobby; they have a good time. They approach it in much the same way as they would any other contest. They work at it assiduously, mainly at election time, but they do not take it too seriously. Still others take local politics too seriously. Being a Liberal or Conservative is of almost religious significance; anyone who is not with them is a political heathen. The first category gets the business done. The second provides the interest and colour. The third, influential in small contests, is always a source of problems and a barrier to progress.

The significance of effective organization is increased by the relatively small number of voters and the small majorities. There is an average of less than 2,000 voters for each member of the legislature, and majorities of less than fifty are common. Workers and candidates cannot take for granted the will of the constituents, even to the point of not calling on a family, neglecting to speak in a district, or ignoring a request for patronage. In one sense this intimacy is democracy at its best because the wishes of the "grass roots" readily find expression. In another sense it is a serious drawback to the Island's government because it is easy for a politician to make unwise decisions and unrealistic commitments in an effort to secure the small majority. Under these circumstances powerful or selfish interest groups can impose their will with devastating effects.

Party organizations therefore feel they must make many concessions to pressure groups. Denominational ones are the most powerful. They are feared the most because of the bitterness that can occur in a small area, and because of the tendency of ecclesiastical interests to precipitate or paralyze official action by threatening to intervene in controversial matters and to thwart the democratic process by use of "gentlemen's agreements" rather than open discussion. Church rivalries are obvious in all Island affairs and whether an individual is Catholic or Protestant is taken far more seriously than in most other provinces. The school system divides citizens from grade one, and the parish, social, and political systems maintain the division. In party organizations the result is obvious in the selection of officers, the awarding of patronage, and the appointment of judges and senators. The "turn" is evident in almost all appointments — now a Catholic, now a Protestant. This practice, on top of political patronage, has a damaging effect on government, because it often supersedes qualifications. For example, appointment of an official is often made from only a quarter of the persons eligible after political and denominational affiliations have been considered. The weak appointments that result have been depressingly obvious for many years.

Another powerful, but far more constructive, pressure group is the agricultural organization, such as the Federation of Agriculture, the Women's Institutes, and associations concerned with various activities such as potato growing and dairy farming. The dominance of agriculture on the Island assures its importance in both parties. The dependence of other industries on agriculture prevents a large gap from developing between their interests and those of the farmers.

It is surprising that the small size of the province and its constituencies and the close relationships among its social and political agencies have not minimized the principle of representation of interest groups in public organization. On the contrary this principle has been emphasized to the point where it has become undemocratic and grossly inefficient. The problem of pressure groups is evident throughout the province; they insist on their "rights" in the tiniest constituency and the smallest committee. Patronage and public works are carefully distributed by county and by district. Excellent appointments and projects are often sacrificed because authorities are prevented from taking an Island-wide view of their responsibilities. For example, it is difficult to get local authorities to understand that a major concentration of capital and effort for one industry in one area is often more productive for *all* than their piecemeal distribution over a number of districts. The latter results in a host of inefficient small economic projects and no really effective industry. Most governmental projects in the province are difficult enough to carry out, but it is even more difficult to rally general support for them from the numerous interests that oppose them or insist on some compensatory advantage. In fact political as well as financial costs are attached to almost everything the Island government does and much provincial politics is devoted, not to actual government, but to the interplay that results from overemphasis of the representation principle.

This over-emphasis sharpens the acquisitive instincts of Islanders. The politics of acquisition and the consequent maneuvering are common in all federal systems. It is quite natural for the smallest partner to demand its share and to be determined to have the privileges enjoyed by the larger partners. The Island has acted in this manner in its federal-provincial relations and to an even greater extent in its internal politics. The efficiency of government depends substantially on the way it makes use of the ability, money, effort, and time that society can reasonably devote to public business. Only a limited proportion of these resources can reasonably be devoted to the mechanics of administration and politics; the major part must go to the services necessary to society. Herein lies one of the serious problems of Island politics: because the mechanics of politics is so extensive in the Island's large system, the process of "getting" for limited advantage too often displaces the process of "doing" for the benefit of all. Every district that wants something because another district has got something, every denomination that will not tolerate an advantage to another unless it gets a favour, and every organization and individual that puts a price on its citizenship add to the getting process and too often subtract from the necessary doing process. For example, the money spent on the construction of many miles of unnecessary paved highway would have paid for many valuable services that the Island has been forced to do without; and the appointment of people of doubtful competence to responsible positions merely because they belonged to a particular denomination or came from a particular district has deprived the Island of much ability and cost it many mistakes.

The high cost of politics on the Island has one compensation. Everyone is interested and the opportunities for participation are numerous. The large number of organizations in the province provide many forums for political discussion and stepping stones to public life. Governmental officials and institutions are not distant phenomena seen only by a small portion of the citizenry; they are in the immediate neighbourhood. Gilbert and Sullivan described this kind of situation in "The Gondoliers":

> "And Party Leaders you might meet
> In twos and threes in every street
> Maintaining, with no little heat,
> Their various opinions."

In one sense officials suffer the disadvantage of working in full view of everyone, but in another sense there is a very real and strong link between government and citizens which is a source of the pride and interest without which a democracy cannot thrive. There are difficulties no doubt —

> "Yet the duties are delightful, and the privileges great;
> But the privilege and pleasure
> That we treasure beyond measure
> Is to run on little errands for the Ministers of State."

III. PARTY ORGANIZATION

The intimacy of the political setting in Prince Edward Island makes party organizations highly personal. There is, therefore, a tendency to interpret the rules to conform to local practice and to the circumstances of the moment. If no one is interested in an annual meeting it can be permitted to lapse; an ineffective committee can be ignored; a rule can be interpreted with elasticity to permit or justify an action.

Both parties have provincial organizations. The officers are chosen, if possible, from the leaders of the district associations. An annual meeting is held but it is usually of interest only just before an election or when it is combined with a convention to select candidates. Both parties have women's organizations but their functions are largely social; the ladies make their major contributions through the main associations. Recently young people's political clubs have flourished with the rising interest of youth in public affairs and especially with the lowering of the voting age to 18 in 1967. There are student political clubs in the university and in some larger high schools. It is already an interesting question whether or not a young person, who joins a club because his friends do regardless of his family's political affiliation, may change his mind when he becomes older.[5]

Both parties changed their intermediate organizations after the recent federal redistribution. The old Prince, Queens, and Kings county associations were replaced by associations for the new federal districts: Egmont, Malpeque, Hillsborough, and Cardigan. These associations operate for both federal and provincial elections and are expected to include representatives of provincial districts; indeed, the Conservative constitution makes this mandatory in the selection of directors.

Most of the business of the provincial organizations is handled by an executive committee consisting of the officers, past presidents, representatives of provincial district and federal constituency organizations, and representatives of the women's and youth groups. Other committees handle special details such as finance, membership, and publicity. This apparatus works with sporadic efficiency. By and large it is lively before and quiet after an election and it is much more active when the party it supports is in power. Each of the district and constituency groups has a similar organization.

The poll organization is the basic unit of the party machinery and it maintains the closest contact with the voters. There are 292 polls in 250 polling divisions on Prince Edward Island. For each poll organization there is a poll committee with a chairman and secretary and from five to twenty members (depending on the size of the poll), all selected by an advertised annual meeting of party members in the poll. The duties of this unit include organizing party workers at election time, scrutinizing voters' lists, canvassing voters, arranging transportation to the polls, and assisting the candidates. The organization also sends delegates to meetings and conventions of the party and shares in the work of the larger groups. All poll organizations are active at election time; between elections some are dormant, but some keep busy by maintaining contacts with members and voters, handling patronage, and distributing information.

The most spectacular work of the party organizations is in the planning and staging of ordinary conventions, leadership conventions, annual meetings, and political meetings. A large portion of the constitution of each party is devoted to these gatherings, which provide the best illustration of how the party machinery works.

The party convention is both the focal point for publicity, celebration, and propaganda and the instrument for the selection of candidates. It has always been the occasion for rousing party expressions of self-confidence and, occasionally, high jinks. Today, however, with the attentions of television, radio, and the press, it has also become a highly organized and efficient machine for impressing the public as well as for getting business done. Conventions must be held often enough to serve these purposes and yet infrequently enough to allow party enthusiasm and public interest to accumulate. The district conventions are usually held in the months immediately prior to an expected election. The provincial convention is held when a party leader must be chosen, when a leader needs an expression of confidence, or when the benefits of a major publicity effort are required.

At the thirty-two district conventions which take place within a few weeks party leaders speak on the issues of the day, extol one another's virtues, and receive votes of confidence from their supporters. Attending the conventions are chairmen of committees, five-man delegations from poll meetings who vote on official matters, and other party members who participate in the business and enjoy the proceedings. Resolutions are passed and sent to appropriate authorities. Party leaders often make special announcements in order to get a headline in the press reports of the proceedings, which inevitably attract less attention as the many conventions take place. The effectiveness of these gatherings depends on the ability of the organizers, on whether the constituency concerned is sure, doubtful, or a lost cause, and on the extent of the contest for nominations.

Candidates for nomination are subject to the judgment of officers, chairmen, and other voting delegates who were previously selected by poll meetings. The five delegates from each poll are selected sometimes without a contest, perhaps from the members of the poll committee, and sometimes after bitter rivalry among supporters of particular candidates for nomination. The "packing" of delegations is common and persons working on behalf of candidates must watch the proceedings carefully from the very first poll meetings. At the convention the delegates are assiduously wooed by the candidates and their supporters. The delegations sometimes vote as a body; usually, however, they vote as individuals.

The procedure at conventions varies widely and is often informal. Nominations can be made from the floor or by a nominating committee. Movers and seconders sometimes make elaborate speeches and sometimes they content themselves with a simple declaration. Those named accept with alacrity

5The formal details of party organization are set forth in the constitution of the Prince Edward Island Conservative Association dated September 1966 and that of the Prince Edward Island Liberal Association dated November 1967.

and pride, although occasionally someone who is nominated as a tribute grace-fully declines. If there are only two nominees (perhaps the sitting members) there is no contest and they receive acclamations. If more than two persons are named there are one or more ballots, with the person receiving the lowest number of votes dropped at each one. The winners are declared elected to resounding cheers, the losers spring forward to declare the vote unanimous, and the wives of the winners are led up to the podium for congratulatory embraces. This last procedure, which was not common in earlier days when wives usually stayed home or at the back of the hall, developed slowly as women's interest in politics increased and as press and television photog-raphers came to play an important role in covering conventions.

The provincial convention brings together federal and provincial sitting members, defeated candidates, members of the executive, and district, con-stituency, and poll delegates from all parts of the province. It is a rousing affair held in a coliseum of appropriate size. The media and the public take a lively interest and music, entertainment, decorations, and refreshments entice and please the crowd. It is the party's biggest opportunity, short of an election, to relay its messages to the public, and also the chance for candidates to vie for the leadership.

This procedure replaced the practice followed in Island politics until 1950 of always selecting party leaders in the caucus. Whether a party was in power or in opposition, its sitting members in the legislature made the selection, even at times when this group was very small. Occasionally there was an obvious successsor to a retiring leader, and the transition was made with ease. Often there were several aspirants and much manoeuvering took place in the limited confines of the caucus. Indeed one man's vote often determined the winner. Although the winner was never repudiated by the party, the process by which he won often caused dissatisfaction. This occurred partic-ularly with respect to commitments he might have had to make to individual colleagues in the process of securing support, to the fact that the party had little or no voice in making the choice, and to the sitting members' advantage over other possible candidates. The caucus occasionally found it difficult to support a controversial leader whom, perhaps, one member might seek to undermine, or to dispose of a leader whose effectiveness was over and who would not resign.

Whatever the shortcomings of the convention, its voice is clear and final. Such a voice was necessary in 1950 when the Conservatives held their first convention to select a leader (R.R. Bell replaced W.J.P. MacMillan) and in 1961 when the Liberals held their first convention to confirm the leadership of the incumbent (A.W. Matheson was challenged by J.W. MacNaught). The mere demand for a convention forced a decision to be made on a difficult party problem – in the one case delayed retirement and in the other internal rivalry. Although the problems remained, the leadership was clearly de-signated by the convention, something the caucus was unable to do. Both parties now follow the practice of selecting their leaders by convention. Premier A.B. Campbell is the first Liberal leader and Opposition Leader George Key is the third Conservative leader to be so selected. It is significant that Mr. Campbell had been in the legislature for just a few months and Mr.

Key and his predecessor W.R. Shaw were without a seat when they were chosen party leaders.

The constitution of the Prince Edward Island Liberal Association now provides that the Executive Committee of the party shall call a leadership convention "whenever it becomes necessary to select a Provincial Leader" and a provincial convention "at such time and place as the circumstances may warrant," in any case at least once every four years. Voting delegates comprise all former and sitting Liberal members of the Senate, House of Commons, and provincial legislature, "non-elected" Liberal candidates in the most recent federal and provincial elections, the president and officers of the provincial, constituency, women's, young Liberals', and university Liberals' organizations, the presidents of the district associations, and five poll delegates from each official polling division. The Executive Committee is specifically charged with the arrangements of the convention.

The Conservative party constitution is in some ways more flexible. For instance it is not specific about procedure for leadership conventions although the actual procedure is similar to that of the Liberals. Conservative voting delegates include candidates nominated for a coming election; only if there are no such candidates are the candidates of the last election included.

The formal provisions for holding conventions tell only part of the story. No one expects the clarion call of untrammeled democracy to come out of such gatherings. In preceding weeks there is much manipulating of opinion and bargaining for commitments, as leadership candidates work tirelessly in the glare of publicity. In a close contest every sentence in a nomination speech, every handshake, every interview with the press, and every conversation in a back room, may contribute to victory or defeat. Nothing must be taken for granted. Skulduggery must be expected and countered; one candidate lost by a narrow margin in a recent convention because some of the voting delegates supporting him were taken "out back" by his opponents and treated with refreshments until after the ballots were cast. Most of all, however, the candidate must present an image for the occasion that will impress the viewers on television and the multitude in the hot, noisy auditorium for whom he must perform in the demanding glare of spotlights and with the restricting limitations of microphones.

There are two kinds of political meetings that take place at election time. One is the great rally of party faithfuls and interested or curious citizens in a district where there is a lively contest. At this type of meeting a battery of prominent speakers and crowd-pleasing entertainment are provided in a packed hall as background for the exhortations of candidates and the enlightenment of public opinion. The other kind of meeting is the much quieter, perhaps dreary, gathering, held in an area that the party has given up for lost. Speakers and candidates know there is little cause for enthusiasm in such an area and listeners must be coaxed to attend. The speeches and the routine are much the same in all meetings. Those who must accompany candidates expect to hear the same ideas repeated again and again, and the press reporters generally find it increasingly difficult, as the campaign progresses, to glean some fresh news for their readers.

These kinds of meeting are comparatively modern on the Island. Until thirty years ago the joint political meeting was common. Representatives of both sides filled the halls to capacity to hear opposing candidates debate the issues of the day under the watchful eye of an independent chairman. These were lively meetings highly charged with excitement and always interesting and newsworthy. Candidates had to speak in the presence of their opponents who had a chance to present the other side of the arguments. The candidates' supporters cheered and the opponents' supporters booed; hecklers tested their patience and their ingenuity. Today's meetings present only one side and cheering predominates. While the older, more rowdy, meetings favoured the debaters and penalized the shy candidates, it can be argued that democracy has lost something important in the change.

Another major factor in party activities is the altered position of the newspapers. Until recently the *Guardian* was Conservative and the *Patriot* Liberal. Each reported on platforms, candidates, and meetings in a partisan manner, and its editorials praised one side and criticized the other. Those who read only one paper got a slanted interpretation of political events; but those who read both got not only both sides of issues but also an enormous amount of news because there was stiff competition between the papers. In addition, the newspapers provided continuous practice in assessing the relative significance of conflicting opinions. Today the papers are owned by one syndicate. Advertising displaces the long reports and speeches. Television competes for the political news. The biased thunder has gone from the editorials. The *Guardian* is now independent with a Conservative slant; the *Patriot* is independent with a Liberal slant; it takes a major issue to increase the slant. Whether or not this change has been a good one for the newspapers' readers is debatable. Certainly for the parties it has removed a formidable weapon for defending virtue and fighting political opposition.

An important factor in all this political activity is the limited number of people served. No other group of 109,000 people in Canada have so many party gatherings and so much political machinery. Socially there is no question of the amount of fun Islanders have with their politics. Psychologically party politics offers a release for the Islanders' energies and their combative instincts. It brings Islanders together as few other activities can do, and continuously reminds them of their responsibilities as citizens. It is also evident, however, that, as often happens where there is too much of a good thing, politics is overdone on the Island to the detriment not only of other activities but of politics itself. While recognizing the advantages of the political machinery, we should now examine the issues with which it deals and the efficiency with which it operates.

IV. THE POLITICAL ISSUES

No issues clearly divide the Liberals and Conservatives in Prince Edward Island. No theory, no policy, and no political action can be identified with either party; each has advocated and opposed everything, depending on whether it was the party in power or in opposition at the time.

Third parties have played no significant part in Island politics. Independent, Progressive, CCF or NDP candidates have never posed a threat and have no effective organization. With one exception (J.A. Dewar, who sat as an Independent from 1919 to 1923), no one from any of these groups has ever won an election and almost all have lost their deposits. Agriculture has always been the dominant industry. The wishes of the rural population have been major factors in party strategy, and the farm vote is well represented in both main parties. There is no big business and industrial labour is not numerous. Consequently there has been no area of political interest with which third parties could identify themselves. Because both parties have appealed to the same electorate for a century and the issues debated in the Legislature have changed little in that time, variations in party politics have not been encouraged.

The issues that the parties dispute in elections and in debates in the legislature, that cause most maneuvering within the parties, and that influence directly the administration of government fall into a few main categories: denominationalism, transportation, federal-provincial relations, patronage, public works, and agriculture, in roughly that order. In the past five years industrial development has also been a lively subject for discussion.

Denominationalism plays such a large part in Prince Edward Island politics that it might well be said that the Island has four political parties: Liberal, Conservative, Catholic, and Protestant. Everyone is publicly labelled from the moment of birth or entry into residence, and his approach to public affairs is clearly dictated by his allegiance. The history of Island politics has shown the major role of denominationalism. Today, in almost every phase of public activity, ecclesiastical aggrandisement and inter-church rivalry are powerful forces and major obstacles to be reckoned with by anyone seeking to inaugurate any policy or project. More public business has been disrupted by church politics than by any other single issue. This problem alone has done more than anything else to add to the cost and uncertainties of governmental business. The denominational issues are of two kinds: actual disputes over education and social services in which churches have a direct interest, and hidden maneuvering — apparent in most matters — concerning ecclesiastical advantage in securing money, patronage, or power. Some of the arguments, fear of arguments and reprisals, compromises, and gentlemen's agreements that have been caused by denominationalism have been open. However, because of the bitterness of earlier days, which almost ended government in the Island, most denominational forces now operate underground. As a result, the public does not have an opportunity to hear the arguments and discuss them intelligently — no matter how much money is allotted to fulfilling a denominational wish, no matter how good a project is that is being obstructed by denominational opposition, and no matter how inept might be a denominational appointment to a public office. Church politics is the one force exempt from the democratic process in Prince Edward Island.

Transportation is of interest to everyone on an island that must communicate and trade with the mainland. It is also a major source of jobs, contracts, and political influence at the local level. Both parties feature it in all their manifestos and every legislative session is concerned with it. When the Island entered Confederation the British North America Act guaranteed "efficient and continuous communication with the mainland" to be provided by the federal government, and since then the Island has seen to it that

Ottawa has lived up to this promise. The ferry services and the trans-Canada highway have always been topics for debate. The provincial opposition party can always find something wrong with these services and every government has featured in its propaganda its efforts to get still better transportation agreements than did its predecessors. In recent years the causeway has been a *cause célèbre*; no speech is complete without it, and its varied implications provide endless sources of fascinating discussion.

For its size and population the Island now has the finest network of roads of any province in Canada. It has built, and must maintain, 1,500 miles of excellent paved highway and 3,330 miles of secondary roads. Building additional roads is the provincial government's main task and each administration carefully indicates what it has done or will do in this area of development. Paving is the best vote-getting process there is and each district must get its share. Many of the Island's roads are vital arteries of commerce; others, however, must be among the least travelled ones in Canada. No one can afford to call a halt and road-building proceeds until, as some people joke, the Island might sink beneath the weight of concrete.

Railroads have been the cause of much discussion in Prince Edward Island as they have been throughout Canada. The federal government took over the Prince Edward Island Railway at Confederation and the line eventually became part of the CNR. It has never paid its way, but it has been an essential part of Island commerce. Although today, with competition from airlines and truck transports, its business is dwindling steadily, the Island will not part with it. Politicians protest vigorously any curtailment of its services. Whether or not there should be a railway on the causeway is a choice subject for debate.

Finance is a normal source of discussion in any government. The Island, as the smallest province, demands a share of the nation's funds commensurate, not with its size and population — for the Island could not live on a sum based on such proportions — but with its status as a province. For this reason the Island has always resisted per capita and matching grant arrangements; provincial officials have debated at great length among themselves and with federal authorities regarding suitable financial agreements. Because the provincial government has nearly always been of the same political allegiance as the federal government, the opposition party has been able to use provincial finance as a potent weapon of attack.

The fact that two-thirds of the provincial government's revenue now comes from Ottawa in the form of miscellaneous grants and payments puts the local treasury in the role of an agent for the distribution of federal funds. This role weakens the local taxpayers' understanding of their own financial responsibility. The Island government finds it difficult to say, "If you want you must pay"; the answer from the taxpayers would probably be, "Why are you not getting more from Ottawa?" The role of agent also enables the provincial government to excuse its own lack of action or mistakes by blaming the federal government for not giving it enough money. Furthermore, the channeling of federal funds such as university grants through the provincial treasury instead of direct to institutions greatly increases the power of the provincial government over those institutions and puts them in a position of complete dependence on the government and on its ability to raise money and make good decisions. This procedure further diminishes the taxpayer's understanding of public finance. In the case of the university, for example, it tends to encourage the interpretation of educational policy by the limited interests of local administration and politics with a resulting weakening of the national interest or the interest of the university itself. These difficulties, which are experienced to a varying degree in all provinces, are particularly evident on the Island because of the high dependence on federal funds and the relative inability of the smallest province to dictate terms to Ottawa or to relieve the overwhelming pressures of local politics on public finance.

Patronage in Prince Edward Island is an unusually large encouragement of political participation, party loyalty, and attention to the government's wishes. The governorship, seven judgships, four senatorships, a speakership, and the ten cabinet posts are attractive dignities. Many positions in the province are at the disposal of the government. It is always apparent what firms and individuals are currently in favour as suppliers of goods and services. As the constitution of the Liberal party directs, "The Patronage Committee shall keep records of service and contributions of party supporters and shall make recommendations for patronage benefits." What is unique about this arrangement is the extent to which the large amount of patronage in a small population enhances the power of the provincial government and increases the proportion of political activity motivated by the hope of patronage.

Public works are a major interest of both parties and a lively cause of controversy. The parties as well as the public have widely encouraged public works despite the fact that the population is the same as it was a century ago, and the productive capacity of Island industry has not increased relative to that of the nation or relative to the amounts spent on public works. The parties do not argue about whether or not public works are justifiable — politically no one wants to say "No" to demands in small places — but why there are not more of them. Consequently one does not travel far in the province without being amazed at the amount of public works for 109,000 people. The wisdom of supplying and maintaining so many of them is inevitably questioned when one notes the less politically popular services that are not adequately provided. The wisdom can be questioned further because of the scattered and marginal benefits of public works. With the compartmentalization of politics into districts, it is difficult to encourage works of a more general and often more efficient and productive nature, which would benefit the whole province and raise its industrial capacity.

As agriculture is the main industry, it is always an important subject of dispute and it generally prevails over other considerations. Both parties must go out of their way to do things for the farmers whose support they must have. What debate there is is usually on how much the government has done and how much the opposition can blame the government for drops in prices or production of farm products.

The Island has a strong tradition of education, and provision of educational facilities is itself not a subject of dispute. The real issues of education have been denominationalism and the need for public works because they, rather than actual educational needs, have so often dictated whether or not institutions, facilities, or services should be provided or obstructed in a particular district or for a particular group or for the province as a whole.

Fortunately for local politics, broader issues periodically enlarge the scope of party interests because the provincial party machinery is also used for federal politics. Because of the Island's status as a province, its officials participate in national governmental and party activities and conferences to a much greater extent than the province's size and population would otherwise warrant. This participation contributes to the officials' appreciation and enjoyment of public life as it compensates for the limiting responsibilities of local politics by providing a wider sphere in which to offer opinions and talents.

All these issues combined in the 1960's to make a major change in the administration, the economy and the fortunes of the province and, by the end of the decade, even to alter profoundly its system of responsible government. Both parties and most of the pressure groups were involved. The Conservative government of W.R. Shaw embarked on a food processing and shipbuilding project in Georgetown which failed because of ministerial inexperience and interference, bad management and singularly naive attempts at business planning, all of which were subsequently investigated and condemned by a royal commission. The resulting financial disaster, which was inherited by the Liberals under A.B. Campbell in 1966, drained the local treasury. The causeway, which had already begun, had committed whatever special funds the federal government could reasonably be expected to spend on the Island. Nevertheless the provincial government proceeded to negotiate a new project of its own with Ottawa in the form of a comprehensive development plan. It got the plan but the causeway was immediately stopped and abandoned and the federal government saved a great deal of money in the deal. These successive events were criticized severely in the national press and the Island lost much of the good will and sympathy which it had long enjoyed. Despite the already large number of institutions and officials on the Island the federal government sent an enormous task force to Charlottetown. This group literally took over the government and the development plan proceeded to embrace every aspect of Island life. Opposition politicians raised a storm over the extent of the takeover, the competence of the planners, the transfer of power from ministers and civil servants to the planners, the size of the resulting bureaucracy, the lack of information, the by-passing of the legislature, and, in general, the loss of responsible government. The affair caused speculation elsewhere on the consequences of this unusually detailed intervention of the federal government in provincial jurisdiction.

V. THE EFFICIENCY OF THE MACHINE

The duty of a democratic government to perform certain functions is generally understood by the people. Less understood is the cost of administering these functions and of maintaining an expanding political and official establishment. Prince Edward Island provides an example of the high cost in money and effort of political overhead. It also illustrates how individual and community effort and responsibility decrease as a large government takes over an increasing proportion of the activities of the society.

The large system and the rewards of politics on Prince Edward Island encourage active political affiliations and close associations with government. Almost anyone's party label is known. Governmental patronage is important in many careers. Because government is so omnipotent and close to the people there is a great tendency toward the "let the government do it" attitude. Whole communities depend exclusively on public enterprises. The benefits are obvious in a social service age, and the democratic theory of people and their government being close to each other is more than adequately honoured. The result of this process, however, is the inclusion in governmental activities and the civil service of a large number of people interested and experienced in, and occupied with, purely political activities as distinct from actual government. The work performed by them regardless of need, in response to purely political demands or in the hope of attracting political support, comprises an ever increasing part of the government's programme to the point where much of the work is a waste of time and money and overshadows more important functions. Furthermore, as this work grows the supply of able people in the small Island society who are available for government service diminishes and the government must call on less competent people.

Another result of the large political emphasis in government administration is the discouragement of imaginative private enterprise by the desire of the government to concern itself with every phase of activity that may bring it credit and by the inertia among people who look to the government for action rather than act themselves. There is every sign that the Island is far behind other provinces in non-governmental activity, especially in industry. When the government itself has attempted to fill the gap by engaging in industry, it has been unsuccessful because governmental personnel have been unable to provide industrial leadership and the government could not resist the temptation of running industry by political standards. The fiasco in Georgetown in the 1960's, for example, was a hopeless mixture of business and politics brewed by people who tried food processing and ship-building without knowing very much about either. The loss in 1969 of the causeway to the mainland which had been approved and commenced was another example: the provincial government demanded too much of the taxpayers of Canada by seeking an expensive federal economic improvement plan at the same time. Because of its dominant position the Island government finds it difficult to acknowledge its inability to handle major projects and to permit initiative and leadership from non-political sources with non-political motivations.

Probably the most serious effect of the large political system on personnel, however, is the fact that dominant government alone cannot attract and hold able people. Where there is too much emphasis on the political standard of measurement, too much looking inward at itself by the government rather than outward at other thriving enterprises, and too much concern with maintaining the establishment for its own sake, good people leave. The Island exports a dangerously large portion of its able young people; the dominance of politics is among the main reasons. It must be emphasized that this statement is not a reflection on the nature of politics but on the amount. In abnormally large quantities politics discourages other enterprise, and imposes its methods and interests on them. Important as it is, politics or politically supported activity is not everyone's preference as a career or as a means of promoting a career or an enterprise.

The justification for a government in Prince Edward Island and the efficiency of political, social, and economic life in the province would be greatly increased if the size and functions of the government were cut by one-third. The reason is the operation of Parkinson's Law. Work, Parkinson said, expands in importance and complexity, not with its real significance, but with the time to be spent; and the number of officials are not related to the quantity of the work.[6] The Prince Edward Island government exemplifies Parkinson's Law and the desires of officials to seek control, multiply subordinates, engage in paper work, make work for one another, and, ultimately, to discourage or prevent non-political enterprise.

A partial solution to the problem, often found elsewhere but not yet sufficiently tried in Prince Edward Island, is the separation of party politics and civil service administration from some public enterprises. Parties and their activities are essential to the selecting and changing of governments and to the process of making public officials responsible to the people. But they are not always essential or desirable in the direct operation of public business. It is not always possible to keep them out of public business in the larger systems. It is far more difficult to make the separation in the smaller ones. Nevertheless the emergence everywhere of the public trusts has provided a combination of public enterprise and professional initiative that neither civil service nor party personnel has been able to give to the management of essential services. Despite some weaknesses, most of these trusts have worked well. It is significant that Prince Edward Island had to wait until 1964 to get its first trusts — an industrial corporation, a university, and a centennial commission — the first public organizations in the province to be free, at least initially, of party politics and departmental management.

The administrative aspects of governmental expansion do not concern us here. The political aspects can never be removed in any democratic government. In Prince Edward Island they tend to be too obvious because governments are so close to, and so dependent on, the party process and the powerful pressure groups. Governmental involvement in some project or function, however suitable or necessary that involvement may be, can be demanded and often implemented simply because it sounds well in a platform or pleases an interest group. Every such involvement increases the establishment and decreases the scope for and initiative of non-political enterprise. The point has been reached where the amount of administration and politics is too large in relation to what it does for the people of the Island and to the province's production in goods, services, and social amenities.

Having ministers of the Crown, for example, is of course essential to the Island's parliamentary system. It is also useful to political parties in power by providing titled leadership in political processes. But ten of them, all with portfolios and deputy ministers, is difficult to justify when the actual business each handles amounts in significance to little more than that looked after by a clerk in a city or county elsewhere. Moreover competent ministers are scarce because the number of elected members from which a premier must choose his colleagues is so small. Under the circumstances it is too easy for ministers to get into mischief or take themselves too seriously by getting into activities that they are not supposed to handle or for which they do not have enough competence. Until the 1940's premiers distributed almost all the portfolios among a few senior ministers and retained other colleagues as part-time ministers without portfolio. Politics made it impossible to maintain this distinction, however, as portfolios increased in number and were divided among all the chosen. As each minister and deputy expanded his organization and looked for more to do, the cabinet inevitably got involved in minutiae and had less time for the general executive functions for which it was intended. Political organizations and the public, in turn, expected and demanded this attention to minutiae, the process spiraled, and matters of real significance were neglected. "We have a cabinet of eight members and a presiding officer!" said Hon J.D. Stewart, Minister of Tourist Development and Municipal Affairs and Provincial Secretary, in the legislature in 1964. "Too large, too cumbersome, too voluble — the same as this House — [Laughter] — too many squeaking wheels. Let us be sensible for goodness sake. Let us get down to size; let us cut this unwieldy thing to a workable size; not more than five members and a presiding officer."[7] "This," said Opposition Leader and former Premier A.W. Matheson, "is good, sound advice,"[8] Yet two years later the cabinet was increased by another minister.

If the legislature, cabinet and civil service and the functions they perform were reduced by one-third, all three would undoubtedly work better and more efficiently. Political party organizations would in turn be reduced in size. Their units would work in larger areas and with larger issues. Because their contacts with voters would be less parochial, the issues would be more worthy of their effort. Because their contacts with elected representatives and ministers would be with fewer men with more to do, their leadership would be stronger. A greater number of necessary non-governmental enterprises might well be encouraged. As for the citizens, politics might take up a little less of their lives and perhaps make way for a desirable increase of their initiative in other directions. This initiative should encourage what the Island needs most and what government cannot provide — new business, new industry, new and improved methods in primary industries and in production as well as in the arts and in cultural and educational leadership and research. These alternatives to political, and often non-productive and non-essential, activities would develop the province because they are productive, provide more rewarding employments, and train and attract able young

[6]C. Northcote Parkinson, *Parkinson's Law* (New York: Ballantine Books, Inc., 1957). pp. 15 and 16.
[7]*Speeches of the Prince Edward Island Legislative Assembly*, 1964, March 17, 1964, p. 456.
[8]*Ibid.*

TABLE I

Party Tenures of Office with Years of Formations of Governments and Names of Premiers

Party	Year	Premier
Liberal	1851	George Coles
Conservative	1854	John Holl
Liberal	1855	George Coles
Conservative	1859	Edward Palmer
Conservative	1863	John H. Gray
Conservative	1865	J. C. Pope
Liberal	1867	George Coles
Liberal	1869	Joseph Hensley
Liberal	1869	R. P. Haythorne
Conservative	1870	J. C. Pope
Liberal	1871	R. P. Haythorne
Conservative	1873	J. C. Pope
Conservative	1873	L. C. Owen
Coalition	1876	L. H. Davies
Conservative	1879	W. W. Sullivan
Conservative	1889	Neil MacLeod
Liberal	1891	Frederick Peters
Liberal	1897	A. B. Warburton
Liberal	1898	Donald Farquharson
Liberal	1901	Arthur Peters
Liberal	1908	F. L. Haszard
Liberal	1911	James Palmer
Conservative	1911	J. A. Mathieson
Conservative	1917	A. E. Arsenault
Liberal	1919	J. H. Bell
Conservative	1923	J. D. Stewart
Liberal	1927	A. C. Saunders
Liberal	1930	W. M. Lea
Conservative	1931	J. D. Stewart
Conservative	1933	W. J. P. MacMillan
Liberal	1935	W. M. Lea
Liberal	1936	T. A. Campbell
Liberal	1943	J. Walter Jones
Liberal	1953	A. W. Matheson
Conservative	1959	W. R. Shaw
Liberal	1966	A. B. Campbell

people by giving them challenging opportunities. In turn the government itself will become more significant as the province becomes more self-sufficient.

The Island has all the physical assets to enable its people to lead a varied, interesting, and rewarding life. Its government gives it an identity and prestige of which its people are proud. Its politics serves that government in the recognized ways of democracy. But just as too much power may render dangerous a vehicle which it propels, a surfeit of politics on the Island may make unstable the democracy which it serves and ultimately cause the Island to lose its government altogether. While the nation itself is discussing constitutional change, the Island might well consider the advisability of overhauling its own system after two hundred years of operation.

The Island is a tribute to the flexibility of the British type of constitution which permitted it to be established and equipped as a political unit. It is a tribute to Confederation which enabled so small a place to be a full partner and allowed it to be treated with generosity and even affection. It is an interesting laboratory of politics where a long experiment has been conducted on the consequences of permitting man's political actions and associations to overshadow and permeate all other aspects of his society while at the same time retaining many essentials of democracy. As in all laboratories, there is noise and smell from time to time, but everyone is occupied and the results are always interesting, sometimes even startling. And, in the valuable tradition of laboratories, may not the Island's political apparatus indicate with reasonable accuracy what can happen, in similar circumstances, in larger constitutional installations?

* QUEBEC *

"Heaven is Blue and Hell is Red"

VINCENT LEMIEUX

I. HISTORICAL BACKGROUND

An old Quebec legend attributes the above saying, used as the chapter title, to a priest who, from his pulpit, exhorted his parishioners to vote for the Conservative party, known as the "Bleus," rather than the Liberals, known as the "Rouges." Many Quebec voters have never regarded these parties in terms of heaven and hell. Nevertheless, the old rivalry between the two major parties has dominated the provincial political scene for the past one hundred years.

The most constant characteristic of provincial party politics in Quebec has been the two-party system. From time to time a third party or a splinter group from one of the two major parties has threatened to disrupt the system traditionally dominated by Conservatives and Liberals or Union Nationale and Liberals. Such parties have never been successful. The most serious threat occurred during the 1930's when the Action Libérale Nationale, a dissident wing of the Liberal party, joined forces with the Conservatives. In 1936, this alliance became the Union Nationale party. The Conservative representative from Trois-Rivières, Maurice Duplessis, became the leader of the new party and held this position until his death in 1959. In 1944, 1948, and 1966, respectively, the nationalist Bloc Populaire, the créditiste Union des Electeurs, and the separatist Rassemblement pour l'Indépendance Nationale and the Ralliement National tried unsuccessfully to gain a toehold in the Quebec Parliament. In 1944, however, the Bloc Populaire did manage to gain four of the ninety-one seats, but the créditistes in 1948 and the separatists in 1966 did not elect a single representative.

The difference between the two major provincial parties has never been as extreme as the difference between heaven and hell. Nevertheless, the parties' ideologies and policies through the years reveal differences that have been virtually constant. There have been three lengthy phases since 1867 that point out these differences.[1] In the initial period, which lasted until Laurier's victory in 1896, the two big provincial parties confronted each other for the most part on nationalist and religious issues. At the beginning of this period, the Conservatives were the Confederation party in Quebec, as they were in all of Canada, with only one extremist wing of the Liberal party opposing them on this issue. Disputes of a religious nature often overshadowed the nationalist squabbles. There were elements in the Liberal party who wanted separation of church and state as well as greater individual freedom in religious education. This movement was opposed by most of the Catholic bishops in Quebec, who gave their support to the Conservatives. Nevertheless, throughout this entire period the provincial Quebec Liberals, together with the Quebec Liberals in Ottawa, proved to be more provincialist than the Conservatives. During this era the Liberal opposition was most active in 1886, after Riel's execution and the accession to power of Mercier's "parti national." Mercier drew support from the Liberals, the National Conservatives, and the Ultramontanes. The last-named, who advocated an alliance between the Church and the State with the Church dominating, had always been in the Conservative ranks, and their battles with the Rouges of the Liberal party raged through the second half of the nineteenth century. For this group to find itself with Mercier's Liberals was indicative of the times. Although the Conservatives defeated Mercier in 1892, it was the last time this party achieved a victory in Quebec provincial elections. From 1897, immediately following Laurier's victorious appearance on the Canadian scene, the provincial Liberals took over the government and held power until 1936. This long tenure forms the second phase of Quebec provincial politics.

It is interesting to note that during the entire second period the Quebec voters consistently preferred the Liberals to the Conservatives at the federal level. Ottawa became the norm for the provincial vote. The provincial Conservatives suffered from the federal Conservatives' policies, which antagonized the nationalistic feelings of the Quebec voters. The religious quarrels of the nineteenth century had died away; furthermore, the two parties hardly differed on economic and social issues until Taschereau became premier in 1920. His government systematically encouraged the industrialization of Quebec through private enterprise. However, opposition to this policy came more from the nationalists than from the Conservative party, which had no organized basis on which it could conduct an effective offensive against the Liberals.

It took the smell of corruption coming from a regime that had lasted too long and, even more, the economic crisis of the 1930's to finally defeat the Liberal government. Yet the final blow was delivered by a splinter group from the Liberal party, the Action Libérale Nationale, which, allied with the Conservatives, left no more than a majority of 6 out of the 90 seats to the Liberals in 1935. The two opposition parties then formed the Union Nationale party, which crushed the Liberals the following year. The special characteristics of this period made economic and social matters as important as, if not more important than, the national question in the struggle between

[1]A similar division into three periods, as well as a more detailed study, can be found in Jean Hamelin et al., "Les élections provinciales dans le Québec," Cahiers de Géographie de Québec, October 1959—March 1960, pp. 5-207. See also Herbert F. Quinn, The Union Nationale: A Study in Quebec Nationalism (Toronto: University of Toronto Press, 1963).

the opposition and the Liberals. In 1939, however, with the threat of war, the Liberals regained control of the government. The federal ministers from Quebec had forcefully intervened in the campaign, threatening to resign if the Union Nationale were re-elected. Their resignations, they claimed, would leave the field wide open for the imperialist conscriptionists. Nevertheless, the federal Liberals called the conscription vote and, in the view of the Quebec electorate, bore a stigma for bolstering the cause of centralization of power during the war years. The Union Nationale took advantage of this situation and got elected by a narrow margin in 1944; they stayed in power until 1960. They managed to do this by directing all their campaigns against the Ottawa Liberals with whom the provincial party was closely identified. Little by little, the Quebec Liberals came to rely on social and economic policy. Finally, they took advantage of the successive deaths of Duplessis and Sauvé as well as the end of the Liberal reign in Ottawa and gained power by a small majority in the 1960 elections. They won again in 1962, but in 1966 the Union Nationale gained a slight edge over the Liberals in terms of the number of seats won, even though they obtained only 40 per cent of the popular vote compared to 47 per cent for the Liberals.

From any point of view, 1936 — the year the Union Nationale party was formed — was an important turning point in provincial politics and in the history of Quebec provincial parties. For the systematic study of Quebec provincial parties, only this recent period, which opened with the end of the 39-year Liberal reign, will be considered. After party ideologies and policies are examined, a study will be made of the electoral supporters. Another section will be devoted to the social structure and organization of parties. In the last, most general section, the Quebec provincial party system will be reviewed, giving particular emphasis to recent changes.

II. PARTY IDEOLOGIES AND POLICIES

In Quebec, as elsewhere, the main objective of all political parties is to obtain enough votes to gain political power. To reach this goal, parties must present ideologies and policies that will persuade a sufficient number of voters to vote for them.

In view of this, a great distinction can be made between the external ideologies and policies and the internal ideologies and policies of Quebec provincial parties. We define external ideologies and policies as those referring to Quebec's position in the Canadian federal system. By internal ideologies and policies, we mean those referring to groups and communities inside Quebec.

A. External Ideologies and Policies of Provincial Parties

Since 1936, and even earlier, at least one of the Quebec provincial parties has attached a great deal of importance to its external ideology and policy. It was noted earlier that until 1936 the Liberal party was the more provincialist and the more autonomist of the two parties. The situation was reversed after 1936 with the formation of the Union Nationale, a strictly provincial party. The Liberals and their leader Godbout became identified in the war years to follow with conscription and federal centralization of power. In the elections of 1944, 1948, 1952, and 1956, the Union Nationale successfully exploited the conflict between its autonomist policy and the Liberal position of centralization. The longer the federal Liberals stayed in power in Ottawa, the easier this task became. Furthermore, the Quebec Liberal members in Ottawa were unable to restrain themselves from intervening in the provincial electoral campaigns. The Union Nationale used this fact to identify provincial Liberals with those in Ottawa. Another factor that aided the Union Nationale was that Godbout, the leader of the provincial Liberal party, was succeeded by Georges-Emile Lapalme, who had been one of the federal members of Parliament.

The Ottawa Liberals (who were identified with those in Quebec) were not only accused of over-centralization; they were also reproached for their excessive generosity to African and Asian countries, since it was felt that this had not been in the best interests of Quebec. In 1956, when Polish eggs were flooding the Quebec market, the Union Nationale widely circulated a denunciation blaming the federal government for its complicity in the matter.

This situation lasted until the late 1950's, when the Conservatives defeated the federal Liberals. The Union Nationale could hardly identify the provincial Liberals with an Ottawa government that favoured centralization, when the government there was a Conservative one. Paul Sauvé, Duplessis's successor as leader of the Union Nationale, even began negotiating with Ottawa in order to resolve such problems as subsidies to Quebec universities. Duplessis's attitude toward negotiation with Ottawa had always been completely negative.

During the 1950's the provincial Liberals had had little success in bringing the debate with the Union Nationale to any ground other than that of federal-provincial relations. But when they took over the government in 1960 and found themselves dealing with a Conservative government in Ottawa, they were in a good position to formulate their own autonomist philosophy and to practice a policy of guerrilla warfare against Ottawa. They did this, however, in a more positive fashion than had Duplessis, by accepting the principle of negotiation. In their negotiations, the young specialists recruited by the Liberals displayed a degree of competence that had not been customary in Quebec spokesmen.

It is true that from 1963 the Quebec Liberal government had to deal with a Liberal government in Ottawa. However, in 1964 there was a separation in the Liberal party structures — between the Quebec provincial federation and the Quebec wing of the national federation — that left the provincial Liberals plenty of room to maneuver in their dealings with Ottawa. This separation was a sign of the times, as was the formation of the two separatist parties, the Rassemblement pour l'Indépendance Nationale and the Ralliement National. As an indication of the political trend, in the provincial election of 1966 all four parties involved advocated a nationalist philosophy. Both "third parties" proclaimed themselves as separatist parties. The Union Nationale's new slogan was "Egalité ou Indépendance" ("Equality or Independence"), taken from the title of a book by the party's leader, Daniel Johnson.[2] The Liberals proposed to continue the battle they had started six years earlier for greater sovereignty for Quebec.

B. Internal Ideologies and Policies of Provincial Parties

Concerning external ideologies and policies, the Quebec provincial parties have been distinguished from each other by the degree to which they favour nationalism. The distinctions between these parties have not been so evident in their internal ideologies and policies. It is particularly difficult to refer to them as being right or left, assuming these terms represent ideologies and policies designed either to maintain or to reduce the differences between individuals and between groups of a society. Since 1936 neither one of the two parties has had a policy that has been at all constant in terms of right or left.

The measures taken by the Union Nationale from 1936 to 1939 and after 1944 with the intention of improving the standard of living of the farmers (extending the supply of electrical power in rural areas, liberalizing credit, etc.) can be considered leftist, since they reduced the difference between this class of Quebec society and other more favoured classes. Similarly, the campaign of the Union Nationale in 1962 to raise the minimum salary of the province's workers to $1 per hour and to reduce the taxes of low-wage earners can also be considered leftist. In spite of these measures (or electoral promises) one cannot disregard the fact that under Duplessis the Union Nationale was also a party clearly anti-union and very sympathetic to the economic and financial interests that filled its electoral coffers.

Since 1936 the Liberals have not been much different in this regard. It can be noted, however, that in the 1966 convention the radical wing of the party fought with some success to permit publication of party finances. In the 1950's, as in the 1960's, the Liberal party has consistently been more favourably disposed to unionism than has the Union Nationale. Whether or not this was due to the fact that the party happened to be in power at the time, the Union Nationale, nevertheless, brought to a vote all the laws that to some degree restrained the freedom of Quebec unions. The Union Nationale was also in power when the workers of Asbestos and Murdochville were clubbed by the provincial police.[3] In contrast, the Liberals have been committed to the return of a certain amount of union liberty and to measures as bold as the right of civil servants to strike. The Liberal government of 1939 to 1944 and, even more, of 1960 to 1966, was different from the Union Nationale government since it paid less attention than the Union Nationale to certain groups or specific areas that had been surpassed by technical progress or, in more general terms, that did not benefit from the modernization available to other groups or areas of society.

All of this indicates that although there are differences in the ideologies and particularly in the policies of the two major Quebec provincial parties, the parties cannot be accurately defined as being left or right. The differences refer rather to the conception that each party has of its role in government as well as to the means it employs to achieve this involvement.

In general, then, the Liberal party is more interventionist than the Union Nationale, in the sense of favouring not a police state but a state that dispenses goods and services. From 1944 to 1960, the annual expenditures of the Province of Quebec increased from slightly less than $100 million to slightly less than $500 million; during a period only one-third as long — that of 1960 to 1966 — expenditures increased from less than $500 million to more than $1 billion. This was largely due to the Liberal party's social welfare measures designed to serve society in general. The Union Nationale has been more concerned with specific areas and classes that have been the most deprived, either economically or culturally. Because of this, the Union Nationale has been more electorally-minded than the Liberal party.

Without exaggerating the differences between the two parties, several concrete illustrations will nevertheless point out that these differences are real. Nationalization of electrical power is a good example, since it was an issue throughout most of the period under study here.[4] In the early 1930's Dr. Philippe Hamel started the fight to establish a public commission on electricity, but the nationalization of all the electrical companies was not accomplished until after the 1962 provincial election. Until 1939 the two parties talked much about the "electricity trust," and certain steps were taken to remedy the situation. However, it was not until the end of the Godbout regime, in March 1944, that Hydro-Québec was formed as a provincial hydro-electric commission by nationalizing the Montreal Light, Heat and Power Company.

During the debate over nationalization the arguments used by each side illustrate the differences between the two parties. The Liberals talked of rate reduction for the small consumer, of the public interest (i.e., of the entire population), of an economic and social equilibrium, and of the industrial and commercial development of the province. Seldom did they refer to specific classes of society other than farmers and settlers who stood to profit from the installation of electric power in rural areas, which nationalization would make possible.

Duplessis, who saw in nationalization a "state capitalism resembling Bolshevism," admitted that rural electric power was a pressing need. But, according to him, the only way to proceed was to establish farmers' co-operatives. Eighteen years later Daniel Johnson, the Union Nationale leader, also opposed the nationalization of electric companies as proposed by the Liberals. He was in favour of partial nationalization only as the means most likely to reduce the rate and improve service. He asserted that the Union Nationale had first to improve the situation of the less favoured classes. He stated during his campaign in 1962: "What the province really needs is not

[2]Daniel Johnson, *Egalité ou Indépendance* (Montreal: Editions Renaissance, 1965).

[3]On the Asbestos strike and its significance in the political evolution of Quebec, see Pierre E. Trudeau *et al., La grève de l'amiante* (Montreal: Les Editions Cité Libre, 1956).

[4]For a brief study of the various campaigns for the nationalization of electricity from the early 1930's to 1962, see Claude Boileau, "Les partis provinciaux du Québec et le problème de la nationalisation de l'électricité" (M.A. thesis, Université Laval, 1966).

nationalization of electricity, but full employment and a more humane policy which gives more to those who are in need and less to those who are prosperous."[5]

This position of the Union Nationale was substantially different from that of the Liberal party which, even more than in 1944, talked of industrial development, of the general building up of the number of employed, of gaining control of the economy, and of the well-being of Quebec. When René Levesque, the chief promoter of nationalization, spoke of those who would gain by this step, he referred to farmers and to families residing in the isolated areas of Quebec. However, he concerned himself as much, if not more, with the engineers and technicians of Quebec who would also benefit, and with the population in general, the consumers, the taxpayers — classes significantly less specific than those to whom the Union Nationale appealed.

Some of the same distinctions are found in the social policies of the two parties and in their policies regarding subsidies to agencies receiving aid from the State. Duplessis opposed social measures coming from Ottawa not only because he maintained they were anti-constitutional, but just as much because he was opposed to the ideology that inspired these steps. As he said, "The best system is that which depends the least on the State." The Union Nationale government adopted certain social measures and did not overlook the subsidization of organizations such as municipalities, school boards, and co-operatives. But these measures and subsidies were usually restricted to categories or organizations representing the least favoured elements of the population, or else they were not statutory.

In opposition, the Liberals proposed, from 1950 onwards, more universal or statutory social policies and subsidies to state-assisted organizations. These were put into effect from 1960 to 1966. For example, hospitalization insurance became effective a few months after their 1960 victory, and standardization of subsidies to municipalities and school boards was realized a short time later. After the Union Nationale returned to power, health insurance became a problem. The Liberal party was in favour of a universal plan as proposed by the Castonguay Commission; the Union Nationale government avoided taking a definite position on this question.

In nearly every area of governmental activity, differences of this nature can be observed between the Liberal party and the Union Nationale. Between 1944 and 1966 the most interventionist and most collective features of the Liberal ideology and policy were apparent in the domain of education. After the Liberals came to power in 1960, a total reform of the entire school system was started. The Union Nationale government had occupied itself for the most part with the building of schools and with non-statutory subsidies to school boards. Similarly, a difference between the two parties can be noted in the area of municipal affairs. The Lesage government talked of a voluntary merger plan to be followed, if necessary, by an obligatory plan for the municipalities. The Johnson government, which succeeded the Lesage government in 1966, did not discuss the matter further. Again, on the matter of highways, the Liberals gave top priority to the construction of superhighways; the Union Nationale always gave precedence, at least in certain public declarations, to rural and regional highways.

These differences between the internal objectives of the Union Nationale and the Liberals can be seen most clearly by comparing the Duplessis regime from 1944 to 1960 with the Lesage regime of 1960 to 1966. The differences are less distinct in the period from 1936 to 1944 and even less before 1936. When the Union Nationale returned to power in June 1966, these differences again diminished, just as differences concerning the external objectives of Quebec began to fade at this time, if not earlier. In the last part of this section an attempt will be made to explain this rapprochement between the two parties, as well as to outline the limits of such a situation.

C. Causes and Limits of the Rapprochement between the Parties

There are at least two causes for the rapprochement that has developed, particularly since 1966, between the ideologies and the policies of the two major Quebec provincial parties. The first and unquestionably the more important is concerned with the strengthening of the Quebec public administration, specifically the strengthening of its higher management. In 1960 the Lesage government began to recruit specialists from Quebec universities and from the federal public administration. Some of them became deputy ministers or directors-general; others acted as advisers to the premier. Except in a few instances, they retained their positions after the 1966 Union Nationale victory. They have continued to influence ministerial policies and, in the case of the advisers to the premier, general governmental policy. This has resulted in a parallelism, in several areas, between the policies of the two governments.

The greatest correspondence between the two parties can be found in the ministries and in those areas well equipped with specialists. The most obvious case is that of the Ministry of Education, where the Union Nationale has continued the Liberal policies. It is also evident that the similarity between the Liberal and Union Nationale governments in their policies towards Ottawa is largely due to the fact that some civil servants in the Department of Intergovernmental Affairs (previously the Department of Federal-Provincial Affairs) and some advisers have served under both governments.

On the other hand, the policy of the Union Nationale differs the most from that of the Liberals in the ministries whose senior administrations had not been strengthened by the Lesage government. In the area of municipal affairs, for example, the Union Nationale quickly made a break from the merger plans of the preceding government.

A second cause for the similarity between the two parties is the Union Nationale's desire to modernize their party. In the final years of the Duplessis regime, the Union Nationale party came to be associated more and more, in certain centers, with political corruption as well as with anti-unionism. Furthermore, the party was accused of designing its policies mainly (if not exclusively) to win votes. The Union Nationale government that was elected in 1966 — in particular its leader, Daniel Johnson — made great efforts to erase this image of the old Union Nationale. It declared itself against patronage; it moved closer to the intellectual and university community, particularly

5*Le Devoir* (Montreal), September 20, 1962, p.1.

at the party convention in March 1965; it wished to involve interest groups in the preparation of the electoral program of 1966; and it gave certain guarantees to the labour unions. Meanwhile, the Liberal party marked time after their great activity in the early 1960's and fell into disfavour among several sections of the population. The result was that the programmes of the two parties, which were very different in 1962, were much less so in 1966, and that the policies of the Union Nationale government corresponded in many areas to those of the Lesage government.

It can be expected that this desire for modernization will last. It is less certain that the senior civil servants who inspired the policies of the Lesage government and who continued to inspire those of the Johnson government will be able to protect their positions of strength for long. It is quite possible that other specialists with different ideas will be acquired, or that strong-willed ministers of opposing points of view will assert themselves. In any case, the Union Nationale remains less interventionist, or at least slower to intervene, than the Liberal party. It also continues to prefer specific rather than collective means, or at least it searches, more than the Liberal party, for ways to make collective measures more specific. These differences in the ideologies and the policies of the two parties, even though they are now more subdued than previously, are enhanced by other factors, such as the difference in their electoral supporters as well as the difference in their social make-up and their organization. These are some of the formidable obstacles preventing a greater rapprochement between the two parties, and they will be treated in the following two sections. The conclusion will then sum up the features that are uniquely characteristic of the provincial party system of Quebec.

III. ELECTORAL SUPPORTERS OF THE PARTIES

The electoral supporters of the two main parties of Quebec have been clearly distinguished from each other since 1936. First, the geographic distribution of each party's supporters will be examined. Concerning this, the result of the disproportion of the electoral districts will be noted. An examination of socio-economic characteristics of the electorate will follow. The last part of this section will comprise a brief study of the stability of the electorate since 1936.

A. Territorial Foundations of the Parties

If Quebec is considered in terms of ten large electoral areas, distinctions can be noted in the support each region has given to the two main provincial parties since 1936. Table I gives the total number of elections held from 1936 to 1966 within the constituencies of each region, and the number of these elections won by the Liberals. The areas can be rated according to Liberal strength on the basis of the proportion of elections the Liberals have won in each area.

From 1936 to 1966, the Liberals have found their strongest support in the metropolitan area of Montreal, as well as in three rural areas: Côte Nord,

TABLE I

Proportion of elections won by Liberals from 1936 to 1966
in ten regions of Quebec.

District	Total number of cases	Liberal victories	Ratio
Côte Nord	9	6	.67
Métropolitain (Montréal)	149	98	.66
Nord-Ouest	41	19	.46
Bas Saint-Laurent—Gaspésie	63	25	.40
Montréal (non-Métropolitan)	198	74	.37
Cantons de l'Est	63	23	.37
Québec	170	58	.34
Saguenay—Lac Saint-Jean	32	9	.28
Trois-Rivières	81	17	.21
Outaouais	36	7	.19
Total	842	336	.40

Source: Reports of the Quebec Chief Electoral Officer and the *Canadian Parliamentary Guide*.

Nord-Ouest, and Bas Saint-Laurent—Gaspésie. The first two have been populated relatively recently. Conversely, the Union Nationale has its strongest base in the areas where the population has been settled the longest and where the movement of the population has been relatively slight for the past fifty years.

The Liberal party has, since 1939, obtained greater support from the cities than it has from the rural areas. This is illustrated by the party's great strength in the metropolitan area of Montreal. This theory can be applied not only at the regional level, but also at the levels of the constituencies and the municipalities, and even at the individual level.

Jean Hamelin, Jacques Letarte and Marcel Hamelin,[6] as well as Paul Cliche,[7] have shown in their studies of the provincial elections that from 1944 to 1956 the Liberals had greater success against the Union Nationale in urban rather than in rural constituencies. This was less clear in 1960, although the Liberals won in twenty-nine of the forty-eight constituencies where city-dwellers constituted more than 60 per cent of the population, and in only twenty-two of the forty-seven constituencies where city-dwellers constituted less than 60 per cent of the population. In 1962, however, the Liberals won in thirty-seven of the forty-eight most urban constituencies, and in only twenty-six of the forty-seven least urban. In 1966 the Union Nationale won in only one-third of the thirty-nine constituencies that were more than 80 per cent urban; on the other hand, they won in forty-two of the sixty-nine other constituencies, or in two-thirds.[8] In most studies of the provincial constituencies

[6]Hamelin *et al.*, "Les élections provinciales dans le Québec."

[7]Paul Cliche, "Les élections provinciales dans le Québec, de 1927 à 1956," *Recherches sociographiques*, July-December 1961, pp. 343-365.

[8]In these three elections (1960, 1962, and 1966) the percentages of urban voters by constituency have been established from the census figures of 1961.

TABLE II

Attitudes to the Liberal government in 1962, relating to the degree of
urbanization of place of residence.

| | Place of residence | | | |
	Montreal	Other cities	Towns	Rural municipalities
Percentage of voters favouring the Liberal government	62	57	56	35
Total number of cases	299	273	95	80

Source: Groupe de Recherches Sociales, *Les Préférences politiques des electeurs québécois en 1962,* Montreal, 1964.

of Quebec the same phenomenon has been established: rural localities are generally more favourable to the Union Nationale than are urban localities and, conversely, the Liberals have stronger support in urban rather than in rural localities.[9]

Finally, polls taken before the elections of 1960, 1962, and 1966 have confirmed this difference at the individual level. In the three elections, except perhaps in 1960, there was a very clear relation between the degree of urbanization in the voter's area of residence and the voter's attitude to the Liberal government. This is well illustrated, for example, in Table II, which contains figures taken from a poll made before the 1962 election.

B. The Effect of the Disproportion of Electoral Districts

The great inequality in the number of voters in each provincial constituency has favoured the Union Nationale since 1939. Twice, in 1944 and 1966, they won more seats than the Liberals even though they obtained a smaller percentage of the vote.

The elections of 1952, 1956, and 1960 provide a good illustration of the effect that the disproportion in the electoral map has had on the election results. In 1960 the Liberals obtained almost the same percentage of votes as the Union Nationale had received in 1952 and in 1956, and the latter obtained almost the same percentage as the Liberals had received in these two elections. Nevertheless, in 1952 and in 1956 the Union Nationale won sixty-eight and seventy-two seats, respectively, compared to twenty-three and twenty won by the Liberals. In 1960 the Liberals won only fifty-one seats compared to forty-three for the Union Nationale.

The most extreme result of the inequality of the electoral map occurred in the election of 1966. The Liberals received 47 per cent of the popular vote but won only fifty-one seats. The Union Nationale received only 40 per cent of the popular vote but won fifty-five seats. The disparity in the electoral map — even more than the third parties, which hurt the Liberals more than they did the Union Nationale — accounts for these lopsided results. The situation is clarified by noting that the Union Nationale was victorious in twenty of the thirty constituencies with less than 20,000 voters and in twenty-seven of the

TABLE III

Relationship between socio-economic characteristics of electoral constituencies and Liberal victories in these constituencies from 1956 to 1966.

	1956	1960	1962	1966
Liberal proportion of victories in all constituencies.	.22 (20/93)	.54 (51/95)	.66 (63/95)	.47 (51/108)
Liberal proportion of victories in constituencies where non-French Canadians comprise more than 20 per cent of the population.	.43 (10/23)	.58 (14/24)	.75 (18/24)	.84 (26/31)
Liberal proportion of victories in constituencies where those with at least a secondary education represent more than 40 per cent of the adult population.	.47 (9/19)	.65 (13/20)	.95 (19/20)	.77 (24/31)
Liberal proportion of victories in constituencies where professional people, administrators, and technicians make up more than 15 per cent of the labour force.	.29 (12/42)	.60 (25/42)	.86 (36/42)	.56 (30/54)
Liberal proportion of victories in constituencies where the average salary for men is more than $3000.	.26 (11/43)	.62 (28/45)	.84 (38/45)	.57 (34/60)

Sources: Canada Census (1961), Reports of the Quebec Chief Electoral Officer, and the *Canadian Parliamentary Guide.*

forty-nine constituencies with between 20,000 and 40,000 voters, but won in only eight of the twenty-nine constituencies with more than 40,000 voters.[10]

C. Socio-economic characteristics of the electorate

To demonstrate that city-dwellers are generally more inclined to the Liberals than to the Union Nationale and that the opposite is true in rural areas does not present the complete picture. Socio-economic categories must be examined to determine whether or not there are significant differences in party support along these lines. An accurate analysis of these differences requires a detailed statistical study of successive public opinion polls. Unfortunately, none were made before the late 1950's. Therefore, this study is limited to the provincial elections of 1956, 1960, 1962, and 1966. In Table III,

[9]See, for example, Michel Chaloult, "Les études locales et régionales," in *Quatre élections provinciales au Québec: 1956—66,* Vincent Lemieux, ed. (Quebec: Les Presses de l'Université Laval, 1969).

[10]On this subject see Vincent Lemieux, "Les effets imprévus de la loi et de la carte électorales nouvelles," *Socialisme 66,* October-December 1966, pp. 107-118.

several relationships are revealed at the constituency level between the results obtained by the Liberals in 1956, 1960, 1962, and 1966 and the socio-economic characteristics of the electorate, based on certain data from the 1961 census.

It is apparent that there is a positive relationship between each of the four variables utilized and Liberal victories from 1956 to 1966. The Liberals won proportionately more victories in constituencies where these variables — non-French-Canadian population, levels of education, number of professional and skilled people, and average salaries — were higher than in the province at a whole.

Among the four variables, the one concerned with educational background seems to maintain the strongest positive relationship with Liberal victories. Three times out of four — in 1956, 1960, and 1962 — it ranked first in Liberal proportion of victories. In 1966 it ranked second, behind the ethnic variable. This fact is worthy of note, as the ethnic variable constantly increased in its Liberal proportion of victories from 1956 to 1966. The three other variables decreased in this proportion in 1966, after steadily increasing from 1956 to 1962.

In 1956 the ethnic and educational variables appear to have played more important roles than the others. In 1960 the four variable factors had almost equal importance. In 1962 the educational variable dominated, while in 1966, as in 1956, the ethnic and educational variables seem to have been the most important factors.

These relationships at the constituency level are apparently just as applicable in the case of individual voters. The following data cannot feasibly be presented in a single table, because the statistical categories differ from one election to another.[11]

The ethnic variable will be treated first. According to a poll made on the eve of the 1960 election, whereas only 43 per cent of the voters of Montreal intended to vote for the Liberals, 50 per cent of those who were not French-Canadian intended to do so. Just before the 1962 election 78 per cent of the English-speaking voters of Montreal favoured a Liberal government, compared to only 58 per cent of the French-Canadian voters. Outside of Montreal, this percentage was 55 per cent of the English-speaking and 53 per cent of the French-speaking population.

It is even more probable that a voter with a high level of education will support the Liberal party. Just before the 1960 election, 33 per cent of the voters with less than nine years of schooling intended to vote for the Liberals, as opposed to 37 per cent of the voters who had more education. The 1962 figures appearing in Table IV are even more indicative of this trend, which may have been accentuated by the fact that the Liberals were then the governing party.

Concerning occupations, the data prepared show that on the eve of the 1960 election, 41 per cent of professional people and managers preferred the Liberals to the Union Nationale, compared to 34 per cent of the skilled workers. Just before the 1962 election, 58 per cent of the voters were satisfied with the Liberal government. The proportion was 76 per cent among professional people and highly specialized technicians, 67 per cent among office workers and salesmen, and 65 per cent among salaried executives. This is in contrast to only 43 per cent of the labourers and domestics, 49 per cent of skilled workers,

TABLE IV

Percentage of voters favouring the Liberal government,
according to number of years of education (1962).

	0 to 4 years	5 to 8 years	9 to 12 years	13 years and over
Percentage favouring the Liberals	46	52	58	72
Number of cases	76	372	276	90

Source: Groupe de Recherches Sociales, *Les préférences politiques des électeurs québécois en 1962,* Montreal, 1964.

and 51 per cent of small proprietors and small businessmen. Again in 1966, according to a poll that found 57 per cent of the electorate intending to vote for the Liberal party, 75 per cent of the white-collar workers who expressed their preference intended to vote for the Liberals, compared to only 50 per cent of the labourers.

Finally, according to the results of the polls used, there is a strong probability that a Liberal party supporter will have a high rather than a low income. In 1962, while 58 per cent of the voters were satisfied with the Liberal government, this proportion was only 46 per cent of those whose declared net income did not exceed $3,000, but it was 65 per cent of those whose declared net income was over $5,000. In 1966, more than 90 per cent of the voters earning over $8,000 intended to vote Liberal, compared to only 50 per cent of those whose income did not exceed $3,000.

It can be concluded that on both the constituency and the individual levels there has been a pronounced relationship since 1956 between the socio-economic factors of ethnic origin, education, occupation, and income and the vote for the two main provincial parties of Quebec. Generally, there is a greater likelihood of finding support for the Liberal party if the voter or the constituency is one with a high level of education, occupation, and income. There is also a greater likelihood of finding Liberal supporters among non-French Canadians or in constituencies where there is a relatively large number of voters who are not French Canadians.

D. Stability of the Electorate since 1936

It was demonstrated earlier that since 1939 support for the Liberal party has been stronger in cities than it has been in rural areas, and that the opposite has been true for the Union Nationale. On the other hand, the Liberals'

[11]In the following data the results of three polls have been used. These were made on behalf of the Liberal party of Quebec before the elections of 1960, 1962, and 1966. The results are contained in the following reports: Groupe de Recherches Sociales, *Les électeurs québécois. Attitudes et opinions à la veille des élections de 1960,* Montreal, 1960; Groupe de Recherches Sociales, *Les préférences politiques des électeurs québécois en 1962,* Montreal, 1964; Société de Mathématique Appliquée Inc., *Evolution du Québec,* Montreal, 1966 (confidential).

long domination before 1936 was primarily due to their massive rural support. At that time the Conservatives did much better in the towns than in the country.

This indicates that the elections of 1935, 1936, 1939, and 1944 were elections of realignment in some constituencies. On the one hand, several constituencies on the Island of Montreal that had been Conservative strongholds until 1939 turned to the Liberals in the 1939 election and remained faithful to them afterwards. This was the case, for example, with the wealthy English-speaking areas of Notre-Dame-de Grâce, Outremont, and Westmount. On the other hand, the Union Nationale took over the rural constituencies around Montreal and Quebec, which had remained faithful to the Liberals until 1939 or 1944, and held on to them afterwards almost without exception.[12]

In 1944 and 1948 two important third parties affected the votes polled by the two main parties. In 1944 the Bloc Populaire, a nationalist party, ran candidates in ninety-one constituencies. With André Laurendeau as its leader, the party obtained 15 per cent of the vote and elected four members. In 1948 the Union des Electeurs, a créditiste party, ran candidates in ninety-two constituencies. The party received 9 per cent of the vote, but none of its candidates were elected. The Union des Electeurs's strongest concentration was found in the city of Quebec and its environs, as well as in the Cantons de l'Est, the Nord-Ouest, and in Saguenay—Lac Saint-Jean. By contrast, the Bloc Populaire was primarily a Montreal party and, in general, more urban than the Union des Electeurs.

In 1948 the Liberals won in only eight constituencies out of ninety-two and were reduced to holding little more than the Island of Montreal. In 1952, following the Union Nationale's anti-union position taken at the time of the Asbestos strike, the Liberals won back several constituencies in Montreal and in other areas where union workers were relatively numerous. Most of these constituencies were retaken by the Union Nationale in 1956, although that year they lost several constituencies with half-urban and half-rural populations – in Abitibi and Bas Saint-Laurent, as well as some rural constituencies with a relatively high proportion of English-speaking people.

The Liberal victory in 1960 was largely due to the party's ability to regain some rural constituencies, particularly poor rural constituencies with a high proportion of farmers. It was pointed out earlier that the classification of electoral supporters on the basis of the urbanization of their area of residence is not as clear for the election of 1960 as for the preceding or later elections. Also, in 1962 and 1966, with the Liberal party in office, the variables of occupation and income seem to have been more significant than in 1960. This indicates some neutralization, in 1960, of the socio-economic differences between the two parties' supporters and, in particular, a temporary return of some farmers to the Liberal party. A public opinion poll made before this election also indicates that 38 per cent of the farmers intended to vote Liberal, as opposed to only 35 per cent of all the voters.

On the other hand, in 1962 and 1966 the percentage of farmers favourably disposed to the Liberals was clearly smaller than the percentage of all voters who favoured that party. According to polls made for the Liberals, these percentages were 40 and 50 per cent, respectively, in 1962. In 1966 57 per cent of the voters intended to vote for the Liberals, but only 51 per cent of the farming population intended to do so.

These percentages and others cited indicate how large the differences were in 1962 between the two parties' supporters. Never — before 1936 or after — has there been such a contrast between the two parties. In 1962 the Liberal party was largely the party of city-dwellers, non-French Canadians, educated people, people with high occupational levels, and people with high incomes. Conversely, the Union Nationale party was supported just as strongly by the rural population, people of little education, people with low occupational levels, and people with low incomes.

The contrast was less in 1966, although the opposing factors continued to remain important. At least one of them will be emphasized again — the one concerning non-French Canadians who supported the Liberal party, and the French Canadians who were more disposed than in 1962 to the Union Nationale. Two third parties, one separatist — the Rassemblement pour l'Indépendance Nationale (RIN) — the other separatist and créditiste — the Ralliement National (RN) — obtained respectively 7 per cent and 3 per cent of the votes cast in 1966. Some of the data suggest that the RIN supporters resembled those of the Liberals, other than the English-speaking people who would not be expected to back a separatist party. There is on the other hand a great similarity between the RN supporters and those of the Union Nationale.

According to a public opinion poll taken before the 1966 election, only 4 per cent of the voters questioned indicated an intention to vote for the RIN, but the proportion was 6 per cent of those with an income between $5,000 and $8,000, 9 per cent of the young people between 18 and 24, and 25 per cent of the student population. According to the same poll, 13 per cent of those questioned indicated they would vote for the RN. It was the choice of 25 per cent of skilled workers, only 7 per cent of white-collar workers, and only 2 per cent of those with an income over $8,000.

The electoral stability of the Union Nationale is apparently greater than that of the Liberal party. Except for the 1936 election, in which the Union Nationale obtained 57 per cent of the votes cast, its success has varied from 52 per cent in 1956 to 38 per cent in 1944. This is a fluctuation of only 14 percentage points, compared to a variation of 21 percentage points in the Liberal vote during the same period. The Liberals obtained 57 per cent of the vote cast in 1962, but only 36 per cent in 1948. The Liberals' portion of the vote dropped from 57 per cent in 1962 to 47 per cent in 1966; at the same time, the Union Nationale's percentage only changed from 42 to 40. Since 1936, the votes polled by third parties seem to have affected the Liberals much more than the Union Nationale. This, among other things, explains the greater electoral instability of the Liberals.

[12]For more details see Vincent Lemieux, "L'analyse hiérarchique des résultats électoraux," *Canadian Journal of Political Science*, March 1968, pp. 40-54.

IV. SOCIAL STRUCTURE AND ORGANIZATION OF THE PARTIES

The differences established between the two main Quebec provincial parties in terms of their electoral supporters can also be found in relation to their social make-up, or in other words, the social characteristics of their members. Since precise data is not available concerning general party membership, this study will be limited to the candidates and members of the legislature, who typify only the leaders of the provincial political parties. This will be followed by an examination of the structures of the party organizations and, finally, the function of these organizations in their relations with the voters.

A. Characteristics of the Candidates and Elected Members

As in the preceeding section this analysis will be based on the most recent elections, for the most part those since 1956. Generally, the successful candidates from 1936 to 1956 had less formal education than those after 1956. Likewise, there were more manufacturers and businessmen and also farmers and workers among the successful candidates during these twenty years than there were afterwards. Since 1956 the proportion of legislative members who were professionals and also semi-professionals — particularly those from the educational sectors — has increased at the expense of the manufacturers, businessmen, workers, and farmers. Finally, it is not surprising to learn that the number of elected members born in medium-sized Quebec cities, as well as in the metropolitan areas of Montreal and Quebec, has been steadily increasing.[13] When classified on the basis of these characteristics, the candidates and elected members of the Liberals and the Union Nationale from 1956 to 1966 form two rather different groups.

It can be seen from Table V that the differences between the two parties' candidates correspond exactly to the differences already noted between their electoral supporters. Like the Liberal voters, the Liberal candidates generally have more education than the Union Nationale candidates and belong to occupational categories that are higher up the social ladder than those of the Union Nationale candidates. There are more key figures in the Union Nationale who were born in localities with a population under 25,000 than there are in the Liberal party. This difference corresponds to the support that the Union Nationale receives from rural areas, which is much greater than its support from cities.

Table V illustrates other differences between the parties. The fact that 30 per cent of the elected Union Nationale candidates had been mayors, compared to 14 per cent of the elected Liberal candidates, illustrates the greater local basis of the Union Nationale party. However, this difference does not appear between the parties' defeated candidates. Generally, the characteristics of the defeated candidates of both parties resemble each other more than do those of the elected members. Concerning the levels of education and occupation categories, the characteristics of the elected and defeated candidates of the Union Nationale resemble each other more than do those of the

TABLE V

Characteristics of candidates and elected members of the Liberal and Union Nationale parties from 1956 to 1966.

	Liberal Party		Union Nationale Party	
	Percentage of elected candidates	Percentage of defeated candidates	Percentage of elected candidates	Percentage of defeated candidates
Place of Birth				
Localities of less than 2,000 inhabitants	28	41	37	28
Localities with a population between 2,000 and 25,000	29	23	40	27
Localities with a population over 25,000 (excluding Montreal and Quebec)	12	12	6	9
Montreal and Quebec	29	23	13	28
Unknown	2	1	4	8
Level of Education				
Having a university education	62	50	54	50
Having no more than a secondary education	30	41	33	37
Having no more than an elementary education	1	1	6	5
Unknown	7	8	7	8
Occupational Level				
Professionals	59	40	48	38
Semi-professionals	8	12	7	10
Manufacturers and businessmen	26	39	34	43
Employees and workers	2	3	3	2
Farmers	4	6	7	4
Unknown	1	—	1	3
Public Careers				
Former Mayors	14	15	30	16
Former members of Chambers of Commerce	46	49	40	47

Source: Robert Boily, "Les candidats élus et les candidats battus," in *Quatre élections provinciales au Québec: 1956—66*, Vincent Lemieux, ed. (Quebec: Les Presses de l'Université Laval, 1969).

[13]The data on the elected and defeated candidates of the two parties are taken from Robert Boily, "Les candidats élus et les candidats battus," in *Quatre élections provinciales au Québec: 1956—66.*

elected and defeated Liberal candidates. This indicates that those voting for the Union Nationale pay less attention to the socio-economic status of the candidates.

B. Official and Non-official Party Structures

It must be emphasized again that the elected and defeated candidates of the two big Quebec provincial parties are only representative of the leadership of their parties. No data is available concerning other political party members, and only approximate numbers are known. In 1966 on the eve of the election the Union Nationale claimed to have 150,000 members. This number is approximate, however, because the party has not collected membership fees since 1965. Moreover, even though this fee was only $1 per year, very few members paid it. The number of Liberal party members is also approximate since the party adopted a measure in 1966 allowing the constituency associations to decide whether or not to levy a membership fee. In 1966 there were about 70,000 Liberal party members who owned party cards whether or not they had paid a membership fee. In 1966 the Rassemblement pour l'Indépendance Nationale listed approximately 10,000 members who paid the annual fee of $7. The Ralliement National has had difficulty gathering even a few thousand members. In total, provincial party members number about 250,000 or 8 per cent of the total number of voters, which was more than 3,200,000 in June 1966.

The official structures of the Quebec provincial parties have not developed evenly. In this regard the Liberal party is far ahead of the Union Nationale. In 1955 the Liberals' constituency associations united to form the Quebec Liberal Federation. The Union Nationale did not start to build any official structures until 1965, and these are still not fully developed.

In establishing official structures, the Union Nationale has limited itself to a National Council, defined as the directive agency of the party. This council is formed of all Union Nationale M.P.s and Legislative Council and of three representatives (one man, one woman, and one youth) from each electoral constituency in the province. It is managed by a committee consisting of the party leader, five M.P.s or legislative councilors, and five other members chosen from the representatives of the constituencies. In October 1965, the directors of the National Council approved a project to establish a constitution uniting the constituency associations. However, these associations took little account of this project.

The Union Nationale resolved at their March 1965 meeting to hold a party convention at least every two years. Nevertheless, no convention was held in either 1966 or 1967. It was suggested at the March 1965 meeting that the Council appoint several committees to assist it in its work. National Council regulations anticipate the formation of such committees. However, they have not been established; the only two committees that actually seem to function are the policy committee and the finance committee, both created as a result of the 1961 convention. This convention, at which Daniel Johnson was elected party leader, was the first one held by the Union Nationale in its twenty-five years of existence.

The Union Nationale has in its Montreal and Quebec offices, as well as in other offices throughout the province, some permanent and semi-permanent employees who work primarily on party organization and strategy. There are also some employees who work directly for the party leader. The Union Nationale has as many, if not more, of these permanent and semi-permanent employees as has the Liberal party. However, the Liberal official structures are much more developed.

The nominating conventions of both the Union Nationale and the Liberal party follow similar procedures. In both cases, the provincial party management can intervene. However, they seldom do. When they have intervened, they have not always been successful in securing the nomination for the man of their choice. The constituency associations and their leaders in both the Liberal party and the Union Nationale control the conventions to some degree throughout the province, except perhaps in some Montreal constituencies where an outsider can usually succeed in getting nominated.

The official Liberal party structures are much more complex than those of the Union Nationale. These official structures must be considered, even though they are often duplicated by non-official ones. The Quebec Liberal Federation is built on the foundation of local associations, each of which is directed by an executive council. The local associations are grouped into constituency associations, each with its own executive council. There are twenty regional groups of constituency associations. The constituency associations are also represented in the party's general council. Local constituency associations organize conventions to elect their officers. Furthermore, the constituency associations and the regional groups each form eight permanent committees — the convention, constitutional, financial, ethnic groups, organizational, propaganda, legal, and policy committees.

The same committees are found at the provincial level. The principal officers of the Liberal Federation at this level are the president, the secretary, and the treasurer, who are elected for one year with the possibility of a one-year extension. Together with the provincial party leader and three of the party's M.P.s they form an executive committee which, between the meetings of the superior council, administers party business. The superior council is composed of about fifty members. In addition to the executive committee members, there are seven M.P.s, the presidents of the twenty regional groups, and representatives from the Women's Liberal Association and the Young Liberals.

The general council is an even larger organization where the members of the superior council join all the other Liberal M.P.s, the presidents of each constituency association, representatives of the Women's Liberal Association and the Young Liberals, representatives of non-French-Canadian ethnic groups, as well as the presidents and secretaries of the permanent committees of the Federation.

The official structures of the Quebec Liberal Federation are obviously quite complex. They require many elective posts and managerial or consultant organizations, many meetings, assemblies, and conventions. It is evident that these structures have not been considered as a tool for winning elections. This is why in many localities and in many constituencies there has not been much concern with official structures, which are duplicated by less official structures organized specifically with the electoral contests in mind. This is a cause of conflict, or at least some tension, which is not found in the Union Nationale.[14] For example, in many cases the chief organizer of the locality or of the constituency is not the president of the local association or of the constituency association. Sometimes he does not even belong to the executive council of these associations. In spite of the fact that all requests coming from Liberals should be made to the associations rather than to the deputy or the administrations, influential party members frequently approach these officials, whom they can influence more than the officers of the associations. Furthermore, in nearly all cases the regional groups exist only on paper, and most Liberals ignore them.[15] In any case, to understand the party organizations' functions, the study of official and non-official structures must be integrated. Such a study of party organization will also permit an integration of the developments previously discussed and thus provide a background for the analysis of the party system in Quebec that will be made in the conclusion.

C. The Party Organization

The Liberal and Union Nationale party structures rather faithfully reflect what has been noted about the ideologies and policies of these two parties and the characteristics of their supporters. It is not surprising that the party more interventionist in provincial politics and the one with greater support in urban and middle-class circles has more developed official structures. Conversely, it is not surprising that greater importance is given to electoral organization and strategy in the party that is more preoccupied with its political impact on different sectors and social classes.

These differences are evident if one observes the structures in operation. The parties then appear to be organizations pursuing definite goals through their ideologies and policies. The most important goal is to gather enough votes to be able to form the government. Our study will be limited to this goal around which, in parties such as the Union Nationale and the Quebec Liberal party, all other goals gravitate. It can be seen how integrated, in pursuit of this goal, are the phenomena discussed in the three main sections of this study: the ideologies and policies of the parties, the characteristics of their electoral supporters and, finally, the social composition and the structures of the parties.

The two major provincial parties of Quebec have always exploited the voters' traditional identification with either the "parti bleu" or the "parti rouge." Unfortunately, statistics are not available on the proportion of voters who continue to identify strongly with these traditional parties, nor are they available on the socio-economic characteristics of voters in areas where this proportion might be high. However, in every election since 1936 the two major parties have each obtained at least 36 per cent of the votes cast; it can therefore be concluded that many Quebec voters have always voted for the same provincial party or have at least identified with one party rather than the other. There is also a general belief that partisan traditions remain stronger in rural rather than in urban areas. These traditions would then be useful to the Union Nationale more than to the Liberal party.

Nevertheless, the parties' organizations will be able to rely less and less on attempts to retain the traditional vote. Multiple factors including urbanization have gradually weakened partisan traditions, particularly since the end of the 1950's. The astonishing success of the Créditistes in the federal elections of 1962 and 1963, as well as the two changes of regime at the provincial level in 1960 and 1966, indicates the erosion of the partisan traditions that had contributed to the electoral stability of the 1940's and 1950's at both provincial and federal levels. When speaking of this situation, the election organizers agree more and more that partisan traditions are no longer important and that the vote has become increasingly unpredictable.

Whether it is a cause or an effect of the weakening of partisan traditions, candidates nominated by the parties frequently have almost no party experience. These candidates obviously do not arouse traditional identification with the party they represent. This lack of party identity is particularly noticeable in several of the Union Nationale candidates in the elections of 1966, and with more than one eminent minister of the Lesage Cabinet.

The party organizations have made more material appeals to the voters, such as the distribution or promise of various goods and services that depend on government action. It is well known that in Quebec some of these goods and services have traditionally been distributed to voters as patronage. This patronage, which reached its peak under the Duplessis regime, was not limited to employment in public offices. Contracts, purchases, subsidies, and pensions also led to relationships of patronage between the parties and the voters. Moreover, as Quinn has illustrated,[16] in addition to individuals, there were municipal councils, school boards, factories, and co-operatives who profited from patronage. The governing party was thus assured the support of the local elite directing these organizations.

It cannot be said that all political patronage has disappeared in Quebec. The Liberals, for instance, have been accused (not without reason) of having replaced "small" patronage with "big" patronage, involving powerful individuals who contribute large sums to the party's coffers. However, the Salvas Commission, the reform of the civil service, and the new electoral law in Quebec have drastically limited party patronage during election campaigns. Therefore, the use of such means to win electoral support is becoming increasingly dangerous for the parties.

Patronage in Quebec has been greater in rural than in urban areas because in rural areas social relationships are more personalized, there is greater economic poverty, and there is a greater lack of information on

14See Paul André Comeau, "La transformation du parti libéral québécois," *Revue canadienne d'Economique et de Science Politique,* August 1965, pp. 358—367.

15This situation exists at least in Bas Saint-Laurent–Gaspésie, as shown in Michel Chaloult, *Les partis politiques dans le territoire-pilote,* Bureau d'Aménagement de l'Est du Québec, February 1966.

16See Herbert F. Quinn, "Administrative and Electoral Practices under the Union Nationale," in *The Union Nationale.*

bureaucratic processes. A reduction in patronage largely affects the governing party, which obviously is the one that uses it the most. These factors were important in the decline of the Liberals in several rural constituencies in 1962 and, even more, in 1966. This situation will affect the Union Nationale even more, since the party's policy and the party's supporters rely more on patronage.

Finally, even the ideologies that the provincial parties of Quebec have traditionally offered to their voters no longer have quite the same impact since the "quiet revolution." It was noted in the second section of this study that, since 1960, all Quebec provincial parties have become nationalistic to some degree. But the negotiations that the Liberal and the Union Nationale governments have undertaken with Ottawa on specific and sometimes rather technical questions have made their attempts to exploit a traditional nationalist ideology more difficult.

In conclusion, it will be indicated how these transformations taking place within the Quebec party system are linked to more general transformations that are taking place within the Quebec political system and for which the parties are largely responsible.

V. THE PARTY SYSTEM OF QUEBEC

In the late 1950's and the early 1960's the party system of Quebec started to undergo radical changes. These have been determined by more general changes in the political parties' environment and, more specifically, in the Quebec political system following the "quiet revolution."

For about sixty years, from the end of nineteenth century to the late 1950's, the party system of Quebec was relatively stable in spite of the creation of the Union Nationale in 1936 and the accompanying disappearance of the Conservative party. A close examination indicates, as noted earlier, that after 1936 the two main parties somehow exchanged some of their positions without causing basic changes in the system itself. The only apparent change was that one of the two provincial parties, the Union Nationale, was not affiliated with one of the two big federal parties.

This study indicates no basic changes in the Quebec party system resulting from the 1936 turning point. Just as before 1936, there was an autonomist governing party and an opposition party that was less autonomist or completely federalist. After 1936, as before, the party in power had the monopoly on patronage and did not fail to exploit it for electoral goals. This explains the governing party's successes in rural areas; these areas, which strongly supported the Liberal party before 1936, started after this date to support the Union Nationale just as strongly. Finally, after 1936 there were not any major modifications in the social composition of the parties or in their organization. These parties had no official structures; they were dominated by members of parliament and were for the most part groupings of election workers. The incentives offered to these election workers and to the voters were the traditional incentives referred to earlier: identification with the party and its leaders, goods and services obtained by way of patronage, and abstract ideologies on the internal and external problems of Quebec.

The Bloc Populaire in 1944 and the Union des Electeurs in 1948 threatened the stability of the system. Hindered by the electoral system and, more basically, by the temporary character of the economic and political situation to which they were responding, their threat was short-lived.

This stability of the party system is also explained by the very conservative character of the parties' actions and, even more, by the apparent stability of the society in which the parties found themselves. During the first half of the twentieth century the successive governments of Quebec enacted very few important laws capable of changing the face of society. Moreover, neither the electoral map nor the electoral law underwent important modifications during this period, except for some amendments to the law enacted by the famous Bill 34, which changed the election rules in favour of the governing party.

Although Quebec society, as early as the 1920's, was in fact beginning to change considerably, these changes remained hidden for a long time by political resistance, especially by the dominating ideologies created by the political parties in their resistance to social change. Ths state of affairs was upset by what has been called the "quiet revolution." This is not the place to make a detailed analysis of this phenomenon. However, it can be stated that, of the social agents who started this "revolution" and saw it through its initial stages, none exerted more influence than the Quebec Liberal party and the government it formed after its victory in 1960.

At least five important series of measures that the Lesage government brought about have greatly contributed to the transformation of the party system in Quebec. These measures were not adopted solely because of the action of the Lesage government. It is evident that several of them originated with and were supported by the public and forces other than the Liberal party. Nevertheless, at one time or another during the process of decision-making that led to the adoption of these measures, the role of the governing party was decisive. These five series of measures, which have already been mentioned in this study, are the following:

(1) The reform of the civil service started by the Union Nationale government of Paul Sauvé produced a strengthening of the higher management of public administration. After a few governmental delays, this reform led to trade unionism in the civil service and also to a new labour code permitting civil servants to strike.

(2) When this new labour code and the famous Bill 60 creating the Ministry of Education were being considered, the government not only allowed but also solicited the intervention of the interest groups concerned. The Lesage government established new rules that made possible the inclusion of interest groups within the processes of political decision-making.

(3) Under the Lesage government major political measures were adopted, such as hospitalization insurance, the reform of the education system, the reform of the civil service, the nationalization of electric power, and the construction of superhighways. By these general political measures, wealth was more collectively distributed among the electors. In the case of educational

reform, for example, the general level of scholarship in the province has already been raised.

(4) In the sphere of federal-provincial relations, the Lesage government, continuing the action started by Paul Sauvé, entered into close negotiations with Ottawa. The Lesage government had the assistance of small teams of specialists from inside as well as outside the ministries. These negotiations, which ended with important gains for Quebec, have contributed in a complex and still rather obscure fashion to the development of separatist movements and parties. At least three factors favourable to this development can be indicated. These factors are linked with government action, although the results were not anticipated by the government. Firstly, the advantages that were obtained in the negotiations have resulted in a desire to obtain much more. Secondly, there have been obstacles over which the government has stumbled in its negotiations with Ottawa. As a result of these obstacles it has been argued that no further progress is possible in the reform of the Canadian political system. Lastly, the ideological arguments exploited in this struggle with Ottawa have created a climate favourable to the expression of separatist arguments. Certainly other more fundamental factors are behind the rise of separatist movements in Quebec, but those just listed cannot be ignored.

(5) Finally, the Lesage government enfranchised the young people between 18 and 21 and introduced amendments that have considerably modified the electoral laws of Quebec. In particular, by the strict control of electoral spending the governing party, which usually has more money to spend on elections, lost the advantage it once had over the opposition party. The new law, however, was designed to keep third parties at a disadvantage. The Lesage government was less aggressive in reforming the electoral map and satisfied itself with the creation of 12 new constituencies in metropolitan regions and another in the Saguenay–Lac Saint-Jean region. This timidity proved fatal to them on June 5, 1966.

These measures and their consequences have produced radical transformations in the Quebec party system, the results of which cannot yet be determined. The most obvious of these transformations is in the increase in the number of parties. Increased activity between Quebec and Ottawa, as well as the Quebec political situation since the late 1950's, has led to the appearance of separatist parties, which unlike the third parties of the 1940's seem as if they will remain for a long time on the provincial political scene. Already the Rassemblement pour l'Indépendance Nationale has affected the Liberal party in the 1966 election, and other similar surprises must be expected in future elections.

These measures have also produced a rapprochement between the two large parties in regard to their external ideologies and policies. From the end of the nineteenth century up to the late 1950's one of the two main provincial parties of Quebec was relatively autonomist and the other relatively federalist; since the 1960 Liberal victory, this distinction no longer applies. The two parties are both autonomist and have proposed greater powers for Quebec within the Canadian confederation.

This neutralization of the differences between the external ideologies and policies of the two parties has made more evident the differences between their internal ideologies and policies. These differences, although never very noticeable, had been taking shape since the early 1950's with the accession of Georges-Emile Lapalme to the Liberal party leadership. When the measures referred to earlier were adopted by the Lesage government, these differences became more apparent. Those measures, however, were also due to pressure from senior civil servants and from government advisers for greater state intervention and for measures more general than those that had characterized the Duplessis government.

At the same time, the socio-economic differences between the supporters of the two parties became more apparent in the late 1950's and the early 1960's. Exact figures are not available on earlier periods, but it would be surprising if the polarization of a socio-economic order within the electorate would be as evident before the 1950's as after.

The 1966 election ended this polarizing movement, and even initiated a rapprochement between the internal ideologies and policies of the two parties. On the one hand, the Union Nationale's proposed programme was somewhat similar to that of the Liberals. On the other hand, there was opposition to the Liberal programme as evidenced by the public attitude to some of the Liberals' policies (on education in particular). The Liberals did not present any general proposals in their platform that were as significant as those proposed in 1960 and 1962. Furthermore, as noted earlier, an analysis of the 1966 vote, compared to that of 1962, reveals a lessening of socio-economic differences between the parties' supporters.

Party organization has been affected very little by transformations resulting from the "quiet revolution." The structures of both parties have remained almost the same as they were before 1960. It was noted earlier, however, how most of the traditional appeals used by the political parties are no longer available or at least are limited, and how this has caused serious problems for the parties in their attempts to secure votes. For this reason, among others, the five measures enacted at the time of the "quiet revolution" have started to alter the parties' organization or at least have started to weaken their traditional forms. The growing efficiency of the public administration has caused the opposition party to call increasingly on experts who can hold their own with those of the government. The growing importance of pressure groups has forced the parties to take notice of them. The Union Nationale boasted, in 1966, of having built its programme from the suggestions made by a large number of these groups. The severity of the electoral law, the general nature of several governmental measures, and the increased level of education and sophistication of the electorate have made many of the old-style candidates and election workers obsolete.

In conclusion, these parties as well as the separatist parties are confronted with the challenge of creating new organizations. This challenge is the most critical one they will have to contend with in the coming years. Only organizations more open and more democratic than before will permit the parties to counter the other rising political forces. Such a transformation would especially enable the parties to develop increasingly complex policies and to obtain voters who would be able to really subscribe to and participate in them. This is the most fundamental area of this study and the basis on which the future of the provincial party system in Quebec will probably develop.

Postscript

There have been important changes in the pattern of provincial party politics in Quebec since the present study was written in 1968. Two new parties have appeared. The Parti Québécois was created at the end of 1968 and soon absorbed the Rassemblement pour l'Indépendance Nationale and the Ralliement National to form a unified separatist party under the leadership of René Lévesque, a dissident Liberal. The Ralliement Créditiste decided in 1969 to enter provincial politics and in January 1970 selected Camille Samson as leader of the new provincial party.

The new parties received their first test in the election of April 29, 1970. Both the Union Nationale and the Parti Libéral du Québec entered the election under new leadership. Daniel Johnson died in September, 1968 and was succeeded by Jean-Jaques Bertrand, whose leadership was confirmed by a convention of the Union Nationale in June 1969. Jean Lesage retired from politics at the end of 1969, and Robert Bourassa, 36, was chosen as Liberal leader by a leadership convention in January 1970.

The appearance of new parties and leaders led to new positions with respect to constitutional (or "external") questions. The Liberals assumed a strong federalist position, in opposition to the quasi-separatism of the Parti Québécois. The Ralliement Créditiste gave moderate support to federalism, and the Union Nationale, treading carefully between commitment to either federalism or separation, gave Ottawa four years to develop a federal constitution acceptable to Quebec; if, at the end of that time, Ottawa's proposals were unsatisfactory, the question of separatism would be put to the people of Quebec in a referendum.

From an "internal" point of view, both the PQ and the RC publicized themselves as "new parties" in opposition to the "old parties" — the UN and PLQ.

On the other hand, the PQ and the Liberals shared a progressive image, compared to the apparent conservatism of the UN and the RC. The organization of the PQ had far more in common with that of the Liberals than with either the UN or the RC. At election time, the PQ claimed a membership of 70,000. The RC had only a few thousand members — but these were very active.

The 1970 election gave seventy-two seats to the Liberals, seventeen to the UN, twelve to the Ralliement, and seven to the Parti Québécois. But the PQ received 24 per cent of the vote, against 20 per cent for the UN and 10 per cent for the Ralliement. The Liberals captured 45 per cent of the vote, a margin of victory over the Parti Québécois of 21 per cent.

Early analysis of the vote showed that the Liberals received massive support from the English-speaking electorate. Otherwise Liberal support showed no salient characteristics. There was a negative relationship between age and the PQ vote, but a strongly positive one between education and PQ support:

students and young professionals and semi-professionals were among the most active supporters of the party. The relationship between age and the UN vote was positive; in terms of occupations, UN support was strong among "small independents" (farmers, small businessmen, retailers, etc.). In the case of the Ralliement, there was a negative relationship between years of instruction and the vote. Much of this party's support was from skilled and semi-skilled labour.

In view of the foregoing one can conclude that the 1970 election was a very important one for Quebec – perhaps the most important since 1936. From the UN point of view, at least, both were elections of "realignment." But while the two party system survived the 1936 election, one may well wonder if it will manage to do so after 1970.

* SASKATCHEWAN *

Parties In a Politically Competitive Province

JOHN C. COURTNEY AND DAVID E. SMITH

Political parties in Saskatchewan have both generated and reflected the colour and the intensity of the province's politics. Since the creation of the province in 1905, individuals and groups have organized, sustained and utilized various political parties for protective as well as representational purposes. Cognizant of the division of powers inherent in Canadian federalism, Saskatchewan voters have not hesitated to change their party allegiances from one election to another and from one level of government to another. Indeed, parties themselves have joined in the game on more than one occasion by dissociating themselves from their Ottawa namesakes in order to prove to the electorate their worth as protectors of the province's interests. Federalism has made this form of politics possible; protection of economic interests has made it necessary.

I. THE HISTORY OF THE SYSTEM

Whatever other influences may have been prominent in the development of Saskatchewan politics, the farmer and the federal system must be given prime recognition. Any historical survey of the province cannot fail to focus upon their contribution to the distinctive features of Saskatchewan's political system. Given a one-crop economy, the significance of the farmer is hardly surprising; his opinions and his policy demands are bound to shape the political society. What is surprising about the Saskatchewan farmer, however, is his continued opposition to direct action in politics. The differences between the politics of Saskatchewan and those of other Prairie provinces are largely traceable to the Saskatchewan farmer's rejection of direct political action and to the fact that all provincial parties since 1905 have found it profitable to cater to him.

More surprising, however, has been the federal system's contribution to the development of the province's political system. Although it is hardly unexpected to find national politics affecting provincial developments to some degree, the federal contribution in Saskatchewan has been sustained and continuous. Federal government is widely accepted as a "method of dividing powers so that the general and regional governments are each, within a sphere, co-ordinate and independent."[1] Such a definition, by stressing division of powers, implies that the two levels of government enjoy a greater degree of independence than has been the case in Saskatchewan for the past sixty-odd years. Intergovernmental dependence, which has been notable during this period, may therefore be explained less by constitutional or legal ties than by common political interests.

Thus, while federalism introduces an additional dimension to the political system by providing two levels of government instead of one and by establishing between them a series of countervailing pressures, it also introduces a mechanism to resolve the conflict between centralizing and decentralizing forces — the national party system. This is not to say that national parties in a federal system do not experience conflict generated by the federal experiment. Indeed, one of the theses of this chapter is that much of the history of Saskatchewan politics may be understood only in terms of such intraparty conflict, which has underscored the value of partisan attachment for politicians at both levels of government. This allegiance to partisanship needs to be emphasized, for it has been a characteristic of Saskatchewan politics. In 1905 the territorial tradition of nonpartisanship was discarded; in 1917 an opportunity to return to nonpartisanship was rejected; and after 1930 the founders of the Co-operative Commonwealth Federation eschewed the example of UFA group government in Alberta for traditional party politics.

A. The Introduction and Operation of the Original Party System

Before 1896 nonpartisan politics prevailed in the North-West Territories. After that date and until 1905 the national two-party system appeared in federal contests but was excluded from territorial politics. The reasons for the delay were simple. There was little dispute about the Territories' goals and a general conviction that, in dealing with Ottawa, these goals could be achieved more quickly and completely if members of the Assembly spoke with a single voice. On local matters some distinction was made between "government" and "opposition" members, but it was neither rigid nor enduring.[2] Federal political distinctions became manifest at the local level only as the Territories were on the eve of achieving provincial status, when the Laurier government revealed the sections of the Saskatchewan and Alberta Autonomy Bills relating to the educational rights of minorities and federal retention of natural resources.[3] Both provisions were attacked by the territorial premier F.W.G.

---

[1]K.C. Wheare, *Federal Government,* 4th ed. (New York: Oxford University Press, 1964), p. 10.

[2]For more on the politics of the North-West Territories see Evelyn Lucille Eager, "The Government of Saskatchewan" (Ph.D. thesis, University of Toronto, 1957), pp. 41-45.

[3]*Statutes at Large,* 4-5, Edward VII, c. 3 and c. 42 (1905), "An Act to establish and provide for the government of the Province of Alberta (Saskatchewan)."

Haultain, a nonpartisan territorially but a Conservative federally, as derogations of provincial rights.

What is significant is that federal issues — the perennial religion-school question and a potentially contentious natural resources policy — were injected into provincial politics. Neither issue had been current in the Territories before 1905, but in that year the former was to help bring Liberal governments to power in Saskatchewan and Alberta and the latter was to become a principal object of attack for the new Conservative opposition.

The demands for unity inherent in Canadian federalism in 1905 induced the central government to seek friendly administrations in the new provinces. Initially it seemed that Ottawa would be only partially successful, since Haultain, territorial premier for eight years and a supporter of autonomy, was the logical choice as premier of one of the provinces. However, his vow to raise the school question in Saskatchewan and Alberta following independence and his public denunciation of the Autonomy Bills in by-election campaigns on behalf of the Conservative candidates in Ontario gave the federal Liberals reason to ignore him.[4] Normally, the federal government has no role to play in the selection of a provincial premier, for it is the Lieutenant-Governor's task to seek out the leader of the party that commands the greatest support in the legislature. However, in this instance the Lieutenant-Governor had to determine which leader, Walter Scott of the Liberals or F.W.G. Haultain of the Conservatives, would likely command support of a majority in the yet-to-be-elected assembly. In making this choice, the new Lieutenant-Governor of Saskatchewan, A.E. Forget, who had also been Lieutenant-Governor of the North-West Territories between 1898 and 1905 appears to have used "the personal discretion of the Crown . . . frankly and openly in the interests of the central government and the Liberal party."[5] In his defence he could point to the results of the 1904 federal election in which the Territories elected seven Liberals and only three Conservatives to Parliament. Later, after December 13, 1905, he could also point to the success of Walter Scott's Liberal government in securing sixteen of the twenty-five seats (see Table I), but by then the Liberals' accession to power had been accomplished by the Lientenant-Governor's action.

There seems little doubt that Forget's sentiments were disposed toward the Liberals. However, it is less certain that he acted under direction of Ottawa. Whether or not he did so act is less important than the fact that the discretionary power of the Lieutenant-Governor, so often derided in Canadian political literature, in this instance proved determinant. The Lieutenant-Governor was originally envisioned by the Fathers of Confederation as a federal officer. Despite the office's evolution in quite an opposite direction in other provinces before 1905 and in Saskatchewan afterward, at that time and in that province Mr. Forget acted as a federal officer. The imprint of federal politics was thus stamped unavoidably on Saskatchewan's first government and, naturally, on its first opposition.

It was anticipatory of later political development that Saskatchewan's first opposition should seek temporary refuge in a special provincial organization. Until 1911, when the federal and provincial Conservative organizations were merged, the opposition actually referred to itself as the

TABLE I

The Popular Vote and Legislative Seats Won by Parties in Saskatchewan Provincial General Elections, 1905–71

Election	Total Popular Vote	Total Number of Seats	Liberal Percentage of Popular Vote	Liberal Percentage of Seats	Conservative Percentage of Popular Vote	Conservative Percentage of Seats	Social Credit Percentage of Popular Vote	Social Credit Percentage of Seats	CCF Percentage of Popular Vote	CCF Percentage of Seats	Others Percentage of Popular Vote	Others Percentage of Seats
1905	34,057	25	52	64	47	36	—	—	—	—	—	—
1908	58,302	41	50	66	49	34	—	—	—	—	—	—
1912	87,632	54	57	85	42	15	—	—	—	—	1	—
1917	187,635	59	57	86	36	12	—	—	—	—	7	2
1921	180,955	63	52	73	3	3	—	—	—	—	45	24
1925	247,764	63	51	79	18	5	—	—	—	—	30	16
1929	361,268	63	46	44	36	38	—	—	—	—	18	18
1934	429,620	55	48	91	27	—	—	—	24	9	1	—
1938	440,273	52	45	73	12	—	16	4	19	19	8	4
1944	397,117	52	35	11	11	—	—	—	53	89	1	—
1948	492,906	52	31	36	8	—	8	—	48	60	5	4
1952	537,962	53	39	21	2	—	4	—	54	79	1	—
1956	551,698	53	30	26	2	—	21	6	45	68	1	—
1960	679,243	55	33	31	14	—	12	—	41	69	—	—
1964	666,497	59	41	56	19	2	—	—	40	42	—	—
1967	411,109	59	46	61	9	—	—	—	45	39	—	—
1971	444,003	60	43	25	2	—	—	—	55	75	—	—

Source: Evelyn Lucille Eager, "The Government of Saskatchewan" (Ph.D. thesis, University of Toronto, 1957), p. 344; statements of election results for 1960 and 1964, issued by the Chief Electoral Officer for Saskatchewan, *Star-Phoenix* (Saskatoon), October 12, 1967 and June 24, 1971.
The percentages may not add up exactly to 100 due to rounding.
The decrease in voter turnout in 1967 is accounted for, in part, by the replacement of multi-member constituencies in Regina, Saskatoon, and Moose Jaw by single member constituencies. However, the turnout throughout the province was the lowest in two decades.

[4]*The Leader* (Regina), June 28, 1905, p. 5. In late May and early June, Mr. Haultain, along with R.B. Bennett and other prominent Conservatives, campaigned in the federal by-elections of London and North Oxford in Ontario. The Autonomy Acts for the new provinces were principal issues in these campaigns. See *The Leader*, May 31, 1905, p. 4; and June 14, 1905, pp. 1 and 4.
[5]John T. Saywell, *The Office of the Lieutenant-Governor* (Toronto: University of Toronto Press, 1957), p. 106.

Provincial Rights party. This policy of 1905 to 1911 reflected the personal views of F.W.G. Haultain before he was appointed to the bench in 1912, but it also proved to be a strategic move.

Since most of the electorate was composed of farmers, and a large number of them wheat farmers, their interests had to be given first consideration by any government. The Liberal government of Walter Scott (see Table II for a list of Premiers of Saskatchewan) acknowledged the farmers' importance by actively soliciting the views of their provincial organization, the Saskatchewan Grain Growers' Association, and by inducing SGGA personnel into the cabinet.[6] On the basis of this consultation it regularly introduced legislation favoured by the farmers; the best example, but by no means the only, was an act adopted in 1911 that incorporated and helped finance the Saskatchewan Co-operative Elevator Company.[7] In return for this solicitude, the farmers reciprocated by eschewing direct political action and favouring the Liberals with their votes.

The farmers' attachment to the Liberal party, both federally and provincially, was natural on other grounds as well. The vast majority of them had immigrated to Saskatchewan in the early 1900's from Ontario, the United States, the British Isles, and Central Europe. In such a situation "the Liberals held trump cards. They were the government in office at a time when hopes were high, conditions buoyant. Many newly enfranchised voters of 1905 had no political tradition and were persuaded to vote for the same party that federally offered homesteads and a new life."[8]

One casualty of this goodwill between the farmers and the provincial Liberal government was the opposition party. There was little it could offer as an alternative to the government other than a more efficient administration. Following the 1905 election this was exactly what the Conservatives, as the Provincial Rights party, did offer, although they usually elaborated their campaigns with general attacks on partisanship and demands for provincial control of resources.[9] While their platform was not likely to dislodge large numbers of Liberal supporters, it did provide a single focus of opposition, independent of Conservative sentiment, for all who opposed the Saskatchewan Liberal government. To the extent that it accomplished the task of monopolizing the opposition, the Provincial Rights party until 1911 and the Conservative party afterward functioned as the principal minority party or "moon," to use Samuel Lubell's solar analogy of the American party system.[10] That Saskatchewan politics differed this early from other prairie provincial politics — for example, politics in Alberta — is evidenced in this monopoly of opposition in the former province and its dispersion in the latter.

B. The Original Party System under Attack

The first six years of the province's political history were marked by the entrenchment of the Liberal government. In the view of one scholar, "gerrymandered representation, the work of the partisan civil services, energetic development policies and sensitivity to the wishes of the provincial farm organizations and the women's suffrage and temperance movements, kept the

TABLE II

Premiers of Saskatchewan 1905–71

Premier	Term of Office	Governing Party
Walter Scott	1905-16	Liberal
W.M. Martin	1916-22	Liberal
C.A. Dunning	1922-26	Liberal
J.G. Gardiner	1926-29	Liberal
J.T.M. Anderson	1929-34	Co-operative*
J.G. Gardiner	1934-35	Liberal
W.J. Patterson	1935-44	Liberal
T.C. Douglas	1944-61	CCF
W.S. Lloyd	1961-64	CCF
W.R. Thatcher	1964-71	Liberal
A.E. Blakeney	1971-	NDP

*Composed of Conservatives, Progressives, and Independents.

Liberal party in power" in both Saskatchewan and Alberta.[11] Furthermore, the provincial Liberals in this period also benefited from federal patronage. The first major disturbance to this pattern of politics occurred when the Conservatives defeated the Liberals in the federal election of 1911. Since the Saskatchewan Conservatives had spent so much energy attacking an unsympathetic but meddling federal government, they might have been expected to benefit from this change in federal political fortunes. To some extent they did, since they and their supporters became the recipients of federal patronage. However, these gains were more than offset by the federal Conservatives' image as a high-tariff party, opposed to the policy of reciprocity with the

[6]This relationship existed from territorial days when W.R. Motherwell, later the first minister of agriculture in Saskatchewan, was one of the founders of the Territorial Grain Growers' Association. Other government personalities prominent in the Association and the Saskatchewan Co-Operative Elevator Company until the 1920's were C.A. Dunning, George Langley, Charles Hamilton, and John Maharg, all of whom were ministers of agriculture in this period.

[7]Paul F. Sharp, *The Agrarian Revolt in Western Canada* (Minneapolis: University of Minnesota Press, 1948), p. 39.

[8]John H. Archer, "The Political Development of Saskatchewan" (Saskatoon: University of Saskatchewan, mimeo., 1960), p. 9.

[9]These perennial issues, discussed in both electoral and legislative debates, are noted by J. Castell Hopkins in *Canadian Annual Review* (Toronto: The Annual Review Publishing Company). See, for example, *Canadian Annual Review* (1913), p. 637; and *Canadian Annual Review* (1920), p. 795.

[10]Samuel Lubell, *The Future of American Politics,* 2nd ed., rev. (New York: Doubleday and Company, 1956), pp. 210-218.

[11]Denis Smith, "Politics and the Party System in the Three Prairie Provinces, 1917-1958" (B. Litt. thesis, Oxford University, 1959), p. 15. A decade later during the provincial general election of 1921 Premier Martin reiterated the value of patronage in the civil service: "We have a Civil Service Commissioner whose duty it is to provide for appointments in the Civil Service, but I do not hesitate to say that in the filling of the more important positions the responsible head of the Department affected makes the selection." *Canadian Annual Review* (1921), p. 811.

United States that was widely supported in the West. Nevertheless, the provincial Conservatives could find some solace in the results of the 1911 federal election. For the first time since the province's autonomy the provincial Liberal government lacked the support of a sympathetic federal government. According to the Lubell thesis, if the farmers switched their allegiance from the Liberal government, the minority party would be the chief beneficiary. After 1911, therefore, it was clear to the Liberal leadership that the farmers must be kept loyal at any cost or they would alter the existing party system.

The vulnerability of that system became apparent in 1916 and 1917 with the spread of the Non-Partisan League to Saskatchewan from Alberta.[12] Overtly the League was not particularly successful; in the provincial election of 1917 it elected only one member to the Legislative Assembly of Saskatchewan and that was by acclamation, since the individual was also the candidate of both the Liberals and Conservatives. The League's influence lay in its theory of nonpartisanship, which deprived the Conservatives of their principal election plank, and in its practical successes in North Dakota, which challenged the achievements of the Liberal party. The League quickly realized that it could not duplicate its earlier electoral victories by the same methods it had used in the United States. In particular, the presence of party discipline and the absence of the direct primary meant that its candidates had to enter Canadian politics as third-party candidates. Under the single-member-district, simple-plurality-vote electoral system the procedure of entering third-party candidates would probably be unsuccessful unless the new party could attract a wide following among the organized farmers. In articulating many of the farmers' demands and in depicting itself as the political arm of the SGGA, the League presented the first real threat to the Liberal party's monopoly of farmer support. Although it failed to capture the farmers' organization, it did infuse them with a new militancy for direct political action. In Saskatchewan this militancy led to an even closer liaïson, in personnel and views, between the SGGA and the Liberal government.

The Non-Partisan League's attack on the original party system of Saskatchewan was crucial to that system's later disintegration. It was particularly destructive since it coincided with renewed strains in federal politics. In 1917 the national Liberal party split between Laurier and Unionist Liberals on the question of forming a coalition government with the Conservatives. The provincial Liberals, who felt they had to choose between the two national Liberal factions, recognized that their choice was complicated more by consideration of their personal loyalty to Sir Wilfrid Laurier than by their concern for the effects of coalition on party organization. For many Liberals, including such prominent Saskatchewan figures as George Langley, W.R. Motherwell, A.P. McNab and G.A. Bell, the Conservative party was so tainted by big business that coalition would amount to guilt by association for the Liberals in the West. For others such as J.A. Calder, former provincial Minister of Railways and now federal Minister of Immigration and Colonization, union was necessary for better administration of the government's war policy including the implementation of conscription.[13] Premier W.M. Martin was concerned that coalition would associate Liberals with the Borden government's discriminatory wartime Elections Act, which prejudicially affected the voting rights of many British subjects of German and Austro-Hungarian origin who had entered Canada since 1902. There were over 32,500 of these people in Saskatchewan in 1916.[14]

Within two weeks of the announcement of Union Government, Mr. Calder announced that a National Government Association of Saskatchewan had been formed under his direction. Calder was the recognized head of the Saskatchewan Liberal party machine and with his knowledge of provincial politics plus Conservative financial contributions the cause of Union Government seemed assured.[15] It was Calder's own opinion that "Liberalism in its truest and broadest sense [would] not suffer" from the experiment. This was an optimistic judgment. Federal party lines, which for over a decade had separated provincial parties, were blurred, and consequently party distinctions in the province were further weakened.

Another federal event, in part related to conditions arising from the war and in part derived from earlier grievances, influenced provincial political development. A national farmers' movement began to take definite shape in 1918, when the Canadian Council of Agriculture adopted a programme entitled the "New National Policy", which included a renewed demand for reciprocity with the United States in the trade of farm products. Response from farmers' organizations was favourable to political action, especially after the new Liberal leader, W.L. Mackenzie King, indicated that he did not concur completely with their demands for revision of the tariff. This was followed by farmer successes in federal by-elections in the East and the West and was capped by the victory of the United Farmers of Ontario in the 1919 general election in that province.[16]

C. The Farmers in Saskatchewan Politics

These wartime and post-war developments weakened traditional party allegiances in the West and at the same time presented the farmers with the alternative of direct political action to secure their policy demands. It was safe to predict that once the farmers were confident of success in federal contests, they would turn their sights on provincial politics as well. Because of their long-time close association with the SGGA, the Saskatchewan Liberals were particularly sensitive to the effect farmer unrest would have on their

---

[12]The electoral activities of the Non-Partisan League and its entrance into Canada are described in Sharp, *Agrarian Revolt*, chs. 5 and 6.

[13]*Canadian Annual Review* (1917), p. 615.

[14]Dominion Bureau of Statistics, *Census of the Prairie Provinces, 1946: Population* (Ottawa: King's Printer, 1949), I, 247.

[15]Smith, "Politics and the Party System," p. 38. See also *Canadian Annual Review* (1917), p. 615.

[16]W.L. Morton, *The Progressive Party in Canada* (Toronto: University of Toronto Press, 1950), pp. 82-85.

electoral fortunes. They were also aware that their vulnerability arose from their association with the federal Liberals, whose trade policies were unpopular with the farmers. Since there seemed little chance of altering these policies to make them more palatable to the western farmer, the alternative was for the Saskatchewan Liberals to dissociate themselves from the federal party. They did this in 1919 and the following year extended their "dissociation" to all federal parties. In the words of Premier Martin: "I will not be responsible for the organization nor for the policies of any federal political party."[17] What the Provincial Rights party had done from 1905 to 1911 was now to be duplicated by the Liberal party.

This break was in response to a potential threat. At its annual convention in 1920 the SGGA debated a motion to establish a provincial political organization that would nominate and support independent candidates. The convention finally resolved to appoint a committee to draft a provincial political platform for submission to local and district conventions and to the next annual convention. However, little interest was shown in this proposal afterward. In 1922 the annual convention of the Association further resolved to create a committee to assist provincial constituencies wishing to organize for direct provincial political action. That year the Grain Growers nominated an "Independent" candidate to run in a by-election but he was defeated by a Liberal. In 1924 the resolution of two years earlier was rescinded by the annual convention and the Association's interest in direct political action ceased.[18]

The organized farmers' threat to the supremacy of the Liberal government was thus checked five years after it had appeared. The government's ability to control farmer unrest in this period illustrated several important features of Saskatchewan politics. Obviously, it proved that dissociation from federal politics was possible. In this particular instance it allowed the Liberals to assume the role of "real" spokesmen for the farmers. As such they could attack other parties, including the farmers' movement, for their federal alignments. It became increasingly embarrassing for the farmers, and later the Provincial Progressive Association, organized in 1924, to denounce the old Liberal sin of federal connections when at the same time they advocated provincial support for the federal Progressives. An example of the difficulties that could arise occurred in 1921 when J.A. Maharg, President of the SGGA and provincial Minister of Agriculture, resigned from the Martin government because the Premier was supporting a local Liberal candidate in the federal general election. The Premier defended his action claiming he was not opposed to individual support of federal candidates but only to provincial party support of federal parties. The Premier stated that Mr. Maharg had resigned "because he could not force me and the whole of the Government into a position where we were to be a cog in the machine of the Federal political party".[19]

The organized farmers' failure to establish a separate political organization at this time was also due to objections to the scheme raised by the leaders of the SGGA.[20] They were convinced that there was no practical alternative for the farmers to the policies offered by the Saskatchewan Lib-

298

erals. As evidence of their support for these policies, a number of prominent SGGA officers co-operated with the government. Mr. Maharg's acceptance of the post of Minister of Agriculture was one example; another was the appointment of Maharg and J.B. Musselman, the Association's recently-retired secretary, to the executive of the government-supported Saskatchewan Co-operative Elevator Company in 1922. Both men feared that any attempt to transform the SGGA into a political party might destroy its existing unity on economic matters. It was their belief that the farmers should try "to build up an organization which would unite, within its ranks, the largest percentage of farmers, through which they could work effectively in raising their industry".[21]

This attitude, which was generally held by the leaders of the Saskatchewan farmers, was significant not only for political developments in the province in the early 1920's but also for developments a decade later, when the Co-operative Commonwealth Federation was founded. In rejecting direct political action by the farmers, the Saskatchewan leaders were also rejecting the theory of group government then being expounded by Henry Wise Wood of the United Farmers of Alberta. Wood's thesis was that economic groups or classes were the basic units of politics; that traditional parties ignored this truth because they sought support from whoever would give it by compromising principles and balancing interests; and that, as a consequence, traditional parties lacked a unifying principle save subservience to "plutocracy."[22] The conclusion of his analysis was that democracy, which he defined as absence of exploitation of man by man or class by class, could never be achieved until group government was introduced.

The theory appealed to many western farmers because it appeared to substantiate many of their prejudices about eastern financial control of the traditional parties. In Alberta the UFA entered politics directly and refused to co-operate with any established political group that did not subscribe to Wood's theory. The size of the organization, the concentration of its vote outside of the cities, and the malapportionment of the province's constituencies in favour of the rural areas guaranteed it electoral victory. By refusing

[17]*Canadian Annual Review* (1920), p. 755.

[18]For a review of the SGGA's discussion of this topic at its annual conventions from 1920 to 1924, see *Canadian Annual Review* (1920), pp. 722-776; (1921), pp. 779-780; (1922), p. 782; (1924), pp. 417-418.

[19]*Canadian Annual Review* (1921), p. 794. For further on the same topic, see also *Canadian Annual Review* (1923), p. 715.

[20]For further on the farmers' flirtations with provincial politics, see F.W. Anderson, "Farmers in Politics, 1915–1935" (M.A. thesis, University of Saskatchewan, 1949), pp. 62 ff.

[21]*Canadian Annual Review* (1924), p. 418.

[22]Wood's distinctive theory of group government is presented in: C.B. Macpherson, *Democracy in Alberta: Social Credit and the Party System*, 2nd ed. (Toronto: University of Toronto Press, 1962), ch. 2; William Kirby Rolph, *Henry Wise Wood of Alberta* (Toronto: University of Toronto Press, 1950), pp. 63-66. For the opinion of Saskatchewan farmer leaders on this theory, see *The Grain Growers' Guide*, November 26, 1919, p. 16; December 17, 1919, p. 18.

to follow the UFA's example and act as a tightly knit group based on occupational interests, the Saskatchewan farmers may well have denied themselves similar electoral success. However, their decision made possible the continuation of partisan politics in the province. The decisions made by the farmers of Alberta and Saskatchewan in the 1920's are a major cause for the different political evolutions of those provinces to the present day. By deciding to enter politics directly, the UFA destroyed the Alberta Liberal party both as a governing and opposition body; by refraining from direct political action, the SGGA helped preserve the Saskatchewan Liberal party.

Of course, the SGGA's decision of 1924 did not bind all farmers; throughout the remainder of that decade the Farmers' Union of Canada, the United Farmers of Canada—Saskatchewan Section (the successor of a union of the SGGA and the FUC) and those farmers who supported the Provincial Progressive Association frequently flirted with proposals for a farmers' party in provincial politics. Yet there was never widespread agreement in support of the idea. Such political activity as did occur was characterized as much by demands for governmental and electoral reform as by promotion of particular farmer interests.

The results of the 1925 provincial election, in which the Liberals won fifty-one out of the sixty-three seats, indicated the strength of that party. Furthermore, the actions of J.G. Gardiner, who became premier in 1926 when C.A. Dunning went to Ottawa, demonstrated a return to the old style of politics. According to one observer, Gardiner was a machine politician who made no distinction between federal and provincial politics.[23] No attempt was made to hide renewed connections with the federal Liberal party and, indeed, Mr. Dunning's policies as premier appear to have made him suspect of Progressive sympathies in his successor's partisan eyes.[24]

The vitality of the rejuvenated Liberals was tested in 1929 and for the first time in twenty-four years was found wanting. Part of the explanation for the Liberal defeat rested in the faulty operation of its party machine,[25] but there were several other reasons for failure. Most significantly, the issue of religion in the public schools was elevated, partly through Ku Klux Klan agitation, into a major sectarian conflict.[26] The Liberals, as may be seen elsewhere in this chapter, have traditionally received support from large numbers of Roman Catholic voters. Therefore, if non-Catholic voters were to indicate their religious prejudices politically, it was bound to affect adversely the Liberal party. That the issue was a major one may be gauged by the new government's speed in amending the School Act to forbid religious emblems and religious dress in the schools.

Other issues in the campaign were fairly typical of previous elections; for example, the opposition candidates pressed for a more progressive policy of natural resource development. On the eve of the Depression the Conservatives ironically included in their platform a plank "to solve the problem of seasonal unemployment." The results of the election gave the Liberals the largest number of votes and the largest number of seats but denied them a majority in the legislature. Refusing to give their support to the Liberals, the newly-elected Independent and Progressive members pledged to co-operate with the Conservatives in a new government on three conditions: that the Conservatives agree to "civil service reform, retention of the identity of each group and freedom in the matter of Federal politics."[27]

The latter two conditions indicated that the old issue of partisan politics was very much alive. This was true throughout the life of the Co-operative Government led by J.T.M. Anderson, a Conservative. Outside the legislature many Progressives disavowed the action of their Progressive assembly members. These members eventually became disenchanted with the experiment, particularly after the formation in 1932 of the Farmer-Labour party, for whose programme they felt considerable sympathy. The Conservatives also found themselves split over the question of co-operation; many "true-blue" Conservatives opposed the Premier's willingness to countenance such diverse support. As the Depression and drought grew more severe, the Premier sought a coalition of all parties, including the new Farmer-Labour party. However, the Liberals and the leaders of the new party were alive to the value of partisan distinctiveness and refused to join a government that now seemed destined for defeat.[28] Added to the provincial burdens of the Conservatives was the unpopularity of their federal counterparts. At no time in Saskatchewan history were federal partisan attachments so disastrous for a party in power as in the provincial election of 1934.[29] The Conservative party, the traditional second party of Saskatchewan politics, was discredited along with its nonpartisan allies. The party's complete defeat, indicated by its failure to elect a single Conservative in a provincial general election until 1964, marked the end of one of the two original parties as well as the end of the short experiment with co-operative government.

In the election of 1934 the Liberal party presented the Saskatchewan voters with a practical partisan alternative to the co-operative experiment of quasi-partisan politics. The success of the Liberals in that election may be

23Professor Smith quotes John Dafoe as saying of Gardiner that he was "a political anachronism — a survival of a stage of political development — which we have definitely passed in the West. I doubt whether he can be modernized." Smith, "Politics and the Party System," p. 185.

24*Ibid.*, p. 186.

25Escott M. Reid, "The Saskatchewan Liberal Party Machine Before 1929," in *Party Politics in Canada*, Hugh G. Thorburn, ed. (Toronto: Prentice-Hall of Canada, Ltd., 1963), p. 55.

26The Ku Klux Klan and its operation in Canada is discussed in Patrick Kyba, "Ballots and Burning Crosses — The Election of 1929," in *Politics in Saskatchewan*, Norman Ward and D.S. Spafford, eds. (Toronto: Longmans Canada Ltd., 1968).

27*Canadian Annual Review* (1928–29), p. 469. It was also part of the agreement that the Government would not resign or threaten to resign except on a direct vote of want of confidence. See Eager, "The Government of Saskatchewan," p. 289.

28Only one Liberal, Charles McIntosh, crossed to the Government side of the legislature. He was offered the portfolio of natural resources. Saskatchewan law until 1936 required newly appointed ministers to stand for re-election in their constituencies. Only two of nineteen such by-elections were contested between 1905 and 1936, one of which was McIntosh's candidacy in Kinistino. He lost to an officially endorsed Liberal. For further discussion of the projected coalition, see *Canadian Annual Review* (1933), pp. 239-241.

29"The Gang's All Here," *Canadian Forum*, XIV (August 1934), 420.

seen as a reaffirmation of faith in partisan politics. This interpretation of the election results is in no way modified by the support given the new Farmer-Labour party. That party, from the time of its inception, also eschewed non-partisanism. These developments once again distinguished Saskatchewan markedly from Alberta, where nonpartisan politics became further entrenched by the victory of Social Credit in 1935.

D. The New Party System

The new party system that appeared after 1934 was again a two-party system, but was now composed of two quite dissimilar parties. The Farmer-Labour party had been formed in 1932 in the depths of the Depression and, to a large extent, was a product of the agrarian discontent of the previous decade. The United Farmers of Canada — Saskatchewan Section, which had been formed in 1926 from a union of the Farmers' Union of Canada and the Saskatchewan Grain Growers' Association, resolved in 1931 to enter politics directly. Their decision was largely determined by the worsening economic conditions in Saskatchewan. But it was also influenced by the fact that the Liberal party, the traditional friend of the Saskatchewan farmer, was out of office; even if the economic situation had not been so bad, the old arguments against direct political action used by Musselman and Maharg in the 1920's would therefore have carried little weight. A new political force in the cities had also appeared in the form of the Independent Labour party led by M.J. Coldwell. Thus, in 1932, it was possible for the two groups, farmer and labour, to unite in a new political party.

An equally important difference between this period and the 1920's was the founding of a new national political party, the Co-operative Commonwealth Federation, shortly after the Farmer-Labour party had been established. Since the CCF was founded as a federation of occupational groups, it rejected the rigid theory of group government enunciated by Henry Wise Wood. Indeed, the farmer and labour groups that met at Calgary in August 1932 and the same groups plus representatives of the League for Social Reconstruction that met at Regina in July 1933 believed that federal and provincial electoral success would be denied to any organization that so restricted its appeal.

Thus, when the Farmer-Labour party presented itself to the Saskatchewan electorate for the first time in 1934, it tried to attract support from as wide a spectrum of the electorate as possible with its distinctive, socialist programme. In this endeavour it enjoyed the backing of a national party organization. But the Farmer-Labour party also had the important advantage of being a Saskatchewan party, originating from the efforts of provincial groups and continuing to possess considerable local autonomy. The wisdom of this strategy was confirmed in the results of the election. While in terms of legislative membership, the party was small, it had the satisfaction of winning 24 per cent of the popular vote and of becoming the sole opposition party in the Legislature. Those who deserted the Liberals, for whatever reason, had only one place to go.

From its emergence in 1932 until its victory in 1944, the new organization acted as a true political party. Its two principal tasks were to attract as much support as it could from the Liberals and to prevent the rise of a challenger to its monopoly of the opposition. To better carry out these tasks the party decided, shortly after the 1934 election, to change its name to the Co-operative Commonwealth Federation—Saskatchewan Section, thereby emphasizing its national character within a provincial context. The following year the UFC "instructed the political directorate [of the party] to formulate plans for setting up a distinct political organization" and thereby removed the image of the party as spokesman solely of the farmers.[30] The party also began to play down its programme of government ownership in favour of government planning. By the time of the 1938 election the CCF party appeared to have established a permanent role for itself as the legitimate, practical alternative to the Liberals in Saskatchewan politics.

That election affirmed the CCF in this role. The most outstanding feature of the contest was the invasion of Saskatchewan by Alberta's Premier Aberhart and his cabinet in an attempt to bring Social Credit to the province. As it happened, only two of the forty-one Social Credit candidates nominated were elected, compared to ten of the thirty-one CCF candidates. But more important than numerical strength was the image of respectability the CCF achieved during the election campaign. The Liberals turned the full weight of their attack against Social Credit, equating it with dictatorship and charging it with trying to make another "Manchukuo out of Saskatchewan."[31] They warned the public against being duped into supporting "Independent" or "Unity" candidates whose politics were unknown and therefore suspect. In an atmosphere so hostile to Social Credit, the partisanship and local origins of the CCF were commended, albeit indirectly, by the Liberals.

Given the disastrous economic conditions confronting the Liberal government and the difficulty of finding practical solutions, the appearance of Social Credit favoured the incumbents by allowing them to focus on a secondary but diverting issue. The results of the election confirmed the wisdom of this ploy, for the Liberals were returned with only a slightly decreased majority. However, these returns warned of future problems for the party. The Liberals tended to do best in areas where farmers were still dependent on federal and provincial relief payments; the CCF picked up support from farmers who had enjoyed good crops in the last harvest.[32]

In the period between 1938 and 1944 the effects of federal Liberal policies on wheat prices and the availability of farm labour did little to help the popularity of the provincial Liberals. At the same time the stature of the CCF was increased as it criticized Liberal policies in Regina and Ottawa. The stature of the provincial CCF in Saskatchewan owed much especially to the activity of

---

30*Canadian Annual Review* (1934), pp. 284 and 285.

31Helen Orpwood, "The Saskatchewan Election," *Canadian Forum*, XVIII (August 1938), 136. See also *The Leader-Post* (Regina), May 16, 1938, p. 1; May 19, 1938, p. 9; June 8, 1938, p. 5.

32Smith, "Politics and the Party System," p. 300; Orpwood, "The Saskatchewan Election," p. 137.

federal M.P.s such as T.C. Douglas and A.M. Nicholson. The one-year extension of the life of the 1938 legislature in 1943 signaled more clearly than any act of the CCF the imminent defeat of the Liberals.

The CCF's success in 1944, when it came to power with fifty of the fifty-five seats, was due to events — drought, depression, and war — and their accompanying frustrations more than to popular support for socialism. The Saskatchewan electorate decided that it was "time for a change" and the CCF presented the only alternative to the Liberal party. The aftermath of victory, therefore, was not a revolution in the province's institutions. The CCF's campaign had concentrated on restoring the province's economy, breaking the Liberal machine, and introducing greater social service benefits; it did not concentrate on nationalizing industry or collectivizing land. What new government ownership there was was only an extension of governmental activity prevalent in Saskatchewan since 1905. It was hardly surprising then that the new Government failed

to replace the present capitalist system, with its inherent injustice and inhumanity, by a social order from which the domination and exploitation of one class by another will be eliminated, in which economic planning will supersede unregulated private enterprise and competition, and in which genuine democratic self-government, based upon economic equality will be possible.[33]

The victory of the CCF in the 1944 election signified the emergence of the new party system. Since that date the Saskatchewan CCF has modified its earlier pronouncements in favour of public ownership and has stressed its distinctive provincial heritage. Only in 1967 did it finally decide to change its name to the New Democratic Party—Saskatchewan Section, having retained the name "CCF" for some six years after the CCF was replaced by the NDP nationally and in the other provinces. The new party system thus bears many of the marks of the old. The Liberal party, which finally returned to power in 1964, continues the old practice of wary allegiance to the federal party and its policies. The distinctive feature of the new provincial party system is the presence of two equally matched parties. The Conservatives continue to wander in the prairie wilderness and Social Credit, after a repeat performance of 1938 in 1956, is a spent force.

II. THE POLITICAL CULTURE

Political culture has been defined as the "attitudes, beliefs, values, and skills which are current in our entire population, as well as those special propensities and patterns which may be found within separate parts of that population."[34] The Saskatchewan political culture has been influenced by a British political heritage, an ethnically diversified population, an agricultural economic base, and a numerically preponderant rural electorate. The overwhelming and continuing importance of these factors, since 1905, helps to explain the simplicity of that culture.

Substructures, "particular [sets] of political orientations . . . distinguish-

TABLE III

Percentage Distribution of the Population of Saskatchewan, by Ethnic Group, 1901–61

	1901	1911	1921	1931	1941	1951	1961
Anglo-Saxon	43.9	54.7	52.9	47.5	44.4	42.3	40.4
French	2.9	5.2	5.6	5.5	5.6	6.2	6.5
German	12.9	14.4	9.0	14.0	14.5	16.3	17.1
Dutch	0.4	0.6	2.2	2.7	4.0	3.6	3.2
Scandinavian	1.6	7.1	7.7	7.9	7.7	7.5	7.3
Ukrainian	1.2	4.5	3.7	6.9	8.9	9.4	8.5
Other	37.1	13.5	18.9	15.5	14.9	14.7	17.0

Source: Dominion Bureau of Statistics, *Census of Canada*, 1961 (Ottawa: Queen's Printer, 1966), Vol. 7.1-6, Table 3.

able from others in the system," are not readily apparent in the province.[35] The traditionally close association between the farmer and the government has made permanent conflict between the two unlikely. Similarly, the acquiescence of early Liberal governments in the farmers' demands for public regulation of the economy accustomed the citizens to active government; as a result later transfers of power between "free-enterprise" and "socialist" governments have failed to precipitate major reversals of policy.[36] The principal source of whatever separateness there is in the political culture of Saskatchewan has resulted from the considerable isolation of the non-Anglo-Saxon groups from the province's political system, but even this element of distinctiveness seems to be disappearing as Anglo-Saxon political dominance diminishes. (see Table III).

In 1905 the federal government endowed the province with an institutional structure that was basically British. There was no question then as to whether this was the appropriate heritage for Saskatchewan and there has been general acceptance since that the province would pattern itself after the Westminster model. Since 1905 not only the structure but also its personnel has been predominantly Anglo-Saxon. However, the status of the various

[33]Such was the party's purpose as stated in the opening paragraphs of the Regina Manifesto of 1933.

[34]Gabriel A. Almond and G. Bingham Powell, Jr., *Comparative Politics: A Developmental Approach* (Boston: Little, Brown and Co., 1966), p. 23.

[35]*Ibid.*, p. 63.

[36]This is not to say that changes in government have not occasioned some conflict. For the effects of the change in 1944 on the civil service, see S.M. Lipset, *Agrarian Socialism* (Berkeley: University of California Press, 1950), ch. 12. For the effects of the change in 1964 on the civil service, see Norman Ward, "Regina Changes Guard," *Canadian Forum*, XLIV (September 1964), 127-128; and Meyer Brownstone, "Another View on the Saskatchewan Government," *Canadian Forum*, XLIV (December, 1964), 198-200. See also Professor Ward's reply to Mr. Brownstone, *Canadian Forum*, XLIV (January 1965), 228-229.

ethnic groups has been changing. One indicator of this alteration has been the membership of the Legislative Assembly.[37]

Until 1938, with the exception of the small CCF contingent of 1934, 60 per cent of all legislative members were Anglo-Saxon in ethnic origin; indeed, nearly three-quarters of the Conservative, Progressive, and Independent members of the legislature were drawn from this "charter" group. By 1964 less than 40 per cent of the M.L.A.s could be so classified; for the first time in the province's history this group was under-represented according to its proportion of the total provincial population. Except for the election of 1929, when race and religion were particularly contentious issues, the Liberal contingent has never been so British-oriented as that of other parties. From the first, the Liberals have been ethnically heterogeneous; in turn, French, German, Scandinavian, Ukrainian, and Dutch representatives have found a place in Liberal ranks before appearing elsewhere. It is revealing of the different rates of cultural assimilation for the various ethnic groups that members from the groups mentioned appeared in the CCF ranks, starting in 1938, in the same sequence.

Throughout its history the Saskatchewan Liberal party has also included within its ranks a greater variety of religions and frequently a greater variety of Protestant denominations than any other governing party. Between 1905 and 1929, when the Liberals were drawing, among others, Roman Catholics and even Swedenborgians, the Conservatives drew solely Anglicans, Methodists, Presbyterians, and United Church adherents; later, in 1964, when Liberal membership in the legislature was 35 per cent Roman Catholic and also included Saskatchewan's first Jewish member, the CCF party still drew 50 per cent of its legislative membership from such Protestant denominations as the Baptist and United Church.

One observer has noted the high correlation between Liberal party support and Roman Catholic voting patterns in the 1929 election, when religion in the schools was a key issue.[38] He has traced a similar affiliation of Roman Catholics for the Liberal party in later elections and has interpreted their support as being partly a rejection of the socialist policies of the Farmer-Labour and CCF parties. Despite this correlation, the CCF has been far more heterogeneous in terms of religious representation than was the Conservative party. Moreover, this heterogeneity has been increasing; Roman Catholic members in the legislative ranks of the CCF have almost tripled since 1944.

Other features of religious representation in the legislature have been an over-representation of the United Church and the denominations that comprise it, an under-representation of Lutheran adherents and, in recent years, an increasing under-representation of the Anglican community. Of the religions in the "Other" category in Table IV, the most under-represented have been the Greek Orthodox and Ukrainian (Greek) Catholic. Adherents of these religions have accounted for at least 8 per cent of the declared faiths in Saskatchewan since 1931. However, only five Greek Orthodox members have sat in the legislature, all in the CCF ranks and all elected since 1944; only two Ukrainian (Greek) Catholics, Liberals elected in 1934 and 1948, have sat in the legislature.[39]

The agricultural base of Saskatchewan's economy is one of the most

TABLE IV

Percentage Distribution of the Population of Saskatchewan,
by Religious Denomination, 1901–61

	1901	1911	1921	1931	1941	1951	1961
Anglican	17.7	15.5	15.4	13.8	13.2	11.5	10.3
Baptists	2.7	3.8	3.1	2.5	2.2	1.9	1.8
Lutheran	6.8	11.6	12.2	12.4	11.8	11.0	10.3
Methodist	13.3	16.2	13.4	—	—	—	—
Presbyterian	18.0	19.9	21.5	7.4	6.2	4.0	2.7
Roman Catholic	19.6	18.6	19.6	20.7	22.6	24.1	26.3
United Church	—	—	0.4	26.5	25.9	29.8	32.1
Other	21.9	14.4	14.4	16.7	18.1	17.7	16.5

Source: Dominion Bureau of Statistics, Census of Canada, 1961 (Ottawa: Queen's Printer, 1965), Vol. 7.1-11, Table 1.

notable features of the province's life. In 1961, 37 per cent of the total labour force was classified as having an agricultural occupation, as compared to 21 and 18 per cent in Alberta and Manitoba, respectively.[40] It is only in the last two decades that agriculture has dropped in prominence even to this level; in the census of 1941, 59 per cent of the labour force was classified as being employed in farming. It is understandable, therefore, that concern for agriculture should be traditional in the political life of the province. Consequently, it is surprising that agricultural occupations, according to occupational distribution in the province as a whole (see Table V), have been under-represented in the legislature. It is even more surprising to contrast the Liberal and CCF ministries of Saskatchewan. In the former the professions have traditionally counted for at least 50 per cent of the occupations of cabinet members; in the latter agriculture has always ranked first.[41]

This stress on agriculture is crucial to an understanding of Saskatchewan politics not only because of the large percentage of the electorate involved in the occupation but also because of the lingering scars that remain as evidence of the agricultural catastrophe that befell the province thirty years ago. In their discussion of political socialization and the process through which an individual acquires political attitudes, Almond and Powell state: "Certain events and experiences may leave their mark on a whole society. A great war

[37]For a detailed study of the membership of the Legislative Assembly, see David E. Smith, "The Membership of the Saskatchewan Legislative Assembly: 1905-1966," Saskatchewan History, XX (Spring 1967), 41-63.

[38]Andrew J. Milnor, "Agrarian Protest in Saskatchewan, 1929-1948: A Study in Ethnic Protest" (Ph. D. thesis, Duke University, 1962), pp. 60, 62.

[39]These figures do not include new members elected in 1967 and 1971.

[40]James A. Munger, Housing and Environmental Conditions in the Prairie Provinces (Saskatoon: Canadian Centre for Community Studies, 1966), p. 82.

[41]The legislators' occupations were derived from their nomination papers, where possible. Otherwise, reference was made to the Canadian Parliamentary Guide.

TABLE V

Percentage Distribution of the Male Labour Force in Saskatchewan,
15 Years of Age and Over, by Occupation, 1911–61

	1911	1921	1931	1941	1951	1961
Proprietary & Managerial	3.7	6.0	4.8	5.1	7.3	8.1
Professional	1.7	2.1	2.4	2.8	3.6	5.6
Clerical	1.7	2.5	2.2	1.9	3.0	3.6
Agricultural	67.3	70.9	66.6	67.4	56.4	43.2
Others	25.6	18.5	24.0	22.8	29.7	39.5

Source: Dominion Bureau of Statistics, *Census of Canada* 1961 (Ottawa: Queen's Printer, 1961), Vol. 3.1-1, Table 3.

or a depression can constitute a severe political trauma for millions of individuals who may be involved."[42] The result of such experiences is that people, large numbers of them, may "acquire new conceptions of the role of politics in their lives and new goals for which they may strive."[43]

It hardly seems an exaggeration to say that this was true of Saskatchewan in the 1930's when the principal industry of the province collapsed. In the words of one observer in 1933:

The Ford car has become a horse drawn vehicle, the rural telephone system is breaking down with staggering losses in the number of subscribers each year. Farm products (where there have been crops) supply an ever larger part of the farm diet. Clothing constitutes a problem of the first magnitude; it has been estimated that it would take $30,000,000 to restore clothing to pre-depression standards. The unrepaired houses aggravate a winter fuel problem which has always been acute on the prairie plains. [44]

One of the most important derivatives of this agricultural economy is the predominantly rural nature of the society (see Table VI). In 1961 Prince Edward Island was the only province that had a larger rural percentage of population than Saskatchewan. This is true despite the fact that for the past forty years Saskatchewan has been experiencing a rural-to-urban shift in population and that 448,000 people have moved out of the province altogether.[45] In the 1930's and 1940's, and again in the early 1970's, the population of Saskatchewan actually decreased. The socio-economic effects of these tremendous shifts, other than their impact on the political system, are beyond the compass of this paper.

One notable effect of migration has been on the age structure of the population. There is a "growing concentration of older people in the small villages and towns, of very young people in rural areas, and of middle-aged people in the cities."[46] The political implications of these demographic changes are suggested in the returns of the last two provincial elections. In 1967, of forty-five rural seats (excluding Regina, Saskatoon, Moose Jaw and Prince Albert West) the Liberals captured twenty-eight; in 1971, of forty-four rural seats (the number having been reduced by one through redistribution) the Liberals captured only ten. Thus it appears that the rural electorate, which is essential to the electoral success of any Saskatchewan party, with its

TABLE VI

Numerical and Percentage Distribution of Rural and Urban Population
in Saskatchewan, 1901–61

Year	Total Population	Rural No.	%	Urban No.	%
1901	91,279	85,687	93.9	5,592	6.1
1911	492,432	412,930	83.9	79,502	16.1
1921	757,510	629,888	83.2	127,622	16.8
1931	921,785	734,664	79.7	187,121	20.3
1941	895,992	705,254	78.7	190,738	21.3
1951	831,728	580,710	69.8	251,018	30.2
1961	925,181	527,090	57.0	398,091	43.0

Source: Dominion Bureau of Statistics, *Census of Canada, 1961* (Ottawa: Queen's Printer, 1963), Vol. 7.1-2, Table 1.

special concerns related to an aging and declining population, seeks out the party most sympathetic to those concerns. In 1971 the NDP succeeded in presenting itself as the party most capable of protecting rural interests, as did the Liberals four years earlier.

Today the political culture of Saskatchewan remains essentially unchanged from earlier decades. The institutions are still British, although the personnel is less so. Despite repeated attempts at industrial diversification, Saskatchewan remains essentially agricultural in economic orientation. To appreciate the degree to which the province still depends on wheat and to realize the impact the drought of the 1930's still has on the minds of the people, one has only to note the expressions of concern and, indeed, of fear that accompany prolonged dry spells in the summer. Agriculture remains predominant, and so too does the rural base of the society. The migration of people, ideas, and tastes between farm, town, and city may have disguised the sharp contrasts of earlier periods; it has not eliminated them.

III. THE NATURE OF THE SYSTEM

Given the agricultural, one-crop base of the province's economy, which would imply a similarity in economic outlook throughout the province, it is perhaps surprising to discover that a competitive two-party system has developed in Saskatchewan. In spite of the single, dominant industry, with its

[42]Almond and Powell, *Comparative Politics,* p. 65.
[43]*Ibid.*
[44]G.E. Britnell, "The Depression in Rural Saskatchewan," in *The Canadian Economy and Its Problems,* H.A. Innis and A.F.W. Plumptre, eds. (Toronto: Canadian Institute of International Affairs, 1934), pp. 109-110.
[45]Munger, *Housing and Environmental Conditions,* p. 14.
[46]*Ibid.,* p. 30.

TABLE VII

Vote Cast for Two Major Parties in Saskatchewan and Alberta

Percentage of Popular Vote	Number of Elections	
	Saskatchewan	Alberta
50-54	0	1
55-59	0	0
60-64	3	1
65-69	0	3
70-74	1	2
75-79	3	5
80-84	3	1
85-89	1	1
90-94	2	2
95-100	4	1
Total	17	17

TABLE VIII

Spread in Percentage Points between Popular Vote for Each of the Two Major Parties in Saskatchewan and Alberta

Spread in Percentage Points	Number of Elections	
	Saskatchewan	Alberta
1-5	5	2
6-10	2	2
11-15	3	3
16-20	2	1
21-25	2	1
26-30	2	3
31-35	0	5
36 and over	1	0
Total	17	17

TABLE IX

Percentage of Total Popular Vote Cast for the Two Major Parties in Saskatchewan and Alberta: Median and Mean

	Percentage of Popular Vote	
	Saskatchewan	Alberta
Median	82.3	77.0
Mean	83.9	75.0

310   SASKATCHEWAN

acute vulnerability to climatic conditions, business cycles, and sudden changes in the international demand for wheat, the people of Saskatchewan have not developed a single-party system. There have been, it is true, prolonged periods of one-party dominance: for example, from 1905 to 1929 when the Liberals were in power, and from 1944 to 1964 when the CCF was in power.

Yet by using the measurement of popular vote rather than the number of seats won in the legislature, which has the effect of removing at least some of the bias of the plurality electoral procedure, a truer gauge of party competition is made possible. In ten of the seventeen elections between 1905 and 1971 at least 80 per cent of the popular vote was cast for the two major parties (see Table VII). In seven of the seventeen elections there was a spread of only 10 percentage points or less between these parties (see Table VIII).

The competitive basis of Saskatchewan party politics is even more striking when one compares it with Alberta. The two provinces were created at the same time under similar circumstances, and both had similar economic bases. In only five of Alberta's seventeen elections, compared to ten of Saskatchewan's seventeen, has at least 80 per cent of the total popular vote been cast for the two major parties (see Table VII). In eight of Alberta's elections, compared to only three of Saskatchewan's, the spread between the first and the second parties has been more than 25 percentage points (see Table VIII). The median and mean figures presented in Table IX further support the contention that the Saskatchewan party system has been more competitive than the Alberta system. If it can be assumed that party competition, partisan preference, and political involvement are directly related to voter turnout, as it is fair to assume they are,[47] then the Saskatchewan party system is one of active participation centring around keen competition, for its voter turnout figures are consistently high. This is especially true when contrasted to both Manitoba and Alberta (see Table X). Thus, the absence of single-party dominance and the continued existence of competitive party politics have been traditional characteristics and must now be regarded as essential components of the party system of Saskatchewan.[48]

How can the obvious difference between the Saskatchewan, Manitoba, and Alberta party systems be accounted for? The ability of the provincial Liberal party to deal effectively with dissent for nearly all of the province's first forty years must rank as a factor of considerable importance. On the one hand, the Liberal party's ability to control farmer unrest during the 1920's meant that the theory of group government propounded in Alberta by Henry

---

[47]Howard A. Scarrow, "Patterns of Voter Turnout in Canada," in *Voting in Canada*, John C. Courtney, ed. (Toronto: Prentice-Hall of Canada, Ltd., 1967), p. 107; and Angus Campbell, *et al., The American Voter* (New York: John Wiley, 1960), pp. 96-110.

[48]The point has also been made that farmers who produce for international markets, such as wheat farmers, and farmers who are subjected to economic pressures which they cannot control have both a high rate of organizational activity and a high turnout at the polls. S.M. Lipset, *et al.,* "The Psychology of Voting: An Analysis of Political Behavior," in *Handbook of Social Psychology*, Gardner Lindzey, ed. (Reading, Mass.: Addison-Wesley Publishing Co., 1954), II, 1128 and 1129.

TABLE X

Percentage of Voter Turnout in Saskatchewan, Manitoba,
and Alberta Provincial Elections, 1932–71

Saskatchewan		Manitoba		Alberta	
Year	Percentage	Year	Percentage	Year	Percentage
1934	85	1932	73	1935	83
1938	84	1936	66	1940	75
1944	81	1941	50	1944	69
1948	83	1945	56	1948	64
1952	83	1949	54	1952	59
1956	84	1953	60	1955	68
1960	84	1958	61	1959	64
1964	85	1959	66	1963	56
1967	78	1962	61	1967	63
1971	83	1966	64	1971	73
		1966	64		
		1969	64		
Mean	83		61		67
Median	84		61		66

Sources: Howard A. Scarrow, *Canada Votes: A Handbook of Federal and Provincial Election Data* (New Orleans: The Hauser Press, 1962), pp. 214-223; Chief Electoral Officer, Province of Saskatchewan, Regina; Clerk of the Legislative Assembly, Province of Alberta, Edmonton; Professor T. Peterson, Department of Political Science, University of Manitoba, Winnipeg; *Star-Phoenix* (Saskatoon), June 24, 1971.

Wise Wood was inappropriate to Saskatchewan politics. That machine politics aided in sustaining the Liberal government during this period further indicates the considerable power enjoyed by the Liberal party in the first twenty-five years of the province's history.[49] On the other hand, the dominance of the Liberal party from 1905 to 1944 and, subsequently, of the CCF from 1944 to 1964 made nonpartisan and coalition politics, such as the Bracken-Garson-Willis-Campbell variety in Manitoba, both unthinkable and unnecessary in Saskatchewan.[50] The electorate and the parties in Saskatchewan obviously lacked interest in adopting the forms of parliamentary democracy that both neighbouring provinces were experimenting with, and by so doing helped to promote rival party politics in the province.

Furthermore, in Saskatchewan the need for and desire for co-operative action and involvement has been greater than in either Alberta or Manitoba. Professor John Archer has stated:

The rapidity of settlement and the immensity of the area settled in Saskatchewan was quite unique. The harsh environment, the physical labour required, the need for shelter, water and food, the immensity of the prairies, the never resting wind, the richness of the soil, the littleness of one human in such a setting – these factors led to the gradual evolution of a native philosophy in Saskatchewan. It was not like Manitoba — where settlement was older and the farm land confined to a relatively small area in the south. It was not like Alberta where a strong ranching industry dominated the south and the lure of the Peace River country drew off the restless to the north. In Saskatchewan — English and Estonian, Scot and Slav, American and Armenian, everyone was subject to the same prime factors of hardship, loneliness, cold, drought, fire, frost and hail at the same time. Necessity dictated that each help the other. The wind blew just as chill over the sidehill dug-out of the Norwegian newcomer as it did over the sod shanty of the Minnesota Swede. The prairie fire licked as hungrily around the frame shack of an English remittance man as it did at the log shack of his Galician neighbour. There was the same urgency to get grain threshed before the winter. There was the same need for companionship, for roads, for schools. There were the same dark threats against monopoly and profit mongering when good wheat brought poor prices and disputed grades.[51]

To a large extent, residents of Saskatchewan have been forced to participate in the management of their own affairs and to co-operate with each other in social, economic, and political endeavours. By the mid-1940's, as Professor S.M. Lipset found, there were between 40,000 and 60,000 different elective posts in Saskatchewan to be filled by the 125,000 farmers. In other words, there was one elective position available for every two or three farmers.[52] This vitality of Saskatchewan politics has expressed itself in other ways as well. One of the studies requested by the federal government's Committee on Election Expenses (1966) discovered that the proportion of people in Saskatchewan who were party activists or opinion leaders or who were aware of fund-raising activities was greater than the proportion in any other province.[53]

By virtue of political participation and involvement, Saskatchewan voters over the years have become aware of various issues, policies, candidates, and parties, as well as their alternatives. Provincial politics has been carried out within a framework of discussion, debate, and, if necessary, competition. The very nature of that discussion and debate, beginning in the 1930's and continuing for the succeeding three decades, has forced both the voters and the parties to identify themselves ideologically. Thus, a large portion of the electorate has actively supported the various political parties. By 1967, at the time of the provincial election, 7 per cent of the total population, or 12 per cent of the electoral population, were card-carrying members of either of the two major parties.[54]

[49]Reid, "The Saskatchewan Liberal Machine," p. 49.

[50]For a discussion of the nonpartisan and coalition tradition of Manitoba, see Murray S. Donnelly, *The Government of Manitoba* (Toronto: University of Toronto Press, 1963), pp. 46-70.

[51]Archer, "Political Development," pp. 14 and 15.

[52]Lipset, "The Psychology of Voting," p. 200.

[53]Committee on Election Expenses, *Studies in Canadian Party Finance* (Ottawa: Queen's Printer, 1966), pp. 43, 45, 47, and 135.

[54]The CCF membership was 33,527 and the Liberal membership 30,983. *Star-Phoenix* (Saskatoon), November 23, 1967, p. 3 and information provided by the Saskatchewan Liberal Association.

IV. THE BASES OF PARTY SUPPORT

The search for electoral support by the two major parties in Saskatchewan has led both the CCF and the Liberals to seek support from as large a segment of the total population as possible and as a result avoid adopting rigid positions centring around firm doctrines. While the commitment to social reform, economic planning, and government ownership of certain industries has been greater in the CCF than in the Liberal party, the latter has, with exceptions, been sufficiently aware of the need for electoral support to favour a good deal of positive legislative action. In at least one election (1964), the Liberals in fact appeared to be ideologically to the left of the CCF on a number of social issues.[55] It is, of course, one thing for a party to be progressive or leftist on the hustings; it is quite another matter to be so when elected to power. Although the CCF introduced much in the way of socialized health, welfare, and rehabilitation services and established a number of provincially-owned enterprises when it first came to power in 1944, not too many years passed before the socialists substantially modified a number of their party's policies so that they might broaden rather than restrict their electoral appeal. In point of fact

distinctive features of C.C.F. policy from the time it assumed office in 1944 until its defeat by the Liberals twenty years later did not represent the sharp departure from the practices of its predecessors or of neighboring provinces which was sometimes pictured. Enthusiasm and a reforming spirit were evident, administrative innovations occurred, there was early socialistic experimenting, changes were made and new policies and services introduced; but these occurred within the framework of the existing economic and social order. Neither the claims of its supporters nor the charges of its opponents of the replacement of the old social order by a new one were fulfilled.

In an era of increasing government activity and participation, C.C.F. performance showed a difference more in degree and in timing than in kind.[56]

On the whole, the impression created by the parties' active solicitation for support as well as their legislative records in Saskatchewan is one of moderate democratic socialism versus a peculiar Prairie variety of liberalism. Yet, in spite of such differences as there are between the two parties, there has developed over the years a characteristic unpredicability about the positions they have assumed on various issues of substantial importance. Just as the Liberal party has tended to be illiberal and anti-intellectual on certain issues, so has the CCF shown a strange penchant for conservatism in certain matters.[57] Just as the provincial parties have shown at times a marked tendency toward dissociation from their federal counterparts (the Conservatives from 1905 to 1911, the Liberals under Martin and Dunning, the CCF as distinct from the NDP from 1961 to 1967, and the "Saskatchewan Liberals" under Thatcher),[58] so have the leaders themselves worked against the very principle they advocated by moving freely between federal and provincial politics. Of the ten premiers of the province, six sat as M.P.s either before or after serving as party leader in Saskatchewan; two of those six became federal cabinet ministers, two ran for the national leadership of their respective parties, and in fact, one was successful in seeking that post (see Table XI). All this leads one to believe that Saskatchewan politics has been as much a politics of per-

TABLE XI

Provincial Premiers of Saskatchewan
And Their Prior and Subsequent Involvement in Federal Politics

Premier	M.P. Previously	M.P. Subsequently	Federal Cabinet Minister	Federal Party Leader
Walter Scott	X	—	—	—
W.M. Martin	X	—	—	—
C.A. Dunning	—	X	X	—
J.G. Gardiner	—	X	X	—
J.T.M. Anderson	—	—	—	—
W.J. Patterson	—	—	—	—
T.C. Douglas	X	X	—	X
W.S. Lloyd	—	—	—	—
W.R. Thatcher	X	—	—	—
A.E. Blakeney	—	—	—	—

sonalities as of parties. The truth of this characteristic of Saskatchewan politics is found in the fact that many people in Saskatchewan have tended to identify themselves as being, for example, "Douglas CCF'ers," "Thatcher Liberals," or "Diefenbaker Conservatives."

In terms of federal-provincial voting patterns the Saskatchewan voter is a free agent, for in this political sphere the emphasis is on personalities and issues at the expense of party doctrine and ideologies. To attempt to explain the provincial party system and provincial voting patterns by referring to

[55]Norman Ward, "Saskatchewan in 1964: Two Comments," in *Voting in Canada*, pp. 187 and 188. The Liberals in 1964 campaigned on an extension of medicare to include major drug costs, for example. Once they assumed office the Liberals abandoned some of the progressivism they had assumed on such issues during the campaign and no legislation was introduced to cover drug costs. During the 1967 election Mr. Thatcher stated he would agree to including drug costs in medicare only on the condition that approval be given by the electorate of Saskatchewan through a plebiscite. This case in particular illustrates the ability of the parties to say one thing but do another.

[56]Evelyn Eager, "The Conservatism of the Saskatchewan Electorate," in Ward and Spafford, *Politics in Saskatchewan*, p. 15.

[57]A more illiberal opinion could scarcely have been uttered by a "Liberal" public official than that attributed to Mr. Allan Guy, newly appointed Minister of Public Works, following the 1967 election at the height of the government-university controversy: "If this is the attitude of the faculty towards responsibility then the time will come when we have to take over academic control as well as financial control." *The Leader-Post* (Regina), December 9, 1967, p. 36. When the CCF was in power it displayed conservative tendencies on such issues as movie censorship, liquor legislation, night shopping, and Sunday sports.

[58]During the 1967 provincial election the Liberals campaigned on the slogan "Vote Saskatchewan Liberal," while the CCF urged support on the basis of being "Saskatchewan's OWN Party."

federal party politics would be futile. The 193,000 Saskatchewan voters who elected seventeen Progressive Conservative M.P.s in 1965, felt no particular attachment to the provincial Conservative party in 1967 when all forty-one of that party's candidates failed to get elected and the total vote for the party came to only 39,000. The federal Liberals' inability to elect a single M.P. in Saskatchewan in 1965 came at a time midway between the provincial Liberals' successes in the Saskatchewan elections of 1964 and 1967. In short, the provincial party system is quite detached from the federal party system in Saskatchewan.[59]

The differences between the two major parties are as much a matter of the type of voter supporting one party in preference to another, as they are a matter of ideological distinctions. The following give more support to the Liberals than to the CCF:[60] those with above-average incomes; the more prosperous farmers; voters under forty-five years of age; sales, managerial, and professional occupational groups; Roman Catholics, Anglicans, Jews, and Mennonites; and those with at least three years secondary school education. Alternatively, the following give more support to the CCF than to the Liberal party: individuals with below-average incomes; the less prosperous farmers; voters fifty-five years of age and over; labourers, craftsmen, and transportation and service workers; United Church members, Presbyterians, and Lutherans; and those with less than three years secondary school education. The type of electoral support received by each of the two major parties helps to explain the more conservative position of the Liberal party and the more liberal position of the CCF on public issues. The original liberal-conservative dichotomy of Saskatchewan politics is preserved in the progressive liberalism of the CCF and the newly found conservatism of the Liberals.

V. CONCLUSIONS

During its sixty-odd year history, Saskatchewan has undergone several fundamental changes. The rapid settlement and growth of the early twentieth century was followed by considerable depopulation, changing the province from the third largest in 1931, with 9 per cent of the Canadian population, to the fifth largest in 1961, with 5 per cent of the nation's population. The optimism generated by the favourable prospects for wheat production prior to and following World War I was challenged severely by the events of the 1930's and was realized only by the large wheat crops and foreign sales of wheat during the 1950's and 1960's. In fact, the turn of economic events in the 1960's changed Saskatchewan first from a "have-not" to a "have" province with the third highest per capita income in the Dominion and then back again. At the same time the two major cities of Saskatchewan experienced short-lived, rapid expansion, while the rural population continued to decline at an equally rapid rate as farm consolidation took place and as the agricultural industry became more efficient.

The demographic and social developments of Saskatchewan's history have had a profound effect on the politics of the province. Political parties, understandably, have searched for ways of utilizing — indeed, of maximizing — these developments for their own purposes. Initially the Liberal party was eminently successful in drawing into its ranks the major disputants in Saskatchewan politics. This absorptive capacity of the Liberal party lasted throughout most of the first four decades of provincial history. More recently both of the province's successful parties have acted as compromising agencies, though this has been less characteristic of the Liberals under Mr. Thatcher than it was previously. Consequently the Liberals' concern for individualism and "free enterprise" has not been so great as to keep them from accepting at least some radical solutions to the problems faced by Saskatchewanians; the CCF, for its part, has chosen a moderate position and has assumed the role of the radical, socialist innovator less frequently than the more doctrinaire European parties on the Left. In short, both of Saskatchewan's major parties have proven themselves to be, in varying degrees and with varying emphases, power-oriented, principle-shunning, compromising entities.

As compromising political agencies, the successful Saskatchewan parties have exhibited a number of common characteristics. They have chosen not to become identified with any one group or section of society and have sought consciously to obtain support by way of broadly based electoral appeals. They have divorced themselves, when necessary, from their federal counterparts by establishing separate organizations, adopting distinctive names, and withholding support or endorsement of federal candidates.

Party politics in Saskatchewan has been active, intense, and, for a good part of the province's history, highly competitive.[61] Political participation and involvement are higher in Saskatchewan than in any other province. This is especially striking if one compares the political system of Saskatchewan with the Alberta and Manitoba systems. Partisan politics impregnates, with few exceptions, every issue faced by Saskatchewanians, whether it be the marketing of a particular agricultural commodity or the proposed establishment of a government-operated medical care insurance programme. Party politics, divisive as it may be in such a two-party situation, has at the same time served as one of the few links between the various groups of people throughout the

[59]The blatant attempt to divorce federal from provincial party politics is illustrated by the following comment made by Premier Thatcher during the 1967 election campaign: "I say to my Conservative friends and to my Social Credit friends — if you are for private enterprise, then look at the Liberals. Cough a couple of times, but put your X in the Liberal column. We do it for you federally. You do it for us provincially." *The Globe and Mail* (Toronto), October 5, 1967, p. 7.

[60]The information contained in this section has been drawn from Lipset, *Agrarian Socialism*, ch. 8; David E. Smith, "Questionnaire Response, Voter Turnout and Party Support," in *Voting in Canada*, pp. 115-124; and Courtney and Smith, "Voting in a Provincial General Election and a Federal By-Election: A Constituency Study of Saskatoon City," *Canadian Journal of Economics and Political Science*, XXXII (August 1966), 338-353.

[61]In the 1967 Saskatchewan election eight and in 1971 five constituencies were decided by fewer than one hundred votes.

province. The population — a good part of which is still composed of first- and second-generation Canadians — contains so many different ethnic and religious groups, is so sparsely distributed throughout the province and is so removed from other Canadians, that very few institutions or activities play any role in drawing the various individuals and groups together. Such uniting influences as there are might include, at the very most, the agricultural industry, winter sports, education, and politics. One of the few things common to all residents of Saskatchewan has been the political process; they have not failed to use it in seeking solutions to their many problems.